PHILOSOPHY WITHOUT FOUNDATIONS

ॐ

SUNY Series in Hegelian Studies

William Desmond, Editor

and

SUNY Series in Philosophy

George R. Lucas, Jr., Editor

PHILOSOPHY WITHOUT FOUNDATIONS
Rethinking Hegel

ૐ

William Maker

STATE UNIVERSITY OF NEW YORK PRESS

Production by Ruth Fisher
Marketing by Fran Keneston

Published by
State University of New York Press, Albany

For information, address the State University of New York Press,
State University Plaza, Albany, NY 12246

Library of Congress Cataloging-in-Publication Data

Maker, William.
    Philosophy without foundations : rethinking Hegel / William Maker.
    p. cm. — (SUNY series in Hegelian studies) (SUNY series in
philosophy)
    Includes bibliographical references and index.
    ISBN 0-7914-2099-X (alk. paper). — ISBN 0-7914-2100-7 (pbk. :
alk. paper)
    1. Hegel, Georg Wilhelm Friedrich, 1770–1831. 2. Hegel, Georg
Wilhelm Friedrich, 1770–1831—Influence—Philosophers, Modern.
3. Philosophy, Modern—20th century. I. Title. II. Series.
III. Series: SUNY series in philosophy.
  B2948.M257 1994
  193—dc20   93-42703
                                                  CIP

10 9 8 7 6 5 4 3 2 1

CONTENTS

PREFACE

In a recent essay, Karl Americks noted that while "Hegel's contribution to practical philosophy no longer requires rehabilitation. . . . Hegel's theoretical philosophy, however, continues to be highly suspect. . . . "[1] The aim of this book is to confront and challenge that suspicion. Its central concern is with the nature and status of Hegel's theoretical philosophy, with his understanding of how we are to engage in philosophy and of what results from that engagement. The enduring antipathy to this theoretical enterprise is contested here in this fashion: I argue, in a variety of ways and from various perspectives, that Hegel's texts can be read such that we can rethink those aspects of the traditional picture of Hegel which have continued to cause contemporary philosophers to dismiss him. Finding philosophical significance in Hegel need not force us to ignore or sidestep what has traditionally been the cause of suspicion, his idea of a philosophical system. Indeed, I shall argue that when we have properly rethought what Hegel means by systematic philosophy, we will see that he is *not* a metaphysical idealist who attempts to foist on us a system which is as unintelligible as it is devoid of argument.

In part, this book endeavors to demonstrate that Hegel's philosophy contains some powerful arguments, and to indicate their cogency. Additionally, it aims to show that these arguments are contemporary in a vital sense because they address what I take to be the central questions about philosophy today: Do criticisms of the foundational tradition in philosophy force us to abandon philosophy and its attempt to provide objective truth? Must philosophy be rejected in favor of relativism, nihilism, deconstruction, or genial conversation? I try to show how a rethought Hegel enables us to answer both of these questions in a decisively negative manner. Thus, this book contends not only that Hegel has something worthwhile to say about a variety

of philosophical topics, but that his conception of systematic philosophy—that which still appears most anachronistic in Hegel—is not
only intelligible and defensible but also of contemporary importance.
What I have worked to indicate is that Hegel's philosophy is not
consummately foundational and absolutist, but rather originates in a
critique of foundationalism. Recognizing and understanding this
critique is the basis for rethinking Hegel; indeed, when we have done
so, Hegel's system emerges as a nonfoundational philosophy which
incorporates some contemporary criticisms of foundationalism
without abandoning philosophy's traditional goal of offering
demonstratable, objective truth. Because the Hegel presented here is
an adamant and radical antifoundationalist, some features of this
interpretation run directly counter to the accepted understanding of
Hegel. Nonetheless, I have tried to show both that this nonfoundational
reading is firmly based in Hegel's arguments, and that it does not
require us to dismiss crucial Hegelian claims about the nature of his
system: rather, what is called for is a shift of focus to enable us to
rethink Hegel's idea of systematic philosophy in a new way.

A NOTE ON THE TEXT

Portions of some of the chapters were previously published. Publication details are listed below.

Part of "Reason and the Problem of Modernity" appeared under the same title in *The Philosophical Forum* 18, no. 4 (Summer 1987): pp. 275–303.

Part of "Philosophy as Systematic Science" appeared under the title "Deconstructing Foundationalism and the Question of Philosophy as Systematic Science" in *Reason Papers* 16 (Fall 1991): pp. 95–113.

Part of "Hegel's *Phenomenology* as Introduction to Systematic Science" appeared under the title "Hegel's *Phenomenology* as Introduction to Science" in *CLIO* 10, no. 4 (1981): pp. 381–397.

Part of "Beginning Philosophy Without 'Beginnings'" appeared under the title "Beginning" in *Essays on Hegel's Logic*, ed. George di Giovanni (Albany: SUNY Press, 1990): pp. 27–43.

Part of "Philosophy and Dialectical Method" appeared under the title "Does Hegel Have a 'Dialectical Method'?" in *The Southern Journal of Philosophy* 20, no. 1 (1982): pp. 75–96.

Part of "On the Presumed Blasphemy of Hegelian Absolutism" appeared under the title "Hegel's Blasphemy?" in *The History of Philosophy Quarterly* 9, no. 1 (January 1992): pp. 67–85.

Part of "Hegel and Hermeneutics" appeared under the title "Gadamer on Hegel: 'Taking Finitude Seriously' and the 'Unbreakable Circle of Reflection'" in *The Dayton Review* 17, no. 1 (Spring 1984): p. 69–78.

Part of "The Critique of Marx and Marxist Thought" appeared under the title "Hegel's Critique of Marx: The Fetishism of Dialectics" in *Hegel and His Critics: Philosophy in the Aftermath of Hegel*, ed. William Desmond (Albany: SUNY Press, 1989): pp. 72–92.

Part of "The Dead End of Postmodernism" appeared under the title "(Postmodern) Tales from the Crypt: The Night of the Zombie

Philosophers" in *Metaphilosophy* 23, no. 4 (October 1992): pp. 311–328.

Part of "The Renewed Appeal to Transcendental Arguments" appeared under the title "Davidson's Transcendental Arguments" in *Philosophy and Phenomenological Research* 51, no. 2 (June 1991): pp. 345–360.

INTRODUCTION

Questions about the basic nature and the fundamental status of their discipline have always preoccupied philosophers, and this is understandable. Given philosophy's traditional claim concerning its special status as a discipline—its self-proclaimed role as the queen of the sciences—we ought not to be surprised by the spectacle of continual debate over foundations which the history of philosophy affords. There have been many pretenders to philosophy's queenly throne, and the palace struggles have been frequent and bloody.

But at least since Nietzsche those metaconcerns which previously engendered recurring foundational crises have taken a new twist. Philosophers have come to focus increasingly, and with an increasingly skeptical eye, on the question of the very possibility of philosophy as traditionally understood: as that endeavor which is distinctive, meaningful, necessary, and superior to others because of its capacity to speak in an unconditional and authoritative fashion about what there is, how it is to be known, and how we ought to live.

So, while the tradition of philosophy has always been exceptional owing to its ceaseless generation of revolutions—the procession of ever-succeeding claims to have overcome the errors of the past and, through a redefinition of first principles, to have finally founded philosophy as the first science—the latest revolution appears to be different. It claims for itself the distinction of having rejected not only the errors of the past, but also the whole tradition of laying claim to philosophy as science. In recent years an image of philosophy as being "tormented by questions which bring *itself* into question" has taken hold, along with attempts to effect an end to this torment by bringing the urge which gives rise to it to an awareness of the impossibility of its satisfaction.[1] We are told that the recurring cycle of crises in philosophy can be overcome by a rejection of that self-understanding of philosophy which has inevitably engendered them.[2] What has emerged from the efforts of Heidegger, Gadamer, Derrida, the later Wittgenstein, and the work of Richard Rorty, to mention only the most obvious and prominent names associated with the latest revolution, is a mode of philosophizing (or thinking) which is rooted in a felt need to direct the critical capacities of philosophy upon the traditional conception of the philosophical enterprise itself, in order to effect a liberation from it.[3] Much of contemporary discussion and debate centers around various attempts to analyze and critically reject philosophy's traditional guiding ideal, its aim to be a radical, self-legitimating science, an absolute foundational discipline.[4] The latest fashion in philosophy is to be against foundations. Linked with the demise of foundationalism is the widely proclaimed collapse of modernity. As an attempt to provide objective rational criteria for individual judgments about knowledge and action, foundationalism is seen to be central to providing a legitimation for modern claims about individual freedom: demonstrating that individuals possess the capacity and the right to autonomy seemingly presupposes establishing foundational principles for judgment within subjectivity. Thus, antifoundationalism and postmodernism go hand in hand.

I hesitate to speak of "antifoundational*ism*," insofar as that suffix might suggest a coherent, deliberately united school of philosophers emerging from a shared tradition, writing in a common style, referring to one another's work, and consciously acknowledging both their mutual influences and a univocal positive goal.[5] If antifoundationalism as a school does not exist, at least yet, what does legitimate the use of this collective label to bunch together philosophers who otherwise diverge in many ways is their agreement, not on some specific and detailed positive conception of what philosophy should be and how to realize this, but rather on what it has been and can no longer be. Antifoundationalism is better thought of as a movement of opposition than a coherent positive school, and what unifies it, minimally, lies, as the name indicates, in what it is directed against. Tying together hermeneutics, deconstruction, poststructuralism, posthumanism, postmodernism, neopragmatism, postanalytic philosophy, and postphilosophical philosophy—to mention some of the terms currently in use[6]—is an agreement that foundationalism with its goal of a philosophical science needs to be rejected[7]—insofar as it has not already rejected itself—as well as a sense that this rejection entails certain basic minimal conditions for future philosophy.

Just what is being attacked here? What are we being asked to renounce? Antifoundationalism defines itself minimally as a rejection of what is sometimes called Cartesianism, understood as the modern attempt to legitimate philosophy's claim to be the queen of the sciences through a project of self-reflection which would result in the discovery and legitimation of indubitable truth principles.[8] As understood from the antifoundationalist perspective, the modern project of foundational epistemology arises from the "Cartesian anxiety"[9] that both philosophy and culture generally are in need of "foundations": before rightful truth claims can be justly made, the conditions of cognition which can afford us knowledge must be articulated and shown to be truth-affording. Our capacity to know must be grounded, legitimated, or justified if errors of judgment both cognitive and practical are to be avoided. The path of discovery which is to lead to these cognitive foundations is one of critical reflection, an internal self-investigation in which the knowing subject liberates itself from all preconceptions and prejudices and comes to full consciousness of the nature, limits, and legitimacy of its capacities as a knower. Through attaining this foundational standpoint of self-transparency, philosophy will have legitimated itself in the radical sense of establishing its authority as "first philosophy": the foundational project will result in philosophy's emergence as the super science. For, by establishing its privileged access to the conditions of cognition through critical self-reflection, philosophy will be distinctive both in having grounded itself—by demonstrating its capacity to arrive at foundational knowledge—and, through this self-grounding, in having justified its claim to authority as that discipline which can rightly judge all other claims to know. Philosophy will have legitimated its claim to be the metadiscipline by rending transparent what Rorty refers to as the "permanent ahistorical matrix" in which all knowledge claims— theoretical as well as practical—can and must be founded.

Thus, implicit or explicit in foundationalism are the assumptions: (1) that conditions for knowledge are unchanging and universal; (2) that they pertain to or can be located in the mind or consciousness; (3) that this same mind can mirror to itself its own cognitive conditions and through this, establish both their legitimacy as necessary and its specific authority as the voice which judges adherence to and deviations from them. As I understand the antifoundational movement, it is defined by its effort to reveal these assumptions as mere assumptions and to demonstrate that they are illicit. "Antifoundationalism" as I shall use the term has as its reference a congeries of philosophers who are minimally united by the conviction that future philosophy must be predicated on the denial of (1) through (3).

The locus of antifoundationalism's rejection of this project lies in the conviction that the foundational standpoint of cognitive self-transparency, the "God's eye" "view from nowhere"[10] which affords foundational knowledge of how knowledge is possible, is unattainable. Antifoundationalism's definitive critical claim is to have revealed the impossibility of arriving at a perspective which can oversee the knowledge-affording relation between the mind and its objects, appearances and things in themselves, beings and Being, or language and the world.[11] Without access to such an Archimedean standpoint (from which we could see that and how our representations hook up to what they purportedly represent) we cannot claim to have revealed *the* foundations of knowledge, and, antifoundationalism concludes, it makes no sense to speak of such foundations or to construe philosophy as a foundational science which can articulate conditions of necessity, universality, rationality, objectivity, and legitimacy, either cognitive or practical.

Inseparable from the paramount critical claim denying the possibility of such an autonomous view of things is a rejection of the foundationalist conception of knowledge as a possible object: as something whose 'nature' and 'conditions' can be isolated, analyzed, and subjected to a thoroughgoing and detached critical scrutiny. In contrast, antifoundationalism is rooted in a basic belief in the opaqueness of the knowing situation. For antifoundationalists all knowledge—and all philosophical reasoning—is finite, conditioned, located, perspectival, or contextual: tied to conceptual schemes, embedded in horizons, governed by language games, ruled by paradigms, inseparable from particular historical traditions, inextricable from forms of life or sets of social practices. According to this contextualist view, knowledge and discourse are irredeemably situated: rooted in or wedded to factors whose ineluctable givenness precludes their ultimate transcendence, as well as any hope of rendering these conditions of contextuality fully transparent. Thus, we cannot come to know things as they are in themselves, independent of a point of view, and must forgo all hope of attaining the autonomous, unmediated perspective requisite of philosophy as science.

This autonomy is doubly precluded since all possible knowledge, we are told, is situated, located, or bounded in a twofold way: both embedded in the *particular* givens of the "styles of reasoning" defined by the contingencies of our various linguistic, historical, social, and cultural contexts and practices, and conditioned *generally* by the "framework of givenness"[12] peculiar to our finite subjectivity, to who and what we are as knowers (or language users).

Local rebellions and a conditional liberation from at least some of the particular givens is possible: antifoundationalism itself claims to effect an emancipation from what it sees as the particular and contingent givens which helped to define the foundationalist tradition; more generally, it rejects the notion of absolutes in the sense of there being any specifiable particulars conditioning knowledge, language, or practice which may be said to hold necessarily, universally, and ahistorically. (Were such absolutes discoverable, their specification would complete the foundational project.)

But while we can liberate ourselves from some particular (social, linguistic, cultural, etc.) givens, we can never hope to escape from all such givens. That is, the general condition of our being conditioned by contingent, given particulars (social, linguistic, etc.) is inescapable, for—according to antifoundationalism—escaping from it would mean arriving at a transcendent view of the context of conditioning itself, a perspective outside of all contextuality, beyond all givenness as such. No revolution seeking emancipation from the context of contextuality, from the framework of givenness itself, from the inescapable situatedness of all claims to know, can possibly succeed.[13] Efforts to attain such liberation are doomed to failure because, by not "taking finitude seriously" they comprise attempts to "step outside our skins."[14] To engage in knowing (or to use language) is always and everywhere to participate in an activity whose foundations must remain opaque—and unjustified—since knowing (and language use) cannot proceed without the assumption of some givens which, in establishing conditions for judgment (or expression) first make knowledge (or discourse) possible.[15]

What remain open for possible revision or replacement are the particular givens we happen to be operating from, but such revision or replacement can only take place in a context defined by other givens. That we must always proceed from some givens is unavoidable. This situation then is The Big Given which rules out foundational philosophy. (And it is this situation which I am indicating by the expressions 'framework of givenness' and 'context of contextuality.' These are, so to speak, the transcendental conditions of possibility, the rock upon which the antifoundational position builds—and rests—its case.) The transcendental illusion of foundationalism was rooted in the unwarranted belief that subjectivity could somehow, through liberating itself from the contingently given, attain to transparency concerning the framework of givenness itself, to a position outside of the cognitive, conceptual, or linguistic matrix from which one could survey its principles of operation: the privileged, necessary givens which are immanent in

its structure and which purportedly define the universal and necessary conditions for cognition or discourse. But this could only amount
to a claim to have represented the grounds of representation itself,
to having said that which, because it makes saying possible, cannot
itself be said. It would be tantamount to having pulled oneself up
by one's own cognitive or linguistic bootstraps. Thus the very attempt to transcend the framework of givenness—the iron cage of
contextuality—in order to provide foundational knowledge of it,
only demonstrates its inescapability and ineluctability.[16]

Hence, when antifoundationalism proclaims the myth of the
given (or when it decries the very idea of a conceptual scheme)
what is being described as a myth in need of abandonment is the
foundationalist belief that *certain* givens can be isolated as privileged, as those determinative factors which, in being universally
and necessarily peculiar to subjectivity (or language) ahistorically
define the conditions of all possible knowledge (or provide the system of categories with which we organize experience). What is precisely not a myth, and what seemingly cannot be proclaimed as one
if antifoundationalism is to avoid undercutting its own critical
claims, is our perspectivality or contextuality, our finitude, understood as the necessity that our knowledge claims are founded in
and relative to some givens, to features of our conceptual or linguistic framework which cannot be rendered fully transparent or
explicit.[17]

Thus, while renouncing all hope of a final discovery of eternal,
unchanging, universal grounding conditions, and hence of the image of philosophy as a mirror of nature and a metascience of knowing, discourse, and conduct, antifoundationalism—so far at least—
has not left the traditional arena of philosophy altogether. In renouncing epistemology it has not abandoned all talk of knowledge
and its possibility.[18] Rather, what we are being asked to do is
conceive of knowledge in a different fashion: in such a way that our
urge to think of it as analyzable into finite and specific components,
and as having or needing grounds, is stifled. Despite adamant deni-
als that some sort of a theory of knowledge—an anti-epistemologi-
cal epistemology—is being offered, antifoundationalism has been
accused of self-referential inconsistency.[19] It would seem that in
order for its claim denying the possibility of transcendental, epistemological knowledge to have argumentative force, it must be made
from nothing other than a standpoint which claims privileged insight into the conditions of knowing, the very standpoint whose
possibility is being denied. Some antifoundationalists seem not to
be troubled by this charge of self-referential inconsistency, perhaps

regarding the apparent perversity (from a traditional perspective) of their position as 'showing' something which cannot be 'said,' in the tradition of Wittgenstein of the *Tractatus*.[20]

Whether this Wittgensteinian gambit is a weasel is something I consider at length, especially in Chapter 2, "Philosophy as Systematic Science" and in Chapter 9, "The Dead End of Postmodernism." At this juncture, it is worth noting that the problem—the need to somehow speak about the unspeakable, just in order to assert its inarticulability, or the need to make claims to somehow know the unknowable, in order to make manifest its resistance to cognition (for the sake of articulating the necessary finitude of our knowledge) or the need to engage in meaningless speech, in order to provide a verifiability criterion to rule it out—goes back at least to Kant's first *Critique*. As Jacobi put it: "I need the assumption of things-in-themselves to enter the Kantian system, but with this assumption it is not possible for me to remain inside it." Or as Ramsey put it: "but what we can't say we can't say, and we can't whistle it either."[21] I shall argue that this problem may be endemic to all talk about foundations of knowledge, *both* anti- and pro-foundational, and that antifoundationalism is plagued by difficulties which bear more than just a family resemblance to those it detects in foundationalism.

In any case, the denial of foundationalism and the rejection of its correlative notions of privileged representations, the correspondence theory of truth, and the transcendental subject would thus seem to represent at least a paradigm shift, albeit one which entails a significant reconceptualization of the philosophical enterprise, rather than a wholesale abandonment of philosophy altogether.

Just what "philosophy" in a positive sense is now to be—even whether it is worthwhile to hold on to the term—is somewhat unclear, and given the denial that philosophy can establish its own paradigmatic status, we should expect a diversity of views concerning what postfoundational philosophy should be. Nonetheless, the terms of the antifoundationalist argument against foundationalism, and especially the contextualist understanding of knowledge which it employs in attacking the foundationalist conception, do lead to the defining of certain minimal or basic conditions for future, postfoundational, philosophy. If antifoundationalism's negative, critical project provides us with no specific univocal roadmap for the future of philosophy, it would seem to offer us at least a compass for the charting of our course, as well as a fixed point of departure. Taking our bearings from the correlative primal notions of the finitude (or contextuality) of cognition and the impossibility of absolute, foundational knowledge, we find that *holism, historicism, pluralism,* and *fallibalism* define the points of the antifoundational compass for future conceptual navigation. Consideration of these foundational points of antifoundationalism enables us to bring into focus some broad features of the postfoundational project.

Because the rejection of foundationalism is conjoined with the claim that knowledge is determined by the context in which the knower is located, antifoundationalism generally can be said to endorse holism, that conception of knowledge according to which truth is defined not in terms of correspondence to objects but as the coherence of claims within the frame of reference defined by the tradition, style of discourse, or set of linguistic or social practices in which the knower is located.[22] Because the context of knowledge is not reducible to some set of isolatable mental or mind-dependent qualities attributable to a transcendental subject[23] (or to some set of fixed, isolatable logical, linguistic, or semantic features), it is usually seen by antifoundationalists as determined intersubjectively and in terms of socially conditioned practices. So, coupled with its holistic view of cognition, antifoundationalism generally regards knowledge as socially constituted. Future talk about knowledge will require us to bring into consideration institutions and activities in the life world.[24]

Given that the context, however it is specified, always functions in an over-determinative manner, and because some condition of contextuality must function as a given, no tradition, style, paradigm, language game, or set of practices can be uniquely privileged. Thus the very idea that philosophy is distinctly defined by its authoritative access to the domain of the eternally and universally true must be abandoned. *"Philosophy has become anti-aprioristic."*[25] Rather than speaking of those features which condition cognition and discourse in terms of ahistorical universality, necessity, and immutability, we must see their tentative and historically contingent character. Hence, along with the renunciation of the claim to such privileged access to foundational absolutes, there emerges an effort to reveal and describe the various extra-philosophical and non-rational conditioning factors and assumptions from out of which arose the myth of philosophy and other myths which claim transcendental, ahistorical authority. These conditioning factors are variously described as rooted in social, linguistic, cultural, economic, political, or other contingent givens, in practices and traditions which are human, historical constructs rather than natural or supernatural fixities. Postfoundational philosophy thus tends towards a sweeping historicistic overview of the human condition and offers us various de-mythologizing "genealogies" or "deconstructions"—critiques of attempts to postulate some givens as privileged—in the styles of Nietzsche, Marx, and Foucault.[26]

Coupled with the new humility associated with historicistic debunkings of the foundational illusion about the privileged nature of philosophical rationality, we find the endorsement of a leveling pluralism which purports to contrast with the authoritative, hierarchical outlook of traditional philosophy.[27] Because philosophy can no longer appeal to the privileged domain of the eternally rational *a priori* as its special subject matter, philosophers are counseled to abandon their contempt for the contingent givens which make up the subject matter of other disciplines, and to cease disparaging or devaluing these disciplines and their methods. In contrast, a pluralistic tolerance of styles, techniques, and truths should be adopted along with an acceptance, if not of their incommensurability, then at least of their irreducibility to one, unified True Picture. "There is no God's eye point of view that we can know or usefully imagine; there are only the various points of view of actual persons reflected in various interests and purposes that their descriptions and theories subserve."[28]

Also intertwined with the rejection of foundationalism and the endorsement of pluralistic holism is an espousal of fallibilism: because all claims to know are ultimately unjustifiable and contingent upon contexts or perspectives, they must be consciously regarded as unavoidably conditional, subject to future reevaluation, revision, and possible rejection.[29]

Emerging out of the turn to holism, historicism, pluralism, and fallibilism and tied to its depiction of our entrapment in the framework of givenness, antifoundationalism has also brought about calls for a turn to and an appreciation of the pre-philosophically given as that with which we should concern ourselves. If absolute and final authority and guidance cannot be found in a mythical domain of the eternally rational, then our attention needs to be directed to the ordinary, to the *Lebenswelt*, to praxis, to the given languages, styles, traditions, communities, habits, and practices in which we find ourselves located.[30]

From this perspective, and in conjunction with the aforementioned, an overall goal for postfoundational philosophy would seem to emerge. Its task is to bring us to self-knowledge in the sense that we attain an awareness of the nature and unavoidable limitedness of our conceptual schemes, styles, traditions and points of view—our habits, our ways of behaving. A condition of this knowledge must be the realization that we cannot ever fully escape from or justify them, for no ultimate justification is possible. Thus some antifoundationalists contend that the most philosophy can be is "edifying" and therapeutic.[31] Armed with the special awareness of the limited character of our particular perspectives which postfoundational philosophy provides, we can, and should, focus our attention on the world of the living, on practices and forms of life, and away from the illusory eternal domain of Ideas. Rather than strive for the unattainable authority which the tradition promised, we should instead seek solidarity and community with those who share our habits and work to extend the boundaries of the "conversation of mankind."[32] It would now seem that philosophical wisdom is to be defined as the practical, putatively tolerance-engendering consciousness that we cannot authoritatively demonstrate that our contexts, styles, traditions, and points of view are better than others. This outlook is almost universally defended by antifoundationalists as being in some way or another emancipatory. It is said to lead to openness, to the liberation of the mind, and the expansion of horizons.

Connected of course with the notion that we cannot demonstrate the superiority of our own, or any other, style, tradition, etc. would seem to be the correlative notion that we cannot demonstrate (or have no grounds for suspecting) the inferiority of our own, or any other, style, tradition, etc. Thus, not the least of what is controversial about antifoundationalism is the apparent dogmatism or relativism which it is said either to lead to or to leave us defenseless against. Much has and will be written about this, some of it by way of denying that a rejection of foundationalism entails relativism.[33] As this topic is dealt with below (especially in Chapter 2, "Philosophy as Systematic Science," and Chapter 9, "The Dead End of Postmodernism,") I shall touch on it only briefly at this point.

In asserting our entrapment in the framework of givenness, and by declaring the impossibility of our ever justifying the givens which happen to shape us, antifoundationalism would seem to lead to levelled standards and equated perspectives, and also, curiously, to at least the possible re-emergence of the very perspective-privileging which it purports to oppose. The attempt has been made to defuse the charge of relativism (in a manner similar to that directed against the charge of self-referential inconsistency) by suggesting that foundationalism and relativism are correlative terms: when the specter of foundationalism and the Cartesian "quest for certainty and indubitability" are "exposed and overcome," we are supposed to appreciate that the phantom companion of relativism disappears too.[34]

At best, this response amounts to an attempt to ease the sting of relativism, to cure a fear of it. It is not a demonstration that the phenomenon does not exist nor that its association with antifoundationalism is baseless. Put differently, to hold that relativism is only conceptually compelling insofar as foundationalism is—and that with the realization of the latter's impossibility the former is somehow defused—may be an argument against the charge that relativism will inevitably lead to anarchic nihilism. One can suggest that the realization of a lack of absolute foundations for our beliefs need not lead to *our* abandoning them, or to chaos, if the very idea of such foundations is unintelligible: there may be a false dichotomy between beliefs absolutely grounded and beliefs which, because they have no ground at all, may or ought to be abandoned at whim. This, however, is not an argument against the claim that antifoundationalism leads to relativism. To assert that one need not worry about foundations for standards of cognition and conduct because none are to be found does not amount to a demonstration that, in the absence of such foundations, there are objective standards (in the sense of standards which can compel rational assent), whose authority rests on something more than the arational and contingent force of tradition, custom, habit, or power. But it is with this latter situation— the issue of the nature and legitimacy of authority—that those who charge antifoundationalism with relativism are (or should be) concerned. This concern takes its force from the conviction that antifoundationalism—with its glorification of the primacy of the other-than-rational, contingently given—offers no ground for distinguishing between legitimate and illegitimate authority. There are good reasons to suspect that antifoundationalism leaves us no bases for distinguishing between the authority of reason and the authority of power. Indeed, antifoundationalists siding with Nietzsche question whether this is a distinction that makes a difference (or *différance*).

If antifoundationalism is not merely to avoid the issue and dogmatically assert the correctness of its view (that relativism is a pseudo-problem) it must do more than simply make the above-mentioned response, for it can only appeal to the unconverted as sophistical rhetoric. Short of conversion to the antifoundationalist position, the response, although meant to dissolve the issue of relativism, will appear to the unconverted as simply a manifestation of the relativist position. What antifoundationalism needs to do—and seemingly cannot do without again succumbing to inconsistency—is somehow to show how its denial of foundationalism is compatible with the assertion and affirmation of some critical perspective which can be ultimately defended as more than just the standard of this or that tradition or perspective, as resting finally on something more than an appeal to the contingent givens of our location. Failing such a move, which would force antifoundationalism back into the foundational gambit, its own call for a defense of pluralism and tolerance seem at best shaky (although the antifoundationalist would hold that this is all any position can be) and at worst merely the self-serving trumpeting of certain features of the Enlightenment tradition out of which it emerges and whose death it has proclaimed. The purportedly liberating tendency of antifoundationalism is ambiguous, because if no perspective or tradition is privileged, then not only is there no reason for preferring one tradition or perspective to another, there is equally no reason for *not* preferring it to another.[35]

Thus antifoundationalism's charge against foundationalism—that it is authoritarian because it privileges one tradition, style, etc., over another—can be turned against antifoundationalism itself. One may then wonder to what extent we are being asked to endorse a kind of self-conscious dogmatism, and whether antifoundationalism's pronouncement of our entrapment in the given does not amount to a curious endorsement of, and an apologetics for, contemporary society, or whatever status quo one chooses. Philosophy as therapy would in fact seem to leave "everything as it is."[36] For the demonstration that the emperor has no clothes, that the Enlightenment and liberal tradition of modernity is without final justification, is coupled here with the claim that not only are no clothes to be found, neither are any needed. From the denial that justification is possible, coupled with the loss of foundations, the implication that all discourse is conversation or rhetoric, and the abandonment of the ideal of an autonomous rational standpoint of objectivity, there would necessarily seem to follow a final abandonment, not only of the ideal of philosophy as authoritative, but also of any claim to the critical force of philosophy. The historicizing and contextualizing of the modernist conception of reason, while arguably implicit in the self-critical project which it instituted and which antifoundationalism claims to have completed, would seem also to sever the link between reason and emancipation which this tradition attempted to forge and which antifoundationalists such as Habermas continue to espouse.

Initially, it might seem curious to mention this current received view in connection with Hegel, except perhaps by way of pointing out that his is a version of philosophy diametrically and thoroughly opposed to it. While there seems to be some recognition of the fact that Hegel mounted a critique of certain features of the foundational project,[37] it remains a fixed truism of contemporary philosophical education that he nonetheless unabashedly propounded an absolute philosophical science resting on a claim to having attained absolute—foundational—knowledge. According to one recent commentator, Hegel is "[l]ike other geniuses" in "confusing himself with God. . . . "[38]

Yet it is worth considering whether that view, which would directly and without further ado postulate a fixed and rigid opposition between current skepticism about philosophy and Hegel's position, does full justice both to the serious and complex issues involved, and to Hegel. I believe that such a rigid opposition is one-sided. To hold that Hegel is in disagreement with certain of the postfoundationalist views on the limited possibility of philosophy is certainly correct. Hegel unquestionably believed that a standpoint of autonomous rational objectivity was attainable, that philosophy as a rigorous science was possible, and that the legitimacy of certain features of the tradition of modernity could be established through a demonstration of their character as distinctively rational. In a nutshell, Hegel subscribed to and attempted to defend what I shall refer to as "the thesis of autonomous reason." "Henceforth, the principle of the independence of Reason, or of its absolute self-subsistence, is made a general principle of philosophy . . . "[39] But to assume therefore that Hegel was unaware of the difficulties, pitfalls, and paradoxes consequent upon the foundational project, and to suggest that his attempt at scientific philosophy is precritical—in either the Kantian or Rortian (or both) senses of that term—is a serious misreading of what Hegel was up to.

It can certainly be shown that Hegel was profoundly aware of the inherent difficulties involved in grounding, founding, or legitimating the philosophical enterprise. But not only that. I shall also contend, as curious as this must initially sound, that Hegel's own attempt to render philosophy scientific—the project carried out in the *Phenomenology of Spirit* of 1807, his self-described introduction to science—consists *as introduction* in nothing other than an immanent and thoroughgoing critique of the traditionally conceived manner of establishing philosophy as science. In brief, I aim to show that Hegel proposed to introduce the standpoint of autonomous reason and philosophical science through a radical and consummately destructive *critique* of foundational epistemology and transcendental philosophy. (See especially Chapter 3, "Hegel's *Phenomenology* as Introduction to Systematic Philosophy," Chapter 4, "Beginning Philosophy without 'Beginnings,'" and Chapter 5, "Philosophy and Dialectical Method.") Bracketing issues of historical interpretation, the position argued here is that the way to philosophy as a critical science of autonomous reason is, in part, through a realization of the impossibility of establishing such a science on epistemological foundations, and further, that this realization emerges in and through a thinking through of the foundational epistemological project. In addition, I argue that such a philosophical science fulfills philosophy's traditional aim of attaining a self-grounding discourse which can articulate objective truth, and that such philosophical science is not only compatible with, but is the only consistent articulation of the postmodernist notions of an antimetaphysical, nonauthoritarian, nonsubjectivist and nontotalizing discourse. (Hegel completes the philosophical tradition in a way which already incorporates the legitimate features of the postmodernist critique of it, and he does this without undermining the force of this critique and without succumbing to the problematic features of the postmodernist version of it.) By providing for a conceptualization of autonomous reason tied to a radical critique of foundationalism, this discourse would be nonfoundational; yet, as constructed through the self-constitution of autonomous reason which that critique first makes possible, systematic philosophy would provide a framework—and a legitimation—for modernist claims about the primacy of autonomy and reason.[40]

Therefore, this book presents the unusual thesis that a thoroughgoing critique of foundationalism is the basis for both a reconstitution of the philosophical tradition and a successful legitimation of modernity. I argue that, rather than presupposing foundationalism, philosophy and modernity require liberation from it. Put differently, I contend that contemporary oppositions between philosophy and postphilosophy and modernity and postmodernity are false dichotomies; that the philosophical revelation of the failure of foundationalism is part of the modernist tradition of the self-critique of reason; and that modernity, with its distinctive claims to the rightful primacy of autonomy, can only be legitimated on the basis of a demonstration that the autonomies of thought and action are neither in need of nor can have any foundations.

Thus, in addition to offering a new approach to ongoing debates about the future of philosophy and the status of modernity, a further concern of this book is to address the contemporary historical question of how the modern philosophical project should be interpreted. It presents a reinterpretation or reconstruction of Hegel's notion of systematic philosophy, one which discloses a profound antifoundational argument in Hegel, an argument which provides a basis for addressing contemporary metaphilosophical issues. In addition, insofar as it shows how Hegel based a philosophical system and a defense of modernity on a radical critique of foundationalism, *Philosophy Without Foundations* introduces a revisionist account of the modernist philosophical project: properly construed, the failure of foundationalism leads not to the rejection, but to the vindication of modernist notions of objectivity and rationality.

How can Hegel be read as a source for arguments which address the current crises in philosophy? Chapter 1, "Reason and the Problem of Modernity," presents an overview of Hegel's philosophy as both continuous with while still unique in the modernist project by showing how foundationalism prior to Hegel failed, and how, in responding to this failure, he anticipated many of the critical and positive claims of postmodernism while remaining true to central features of the philosophical tradition and the modern project. At a systematic level, it outlines the common assumptions underlying foundationalism and antifoundationalism, revealing how Hegel's rejection of them provides the framework for his distinctive attempt to legitimate modernity in his systematic project. Chapter 2, "Philosophy as Systematic Science," takes these issues outside of this historical framework; it centers on the contemporary foundationalist-antifoundationalist debate, and shows why this debate has reached an impasse requiring a different approach, and how systematic philosophy provides a response to this impasse. Chapter 3, "Hegel's *Phenomenology* as Introduction to Systematic Science," picks up the twofold themes of reinterpreting Hegel and criticizing foundationalism by showing how reading the *Phenomenology* as such a critique reconciles seeming contradictory claims Hegel made about his system and lays to rest interpretive controversies about the *Phenomenology*. Where "Hegel's *Phenomenology*" looks ahead to the logic and the system, Chapter 4, "Beginning Philosophy without 'Beginnings,'" looks back to the *Phenomenology* from the *Logic*, and again addresses both interpretive controversies about Hegel (pertaining to claims about the nature of logical science and the system) as well as reconstructing and assessing Hegel's arguments about how an immanent critique of foundationalism provides the basis for a foundation-free systematic philosophy. "Beginning" provides a further development of key aspects of the positive outcome of a Hegelian critique of foundationalism for philosophy, laying the basis for the notion that a rejection of subjectivity as foundational need not require an abandonment of objectivity and indicating how Hegel's radical antifoundationalism provides a basis for a nonfoundational system of autonomous reason. Chapter 5, "Philosophy and Dialectical Method," broadens the considerations of "Hegel's *Phenomenology*" and "Beginning" to show how the beginning of a systematic philosophy which the *Phenomenology*'s immanent critique of foundationalism has made possible provides a framework not only for logic, but for Hegel's system as a whole; addressed here in a preliminary fashion are crucial questions regarding the ways in which logic and system can be said to present an argument and how the system is not merely nonfoundational but antimetaphysical as well. Thus the argument (in "Reason" and "Beginning") presenting systematic philosophy as *sui generis*, as capturing features of both the philosophical tradition and of postmodernism's critique of it, are further articulated. Chapter 6, "On the Presumed Blasphemy of Hegelian Absolutism," indicates how this reconstruction of Hegel corrects the traditional interpretive claim that his philosophy is a blasphemous absolutism, and how, unlike contemporary antifoundationalism, the system in fact provides a coherent conceptualization of finitude.

Picking up on further considerations of the system as nonfoundational and of its contemporary relevance are both Chapter 7, "Hegel and Hermeneutics," and Chapter 8, "The Critique of Marx and Marxist Thought." Chapter 7 shows the centrality for hermeneutics of its confrontation with Hegel, and reiterates in the specific context of Gadamer's hermeneutics the fundamental problem with contemporary nonsystematic critiques of foundationalism and the effort to articulate finitude. Chapter 8 indicates how Marx and his followers have profoundly misread Hegel as a metaphysical idealist. Disclosing how Hegel's conception of systematic dialectical philosophy properly construes systematic philosophy as limited, it further shows how this limitation makes a viable critical theory possible, and how Marx, by misunderstanding Hegel's approach, falls prey to the idealism and absolutism he accuses Hegel of. The problematic character of recent attempts to overcome philosophy discussed in earlier chapters is further developed in Chapter 9, "The Dead End of Postmodernism," a critical overview of contemporary postmodernism which focuses specifically on the failure of Rorty's attempts to overcome foundationalism and establish something "postphilosophical." This chapter also provides a further consideration of how nonfoundational systematic philosophy may provide a way of fulfilling philosophy's traditional claim to articulate unconditional objective truth in a manner which nonetheless escapes postmodernism's charges of totalization and absolutism. Chapters 10, "The Renewed Appeal to Transcendental Arguments," and 11, "The Problematic Role of God in Modern Epistemology," again address the formal and the historical issue of foundationalism and the modern project from a contemporary perspective. Chapter 10 presents Donald Davidson's attempt to fulfill certain traditional philosophical objectives as part of the modernist transcendental project, and discloses how it, too, fails. Picking up on a reading of foundationalism's structure introduced in Chapter 6, "The Problematic Role of God" illustrates how appeals to a divine mind throughout the modern foundational epistemological-transcendental project, from Descartes through Nietzsche, both disclose a common gambit and reveal its fundamentally problematic character.

This book challenges contemporary assumptions about philosophy's inevitable demise in the collapse of foundationalism by showing how antifoundationalism remains committed to the central assumptions of foundationalism; additionally, it articulates a radical critique of foundationalism which transcends those assumptions and provides for a discourse which articulates philosophical truth as objective while yet nonmetaphysical and nonabsolutist. By locating the grounds for this response to the current crisis in philosophy in Hegel, it also challenges what has been the received view in contemporary Hegel scholarship.

PART ONE

❧

The Relevance of Hegel

Chapter 1

REASON AND THE PROBLEM OF MODERNITY

Perhaps a new form of systematic philosophy will be found which has nothing whatever to do with epistemology but which nevertheless makes normal philosophical inquiry possible.

—Richard Rorty

The sleep of reason produces monsters.

—Goya

Hegel is back.

—Ian Hacking

At least among those whose philosophical education includes a study of its history, it has long been a commonplace that, in line with his immediate predecessors, Hegel sought to articulate a distinctively modern conception of philosophical rationality or reason in order to address what he regarded as distinctively modern theoretical and practical problems.[1] The problems underlying Hegel's philosophical project can be described as distinctively modern because they concerned two things: on the one hand, theoretical or epistemological issues arising uniquely out of the emergence of modern scientific thought in its break from the prevailing intellectual tradition and, on the other hand, practical issues arising uniquely out of the French Revolution in its break from prevailing social and political traditions.[2] As I shall suggest in more detail, these two revolutionary events were perceived by their philosophical supporters as standing in need of justification or legitimation. In addition, these philosophical supporters felt that, because of the

21

nature of the claims being made in and by these revolutions, this legitimation could only be provided by philosophy.

According to this traditional view, Hegel is at one with his predecessors from Descartes through Kant, Fichte, and Schelling in seeking to provide a standpoint of reason which could articulate, justify, and ground the new conception of our place in the cosmos which follows from an endorsement of modern principles of scientific thought and modern principles of action.[3] Thus, in broadest terms, the core issue or problem of modernity, when looked at philosophically, is that of justification or legitimation, and modern philosophy's major historical theme is the search for an adequate rational-foundational standpoint from which the tasks of legitimation could be accomplished.[4]

If at least some features of the broader context of modern philosophy and of Hegel's thought which I have noted have long since been a philosophical commonplace, it is fast becoming a commonplace of more recent times that both the pre- and postHegelian traditions of modern foundational philosophy have consistently failed in their efforts to provide the sort of rational legitimation for the norms of cognition and conduct which both supporters and critics of modernity perceive as in need of legitimation. Put simply, and in its most contemporary version, the central core of attacks on the modern philosophical-foundational project seems to arise from the conviction that the philosophical standpoint of reason from out of and upon which modern conceptions of knowledge and conduct could be justified—as legitimate because paradigmatically rational—is unattainable.[5] It is argued that reason is unable to attain self-transparency concerning its own conditions, and that the contexts of discourse in which problems of knowledge and conduct are to be addressed are inherently and inescapably extra-rational. Claiming that we are embedded in a web of givenness which resists rational penetration in some final sense, critics hold that criteria of knowledge and conduct must always lack an adequately rational foundation.[6]

In fact, the basic program of the philosophical critique of the claim that modern scientific thought and modern society are distinctively rational is by no means a recent invention. To one degree and in one form or another, the three central tenets of this critical view have been with us for quite a long time. To perceive that the epistemic and practical ideals of modernity have continued to stand in need of a philosophical accounting since their inception, to conclude that the various attempts to provide one have failed, and to make the subsequent critical claim of having unmasked these ideals as false idols—these have long since ceased to be original assertions. One might hold that the philosophical critique of modernity counts as a distinct tradition in its own right. From such a perspective the larger tradition of modern thought can be witnessed as a struggle and a dialectical interplay between those who contend that modern cognitive and social practices have a distinctively rational core, and those who contend that they do not. In this way one may locate the beginning of the antimodernist tradition within modernity with Kierkegaard, Marx, and Nietzsche—the holy trinity of the idea that modern bourgeois society is hollow, corrupt, and corrupting, and fraught with a high degree of systematic self-deception which is mirrored in the vain efforts of philosophers to provide this society with rational justification. Insofar as one can place the origins of philosophical critiques of modernity with these thinkers and these notions, then it is easy to see that variations on these antimodernist themes have been a significant feature in philosophy since their time.

Thus one might wonder which is the dominant trend in modern philosophy as a whole, and whether modern philosophy does not, in an important sense, come to an end with Hegel and his perceived failures. For at least when viewed from an anti- or postmodernist position, postHegelian efforts to provide rational, legitimating foundations for the central tenets of modern thought and society—the efforts undertaken by the schools and traditions arising out of phenomenology and logical positivism—begin to appear now as doomed exceptions to a growing consensus of naysayers: in the burgeoning camp of critics of the modern rational-foundational project we certainly find the later Wittgenstein, Heidegger, Gadamer, Foucault, Derrida, Habermas, Feyerabend, MacIntyre, Davidson, Rorty—and if Rorty is correct, Quine, Sellars, Putnam and Kuhn.[7] Agreement on this seems to be cutting across traditional philosophical boundaries.

One curious thing about this critical tradition is its relation to Hegel. Leaving aside the more recent critics of modernity who ignore Hegel altogether, such as Wittgenstein, or dismiss him outright, such as Heidegger, the views on Hegel of several others— certainly Foucault, Derrida, Gadamer, Habermas, MacIntyre, and Rorty—are complex and often ambivalent.[8] We find, for example, an explicit appreciation and endorsement of aspects of Hegel's phenomenological critique of foundational subject-based epistemology and transcendental philosophy in Rorty, Gadamer, and Habermas.[9] In MacIntyre, and to varying degrees in Habermas, Rorty, and Feyerabend, we find a reiteration of aspects of Hegel's holism: assertions about the contextual embeddedness of knowledge and morality and the irreducibly intersubjective character of cognition and individuality. Broadly, and also in agreement with Hegel, we can find the increasing endorsement of an historicist perspective. For certainly in Gadamer, MacIntyre, and Rorty, we find agreement with its first serious practitioner, Hegel, about the centrality of the history of philosophy for philosophical understanding. And more generally there is increasing agreement with Hegel—most recently for example in postKuhnian philosophy of science—that ideas and theories are intertwined with and incapable of being adequately understood apart from their historical, social, political, and cultural contexts.[10]

On the negative side, though, the relation between Hegel and contemporary critics of modernity is easier to delineate. They all reject in Hegel what they perceive as the character of the philosophical-rational position or standpoint—the system—from which he developed his particular views on knowledge, man, and society. Like others whose rejection of Hegel is complete and unequivocal, they will have nothing to do with Hegel's purported idealistic and metaphysical absolutism, which they identify with his claim to have brought philosophy to the standpoint of an autonomous rational science. What they occasionally wish to do is mine, from the wreckage of his system, those features of it in accordance with their own outlooks.[11]

Given this state of affairs, a question arises which at first seems to be of interest only to students of the history of philosophy, but which has, I believe, extrahistorical and genuinely philosophical significance. How did a self-acknowledged defender of modernity and a participant in the tradition which seeks to find a legitimation for it, a philosopher who espouses the autonomy and self-sufficiency of reason, anticipate and articulate so many of those critical points noted above? This question may take on added weight when one appreciates that, according to critics of the modern foundational tradition, these 'postmodernist' points—antifoundationalism, holism, and historicism—follow from a rejection of the ideal of autonomous reason and are incompatible with it as well as with modernity's claim to a distinctive legitimacy and rationality.[12] To put my question in a more challenging way, it is possible to disentangle a *whole* Hegel from his perceived commitment to absolute idealism? Can we somehow make sense of a Hegel whose agreement with the postmoderns on antifoundationalism, holism, and historicism can be seen not as an aberration, but rather as a consequence of his conception of philosophical rationality? Are antifoundationalism, holism, and historicism, properly understood, compatible with a claim to autonomous reason and a philosophical system? And if this can be worked out, will it suggest—as paradoxical as this may sound—that a philosophical legitimation of modernity, rather than being rendered impossible by antifoundationalism, holism, and historicism, is inseparable from them? Is it possible that Hegel saw these things and worked out these connections?

I believe that the answer to all these questions is yes. In an attempt to sketch the reasons for my belief I shall argue three things.

(1) Hegel's position on—his understanding and defense of—modernity is unique. To an extent not usually recognized, Hegel is an anomalous phenomenon when looked at from either the modernist or the antimodernist perspective.

(2) The seeming discord noted previously between many of Hegel's conclusions and his systematic position—with its commitment to a notion of autonomous reason—may be resolved insofar as we understood the manner in which Hegel undertook the project of a rational legitimation of modernity in and through a conception of autonomous reason. This is the question of whether or not, and if so how, we can reconcile the points where Hegel is in agreement with critics of modernity with his commitment to the project of legitimating modernity and with his belief in the autonomy of reason.

In this regard, my aim is to put forth a revisionist scheme. I want to suggest that we need to reassess Hegel's conception of philosophy as a system and that, while Hegel is deeply concerned with the foundationalist project of his predecessors, he nevertheless breaks with central features of it and is *not* a foundationalist in the sense attacked by, amongst others, Nietzsche, Heidegger, Gadamer, and most recently Richard Rorty, in *Philosophy and the Mirror of Nature.*

(3) If I am correct about these points, then Hegel needs to be introduced into contemporary debates about knowledge and practice along with Rorty's Dewey and MacIntyre's Aristotle.

So the issues I plan to address are three-fold: (1) What are the problems of modernity from Hegel's perspective and how does he attempt to deal with them? (2) How might Hegel's project as a defense of modernity be perceived as in continuity with, while yet as distinctly different from, that of his predecessors in the foundational tradition? (3) Which features of Hegel's treatment of the problems of modernity are worthy of contemporary consideration and how might Hegel be seen as having provided a legitimation of modernity?

I. The Problems of Modernity

The tasks of Hegel's project as a philosophy of modernity arise from
two related sources: first, from a general belief, shared to certain
extents by some of his predecessors, that the decisive breaks from
past authority heralded by the scientific and French revolutions
stand in need of legitimation, and that this legitimation must consist in the discovery, articulation, and clarification of general principles for knowledge and practice in consonance with at least some
of the specific core claims of these revolutions. As I shall indicate,
for Hegel this need for legitimation will appear not only as a need
to reject what the prerevolutionary traditions had regarded as specifically authoritative in matters of cognition and conduct; more
generally and radically, the legitimation of modern notions of cognition and conduct will require for Hegel a demonstrative and thoroughgoing rejection of the idea that the past or tradition in their
givenness—indeed, that *whatever* we might find given—must and
ought to be taken forthwith as authoritative for knowledge and
conduct.[13]

Second, Hegel's own project is more specifically shaped by his
perception of the inadequacies of his predecessors in successfully
legitimating the breaks from past authority announced by the scientific and French revolutions. In general terms, for Hegel the core
of this inadequacy stems from what he sees as these modernists'
attempts to substitute, for the old, privileged and authoritative
givens of the then prevailing intellectual and socio-political traditions, what are new, allegedly *rational* privileged givens as the
authoritative modern principles for cognition and conduct. To anticipate, Hegel's disagreement with this approach to the issue of
legitimation stems from the fact that he sees the task of philosophical legitimation as resting on a thoroughgoing demonstration
of the autonomy of reason from any and all givens, privileged or
otherwise.

But first of all, how is it that these revolutions appear as
decisive breaks from the past and as in need of a legitimation
which will involve a search for new principles of cognition and
conduct? How are the modern approaches to knowledge and action
distinctive? And why is modernity as the outcome of these two
revolutions in need of philosophical legitimation?

As regards the scientific revolution, it constitutes a radical or
revolutionary break from past authority because the new truths
concerning nature which it asserted were out of consonance both
with the teleological tradition of Aristotelian science and with

common sense.[14] Thus, from the point of view of the philosophical supporters of the new science, the legitimacy of its claims seemingly had to rest on the further philosophical or metascientific claim that this approach embodied not simply a new method for arriving at the truth about nature, but rather *the* true and proper method of cognition as such.[15] Hence one major concern of the modern philosophical project becomes defined as an investigation into the foundations of knowledge, an investigation to be conducted in and by the mind, reason, consciousness, understanding—in and by the reflecting subject. For, whether the new method of science was perceived by its inventors and legitimators as rationalist or empiricist in character (whether ideas or sense impressions are its basic foundations), it seemed nonetheless that only an exercise of reason could establish and legitimate this method and its truth claims against the recognized authorities of Aristotle and common sense.[16] Given the deviation of some of the central truth claims of the new science from these traditional authorities, what had to be established in general was that final authority in matters of cognition of nature resides within the mind of the cognizing subject. So, to succeed in this legitimation (a legitimation which would seek to ground the right to freedom of thought in science and the autonomy of science from external authorities), philosophy would have to demonstrate that *all* minds share a common set of cognitive principles sufficient for providing knowledge of the truth. Thus, we have the modern project of foundational epistemology. It sought to show that the ultimate foundations for determining truth lay, not in certain privileged texts or institutions, as the tradition would have it, but rather within the thinking-rational subject, in its possessing access to certain privileged, knowledge-foundational and criteriological givens, be they sense impressions, innate ideas, or *a priori* forms of judgment.[17]

Paralleling the rejection of the authority of tradition in matters of cognition announced by the scientific revolution, the French Revolution was witnessed as heralding a rejection of the authority of tradition in matters of action and conduct, both individual and social, and as thus also necessitating the attempt to establish reason, or the autonomous rational subject, as the final authority for practical judgment. For what was perceived by its philosophical supporters as this revolution's combined assertion of an in principle human equality and a universally shared right to individual autonomy or liberty flew in the face both of common sense and of long-standing social and political tradition. In the former case, these modernist assertions conflicted with the evidence that human beings are by nature unequal, suited for different tasks and responsibilities. In the latter case they conflicted with traditional notions of naturally or divinely ordained hierarchies of rights and privileges, hierarchies seemingly appropriate to the given evidence of human inequality.[18]

Thus again, since neither given tradition nor the given evidence of common sense supported the unprecedented revolutionary claims of equality and universal autonomy now being asserted here in the practical domain, it seemed that their only proper articulation and justification could come from reason. Again, and again because of the unprecedented and radical character of the claims in question, philosophy was called upon to find a new authority—now regarding conduct—located within the individual subject. Paralleling its task in regard to science, the philosophical exercise of reason would have to demonstrate the legitimacy of the ideas of equality and freedom by discovering and articulating those universal principles or grounds for judgement on the basis of which all individual wills could constitute a harmonious social and political world, when once freed from the constraints of tradition and despite the seeming diversity of their particular inclinations. And thus, we have the modern philosophical-foundational projects in the areas of morality, politics, and economics, with philosophers seeking to show that the ultimate foundations for right conduct lie within each and every autonomous subject, in its possessing access to certain commonly shared and privileged behavior-legislating givens, be they desires, natural sentiments, or innate rules.[19]

In broad terms, then, this is how Hegel understood the efforts of his predecessors. He saw rationalists, empiricists, and transcendental idealists all engaged in the task of seeking to discover some given, universally shared bases for knowledge and action within the individual, either as a rational or a natural sensing being. But what prompted him to pursue the process of articulation and legitimation further, and in a decisively different manner than his predecessors? What pushed Hegel on was the conviction—shared by him with contemporary critics of modernity—that the foundational project as undertaken by empiricists, rationalists, and transcendental philosophers was bankrupt and could succeed neither in the specific task of illuminating concrete principles for knowledge and action nor in the general task of legitimating the ideal of individual autonomy itself.[20]

How so? First of all, and as was already clear to Kant, the empiricist foundational project had failed, and necessarily so. For what had originated as a search for universal principles for knowledge and conduct within the domain of the autonomous subject as a natural, sensing being had culminated in Hume's thinking through the empiricist position to its ultimate consequences.[21] These consequences were devastating from a foundationalist and modernist perspective, and not merely because Hume's specific conclusions about knowledge and conduct were antithetical to the modernist outlook. In addition, Hume's skeptical position had been arrived at through the very practice of critical reflection which was seemingly the only possible path to a secure legitimation of the modernist perspective. Through rational-critical reflection Hume had demonstrated that, on strict empiricist principles, matters of knowledge and conduct—of science and morality—are and can only be fundamentally and irreducibly subjective matters of habit and convention, without any ultimate, strictly rational foundations. Consequently he advocated skepticism in knowledge and the hewing to tradition in matters of conduct.[22] Thus, if new foundational principles for distinctively new notions of cognition and conduct were to be established, it became all the more clear in light of Hume that they had to be found, if they were to be found at all, in humans as rational, in reason. In opposition to Hume, it had to be shown that reason contains as given universal principles of judgement on the basis of which humans as rational are capable of constructing, from the sensibly given, a common intelligible world of knowledge and experience and a common and harmonious social world. But, more significantly given Hume's negative achievement *vis-à-vis* rationalist metaphysics, this project as a reply to Hume presupposed showing that reason in fact possesses the power and authority to make such discoveries and claims.

That is, it had to be shown before all else that what reason might claim to find within itself as the privileged and given principles for knowledge and conduct are not in fact arbitrary posits in the style of the rationalist metaphysics which Hume had decisively criticized. Thus Kant, having been awoken from his dogmatic slumber by Hume, called for a critique of reason itself as an unavoidable preliminary task for the future of modern philosophy.

For Hegel, then, it is on this issue—the demonstration of reason's autonomy and the consequent demonstration that reason can rightfully lay claim to possessing an authority which can challenge tradition—that the transcendental projects of Kant, Fichte, and Schelling fail. And it is around this issue—the issue of *how* reason might establish its autonomy, and of what follows from such a demonstration—that we can see Hegel parting company with the whole foundationalist endeavor.

Hegel saw that the confrontation between Kant's, Fichte's, and Schelling's foundational-transcendental rationalism and Hume's skeptical empiricism could only be a standoff, and that the only possible way beyond it to establish the autonomy of reason and the legitimacy of its claims to authority would be by rejecting the whole conception of mind or reason which underlies *both* the skeptical and the transcendental-foundationalist positions.[23] In what sense does Hegel see the transcendental-foundational project as a failure and as issuing in a standoff between foundationalism and antifoundationalism, between modernism and antimodernism? How does he attempt to go beyond this *aporia?* This brings me to the second of my three main points and more specifically to my revisionist claim that Hegel rejects foundationalism as a basis for legitimating modernity.

II. The Hegelian Difference

In brief, the failure of Kant and the transcendental endeavor lies in the fact that this elaborate and complex approach cannot finally meet the objections of Humean skepticism, which is ultimately a challenge not merely to certain specific claims of reason but also and more fundamentally a challenge to the very conception of reason as adequate to making *any* legitimate and authoritative claims about matters of fact. From a Humean perspective the Kantian transcendental gambit could show that, *given* Newtonian science and Lutheran morality, we can reason back in a transcendental fashion to the ultimate principles of judgement which are the necessary conditions for the possibility of these modes of cognition and conduct. But that just these purportedly given modes of thinking and acting are the universally necessary and legitimate modes of cognition and conduct *überhaupt*, that they have not been arbitrarily selected or posited, is beyond the power of the transcendental method to establish.[24] In the face of Hume's skepticism, which challenges reason's pretension to critical authority, the transcendental-foundational approach can only appear as a mode of argumentation which finally establishes nothing with the certainty which it claims. For just what is at stake here is the *exclusive* legitimacy and universality of those modes of cognition and conduct taken in transcendental thought as the original privileged givens whose foundations are articulated and allegedly grounded in the critical project. Thus, the transcendental gambit of assuming their legitimacy—taking them not as some, but as the givens—and then

finding principles in reason which account for them gets one nowhere,[25] at least insofar as one has pursued the more radical self-
critique of reason along Hume's lines.

So, Hume's challenge could be seen as standing, a challenge
echoed in contemporary critiques of modernity and foundationalism
such as Heidegger's. Hume's final challenge was to contend that,
because reason is always and inescapably conditioned by what are
(presumptively) externally given factors, any determinations it might
make by way of issuing a challenge to the authority of extra-rational givens in the name of internally given rules of reason are and
must be arbitrary. As such, these claims of reason ought to be
abandoned in the face of the more primal givens of experience as
conditioned by tradition and convention, the extra-rational background on the basis and from out of which all reasoning emerges.
This claim for the recognition of the primacy of the other-than-
rational might be said to be paralleled in Heidegger's demand that
we attune ourselves to the primordial call of Being which is ineluctably resistant to any rational penetration which would challenge
its authority over us.[26]

How might this state of affairs be viewed along Hegelian lines
as a standoff, albeit one with which those skeptical of reason's
power could be more comfortable? From Hegel's perspective, the
notion that a philosophical impasse has been reached can emerge
when one begins to consider, from a broader outlook, what can be
seen as the *common* assumptions of the anti- and pro-modernists,
the antifoundationalists and the foundationalists.[27]

What are these common assumptions? For one thing, it is not
only that the transcendental philosophers and Hume both reach
their conclusions through critical reflection on the givens of experience. Both Hume and Kant begin their critical reflection with assumptions about the given nature of human experience, seeking to
discover through critical reflection in what respects, and how much
of, given experience is philosophically legitimate. At a higher level
of generality, they also share, in one respect, a common overview of
the nature of reason itself. For both agree, despite their differing
views on the specifics, that reason is and always must be conditioned by certain determining factors, certain inescapable givens.[28]
For Hume these are factors external to reason: in matters of cognition they are the sensible givens which legislate to reason; in matters of conduct they are the passions to which reason is and must
be a slave. For Kant and the transcendentalists the factors that
condition, limit, and determine reason are its internally and in-
nately given *a priori* rules and principles, which must legislate to

the sensibly given manifold in matters of cognition, and which ought to legislate to the passions in matters of conduct.[29] And as Kant concludes the meta-critical lesson of the critical philosophy, although these principles are found in reason they are nonetheless *givens* to which reason must submit itself in any coherent and legitimate exercise of its powers. They are fixed givens beyond which reason must not extend itself no matter how much it may be driven by its very nature to do so.[30]

And thus to Hegel, the point of contention in his times between foundationalists and antifoundationalists—paralleled perhaps in our own—appears as a standoff. It appears as an *aporia* because both positions are based on conflicting and seemingly irresolvable claims concerning what a property critical reflection on experience indicates as the necessary determining and conditioning factors for knowledge and conduct. Both Hegel's pro- and antimodernist predecessors agreed that the rational subject is conditioned and limited in matters of knowledge and action by certain givens. Yet they disagreed on the source, nature, extent, and consequences of this conditioning, and on its limitations. (Moreover, they particularly disagreed on its practical entailments.) Beyond the points of commonality, they disagreed on these particulars because, while they held similar views on the given character of experience, they parted company in their critical accounts of just what is to be found in the deeper analysis of human subjectivity which finally makes this experience possible and which thus establishes the character and range of its legitimacy. Hence, finally, from Hegel's view, each side was incapable of demonstrating to its opponent that what was being presented as the final and ultimately determining and conditioning factors were in fact finally authoritative and determining. On the issue of what provides individuals with legitimate principles and guidelines for knowledge and action, one side holds that it is what is given to the senses by reason, the other that it is what is given to reason by the senses which constitutes these principles.[31]

So we can see Hegel coming to ask if there is any way to get beyond this impasse. (To which the Habermas-Gadamer debate bears at least a family resemblance.)[32] Do the outcomes of the pro- and antimodernist attempts to show specifically what it is that conditions reason in fact show that reason is and must always be conditioned by certain givens? That is, is the only final meta-perspective here something like this: that these conflicting conclusions on just what the determining factors are point to a *general* impotence on the part of reason as regards its ability to ultimately discover just what always conditions and determines it? Must we reconcile ourselves, in the manner of Nietzsche, to the idea that reason must always arbitrarily posit some determinative foundations, foundations which are then remorselessly unmasked as illusory, and so on, *ad infinitum?* Is the only position beyond foundationalism and skepticism one where the life of the mind— and life by the mind—is a tale told by an idiot, full of sound and fury, etc.? Must we resign ourselves to the genial nihilism which regards human existence as pointless positing?[33]

Or—and I take this to be Hegel's view—do the conflicting conclusions perhaps indicate instead that it is a mistake to conclude that reason *must* be conditioned by any *given* factors? Might it be that this general negative conclusion (disagreements about the particulars of what conditions reason aside) follows from the fact that these efforts at critical self-examination always began with the conditioned character of reason as an assumption (so that all that needed to be done was to determine its specifics)? Does the fact of the conflicting conclusions arrived at by foundationalists and skeptics perhaps point to or suggest the possibility that the conflict over conclusions, rather than providing the necessary impotence of reason in the face of the given, stems instead from the fact that, in both of these cases, the process of critical reflection began with certain arbitrarily selected givens as the starting points? Might this metacritical discovery about the ruling assumption of prior efforts point to the possibility of a further self-examination of reason? Might not such a further self-consideration have a different outcome just because and insofar as it does not begin, as its predecessors did, with the assumption that reason is inescapably conditioned by certain givens (either external or internal)? Put differently, might a self-consideration of reason arrive at different conclusions if it did not begin with the assumption that the given features of human subjectivity defined, governed, and limited the nature and prospects of reason? And might not this outcome differ radically from both foundationalism and antifoundationalism, at least as regards reason's capacity for autonomy?[34]

The conventional wisdom, a commonplace going back to Kant and echoed most recently in Gadamer, is that it displays the self-deceptive arrogance of reason to assert its autonomy from the limiting conditions of human finitude and subjectivity. Could not one rather suggest that the deeper arrogance lies in unreflectively presupposing that the conditions of our merely human subjectivity— as they happen to be interpreted at some particular time—delimit the capacities of our (merely human) reason?

How might such an alternative reaction to the standoff emerge? For one thing, it is possible that these conflicting outcomes and the apparent failure of the rational-foundational project in general indicate that from the start it is a mistake to attempt to establish the right of reason to legislate in knowledge and conduct by seeking *givens* in reason; conditions or principles which allegedly ground "given" experience and which need only to be uncovered and made perspicuous. Perhaps the key to demonstrating the authority of reason over what is given to it lies not, *à la* the critical philosophy, in searching within reason to discover given determinate principles in which modern claims about rational autonomy in thought and action are grounded, but rather in first showing that *no* givens, either internal or to external to reason need necessarily condition or determine it in its operations.

Furthermore, could not one argue that an implicit indication of reason's power to transcend what is given might be found in the very efforts of critical reflection to establish the given, reason-determining conditions? These projects, both foundational and antifoundational, aim to specify what they take to be the conditioning and limiting features of reason's operation. But, as Jacobi had already suggested, if an exercise in philosophical-critical reflection can come to specify and articulate these conditions, does not this very exercise and employment of reason indicate that these allegedly reason-determining and limiting conditions can, in some sense, be gone beyond—that the exercise of reason which establishes them is not and cannot itself be *thoroughly* subject to them?[35]

But how might such a demonstration of the potential autonomy of reason be effected? How might it be shown that reason need not necessarily be conditioned in its operations by any givens? Perhaps—and I take this to be the argument of Hegel's *Phenomenology of Spirit*—by working to show systematically and immanently that any process of critical reflection which attempts to establish that reason *is* governed or determined by certain givens (internal or external) is finally aporitic. Displaying the *aporia* would involve revealing that the very standpoint of critical reflection *from which* the conditioned character of reason could be articulated always *eo ipso* shows itself as a standpoint which transcends the allegedly unconditional reason-determining conditions it aims to establish. And this feature of reason's persistent self-transcendence of the purportedly ultimate transcendental conditions which it posits would be shown to emerge just because of reason's alleged capacity to demonstrate the exclusive legitimacy and rulership of these conditions. To establish ultimate limiting conditions, reason must transcend them; once it has transcended them it can no longer claim that they are ultimate. In this way, one might attempt to show immanently that both foundationalism and antifoundationalism are systematically self-defeating.

To what would such a demonstration lead? This question is vital in terms of seeing how different Hegel's rejection of foundationalism is from contemporary antifoundationalism. It could finally come to indicate not only that no *given* conditions can finally be established once and for all as the unconditional, absolute, fundamental principles of reason—a negative point on which Hegel is in agreement with various contemporary antifoundationalists. In addition—and here is one central point of difference—by proceeding systematically in a consideration of attempts to establish such reason-determining conditions, this consideration might finally come to unmask as arbitrary and unfounded that fundamental meta-assumption about reason's own nature in terms of which its operations must always be viewed as conditioned by certain givens. This immanent critique of foundationalism and antifoundationalism might reveal the illegitimacy of what is, for Hegel, the primal further common assumption at work both in foundationalism and antifoundationalism, an assumption he sees as the ultimate and heretofore hidden, unjustified, given operative in all attempts to demonstrate that reason is necessarily and inescapably conditioned by some given or givens.

For Hegel, the hidden assumption underlying the view of reason as necessarily heteronomous is the notion that reason's operations must always and can only be construed according to the model of conscious awareness. This assumption holds that reason must be construed according to that mode of thinking in terms of which whatever is thought *is* always in some way given and fixed in its determinate character in virtue of being there—given—as an object (*Gegenstand*) for a thinking awareness. As a systematic consideration of the legitimacy of this "natural assumption . . . in philosophy," the *Phenomenology* works to show that when the process of critical reflection by philosophical consciousness comes finally to the point of defining and grounding its own presupposed structure, the structure of consciousness, as necessarily determinative for thought, this ultimate act of self-legitimation is and must be one in which the fixed and minimal distinction definitive of consciousness—the distinction between awareness and its object—is eliminated or collapses.[36] For only when this distinction is suspended can consciousness show that what it takes the object to be—its representation of the given—is the correct representation of the given as given. Only at the moment of the elimination of the distinction between thought and its object can the "referential skyhook" requisite to complete the project of foundational epistemology be attained.[37]

This outcome—Chapter VIII of the *Phenomenology*—would show thereby that the view which holds that *all* thought is and *must* necessarily be conditioned by some given cannot critically ground—legitimate *überhaupt*—that very understanding of the nature of thought or reason (the consciousness model) which could finally establish in a philosophically adequate fashion just this allegedly necessary fact. Phrased in a different way, this would constitute subjectivity's immanent, deconstructive discovery that its own constitutive structure—as a structure which seeks to posit foundations—is itself an arbitrary posit.

This metacritical discovery—this critique of critical philosophy, of the unchallengeable primacy of subjectivity, and of the correspondence model of truth—would then reveal that to engage in reasoning with the assumption that reason's operations are and must be conditioned by some given is, at least at this juncture, an arbitrary assumption. And coming to an awareness of the arbitrary character of this fundamental assumption common to foundationalists and antifoundationalists alike would thus open the way to or point to the possibility of, an exercise of reason which possesses at least the potential for genuine autonomy.[38] For insofar as we come to see the arbitrary character of assuming in philosophy that whatever reason conceives must be founded in some given determinacy—something always taken for granted in that process of critical reflection which presumably took nothing for granted— then perhaps a self-consideration of reason can take place which *is* autonomous. This self-consideration of reason may be autonomous in the sense that neither any given determinacy, nor the very structure according to which determinacy is construed as always to some extent given, is illicitly appealed to in reason's constitution of its own domain.

My claim at this juncture is only that the *Phenomenology*, through its immanently critical deconstruction of the standpoint which assumes the impossibility of such autonomy, reveals the possibility for such an autonomous self-constitution of reason. The existence of such a possibility does not, of course, amount to anything like a demonstration that Hegel, or anyone else, has succeeded in creating a system of reason whose concepts are exclusively generated in an autonomous fashion. Nor have I indicated how reason might go about engaging in a procedure of autonomous self-constitution which, even in being autonomous, is not at the same time arbitrary in the determinations it constitutes. These are matters which cannot be gone into here.[39] But, assuming for the sake of argument that Hegel has at least offered a system which can make a plausible, *prima facie* claim to being a system whose determinacies are those of autonomous reason, I will now turn to my third question. What features of Hegel's treatment of the problem of modernity are of contemporary relevance? I will address this question in two parts. Assuming Hegel's systematic philosophy, or parts of it, is a system of autonomous reason. (1) where does this place him in the contemporary spectrum, and (2) in what sense has he presented a legitimation of modernity?

III. Legitimating Modernity

(1) For one thing, and as I have suggested in my remarks about Hegel's assessment of the inadequacies of his predecessors, his position puts him in agreement with those contemporary philosophers such as Rorty who have argued against the foundational epistemological project with its commitment to the primacy of reflective consciousness and the representational or correspondence model of truth. Unlike such contemporary critics of foundationalism however, and as I have also suggested, Hegel's rejection of the adequacy of consciousness as a paradigm in philosophy does not lead him to skeptical, relativistic, nihilistic, pragmatic, religious, or quasi-mystical conclusions which devalue reason and explicitly or implicitly suggest that we must subordinate reason to some other authority. Hegel's systematic philosophy acknowledges no such ultimate authority over reason, be this authority the passions or nature, tradition or convention, the material and economic conditions for the reproduction of the species, the hermeneutic consciousness, the (allegedly) necessary conditions for the possibility of linguistic communication, the will as will to power, God, or the Being of beings. Hegel's systematic philosophy rejects all such foundations, and his critique of foundationalism opens the way for the creation of an alternative conception and system of reason, one whose claim to authority rests solely on its character as having articulated concepts and principles which can be seen to be the exclusive determinations of autonomous reason.

The following should be stressed at this point, for it is a key feature of this revisionist account of Hegel. Any authority such a system of autonomous reason might command does not rest on any claim to be an account of reality as we find it or as it is given. Hegel's systematic philosophy is not; in fact, it is anything *but* a metaphysics, either idealist, materialist, realist, descriptive, or critical. It is none of these simply because the very beginning of the system—following upon the *Phenomenology's* critique—lies in its severing, in and for this system, of all connections with that model of reason (the consciousness or subjectivistic model) which underlies all possible metaphysics. This system rejects at its start that model for philosophical thought which must be presupposed in order to postulate either a contrast (as in realist metaphysics) or an identity (as in idealist or materialist metaphysics) of thought and object or mind and nature.[40]

Hence, and in sharp contrast with Marx, the dialectical generation of categories or concepts in Hegel's system, and the necessity which pertains to this process and to conceptual relations is exclusively intra-systemic. (And hence, for Hegel, even the system of pure reason is limited, although its limitations are strictly self-constituted.) What this means is that dialectical reasoning as a philosophical science and dialectical necessity as a feature of it are exclusively matters of the constitution and relation of thought determinations. Thus the system contains neither an explicit nor an implicit claim as to whether 'reality as we find it'—reality construed according to the model of consciousness—either is or is not dialectical *in re.*[41] In addition, this system is not a transcendental system of categories, principles, or rules in terms of which a thinking subject allegedly must cognize reality construed as what is in some manner given to consciousness.[42] For—and once again as in the case of metaphysics—such a transcendental philosophy presupposes the model of consciousness which takes as paradigmatically and irreducibly given the distinction between subject and object, the exact presupposition which this system rejects as primal and as exclusively and irreducibly authoritative for philosophy at its start.[43]

If this system claims to be neither a descriptive account of reality as it is given nor an account of the forms of thought according to which reality must be cognized, if it is founded neither on a purported—foundational—insight into the fundamental nature of being nor on a purported—foundational—insight into the conditions for the possibility of conscious cognition, what then is this system? Hegel's philosophical system is, I would suggest, *sui generis.* In its fully developed form it is simply the conceiving of reality from the standpoint of autonomous reason, which, more specifically, is that standpoint which rejects the authority both of any specific given and of the framework of givenness itself as demonstrably determinative for reason. Alternatively, it is what we might call *Realphilosophie*, using Hegel's term to describe the system beyond the *Phenomenology* and the *Science of Logic*. And as such—and this is a further feature of its self-constituted limitedness—this system does not deny the reality of anything 'given' external to reason, or to itself as the system of reason. In strict terms, questions of what can be actually established by modes of cognition which assume givenness and which take account of the given in their actual employment fall outside of the system.

So this system does not deny *überhaupt* the factuality of the given or the possibility of modes of cognition appropriate to it. For, as a final, metaphysical conclusion, such a denial would require cognitive reference from within the system to the allegedly given, just in order to establish an idealistic rejection of its ontological ultimacy, and that reference would entail a lapse into the mode of consciousness whose suspension is a precondition for this system's autonomy. Rather, what this system *does* deny is simply that the determinative primacy *for reason* of any such givens can be demonstrated.[44] So this system does not 'absolutize' reason in the sense of denying that there are any limits to it. As noted above in regard to Marx, who from the point of view of Hegel lapses into idealism in postulating reality and history as literally dialectical in character, this system does acknowledge its limits, and it must do so for the sake of its own claim to autonomy. The price of the claim to reason's autonomous self-constitution, as based on a rejection of the given as foundational in and for it, is an appreciation of the self-closure of the system. Insofar as the autonomy of the system rests on a rejection of the philosophical authority of the given, a rejection of the foundational standpoint which assumes the possibility of a referential skyhook, self-closure is entailed in the sense that the completed system of reason cannot return to the framework of descriptive reference which was abjured as operative in and for it at its start. (This is, in part, my revisionist account of the notorious "circularity" of Hegel's system.)

Nonetheless, those features of the system which comprise its autonomy and its self-limitedness are at the same time just those features of it which give it a certain normative force *vis-à-vis* the given. Rejecting the given as a basis for the system does not, as I shall argue, entail a rejection of reason's claim on or against the given. But, it should be stressed once again, systematic philosophy's normative force rests neither on the basis of any descriptive claims concerning the nature of given reality, nor on any descriptive or prescriptive claims concerning what are allegedly those necessary principles according to which reality must be known or cognized. Hegel's is a nonfoundational while still a *critical* philosophy. What I am suggesting is that he avoids the current dilemma of rejecting foundationalism only to fall into uncritical relativism.

What does this mean and how does he do this? It means, amongst other things, that this system of reason, to the extent to which various domains of reality do come to be conceived within it, has critical authority *solely* insofar as we seek to discover what can be conceived from a standpoint which is not founded on arbitrarily selected or postulated givens. That is, it has critical authority solely insofar as we choose to seek to determine what is rational about the real when it is conceived from the standpoint of autonomous reason, *i.e.*, as a category of systematic philosophy. And this means the following, then, for us as human subjects, as conscious aware-ness who live, think, and act in the domain of the given: the critical question of the extent to which some aspect or feature of what we take to be the world as given to us does or does not accord with the demands of reason is an extra-systemic question.[45] In a moment I shall have more to say on this, and on how this system can play a critical role in regard to the given, despite its severance from the given.

In addition, and more specifically as regards the location of this systematic philosophy in the contemporary spectrum, Hegel's rejection of the primacy of subjectivity in and for this system puts him in general agreement not only with those holists who reject the model of isolated subjectivity as adequate for understanding cognition; additionally, in the arena of social and political philoso-phy, he would agree with those critics of modern society who attack what they see as its roots in unfounded conceptions of liberal indi-vidualism.[46] Based as it is on a standpoint of reason which rejects the exclusive primacy of givenness and of the subject. Hegel's con-ception of the rational character of society and its institutions is derived from the notion that individuality and freedom are not givens. In this manner, Hegel parts company with traditional lib-eral theory. For Hegel, individual freedom and individuality itself, when systematically conceived, are seen to originate from and be dependent upon a network of various institutions whose definitive character is more properly thought of as intersubjectively consti-tuted. Thus, Hegel's social and political philosophy does not reject the ultimate worth or legitimacy of individual freedom, as MacIntyre's does.[47] What it does reject is the adequacy of properly understanding the nature and conditions for the actualization of such freedom insofar as it is theoretically conceived in atomistic, egological terms, as it is either in natural right or in contract theory.[48]

So, we can say that Hegel, like the postmoderns, rejects foundationalism and absolute subjectivity while endorsing cognitive and practical holism. But unlike the postmoderns he does this in such a way that this rejection and endorsement are fully rational, and are not only compatible with but also entailed by the idea of autonomous reason which the postmoderns disparage. In addition, as we shall see, the Hegelian endorsements of holism and historicism, unlike those of the postmoderns, are part of a legitimation of modernity and are connected to the preservation of a critical dimension for philosophy. This is an important contrast to the postmoderns' dismissal of or despair concerning such a legitimation and their cheerful embracing of, or moody resignation to, relativism.

(2) In what sense has Hegel presented a legitimation of modernity? And in just what sense is this nonfoundational system nonetheless a critical system *vis-à-vis* the given? How does Hegel reject foundationalism, which seeks a basis for its critical stance in the given, and still avoid relativism?

Insofar as the core idea of modernity is the notion of a human right to autonomy, a right to self-determination in matters of thought and action, then, in Hegel's view, this notion—as it comes to be developed and articulated within systemic philosophy, *i.e.*, as a rational concept—would have the only possible *theoretical* legitimation it can have or needs. It seems to me that a central insight in Hegel's project—paralleling his methodological rejection of a foundation for philosophy itself—is that the modern claim to such autonomy is utterly insusceptible of being founded or legitimated theoretically by an appeal to any facts, any givens.[49] Hegel would agree with MacIntyre that, in this sense, modernity is without foundations. For Hegel as for MacIntyre, both the idea of natural rights and the idea that given principles internal to reason can support these claims to freedom are fictions.[50] But unlike MacIntyre and other critics of modernity, it does not follow from this for Hegel that the absence of such foundations for principles of freedom amounts to an indication of their illegitimacy. From a Hegelian perspective, it is fundamentally contrary to the whole modern idea of freedom—an idea Hegel sees as challenging the immediate and ultimate authority of all givens—to seek its legitimacy in some givens. To put the matter in positive terms, these claims to freedom are fictions in the literal sense of being non-natural human

constructs. Consequently, the legitimation of freedom and the constitution of principles of thought and action in accordance with it
can be undertaken only through an exercise of fully autonomous
reason. But if this is so, how can the system of reason which conceives freedom in these terms have any critical force?

The *prima facie* claim that autonomous reason has the right
and authority to legislate critically to the given can be established
only insofar as it can be shown that no allegedly privileged givens
can be demonstrated as primary and necessarily determinative and
authoritative for reason—the task of the *Phenomenology*. Thus,
finally, the following can be said in regard to the critical dimension
of this nonfoundational system: it can function critically only *insofar* as one acknowledges that claims to authority require some
rational justification—insofar, that is, as one steps beyond a mute
appeal to coercion or force. Then, Hegel claims, if we make this
move, we must finally acknowledge only the authority of autonomous reason itself. For, in the last analysis, it can be shown—at
least according to the *Phenomenology*—that no particular given
which might claim primacy over reason can be fully legitimated in
an adequately rational fashion as something more than an arbitrary given or postulate.

I have argued that the severance of reason from the given in
the self-constitution of its principles—the system's self-imposed
alienation from the world as it is found—is crucial as a necessary
(but not sufficient) condition for the claim that this is a rationally
autonomous system and also for the claim that the system has
provenance as regards the philosophical theory of rational autonomy.
This feature of the system has important consequences in regard to
the system's understanding of how freedom, as rationally conceived,
is to be actualized extra-systematically. For one thing, the system's
self-imposed self-containedness leads in its own right to the idea—
which accords with our non-systematic intuition—that the extra-
systemic actualization of freedom as rationally conceived is, amongst
other things, contingent in part upon the acknowledgment in the
socio-political world of the rightful authority of reason. And reason
alone, as Hegel was well aware, cannot compel this acknowledgment. Hence for Hegel the actualization of the rational freedom
articulated in systematic philosophy is unquestionably dependent
upon historical circumstances and human actions which can be
neither predicted nor ordained by philosophical theory. Thus, both
Hegel's historicist perspective about the contingent and located character of modern freedom and his own philosophy of freedom, and
his cautious views concerning what philosophers can do to actual-

ize freedom follow from his conception of systematic philosophy itself.[51] In this way we can appreciate how a system of autonomous reason, rather than demanding a denial of the contingent, the located, and historically embedded, leads instead to a rational appreciation of them (where by "rational" I mean an appreciation or acceptance which does not absolutize these features of our life world).

Only free choice—the choice, methodologically, to think rationally-philosophically; and the subsequent choice to seek effective acknowledgment of reason as legitimately authoritative in the world of the given—can finally bring systematic philosophy to bear as a critical force in this world. But acknowledging that such choices cannot be rationally compelled—acknowledging that they are free and that nothing given forces us to be rational—only involves a reasonable appreciation of the limits of reason and not a pronouncement of its utter importance. For in any case, the postmoderns' reason-disparaging pronouncements, which assume that philosophy can be critical only insofar as it can be foundational and that, since it cannot be foundational it cannot be critical, are self-sublating. As that thoughtful student of the Hegelian dialectic, Quine, puts it: someone "cannot proclaim cultural relativism without rising above it, and he cannot rise above it without giving it up."[52]

The larger point for Hegel here, given his conception of systematic philosophy and of freedom, is this: philosophical reason as such cannot actualize freedom, nor, as a rational system, can it provide guidelines as to how, pragmatically, one can best go about the activity of attempting to actualize freedom. For Hegel, the task of this actualization, given his systematic conception of what freedom is, is necessarily a task for human action. Thus, Hegel would agree with Aristotle and others that there can be no practical science of politics. Hegel, however, does not take this Aristotelian and postmodern position on the basis of a purported insight into the allegedly determinative givens of human nature which supposedly establish that human affairs must always lack the necessary regularity and universality for *theoria*. Rather, Hegel rejects that idea of a practical science of politics simply because a rational, systematic understanding of the modern principle of freedom as individual autonomy leads to the perception that any attempt to dictate the specifics of this freedom's actualization would be in conflict with this very idea of freedom. In other words, 'rational freedom'—freedom as conceived in systematic philosophy—must be freely realized. Thus such freedom is fragile, for its essential nature is to be a free human construct. Freedom's reality depends upon various circumstances and conditions which can only be guaranteed by human acts and by humanly created institutions. The necessary minimal framework for such action and for the structure of such institutions *can* be rationally perceived. Here systematic philosophy has its proper role, one which cannot be gone into here. (I refer interested readers to the work of K. R. Dove and Richard D. Winfield.)

The point worth stressing here is that reason alone cannot make the institutions and structures of rational freedom real and cannot tell us how best to go about making them real. Again, this is because such judgments—as to whether the world as given is or is not in accord with reason, as well as judgments about how to act in the world—both fall outside of the purview of systematic philosophy. They do so because its claims to autonomy and legitimacy require the suspension in and for the system of that model of cognition in and through which such judgments are made. And this suspension is required since that model itself requires and must assume in its operations the validity for cognition of the given generally and of some given specifically. To make this point in another way—and as Hegel argues systematically in the *Philosophy of Right*—such practical judgments fall outside systematic philosophy because they require contextuality: our location as citizens within the institutional frameworks of particular socio-political institutions and traditions. Like Herr Krug's pen, these cannot be deduced systematically.

So for Hegel, unlike Marx, there can be no strictly philosophical theory of praxis, in the sense of philosophy as a dialectical science of autonomous reason. There can be no philosophical theory of the realization of theory, and especially of a theory of freedom[53] (where "philosophical theory" means one claiming universality, necessity and not descriptive but *pre*scriptive and critical force for its assertions). There is no place in systematic philosophy for those who wish to take on the role of philosopher kings. And so in this systematic philosophy there is missing the paradoxical notion in which rational freedom is reduced to some form of rational necessity, a paradox found, as I see it, in Hegel's predecessors Leibniz, Spinoza, and Kant, and in his successor, Marx.

Similarly located in historical circumstances, as Hegel himself notes, is his own system of thought.[54] Thus again, Hegel's historicism fits in part with contemporary historicism (though his historicistic perspective emerges out of a system of autonomous reason). But, insofar as critics of modernity are incorrect in claiming that we are now in a postmodern age—an issue for rational-empirical discussion and debate, but not for systematic philosophy as such to address—and insofar as we remain committed to the basic notions of the distinctively modern tradition which Hegel saw emerging and hoped to shape—the notions of the rightful autonomy of human thought and action—then his philosophy still remains important, or ought to take on a new importance. And, if we choose for whatever reason to make a commitment to these ideals of freedom, this philosophy retains a critical force against those aspects and features of our given social and political worlds which—in our best extra-philosophical judgment—do not accord with freedom as rationally and philosophically understood. If Hegel is right on these matters, if a nonfoundational but still critical philosophy is possible, then we ought to conclude that our contemporary relativists are wrong. Philosophy is not mental masturbation. If Hegel is right on these matters, if a genuinely distinctive role for philosophy is possible, then we ought to conclude that our fashionable postmodernists are wrong. Philosophers have more to do than to commit philosophical suicide.

In this chapter I have begun to make a case for the contemporary relevance of Hegel's philosophy, arguing that some themes he shares with antifoundational postmodernists are not aberrant features of his systematic philosophy, but are consistent with his radical notion of a nonfoundational system. Many of the themes introduced in this chapter are developed further in subsequent chapters. Historically, Hegel's departure from the modernist foundational project was connected to his objective, in the *Phenomenology*, of developing an immanent critique of foundationalism and the subjectivist model of cognition. The specifics concerning how the *Phenomenology* can be understood in this light are laid out in Chapter 3, "Hegel's *Phenomenology* as Introduction to Systematic Science." How this critique provides the beginning point for a nonfoundational system of autonomous reason is addressed in Chapter 4, "Beginning Philosophy Without 'Beginnings.' " I have also claimed here that Hegel's system is antimetaphysical, that it is self-limiting, that it provides for a coherent understanding of the finite character of knowledge *and* that it is nonetheless a legitimation of modernity, rationality, and objectivity. These themes are also addressed below, in Chapters 5, 6, and 8, where the idea that this system is a critical philosophy is also considered.

In Chapter 2, "Philosophy as a Systematic Science," I tackle in more detail one of the central claims of *Philosophy Without*

Foundations introduced in Chapter 1: the idea that today's strictly dichotomous opposition between foundationalism and antifoundationalism is mistaken. Chapter 2 argues that foundationalism and antifoundationalism are both deeply flawed enterprises, and shows that in their present formulations they appear to be irreconcilably opposed. It then develops the Hegelian insight that they share an underlying assumption about the nature of cognition—that knowledge can only be construed along subjectivist lines. Chapter 2 concludes by showing that when this assumption is subjected to an immanent critique, it may lead to a conception of philosophical knowledge which not only avoids the problems of foundationalism and antifoundationalism but also reconciles certain of their positive notions about knowledge.

Chapter 2

PHILOSOPHY AS SYSTEMATIC SCIENCE

There is nothing more terrifying than ignorance in action.

—Goethe

What is perhaps most distinctive about contemporary rejections of foundational philosophy is the self-understood radicality of these critiques. They claim not to be doing better what their predecessors had attempted, but rather to be putting an end to the philosophical tradition in general. What I aim to do in this chapter is threefold: (1) to consider the basic character of some contemporary attempts to reject philosophy wholesale and to indicate certain difficulties with these attempts; (2) to suggest a method of criticizing traditional philosophy which avoids these difficulties; (3) to outline how such a method both coherently articulates what is valid in contemporary criticisms of philosophy and points the way to a different understanding of what philosophy as a rigorous or systematic science might be.

I. The Contemporary Idea of Deconstruction

Since Nietzsche, philosophy has become increasingly preoccupied with metaquestions concerning both its status and its possibility as a meaningful endeavor. In more recent years, in the works of Heidegger, the later Wittgenstein, Gadamer, Habermas, Foucault, Lyotard, Derrida and Rorty, this metaconcern has been transformed into a concerted effort to analyze and to critically reject or

47

'deconstruct' the traditional guiding ideal of philosophy: its aim to attain a standpoint of objective and autonomous reason and thereby to transform itself into the 'queen of the sciences,' a radical, absolute or presuppositionless foundational discipline which can speak for *the* truth.

The possibility of philosophy in this grand and traditional sense has been disparaged from several different perspectives. All might be said to share in common a belief in, and a desire to demonstrate, the unattainability of the radical self-grounding or self-legitimation which the traditional ideal of philosophy demands. In brief, the deconstructors hold that the philosophical pretension to an aperspectival, presuppositionless standpoint is an unwarranted conceit. Positively expressed, the differing attempts to deconstruct foundationalism variously strive to demonstrate that there are inherent, necessary and non-transcendable limits to thought. I shall call this the thesis of thought's finitude. It is further argued, with differing stresses and in differing ways, that these limits must be taken into account if philosophy, or postphilosophical thought, is to go about its business in a meaningful way.

The contemporary attack on philosophy's ideal of rigorous science takes the shape of a thoroughgoing rejection or deconstruction of foundational epistemology. In aiming to speak of the nature of truth itself and the conditions for its possibility—a precondition for philosophy's claim to be a rigorous science—epistemology claims to discover and ground the necessary conditions for the possibility of true knowing or discourse. And the capacity to do this successfully presupposes implicitly or explicitly that one has attained a metastandpoint of unconditional knowing, a standpoint in which thought is fully transparent to itself, meaning that the epistemological ground or foundation is itself as fully legitimated or grounded as that which is to be founded upon it. Because the standpoint to which foundational philosophy must lay claim is the absolute standpoint from which the determinate character and legitimacy of philosophy as a rigorous foundational science would be articulated, and because epistemology is that endeavor in which claims to such a standpoint are both made and argued for, the attack on the ideal of philosophy as a rigorous science has taken shape specifically as an attack on foundational epistemology.

Positively expressed, the antifoundationalist position asserts that the self-grounding standpoint of absolute knowing to which foundationalism must lay claim is unattainable, in that every standpoint of thought is necessarily one from amongst several possible perspectives, each of which is a limited standpoint unavoidably conditioned by determinative factors which can neither be made fully transparent nor transcended. Such factors might consist in the overdetermined character of the given natural languages in which philosophical thought is articulated. Or, expressing the antifoundationalist position in Heideggerian fashion, it is claimed that the correspondence model of truth—which foundational epistemology presupposes and which promises knowledge as a full revelation and a complete mirroring of what is—is illusory in that every truth-telling or disclosure is also a concealment. Each event of presencing presupposes, as a condition of its possibility, a correlative absencing or concealing. Truth as dis-closure (*a-letheia*) always retains within itself an ineluctable reservoir of closedness or obscurity (*lethe*).

What does the antifoundationalist position have to do with 'systematic philosophy'? Systematic philosophy claims to provide a mode of discourse which is unconditional and absolute in the sense that what comes to be established in this discourse is thoroughly determined by the discourse itself. As self-determining discourse, systematic philosophy articulates the position of autonomous rationality. On the face of it, both the positive and negative points made by antifoundationalism would seem to suggest that, if antifoundationalism is correct, systematic philosophy is impossible. This would seem to be the case because, as self-determining, systematic philosophy lays claim to a standpoint of thought which is presuppositionless and from out of which all of the system's determinacies are generated in a fully immanent manner. Systematicity in systematic philosophy means, first and foremost, this internal immanent or self-generative feature, and the alleged autonomy and rigor of systematic philosophy—its claim to being science—is a function of its immanency, an immanency the condition of the possibility of which is the attainment of a presuppositionless starting point.

The apparently complete incompatibility between systematic philosophy and antifoundationalism arises from the linking of such a presuppositionless starting point with the completion of a project of foundational epistemology which has as its outcome the attainment of a standpoint of self-grounding or self-legitimating thought or reason. This would purportedly function as a determinate standpoint from which the systematic philosopher could lay claim to having uncovered and grounded the conditions for the possibility of knowledge *überhaupt*. The favorite historical example—and the *bête noir*—of the antifoundationalists is, of course, Hegel's system.[1]

Thus, the view which sees systematic philosophy as wedded to foundationalism and as falling along with it holds that 'presuppositionlessness' must and can only consist in a position in which the determinate factors constitutive of knowledge are clearly defined and fully legitimated (such that, these factors having thus been shown to be the necessary preconditions for thought, they are 'absolutes' and not presuppositions in the negative sense of the word).

I shall argue, however, that presuppositionlessness need not—indeed cannot—be construed in this manner. Thus I shall contend that a genuine systematic philosophy which does have a presuppositionless beginning point does not claim to have attained this by successfully completing the project of foundational epistemology in the manner envisioned by antifoundationalists. I shall argue, to use the closing words of Rorty's *Philosophy and the Mirror of Nature*, that " . . . a new form of systematic philosophy . . . which has nothing whatever to do with epistemology but which nevertheless makes normal philosophical enquiry possible"[2] is possible. Furthermore, I aim to show not only that such a systematic philosophy is possible, but also that its possibility is not only compatible with, but itself presupposes, a deconstruction of foundationalism. In making that point, I shall contend that there is an essential difference between a systematic—that is, a thoroughly immanent—deconstruction or critique of foundational epistemology and an *ad hoc* deconstruction. My contentions will be: (1) that systematic deconstruction makes clear the extent to which a nonfoundational systematic philosophy is possible; (2) that it makes possible a coherent, nonparadoxical articulation of the finite character of thought; and (3) that in so doing it thereby avoids various difficulties found in *ad hoc* deconstructions. In criticizing *ad hoc* attempts at deconstruction and in arguing the superiority of systematic deconstruction I shall contend that a major failing of *ad hoc* deconstructists consists in the paradoxical or self-referential character of their assertions that thought is finite and not susceptible to transparent self-legitimation. I shall ague that, as a consequence of this paradoxicality, *ad hoc* deconstructionists are unable to decisively undermine the foundationalist perspective. Lastly, as it is clear that a systematic philosophy which does not begin with epistemological foundations but rather with a systematically deconstructive critique of foundationalism would be something different from what one would expect of philosophy as a rigorous science, I will conclude with a few remarks concerning what I take the nature of such a scientific system of philosophy to be.

II. The Problematic Character of *Ad Hoc*
Deconstructions of Foundationalism

One way to focus on the difficulty with *ad hoc* rejections of foundationalism is to examine the complex character of the issue of dogmatism as it is perceived and addressed by both foundationalists and antifoundationalists. This is an important issue because one of the guiding motivations for both foundationalism and antifoundationalism is a desire to avoid dogmatism, broadly understood as the unfounded assumption that a particular point of view is unequivocally right. For foundationalists, dogmatism can be avoided only by foundational epistemology. For the antifoundationalist, however, it is rather foundationalism itself which leads to dogmatism. By looking more closely at this issue we can see (1) how and why is it that *ad hoc* deconstructions of foundationalism fail as decisive critiques of foundationalism and (2) why a systematic deconstruction is called for if the claim that foundationalism ought to be rejected is to be substantiated.

That one aim of foundationalism is to transcend dogmatism is clear from the works of Descartes, the founding father of foundationalist epistemology and from the works of his followers in modern philosophy who continued and transformed his project. Foundational epistemology's original position regarding dogmatism can be expressed as follows: If the definitive conditions for knowledge are not first established and grounded by means of a preliminary investigation into the nature and limits of knowing, then when we go about the business of making knowledge claims we cannot be certain that we are operating properly. The project of foundational epistemology is needed so that the twin specters of radical skepticism and dogmatism can be laid to rest. For our assumption that we are going about things in the proper way may be unjustified. We may have deceived ourselves (or we may be being deceived) into thinking that we are coming to know the truth when we in fact are not. Mere assumptions concerning the rightness and legitimacy of how we go about the business of knowing must be viewed as so many dogmatic assertions, as unjustified assumptions, resting on faith, tradition, convention or whatever. They amount to untenable appeals to authority and they are not to be accepted until they pass certification by the tribunal of reason. Foundational epistemology achieves this end in two steps. First, it determines whether knowledge as such is possible or impossible.

Having determined the possibility of knowledge, it then supplies a method which allows the systematic verification or falsification of our beliefs, enabling us to create a rationally reconstructed, autonomous and self-grounding culture.[3]

From this perspective, reason is a "natural light."[4] This image is powerful, important, and seductive. In raising the specter of radical skepticism as a possibility for which the absolute certainty provided by foundationalism is the only antidote, the foundationalists shaped a view of reason, mind, understanding or consciousness as a fully self-illuminative faculty. Only if mind or reason can attain to full transparency concerning itself—knowing its own workings as the instrument or medium of knowledge—can the knowledge conditions which constitute its operations be fully justified and grounded, and the twin specters of radical skepticism and blind dogmatism exorcised. This justification and exorcism entail a view of reason as an instrument, faculty, or medium which can only perform this justificatory task insofar as it is itself capable of full self-justification as the epistemologically critical and justifying instrument. Self-justification is required because anything left unjustified—merely assumed as true—would compromise the whole endeavor. Thus foundational epistemology requires a moment of absolute self-transparency in which reason's own operating conditions are known and validated in an unconditional, unquestionable, indubitable fashion. Indeed, one can view the entire development of modern epistemology as a search for that moment of fully self-certain, self-transparent, unconditional, absolute knowing. And one can further see this search as rooted in the assumption—later to be brought into question by the antifoundationalists—that the mind or reason knows nothing better than itself and can attain full clarity concerning the conditions of its own possibility.

What distinguishes the foundationalist view of dogmatism from the antifoundationalist view is the former's linking of dogmatism with the possibility of radical skepticism. For the foundationalist, radical skepticism—the possibility that we could be wrong about everything—is a philosophically genuine possibility which can only be met by an absolute certainty attained through the self-investigation of reason. Given the specter of radical skepticism, from the standpoint of the foundationalist, any and all positions which are not rooted in and justified by a successful foundational epistemology are *eo ipso* unjustified, uncertain, *and* dogmatic, insofar as they claim to be anything more than unjustified and uncertain.

From the point of view of the antifoundationalist, radical skepticism is itself only a by-product of the seductive vision of absolute certainty and self-transparent reason to which the foundationalist is mistakenly attached. As a corollary of the belief in an absolute certainty, the threat, if not the possibility, of radical skepticism is held to disappear once it is made clear that absolute certainty is unattainable in principle. The antifoundationalist assures us that if absolute certainty cannot be attained, then absolute uncertainty makes no sense, since they are correlative terms. In addition, foundationalism's false claims to absolute certainty amount to dogmatism in pretending to provide an unequivocal, exclusive standpoint from which the truth can be established. With the demonstration that absolute self-grounding certainty is an illusion, the Gang of Four which contemporary deconstructionists are accused of nurturing and which they dismiss—radical skepticism, relativism, nihilism and dogmatism—are said to be liquidated.

The difficulty of the contemporary antifoundationalists' *ad hoc* attempts to deconstruct foundationalism by showing that absolute truth or absolute certainty is impossible lies, as the label *"ad hoc"* suggests, in the manner in which these critiques of foundational epistemology are carried out. The essence of the problem is the internal inconsistency of the antifoundationalist position. The problem here concerns the status of the discourse in which, and the status of the standpoint from which, one attacks foundationalism.

The antifoundationalist wishes to assert that the aperspectival, ahistorical metaposition—the standpoint of absolute self-grounding knowing—which the foundationalist aims to attain is an impossibility *in principle.* Correlatively, the antifoundationalist desires to show that *all* human knowing is finite and burdened by inherent limitations which, although they can be philosophically articulated and illuminated, cannot, nevertheless, be removed or transcended. According to antifoundationalists, we have something like a basic insight into or self-awareness of these limits, one which can be philosophically accounted for.[5] It is only the seductions of the powers of reflection which lead us into the illusion that they can be gone beyond. The difficulty for the antifoundationalist concerns the character and status of these claims and the implicit position or standpoint from which they are promulgated.

For one thing, the claim that an absolute standpoint is unattainable *in principle* and that efforts to attain it are thus mistaken and doomed to failure from the start is itself an absolute claim. For the assertion that not only has no one yet succeeded in successfully articulating an absolute philosophy, but that it is in principle impossible to do so, is itself an apparently ahistorical claim to an insight into the true nature and possibility of truth and knowledge.

Undoubtedly, what the antifoundationalist *says* is that unconditional truth claims are not possible, but this claim is itself an
unconditionally true meta-assertion about the nature of truth. From
the standpoint of the foundationalist, the antifoundationalist has a
right to be skeptical about the possibility of attaining an absolute
standpoint through a foundational project, but she has no legitimate grounds to dismiss the project out of hand. Correlatively, the
antifoundationalist's positive assertions concerning finitude also appear as claims which are being made from an absolute, aperspectival
standpoint. One might say that the antifoundationalist is in a difficult position both in regard to what she wishes to assert and in
regard to the position from which she makes her antifoundationalist
claims. Antifoundationalism seems to succumb necessarily to the
self-referential inconsistency of making absolute claims against absolutism and to be denying the possibility of an absolute perspective on the truth from a perspective which itself is absolute. From
the standpoint of the foundationalist, the antifoundationalist's unequivocal claims concerning the impossibility of attaining an absolute standpoint can only appear as question-begging and dogmatic.
For in the foundationalist's eyes, the antifoundationalist is going
about making unconditional claims about the nature of truth and
the conditions and limitations of its possibility—something the
foundationalist claims to do also—*without* going through the effort
of justifying the standpoint from which such claims can rightly be
made.

What is the antifoundationalist response to all this? Sophisticated antifoundationalists such as Gadamer and Rorty seem to be
aware of the charges of paradox and inconsistency to which their
positions open them, but not to be especially troubled by them.[6] If
the foundationalist can respond to their attacks on foundationalism
by raising metaquestions and meta-issues concerning antifoundationalism, the antifoundationalist can respond in kind, although with a certain twist. The kind of metalevel response which
the antifoundationalist can make has its *locus classicus* in the earlier Wittgenstein's notion that certain things which cannot be said—
or cannot be said coherently without violating fundamental limiting principles of discourse—can nevertheless be shown.

The antifoundationalist response might go like this: It may
appear that antifoundationalist claims are unconditional and absolute claims concerning the nature of truth and the possibility of
knowledge; the language of the foundational tradition in which
they must be asserted produces this appearance. But it is the
very nature of the limited or finite character of human knowing

and speaking that they convey this appearance when addressing their own nature. The very metalevel problems which are brought to bear against antifoundationalism reveal the truth of anti-foundationalism in that they *show* at the metalevel what cannot be articulated without this self-referential inconsistency. This self-referential inconsistency is not a problem, but rather a revelation of thought's inescapably limited character, a revelation which appears whenever thought focuses on its own nature. It serves to indicate the impossibility of our ever being able to provide a transcendental grounding for the definitive conditions of finitude, and this disclosure is perfectly consistent with our position. For it is just the impossibility of any such grounding which we are interested in articulating. A consistent antifoundationalism could not do what foundationalism demands, so we are being consistent with our position in refusing to attempt to do so. The charges of paradox raised against antifoundationalism are finally of no importance simply because what foundationalism sees as a paradox to be removed or avoided the antifoundationalist recognizes as evidence for the point he wishes to make: the opacity, the non-transparency of knowledge and truth conditions and the impossibility of attaining a standpoint from which they can be talked about in a fully adequate manner. In addition, in charging antifoundationalism with question-begging and dogmatism it is the foundationalist—from the perspective of antifoundationalism—who is truly begging the question and being dogmatic. For these charges against antifoundationalism can only be made—since they only make sense if foundationalism is a real possibility—by someone who does not see beyond the confines of the foundationalist paradigm. Thus it is the foundationalist who is begging the question and being dogmatic in refusing to be open to the radical questioning of the possibility of foundational philosophy itself. The foundationalist is willing to be a radical skeptic about everything except the necessity of foundationalism. In demanding that the paradoxes of self-reference be successfully dealt with by us, you are demanding that we resolve problems which foundational epistemology cannot resolve itself, problems which our position holds cannot be resolved as their irresolvability is itself indicative of our thesis concerning the finite, non-groundable character of knowing. And in demanding that we ground and justify our antifoundationalist position you are asking us to play your game and to accomplish something which foundational epistemology has not been able to accomplish, and which we claim cannot be accomplished with success. Thus our failure to meet your demands is not indicative of a problem in our position, but of the truth of what we assert about the nature of knowing.

To which the foundationalist might respond: You are trying to modify your position without owning up the consequences of such a modification. The counter charges of question-begging and dogmatism will not work. Foundationalism can admit that as yet no one has succeeded in completing the project; indeed, foundationalism is open to bringing the possibility of foundationalism itself into question, for our demand that a standpoint of justification be sought brings everything into question. But antifoundationalism is not content with making the historically accurate observation that no one has yet succeeded in successfully carrying out the foundational project. Rather, antifoundationalism wishes to dogmatically assert that foundationalism is impossible in principle, that it is a way of understanding the nature and the goal of philosophy which is fundamentally mistaken. Of course, antifoundationalism refuses to engage in the foundational activity which would ground the legitimacy of its 'insights' into the absolute character of finitude. Were the antifoundationalist to do this he would see that he is engaged in much the same project as we are. But unless the antifoundationalist brings his own position into question, the charge of dogmatism is correct. And if antifoundationalism admits that its own position is and remains ungrounded, then antifoundationalism has no basis on which to make unequivocal claims about the possibility of foundational philosophy. If antifoundationalism will admit that the impossibility or errancy of foundationalism cannot be demonstrated from a justified position, then it must also admit that the possibility or impossibility, the meaningfulness, or nonmeaningfulness of foundational philosophy is an open question, which is all that foundationalism asks. The paradoxes of the antifoundationalist position 'show' nothing else but the fundamental wrongheadedness of the antifoundationalist position itself.

Standing back from this dialogue, we might say at this juncture that the foundationalist-antifoundationalist debate has reached a standoff, and that these two positions on the character and possibility of philosophy are separated by an unbridgeable gap. It seems that each occupies a position from which neither can finally speak to the other, for *each* is looking at the philosophical world in a way which is diametrically opposed to the other's, and which precludes the possibility of finding a common ground upon which their differences can be resolved. Both sides approach the question of what philosophy is, and what it ought to do, in such a fashion that their respective visions are incommensurable.

The foundationalist will not be swayed from the fundamental and definitive demand that no truth claims—and especially truth claims about the nature and possibility of truth claims—can be regarded as adequate unless the standpoint from which such claims are made is justified. The foundationalist article of faith is that reason's demands for such justification are self-evident and un-avoidable. Consequently, from the foundationalist point of view, the demands of finitude, while seemingly obvious in being grounded in basic facts about human nature, are contestable insofar as the commonsensical standpoint which asserts them remains un-grounded, and insofar as these demands run counter to the idea of rational accountability. Any critical project can only touch the foundationalist position insofar as it recognizes the demands of reason; to fail to do so is, for the foundationalist, simply to step outside the bounds of philosophical discourse.

The antifoundationalist will not be swayed from the funda-mental and definitive view that no truth claims—and especially truth claims about the nature and possibility of truth claims—can ever be fully justified or grounded. The antifoundationalist article of faith is that the self-evidence of human finitude precludes the possibility of absolute self-grounding. Consequently, from the antifoundationalist point of view, the demands of reflective reason, while seductive, are illusory, and any attempt to attack this prin-ciple can touch the antifoundationalist position only insofar as it recognizes the limits of finitude.

Seeing that foundationalism recognizes the demands of rea-son as primary and antifoundationalism recognizes the constraints of finitude as primary might lead one to the view that there is no possible rational resolution of the controversy, and thus one might conclude that no final demonstration of the correctness or incor-rectness of either position is possible, because they have incom-mensurable criteria concerning what counts as a demonstration. Looking at the matter in this way, one might feel that only a quasi-religious, or quasi-psychoanalytic, conversion from one standpoint to the other is possible; a conversion which consists just in 'coming to see things aright' however this is construed, in the spirit of the latter Wittgenstein.

Now *this* metaperspective on the issue might seem most amendable to the antifoundationalist. In fact, an antifoundationalist might hold that if the foundationalist can be brought to agree with this metaperspective on their differences, then the issue would be resolved in the favor of antifoundationalism. One could imagine a sophisticated antifoundationist saying: "Of course I cannot demonstrate to you that you are wrong in a manner that you find acceptable, for you can always respond to what I say and to what I bring forth as evidence with a demand that I justify the standpoint or the discourse in which or from which I make my claims. And you cannot demonstrate to me that I am wrong in a manner which I find acceptable. But that's the whole point. Just this incommensurability *shows* that the ideal of an absolute metaperspective of knowing which could reconcile such differences is unattainable." To which the foundationalist can respond, once again, that while such a standpoint has not been reached, this in no way proves that it cannot be reached. This metaperspective on the issue will only appear to the foundationalist who does not 'see' that he is 'bewitched' by a 'pseudoproblem' as question-begging.

What is to be done? *Can* anything to be done to resolve this situation or is it truly an impasse? From the point of view of systematic philosophy something can be done. Systematic philosophy holds that a common ground for resolution is attainable in that *antifoundationalism's demand for the recognition of finitude and foundationalism's demand for radical justification can be accommodated.* Both a demonstration of finitude which avoids paradox and an articulation of a self-grounding standpoint which is nonfoundational are attainable. The key to this reconcilation, the effort which literally effects both of these seemingly antithetical goals, lies in a *systematic* consideration of the foundational project. I have labeled this a systematic deconstruction of that project in anticipation of its negative outcome for foundationalism, but in fact its results will be equally negative and positive for both foundationalism and antifoundationalism. The systematic consideration which follows will reveal that *antifoundationalism is right in that our way of knowing is inescapably finite, but wrong in assuming that no other way of knowing is conceivable.* Correlatively, it will show that *foundationalism is right in that a presuppositionless and hence self-grounding standpoint is attainable, but wrong in seeing this standpoint as providing foundations for cognition.* This systematic (and deconstructive) consideration of foundationalism will also be critical of antifoundationalism in that it will show that a consistent recognition of the finitude of our mode of knowing is incompatible with the claim that this mode of knowing is absolute in its finitude; the antifoundationalist view that no other mode of knowing is possible cannot be reconciled with its assertion of the finite character of our knowing. It will be critical of foundationalism by showing that a realization of a presuppositionless standpoint is incompatible with the establishment of foundations of cognition; the foundationalist view that a self-grounding science must begin with determinate conditions for cognition cannot be reconciled with its own realization that such a science must begin without presuppositions.

The way in which a systematic consideration of foundationalism operates is to apply the principles and criteria of foundationalism to the foundational project itself. What I have labeled *ad hoc* deconstructions fail because they assume the correctness of a position antithetical to foundationalism, and thus apply criteria to it which beg the question at issue. Thus foundationalists can always dismiss antifoundationalist critiques as beside the point. To approach foundationalism systematically however, is to approach its prospects for success as, initially, an open possibility. If foundationalism is to be shown defective this must be demonstrated immanently: the demands laid upon foundationalism and the criteria by which it is judged must be its own. What are foundationalism's basic principles and criteria, and how does their application to the foundationalist project lead to its own immanent deconstruction?

III. The Systematic Consideration of Foundationalism

Foundationalism demands that we do not presuppose our capacity to know the truth, but rather that we first establish it by means of a preliminary investigation into the nature of cognition, one which will demonstrate that and how knowledge is attainable. Foundationalism holds that cognition is something which is in need of being investigated because it could go wrong. It further holds that cognition is capable of being investigated in such a way that this tendency toward error can be redressed by laying out the rules for cognition's proper exercise. In holding this, foundationalism commits itself to understanding cognition in terms of a determinate relationship between knowledge and object. Cognition must involve a relation, for if we are going to speak of our being right and wrong, we must have a standard for correctness and something we compare to that standard. On the one hand we must be able to specify knowledge, and on the other that which it is purportedly knowledge of—the object as standard of judgment—if cognition is going to be understood in the manner of foundationalism: as capable of having the conditions under which it both meets and fails to meet a standard specified by an epistemological or transcendental investigation. In addition, the cognitive relation must be understood as something which is capable of analysis in general terms—all instances of cognition must involve certain uniform conditions—if an investigation into it is to result in the kind of foundational knowledge which will serve as a useful prophylactic against error.

In accord with these requirements, foundationalism understands the relation between knowledge and object in terms of the correspondence model: an idea—or, if we make the linguistic turn, a proposition—is true when it corresponds to an objective state of affairs. Just how knowledge and the standard are more specifically conceived makes no essential difference to the character of the foundational project. In line with Descartes' classic distinction between *res cogitans* and *res extensa*, we may construe knowledge and standard as falling into two separate ontological domains, with the standard as an object understood as existing external to an inner dimension of mental awareness in which it is represented. Or, as has become fashionable in more recent times, we may attempt to avoid the problem of bridging inner and outer which 'externalists' confront by going 'internal': refusing to regard knowledge and its object as fundamentally different in character, seeing them rather as distinct components of a larger, ontologically seamless unity (such as the pragmatists' "nature"). The reason that the particular ontological specification of knowledge and standard/object makes no difference—the reason that it is irrelevant for foundational purposes whether they are both conceived as ontologically the same or as different—is simply that all versions of foundationalism minimally require an *ineliminable* epistemic difference: Foundationalism minimally demands that the standard be construed as something which is determined as what it is independently of the knowledge which is to be measured against it, irrespective of whether the character of the determination as independent is construed as following from an ontological difference or not. If the standard is not so construed (as independently determined) there can be no question of an objective test of the knowledge against the standard. (If the domain of that which is to be tested were permitted to determine the standard against which the test is made, objectivity would be sacrificed. A ruler cannot be an objective measure of its own correctness.) Knowledge and standard may both be ontologically ideational, as with Berkeley, or they may both be ontologically natural, as with the pragmatists; but only so long as the standard is construed as determined independently of the knowledge being measured against it (whether it is said to be so determined by God, or by nature, or whatever) does the possibility for a test exist.

Once this epistemic difference which is required for testing has been allowed, the foundationalists' central difficulty of comparing knowledge and object without compromising the validity of the standard as an independently determined measure arises. That is, if we grant the epistemic difference needed for genuine testing—that the standard is determined as what it is prior to and apart from the knowledge of it—the difficulty of showing that knowledge and standard correspond arises whether or not knowledge and object are ontologically different. The attempt to fashion an internalist foundationalism as a response to externalist difficulties cashes out as the introduction of a distinctive without a difference. For the foundational act of comparing knowledge and standard requires that the standard be epistemically distinct in order to be a genuine standard, but also epistemically the same (of the status of something knowable) in order to be something against which knowledge can be compared. But as soon as the standard becomes epistemically knowable—as soon as it comes to be known in the act of making the comparison—its status as an objective standard against which knowledge claims are to be tested is fatally compromised. For once the standard is known, the foundationalist no longer has a guarantee that it is determined as what it is objectively, independent of the foundational knowing act. As this intimates, and as I shall discuss in more detail below, the failure of foundationalism is that it requires itself to satisfy test conditions which cannot possibly be met without compromising the conception of knowledge which it presupposes.

Foundationalism's goals are to show that there is a specific mode of knowing which satisfies this correspondence relation and to specify the general conditions (pertaining to knowledge, objects, and their relation) which make this satisfaction possible. It is when we think through what must be required for foundationalism to succeed that we discover how and why it cannot succeed in grounding its understanding of cognition. In order to demonstrate correspondence, foundationalism must violate or suspend the very assumption that gets the project going: that cognition consists in a determinate relation between its purported knowledge and an object. To put it differently, demonstrating correspondence means attaining to a state of affairs in which what must be presupposed to carry out the demonstration can no longer be presupposed, so that what foundationalism was going to 'found' disappears in the very act of founding it. In short, if foundationalism's demands are to be met, the conditions for its possibility must be violated; the foundational project displays an immanently generated internal incoherence that requires its rejection, and allows us to do so without any need on our part to claim any sort of quasi-foundational, absolute knowledge, as is the case with the *ad hoc* antifoundationalists. How so?

To establish that, and how, a truth-affording relation between (what is purportedly) knowledge and object is possible, foundationalism must demonstrate correspondence between the candidate for knowledge and the object. It must show that 'knowledge' and object are identical in content, in order to establish that the purported knowledge is true, is genuine knowledge; and it must, at the same time, preserve the distinction between knowledge and object. Demonstrating that we have achieved a successful comparison means that the entities being compared must also be distinct from one another, for without the difference, we have no comparison. In addition, without the preservation of a difference between knowledge and its object we have no knowledge to speak of (at least insofar as knowledge is understood in the manner presupposed by foundationalism). Additionally (as noted above) only if the difference between knowledge and object is preserved in the foundational act can it be shown that the knowledge in question is objective, is knowledge *of* the object, and not a mere subjective projection or fantasy. So what foundationalism must establish is a state of affairs in which knowledge and object are at one and the same time in a relation of identity (to demonstrate truth) and difference (to insure that a comparison has been achieved; to insure knowledge, for knowledge is a relation and must have distinct relata; and to insure the objectivity of knowledge). In short, this state of affairs requires identity and difference at one and the same time, for if at one moment (or in one foundational act) identity is established, and at another difference, we cannot be certain that the knowledge identified at the one moment and distinguished at the next are the same.

The problem, however, is that if we have simultaneous identity-and-difference, we no longer have anything that can be picked out and identified as 'knowledge,' on the one hand, and as the 'object' on the other. The state of identity-and-difference between knowledge and object which must be required in order to found knowledge is one in which 'knowledge' and 'object' disappear, for insofar as *both* are identical and different at once, they are neither the same nor different.[7] Or, to put the problem another way, we no longer have a determinate relation here, and foundationalism presupposes that knowledge involves a determinate relation as one in which knowledge and its object are always distinguishable from one another. The fatal problem for foundationalism is that both the identity of knowledge and object and the difference must, but cannot, be attained at one and the same time, if this model of knowledge is to be grounded. They cannot be attained, because attaining them eliminates the model; they must be attained, because if they are not the possibility of truth as correspondence remains in question. Put in another way: foundationalism cannot show both that its knowledge is true and that it is knowledge of an object; it can attain certainty about truth at the price of objectivity, or objectivity at the price of certainty about its truth, but not both.

IV. The Possibility of Systematic Philosophy

Because the very conditions required for foundationalism to succeed have led to the suspension of the model of knowledge which foundationalism sought to ground, this systematic thinking through of foundationalism demonstrates the failure of foundationalism according to its own criteria. Thus it is a thoroughly immanent critique; thus, unlike *ad hoc* antifoundationalism it does not beg the question by presupposing an alternative non-foundational model of knowledge.

If a systematic consideration of the foundationalist project succeeds in effecting the antifoundationalist critique without the problems of *ad hoc* antifoundationalism, how does it also open the way to a systematic science? Put differently, how is the consideration also a partial success for foundationalism and a partial failure for antifoundationalism? It is a partial failure for antifoundationalism in the sense that it is a critique of antifoundationalism's (inconsistent) pretensions to absolutism. Both foundationalism and antifoundationalism presuppose the same model of cognition, the subjectivist model which presupposes that knowledge is always of a determinate other given independently of cognition. Foundationalism presupposes this model in its attempt to establish correspondence; antifoundationalism presupposes it in its assertion that knowledge is inescapably finite because it is grounded in conditions which cannot be rendered transparent. The immanently generated collapse of the subjectivist model reveals that it is finite because it cannot ground itself, but it also shows that one cannot successfully claim, as the antifoundationalists inconsistently wish to claim, that knowing must be understood in terms of this model. If the subjectivist/foundationalist model cannot show how knowledge understood in its terms is legitimate, then it cannot be claimed (as *both* foundationalists and antifoundationalists wish to claim) that this is the only conceivable model for cognition. And thus, foundationalism's self-effected failure to ground its model of cognition is also a partial success for foundationalism because it opens the way to a conception of cognition which is arguably self-grounding. How so?

The specific failure of the foundational-antifoundational model lay in presupposing a determinate difference between knowledge and object. If, as we have seen, this model of cognition collapses when the conditions for its self-grounding are fulfilled, then perhaps this also indicates that the way to attain a self-grounding mode of cognition lies just in specifically rejecting that model. That is, if we begin by deliberately refusing to presuppose any determinate relationship between cognition and its object, a mode of consideration might ensue in which both come to be determined at once. This discourse could then be arguably self-grounding in the sense that nothing *determinate* from outside of the consideration is present to externally determine what comes to be established in it. If that were the case, philosophy as a systematic science would arguably be possible because the demand that this discourse be unconditional or autonomous—not founded on anything externally determined—would allow for the possibility of a strictly immanent determination of the categories of the discourse.

While attaining foundationalism's goal of self-grounding, this systematic science would still be compatible with a *consistent* antifoundationalism for two reasons. For one thing, the very possibility of this systematic discourse would have been conditioned by the self-engendered collapse of the assumption that all discourse must be other-determined, founded on something given as determinate. The collapse of foundationalism is the collapse of this assumption in its failure to ground itself. Insofar as systematic discourse is made possible by the prior suspension of this assumption, systematic self-grounding science would not abrogate the antifoundational insistence that all cognition is in some way conditioned or contextual—made possible by factors external to the cognition itself. Rather, it would articulate the only coherent sense in which this thesis can be maintained: Systematic discourse is conditioned because it has been made possible by the self-refutation of the assumption about cognition which insists that all cognition must begin with something determinate. (Foundationalism asserts that it is the conditions of cognition themselves which are always given *and determinative* of whatever might be thought;

antifoundationalism asserts the same thing, with the qualification that these conditions are opaque. Systematic philosophy asserts that it is conditioned—in the sense of "having been made possible"—by the self-suspension as a foundational principle for philosophy of this foundationalist-antifoundationalist thesis that thought must always be conditioned—in the sense of 'predetermined'—by something already given.) Secondly, this systematic discourse would also be consistent with antifoundationalism because, being based on a thoroughgoing rejection of the unconditional validity of the subjectivist model, it cannot claim to achieve those ends which are part of this model's definition of knowledge. The model which has been suspended defined knowledge as always being knowledge of something given to cognition: 'knowledge' was thus taken to be fundamentally descriptive in character, an account of something present to cognition. As based on a rejection of this model, systematic discourse would make no pretension to supplant descriptive discourse by offering itself as a perfected form of such discourse. Systematic philosophy does not claim to describe the given world in any of the manifold senses in which traditional philosophy has construed that task; hence systematic philosophy is radically nonmetaphysical. However, it does claim to supplant descriptive discourse insofar as it waxes metaphysical by purporting to be unconditional.

Thus, systematic discourse parts company both with foundationalism, which sought a mode of discourse that would be unconditionally authoritative and determinative for all other modes of discourse, and with antifoundationalism, which explicitly or implicitly postulates a relativism in which all modes of discourse are equal.

In Chapter 2 I have tried to show that, despite their real differences, foundationalism and antifoundationalism share an important common assumption about the nature of knowledge. Both are committed to the subjectivist model of cognition, to the notion that knowledge can only be construed as *knowledge of* some given object. But foundationalism cannot demonstrate that such knowledge is attainable, and antifoundationalism cannot demonstrate that knowledge generally is finite in the distinctively pejorative sense that it can only be thought of in terms of such a flawed model. Neither foundationalism nor antifoundationalism succeeds. I have outlined a possible way beyond this model which avoids the problems of both foundationalism and antifoundationalism. The

systematic, immanent critique of the model indicates the proper
sense in which knowledge is finite, and antifoundationalism is correct, for it discloses that the grounding foundationalism seeks cannot be attained insofar as one holds to the subjectivist model that
foundationalism presupposes. But just this disclosure functions at
the same time to liberate us from this model—antifoundationalism
is not correct in its insistence that knowledge must be construed
according to the finite subjectivist model.

In Chapter 3 I shall bring these issues back to the specific
context of Hegel's philosophy, arguing that the immanent critique
outlined in Chapter 2 (in the context of contemporary debates) is
what Hegel has already laid out for us in his *Phenomenology of
Spirit* of 1807. Thus chapter 3 lays the groundwork for my larger
claim that Hegel moves beyond the foundationalist-antifoundationalist standoff and offers a new conception of systematic
philosophy. In challenging traditional understandings of Hegel,
my interpretive contention will be that this reading of the *Phenomenology* functions to address a variety of interpretive problems which have plagued readers of the book who have sought to
understand it as a coherent argument that functions as Hegel's
self-proclaimed "introduction" to science.

Chapter 3

HEGEL'S *PHENOMENOLOGY* AS
INTRODUCTION TO SYSTEMATIC SCIENCE

There's no success like failure, and failure's no success at all.
—Bob Dylan

Contemporary developments in continental thought which have their roots in Nietzsche, which run through the works of Heidegger and Gadamer and perhaps reach their most radical articulation in the writings of recent French thinkers, indicate the extent to which traditional notions concerning interpretation, text authorship, and especially the idea of the 'correct reading' of a text have been brought more and more into question. Serious doubts have arisen as to whether any single interpretation—of a text, idea, historical period, etc.—can be designated as adequate. Central to these doubts is the question of whether historical imbeddedness—the historicity and the immanently perspectival character of consciousness—can be overcome. The issues and problems connected with these questions are many and run deep, challenging at the most basic level the idea of autonomous, objective, and radically 'scientific' reason which has, as an ideal, guided western thought for centuries.

What do these issues have to do with Hegel, and specifically with his *Phenomenology of Spirit*? In recent years, dismay over the failure of interpreters to come to agreement over the *Phenomenology* has led increasingly to the belief that no genuine, comprehensive, and finally adequate interpretation of that work is possible.

Thus, it might be suggested that the case history of *Phenomenology* interpretation provides *prima facie* evidence in favor of the general (and generally negative) views on text interpretation mentioned above. But a second point of connection is much broader and concerns our fundamental understanding of reason. For the *Phenomenology*, as Hegel's declared introduction to science, is meant to indicate how consciousness can overcome its merely perspectival and imbedded character and how, thereby, a standpoint of autonomous objective reason—the standpoint of science—can be attained.

In what follows, I shall contend that the problem of interpreting the *Phenomenology* is rooted in a serious prevailing misunderstanding of how Hegel intended the *Phenomenology* to function as an introduction to a standpoint of objective reason. I shall suggest that the *Phenomenology* can be interpreted in a comprehensive and adequate manner and that such an interpretation is grounded in a new understanding of how the work is meant to introduce science.

One of the most vexing problems confronting Hegel scholars today is understanding the *Phenomenology* in the role assigned to it by its author as the introduction to science, or, to use Hegel's words, the "deduction of the concept of science."[1] In recent years the deeper question has arisen of whether it is even *possible* to understand the work in that manner. Despite the ever-increasing number of works devoted to the *Phenomenology* it has been suggested by several scholars—amongst them Wim van Dooren and most recently J. N. Findlay[2]—that we are still without a satisfactory commentary on Hegel's first book over 170 years since its appearance. This state of affairs has led Otto Pöggeler (and others) to ask whether the *Phenomenology* actually presents us with a coherent argument which leads consecutively from beginning to end and is susceptible to a philosophically reconstructive commentary: Does the book have a genuine argument at all or is it only a collection of related themes whose sequential ordering is more or less arbitrary? Pöggeler doubts whether the *Phenomenology* is even a book at all in the sense of "something fully finished and completed." He contends that "the composition of the work can scarcely exhibit an ordering which springs unequivocally out of the beginning point of the work and remains unproblematic in its unfolding." And in agreement with van Dooren and Findlay he declares, "Despite this return [to the *Phenomenology*] in regard to an attempt at an interpretation of the *Phenomenology of Spirit* we still have not proceeded beyond the first step."[3] Pöggeler contends that, if we are going to be able to grasp the idea of the *Phenomenology*, what Hegel wanted must be understood: To this day "it has not yet become correctly clear what Hegel wanted and what he achieved, wherein he was led as he sought to write an introduction to his system."[4]

I agree with Pöggeler and others that we are still without a satisfactory commentary on the *Phenomenology*. But unlike Pöggeler I am not convinced that the absence of a genuine commentary must be attributed to the fact that the *Phenomenology* as written fails to present us with a cohesive, interconnected argument (or to the fact that Hegel supposedly changed his mind about what he was doing during the course of writing the *Phenomenology*[5]). The absence of a commentary may rather be attributed to our failure to perceive what Hegel wanted when he sought to write an introduction to his system. The clue which will perhaps enable us to proceed beyond the first step in interpreting the *Phenomenology* can be found by turning to the *Science of Logic*. We must focus on Hegel's self-understanding of the *Phenomenology*, that is, on his conception of the role and accomplishments of the *Phenomenology*, as this self-understanding is presented in that work—the *Logic*—whose concept the *Phenomenology* is supposed to deduce. If, as Pöggeler says, an understanding of the idea of the *Phenomenology* requires that we understand what Hegel wanted to do, then it is in the *Logic*, I shall argue, that Hegel informs us both of what he wanted to do and of what he felt he had done in the introduction to his system of science. I shall first attempt to show why we are still today without a satisfactory commentary on the *Phenomenology*. I shall argue that the received view of Hegel's *Phenomenology* as an introduction to science is inadequate because it cannot account for Hegel's self-understanding of the *Phenomenology* as presented in the opening sections of the *Logic* (The "Introduction" and "With What Must the Science Begin?"). Secondly, I shall argue that in these opening sections Hegel presents a clue as to just what he wished to accomplish in the introduction to his science: namely, to overcome the standpoint of consciousness altogether and thereby to attain to the standpoint of science as one of objective, autonomous reason, which Hegel offers us in the *Logic*.

I. The Received View of the *Phenomenology* as Introduction to Science

Although there is disagreement in the received view as to whether the *Phenomenology* presents anything like an argument, and further disagreement about just what this argument might consist in, there *is* a consensus that the aim of the *Phenomenology* as an introduction to science is a positive one.[6] The *Phenomenology* was designed, according to the received view, either to present a demonstrative argument whose function is to establish and ground the nature and validity of absolute knowing, or, according to those who see the argument to be more rhetorical and persuasive than demonstrative, to elevate the reader propadeutically to the level of absolute knowledge and to convince him thereby of its validity.[7] Although there is disagreement concerning the exact manner of the argument, there is agreement that its aim is positive: it is to introduce science or deduce its concept, whether through a rigorous demonstration of the truth and validity of a mode of absolute knowing or through an illustrative recapitulation of the steps to absolute knowing.[8] Although the *Phenomenology*'s manner of proceeding is seen to be original and unorthodox, its aim as an argument is found to be traditional and positive.

This positivity thesis concerning the aim of the *Phenomenology* as the deduction of the concept of science is reinforced by the received view's interpretation of absolute knowing itself. According to this view absolute knowing as the concept of science deduced by the *Phenomenology* stands as a determinate principle or structure of true knowing as such.[9] Whether or not the argument of the *Phenomenology* which leads to absolute knowing is a success is a matter of some debate in the received view.[10] Nonetheless, there is agreement that absolute knowing stands in Hegel's view as absolutely true, actual and scientific knowing and as such constitutes for him the concept of science.[11]

What exactly is absolute knowing, and how does the received view understand it as the foundational principle, the beginning point, of science? Here again we can find agreement among holders of the received view: absolutely true and unquestionably valid knowing is held by Hegel, they argue, to consist in the pure reflective self-knowing of an absolute self-consciousness or absolute subject. Since the *Phenomenology* culminates in absolute knowing with the establishment of the identity of subject and object, this absolute knowing as absolute self-consciousness is seen to be the aboriginal unifying structure in which the necessary interrelation and intermediation of subject and object—of knowing and what is known— are achieved. As such, this structure is claimed by Hegel to be paradigmatic for any and all knowing.[12] The coming to absolute knowing *via* the *Phenomenology* is thus seen to establish what true knowing as such is, and to have thereby deduced the concept of science. The *Logic* is then seen to begin with and rest upon this structure of absolute knowing as its foundational and methodological principle. The logical categories of the science are seen to be generated out of this structure through the self-reflective self-knowing of absolute self-consciousness.[13]

In summation: According to the received view, absolute knowing as the deduced concept of science (1) is seen to be an actual and true knowing; (2) is seen to consist in a determinate relational structure whose elements or poles are subject and object (or subject/object, object/subject); (3) the logical science is seen to rest upon this structure as its presupposition, to have its nature or validity as science grounded in this structure; and (4) to have its logical categories generated out of the reflective activity of this structure of absolute self-consciousness as it engages in self-knowing. It is thus contended that the *Phenomenology* was meant by Hegel—at least originally—to establish the structure of absolute self-consciousness as the principle of absolutely true knowing and thus as the concept of science.

II. Hegel's Understanding of the *Phenomenology* as Introduction to Science

It is my contention that this traditional view of the relation of the *Phenomenology* to the *Logic* is neither in agreement with nor provides a satisfactory accounting for what Hegel himself says in the opening of the *Logic* concerning the *Phenomenology* as the deduction of the concept of science, concerning the nature of logical science and its method, and concerning the beginning of this science and what is required for this beginning.

I shall argue generally, in opposition to the received view, that both the *Phenomenology* as introduction, and absolute knowing as the deduced concept, must be understood *negatively*. Which is to say that, even as the deduction of the concept of science, the aim of the *Phenomenology* is not to establish and ground absolute knowing, embodied in the structure of consciousness, as true knowing *überhaupt*. (The aim is not to establish a structure of absolute self-consciousness as the foundational principle for autonomous, objective reason.) I shall contend that absolute knowing, as the deduced concept which *does* constitute the beginning point of the science, is, according to Hegel, not a true or actual knowing and not a determinate structure or methodological principle for the constitution of science. I shall further show that according to Hegel this science does not begin in or with, nor base itself on a reflective structure of the ego or self-consciousness, and that the *Phenomenology* does not serve to deduce the concept of science by in any way predetermining or grounding the method, manner, or nature of scientific cognition. I shall ague that it is Hegel's claim (1) that the nature, method, and validity of logical science can only be established *within* this science and not prior to it, and (2) that, nonetheless, absolute knowing is the deduced concept of science and that the *Phenomenology* is designed and carried out as the introduction to this science. My aim will be to show that the received view's account of absolute knowing cannot reconcile the following claims made by Hegel in the opening of the *Logic*: that logic begins without presuppositions while the *Phenomenology* is nonetheless the presupposition for the *Logic*, further, that the concept of science or logic cannot be in any way predetermined and that nonetheless the *Phenomenology* is the deduction of the concept of science.[14] Any adequate account of the *Phenomenology* as the deduction of the concept of science must be able to explain these apparently contradictory claims of Hegel's.[15] My positive thesis is that, to make sense of these claims by Hegel, both the *Phenomenology* as the deduction of the concept of science and absolute knowing as the deduced concept must be understood as radically negative, and further that clues in the *Logic* concerning the introduction to his science support this thesis.

"With What Must the Science Begin?" is where Hegel actually informs us how absolute knowing leads to or constitutes the beginning of science. Hegel tells us here that logic begins in or with absolute or pure knowing, that this pure knowing *is* the concept of science and is the result or outcome of the *Phenomenology* and the truth of consciousness (*Logic*: pp. 68–69).[16] We must ask: according to Hegel, is this pure knowing an actual and true knowing which is embodied in a determinate structure taken up in the *Logic* as its constitutive or methodological principle? Does the *Phenomenology* deduce the concept of science by establishing what absolutely true and hence scientific cognition consists in? Both of these key theses of the received view are here denied by Hegel. The latter thesis is suspect insofar as Hegel informs us that "it is the nature of cognition simply as such which is to be considered within the science of logic. . . . [T]o want the nature of cognition clarified *prior* to the science [*vor der Wissenschaft aber schon über das Erkennen ins reine kommen wollen*] is to demand that it be considered outside the science; *outside* the science this cannot be accomplished, at least not in a scientific manner and such a manner is alone here in place" (*Logic*: p. 68). Taken by itself, however, this statement denying the possibility of clarifying the nature of cognition prior to science and holding that it is just the task of science to do this does not itself fully undermine the received view. It could still be argued that the *Phenomenology* comes to determine the structure or principle of scientific cognition which is only subsequently to be elucidated or unpacked in the logic proper. But what Hegel says next rules this out, too. He tells us that we begin in the *Logic* with absolute or pure knowing as the deduced concept which results from the *Phenomenology*. In so doing we begin in or with the "determination of pure knowing" (*Logic*: p. 69). What then is this pure knowing which has resulted from the *Phenomenology* as the "ultimate, absolute truth of consciousness" (*Logic*: p. 68)? Is it, as the received view maintains, some determinate structure or principle of cognition which now merely awaits clarification or unfolding? Is this pure knowing constitutive of knowing as such; is it even a knowing? Hegel's answer to these questions is decisively negative. He proceeds to tell us that in beginning with this pure knowing as "what is there before us," as the outcome of the *Phenomenology*, pure knowing is that which has "sublated all reference to an other and to mediation; it is without any distinction and as thus distinctionless ceases itself to be knowing; what is present is only *simple immediacy*" (*Logic*: p. 69). (A few pages later, Hegel speaks of this knowing as collapsing and vanishing into an undifferentiated unity in such a way that it "leav[es] behind no difference from the unity and hence *nothing by which the latter could be determined*" [*Logic*: p. 73; emphasis added])[17]

According to Hegel then, science, in beginning with the deduced concept as pure knowing begins neither in nor with a knowing or with any *structure* of knowing at all. Further, it cannot be argued that this beginning point has some structure of knowing outside it, such as its *method* in terms of which "simple immediacy" is to be considered. Such a reading is ruled out because Hegel holds: (1) that method or form and content are *one* in his science (*Logic*: pp. 43–44); (2) that "the exposition of what can alone be the true method of logical science falls within the treatment of logic itself . . ." (*Logic*: p. 53); (3) that "the account of scientific method . . . belongs to its content" and "cannot be stated beforehand" but emerges "as the final outcome and consummation of the whole exposition" (*Logic*: p. 43); and (4) that the very immanent and scientific character of this logic consists in the fact that we rid ourselves "of all other reflections and opinions whatever" and take up "what is there before us" (*Logic*: p. 69). Hegel is unequivocal on this point: just in its beginning with the concept of science deduced by the *Phenomenology*, the logic *does not* begin in or with any knowing or structure of knowing, either as the object of scientific consideration or as the methodological or guiding principle for this consideration. Science begins rather with that absolute or pure knowing which, as the outcome and truth of the *Phenomenology* "*hört somit selbst auf, Wissen zu sein.*" In Hegel's mind, the outcome of the *Phenomenology* as the deduction of the concept of science is *negative*. For not only does the absolute or pure knowing in which the *Phenomenology* results cease in and of itself to be a knowing; further, in this self-cessation, what that knowing was as a determinate describable structure—the structure of consciousness—also ceases to be, is eliminated or *aufgehoben*. In beginning with or in this self-cessation of absolute or pure knowing as the deduced concept, science does not begin with the reflective structure of the absolute ego or self-consciousness which subsequently comes to generate logical categories *via* some process of immanent self-reflection. As we saw in his account of how the deduced concept comes to constitute the beginning of science, Hegel makes no mention of such a structure. What he *does* say about the deduced beginning point rules out the possibility of its being some such determinate structure or principle. For "simple immediacy" as the beginning point is "completely empty being" (*Logic*: p. 75), it is "pure indeterminateness" (*Logic: p.* 72) as that which is "without any distinction" within itself and which has "sublated all reference" to anything other than itself (*Logic*: p. 69).

According to Hegel, the deduced concept of science with which the *Logic* begins cannot be any determinate principle or structure of knowing, for he tells us that what the logic begins with "must be purely and simply *an* immediacy, or rather merely *immediacy* itself. Just as it cannot possess any determination relatively to anything else, so too it cannot contain within itself any determination, any content, for any such would be a distinguishing, and an interrelation of distinct moments and consequently a mediation" (*Logic*: p. 70). If Hegel took absolute knowing as deduced concept to be a structure, then he would not speak of it as collapsing into a unity which is "undifferentiated" (*Logic*: p. 74), a unity which leaves "behind no difference" by which it could be determined (*Logic*: p. 73). If Hegel held that the science begins with a determinate reflective principle embodied in an absolute self-consciousness, then he would not hold that it begins with no determinacy either within itself or in relation to anything else. Nor could he hold that "the beginning cannot be made with anything concrete, anything containing a relation *within itself*.... Consequently, that which constitutes the beginning, the beginning itself, is to be taken as something unanalysable, taken in its simply unfilled immediacy, and therefore *as being*, as the completely empty being"[18] (*Logic*: p. 75).

Although Hegel's remarks make it clear that absolute knowing as the deduced concept is not the self-reflecting self-knowing absolute self-consciousness that it is traditionally taken to be, and that the *Phenomenology* does not introduce science by somehow grounding, establishing, or predetermining the nature of true and hence scientific cognition, they do not indicate just how the *Phenomenology* functions to deduce the concept. That is, they do not indicate how the outcome of the *Phenomenology*, in its being the deduction of the concept, leads to the self-cessation of absolute or pure knowing into indeterminateness. Nor do they tell us what the meaning or sense of this deduction is, or how it works. These are questions which we shall turn to below. Nonetheless, that the outcome of the *Phenomenology* as deduction of the concept is taken by Hegel to be a negative one is clear. Hegel tells us further that the beginning of his science is an "absolute beginning" which means, according to him, that "it may not presuppose anything" and "must not be mediated by anything nor have a ground" (*Logic*: p. 70). Rather, he says, this beginning "is to be itself the ground of the entire science" (*Logic*: p. 70: cf. p. 43).

Now, however, we must confront our chief interpretive dilemma. For Hegel *also* asserts, in three separate places in both the "Introduction" to the *Logic* and in "With What Must the Science Begin?" that this science *presupposes* the *Phenomenology*: "The concept of pure science and its deduction is therefore presupposed in the present work in so far as the *Phenomenology of Spirit* is nothing other than the deduction of it" (*Logic*: p. 49; cf. p. 68, p. 60, and p. 48). How then is the *Phenomenology* to be understood as the necessary presupposition for science, as its mediation and as the deduction of its concept, if it is also held that science begins immediately (*Logic*: p. 70), if "not only the account of scientific method, but even the concept itself of the science as such belongs to its content ... and cannot be stated beforehand" because it "has its genesis in the course of the exposition and cannot therefore be premised" (*Logic*: p. 43)? How can the *Phenomenology* be the presupposition which Hegel claims it is if, as he also states, the science begins without presuppositions (*Logic*: p. 70)?

It is my contention that if any sense is to be made out of these seemingly mutual exclusive sets of claims, this sense is not to be found in the received view, with its positive reading of the *Phenomenology* as deduction and its positive—and as we have already shown, mistaken—understanding of absolute knowing as the deduced concept. Clearly, if the aim of the *Phenomenology* as introduction were to be the establishment of the nature of true cognition, and if absolute knowing as the deduced concept of science were to be a determinate structure of actual cognition (from out of which the logical categories are to be generated *via* a process of self-reflection), then the *Logic would* begin in or with a determinate presupposition and it would have its ground outside itself. Only if the *Phenomenology* as the presupposition for the *Logic* is understood to have a radically negative outcome can we reconcile and make sense out of the above mentioned claims and *also* understand Hegel's description of the *Phenomenology* as a *self-sublating* mediation or presupposition for science (*Logic*: p. 69). Understood in that negative manner, absolute knowing is, as Hegel says, a self-sublating or self-eliminating knowing and, as the deduced concept, constitutes the presuppositionless beginning point of science not in its being a knowing but rather in its self-elimination as a presupposed structure of knowing. The reconciliation of Hegel's apparently mutually exclusive claims thus lies in seeing that only a presupposition which is self-sublating, that is, which has a radically negative outcome such as that sketched above, could be a mediation or presupposition for presuppositionless science.

How then are we to understand the *Phenomenology* as the presupposition for presuppositionless science, as the necessary mediation which brings us to the point of an immediate beginning? As I understand it, it is Hegel's contention that the *Phenomenology* functions as the mediation and presupposition for presuppositionless science just in so far as it serves to indicate that absolute knowing, the knowing arrived at by consciousness as its "ultimate, absolute truth"—pure or utterly presuppositionless and self-grounding knowing—is *no knowing* at all. So the mediative function, the function of the *Phenomenology* as the presupposition for presuppositionless science, consists in its revealing the fact that when consciousness' presupposed structure of cognition is brought by consciousness' immanent dialectic to its "ultimate, absolute truth," this consists in the sublation of this knowing as a knowing and in the collapsing or vanishing of the foundational structure of this knowing—the structure of consciousness—into an indeterminate unity. Absolute knowing as the deduced concept of science is the presupposition for the beginning of presuppositionless science because it is the indication that absolutely presuppositionless knowing, that with which the science must begin, is no knowing at all and has no determinate structure. The *Phenomenology* can then be understood as the presupposition for presuppositionless science not because it establishes, grounds or predetermines the nature or principles of true, valid, and scientific cognition—for, according to Hegel that can be done only within the logical science, and because it is done therein he claims this science has its ground within itself and begins without a presupposition. Rather, the *Phenomenology* is the presupposition for presuppositionless science because it indicates what science must begin with if it is to begin without any presuppositions concerning knowing: not with some knowing, but with the self-cessation of knowing understood as the knowing of consciousness, with this knowing's coming to establish itself as absolute. (When the presupposed structure of knowing with which the *Phenomenology* begins— the structure of consciousness—is brought to its absolute self-grounding and self-legitimation, it comes in this absolute self-grounding to eliminate itself.) The *Phenomenology* is the presupposition for presuppositionless science because it indicates the necessity of the radically indeterminate and presuppositionless character of the absolute beginning of philosophical science.

If Hegel is serious—and I take him to be utterly serious— when he says that method and content are and must be one in the science (*Logic*: pp. 43–44, 54), when he says that the ground, the truth, and the validity of logic cannot be established outside it, when he states that logic must begin "without preliminary reflection" and "cannot presuppose any of these forms of reflection and laws of thinking" "for these constitute part of its own content and have first to be established within the science," and when he states that the concept of logic itself "has its genesis in the course of the exposition and cannot be premised" (*Logic*: p. 43), then the concept deduced by the *Phenomenology* cannot consist in a determinate structure or principle of true and scientific knowing. According to Hegel, if science is to be truly radical and self-grounding, it cannot begin with any determinate method, definition or rule of procedure (*Logic*: p. 53, p. 70, p. 72, p. 73, p. 75). And the necessity of understanding this radically negative state of affairs as requisite for the beginning of science is demonstrated by the *Phenomenology* as the presupposition for science. Thus, the *Phenomenology* is not a presupposition for the science because it establishes no principle, method, or ground for the science, and yet it is a presupposition for the science because it shows why such a science cannot have any such external grounding.

How then are we to understand the task, the aim of the *Phenomenology* as introduction to science? As the presupposition for presuppositionless science, the function of the *Phenomenology* must be to show both *that* science cannot begin with any determinate structure or presupposition and *why*, if it is to be pure science, it cannot begin in that manner. Now according to Hegel, what science does begin with in beginning without presuppositions is pure, reflectionless, and unstructured immediacy or indeterminateness, which, he says, is the "ultimate, absolute truth of consciousness" (*Logic*: p. 68). As I understand this, such an outcome of the work presupposed by presuppositionless science must indicate that the role of the *Phenomenology* is to show why beginning with the structure of consciousness as a presupposition in philosophy leads to its elimination or self-cessation as a structure of knowing when its absolute and ultimate truth is achieved That is, the task of the *Phenomenology* as introduction to science is the *critical* task of showing that when consciousness itself comes to demonstrate its absolute truth as a structure of knowing, when consciousness comes to an absolute self-grounding as structure of knowing, then consciousness, as a determinate and presupposed structure, comes to eliminate itself. (Thus, the *Phenomenology* might be understood not as the perversion of the Kantian critical project, but as its ultimate and radical completion. A completion which leads not to the affirmative absolutization of consciousness, but rather, through the consideration of consciousness's attempt at its own absolutization to the immanent demonstration that consciousness cannot be taken as the foundational principle in philosophy.) The outcome of the *Phenomenology* demonstrates that consciousness' attaining to its ultimate and absolute truth in absolute knowing yields 'indeterminateness' as the mediated indeterminateness of the structure of knowing presupposed in the *Phenomenology*. So understood, the *Phenomenology* is a presupposition for science because it comes to indicate indeterminateness as the outcome and truth of consciousness' project, the project defined in the "Introduction" to the *Phenomenology* as consciousness' search for its truth. The *Phenomenology* is not a presupposition in this science in the sense that the *Phenomenology*'s outcome predetermines something in the science. The positive aspect of the outcome of the introduction is precisely the negative one of indicating how the science is *not* to begin—with a presupposed structure or principle of knowing—if it is to be pure and presuppositionless. The *Phenomenology* is not a presupposition since it is, as Hegel says, a self-sublating mediation, in that the truth of consciousness as a presupposition about knowing shows itself to be its own elimination into indeterminateness or immediacy. That the positive character of the *Phenomenology* as introduction lies precisely in its negative outcome, and further, that the beginning point of science, in virtue of this outcome, is both mediated (by the *Phenomenology*) and immediate (because the *Phenomenology* as mediation is radically self-sublating) is also in agreement with Hegel's remarks about the nature of determinate negation (*Logic*: p. 54) and about beginning points generally. Concerning the latter he tells us: "What philosophy begins with must be either *mediated* or immediate, and it is easy to show that it can be neither the one nor the other; thus either way of beginning is refuted." "[T]here is nothing, nothing in heaven or in nature or mind or anywhere else which does not equally contain both immediacy and mediation, so that these two determinations reveal themselves to be *unseparated* and inseparable and the opposition between them to be a nullity" (*Logic*: pp. 67–68).

My contention that the *Phenomenology* as the introduction to science and the deduction of its concept functions in a negative and critical—as opposed to a positive and affirmative—manner *vis-à-vis* consciousness is substantiated by other remarks by Hegel in the *Phenomenology* and the *Logic*. In the "Preface" to the *Phenomenology* Hegel notes the following.

> The standpoint of consciousness which knows objects in their antithesis to itself, and itself in antithesis to them, is for Science the antithesis to its own standpoint. The situation in which consciousness knows itself to be at home is for Science one marked by the absence of Spirit. Conversely, the element of Science is for consciousness a remote beyond in which it no longer possesses itself.... When natural consciousness entrusts itself straightway to Science, it makes an attempt, induced by it knows not what, to walk on its head too, just this once; the compulsion to assume this unwonted posture and to go about in it is a violence it is expected to do to itself.... It is this coming-to-be of *Science as such* or knowledge that is described in the *Phenomenology of Spirit....* This coming-to-be (considering the content and patterns it will display therein) will not be what is commonly understood by an initiation of the unscientific consciousness into Science; it will also be quite different from the "foundation" of Science.... (*Phenomenology*: pp. 15–16)

And in the "Introduction" to the *Phenomenology*, where Hegel posits
consciousness as engaged in a search for the truth by means of a
self-investigation of its modes of knowing ("shapes" of consciousness) he anticipates the outcome of this project in the following
negative manner:

> Natural consciousness will show itself to be only the Notion of
> knowledge, or in other words, not to be real knowledge. But
> since it directly takes itself to be real knowledge, this path has
> a negative significance for it, and what is in fact the realiza-
> tion of the Notion counts for it rather as the loss of its own
> self; for it does lose its truth on this path. The road can there-
> fore be regarded as the pathway of doubt, or more precisely as
> the way of despair. . . . [T]his path is the conscious insight into
> the untruth of phenomenal knowledge. (*Phenomenology*: pp.
> 49–50)

The idea that the *Phenomenology* functions as introduction to science through being a thoroughgoing and radical critique of consciousness is also substantiated by several remarks of Hegel's in
the opening sections of the *Logic*. He tells us: "pure science presupposes liberation from the opposition of consciousness" (*Logic*: p. 49);
and "the liberation from the opposition of consciousness which the
science of logic must be able to presuppose lifts the determinations
of thought above this trivial, incomplete standpoint and demands
that they be considered not with any such limitation and reference
but as they are in their proper character, as logic, as pure reason"
(*Logic*: p. 51).

For Hegel, science—the attaining to an autonomous standpoint for thought—begins when the subject/object distinction of consciousness is no longer taken to be paradigmatic for thought. We
have seen that this ultimate rejection—the "liberation from the
opposition of consciousness which the science of logic must be able
to presuppose"—is the outcome of absolute knowing as the deduced
concept. And we have seen that it is a radical rejection, for the
overcoming of the opposition in absolute knowing does *not* yield
some absolute consciousness or some superpurified transcendental
ego. Rather, when consciousness comes to attain its absoluteness
in absolute knowing—when it comes to an absolute self-grounding
of itself through knowing its object as itself and itself as its object—the determinate difference between subject and object, the
opposition of consciousness which is definitive of consciousness
as a mode of knowing, is eliminated, leaving behind only an

unanalyzable, undifferentiated unity: pure indeterminateness. Further evidence that such an understanding of the role and aim of the *Phenomenology* corresponds to or coincides with Hegel's own self-understanding of the work is to be found in the following remarks from the "Introduction" to the *Logic*.

> These views on the relation of subject and object to each other express the determinations which constitute the nature of our ordinary, phenomenal consciousness; but when these same prejudices are carried out into the sphere of reason as if the same relation obtained there, as if this relation were something true in its own self, then they are errors the refutation of which throughout every part of the spiritual and natural universe is *philosophy*, or rather, as they bar the entrance to philosophy, must be discarded at its portals. (*Logic*: p. 45)

The task of the *Phenomenology* as introduction is thus to transcend the "limited standpoint" by refuting that "prejudice"—that knowing *must* be, in some form or another, knowing as defined by the structure of consciousness—which "bar[s] the entrance to philosophy" and consequently "must be discarded at its portals." It is my contention that the *Phenomenology* fulfills this task in its being a consideration (by the phenomenological "we," the observers of consciousness) of the attempt by consciousness to show that this "relation of subject and object" *can* be "carried out into the sphere of reason." Consciousness in the *Phenomenology* attempts to show that its structure *is* definitive of true knowing as such, that it is "something true in its own self," and that it can thus be taken as the foundational principle or beginning point for philosophical science. But, according to Hegel, when consciousness comes to the point of grounding itself as absolute principle for philosophical science, the knowing attained and consciousness itself as something determinate and presupposible are eliminated. Thus, the *Phenomenology* deduces the concept of science negatively by showing why it is that autonomous, radically pure and self-grounding science cannot begin with any such presupposed determinate structure or principle. The consideration of the attempt to absolutize consciousness in the *Phenomenology* shows, contrary to the traditional interpretation of that work, that consciousness is not an absolute principle for Hegel. And it also suggests—in a manner unappreciated by those who today argue in favor of the notion that all thought is necessarily *limited* owing to its embeddedness in a perspective defined by the structure of consciousness—that consciousness is not an absolute limit beyond which reason cannot extend. Thus, in general terms, the *Phenomenology* argues both against the positive idea of consciousness as the absolute principle for reason and against the contemporary negative idea of consciousness as an absolute limiting condition for reason.

Two central difficulties confront interpreters of the *Phenomenology*: deciphering how it can have an argument, and how it can possibly function as an introduction to systematic science without presupposing science. In Chapter 3 I have suggested that both problems can be solved if we see the function of the *Phenomenology* as immanently critical and its outcome as negative. In presenting this way of reading the *Phenomenology*, I have turned to Hegel's comments about that work in its role as the introduction to his system to argue against the received view which holds that Hegel is a committed foundationalist who wrote the *Phenomenology* to establish an absolute self-consciousness as the foundation for the system. Indicating that the relevant texts fail to support this view, Chapter 3 argues that the *Phenomenology* needs to be understood precisely as the deconstruction of such a foundational point, as a demonstration that the subjectivist model cannot ground its foundational primacy. Read in this way, we can understand in part how this negative outcome nonetheless functions as an introductory mediation for a self-grounding, presuppositionless system through its elimination of consciousness as a foundational structure. It shows why philosophy cannot have any external grounding, any beginning in a given, determinate foundation.

While Chapter 3 stresses the negative, antifoundational nature of the *Phenomenology*, Chapter 4, "Beginning Philosophy Without 'Beginnings,'" takes up the positive side of this negative outcome. It addresses the question of how the subjectivist model instantiated by consciousness can be seen as definitive of foundationalism, and it further explains why the suspension of consciousness effected by the *Phenomenology* makes possible the *Logic*'s constitution of categories as a procedure of radical *self*-determination. Thus an important step is taken in disclosing how the Hegelian critique of foundationalism nonetheless makes possible a realization of philosophy's traditional search for a presuppositionless discourse.

Chapter 4

BEGINNING PHILOSOPHY WITHOUT 'BEGINNINGS'

In no science is the need to begin with the subject matter itself, without preliminary reflections, felt more strongly than in the science of logic.

—Hegel

Understanding Hegel's *Logic* is crucial to any systematic endeavor to understand this most systematic of philosophers. If we are to consider seriously Hegel's claim to have established philosophy as science we cannot avoid a confrontation with the *Logic*. It is in the *Logic* that the scientific status and nature of the system are first established and elucidated; it is to this work that Hegel refers us when questions about the scientific character of rest of the system arise.[1]

But if the importance of the *Logic* is not in question, the same cannot be said about the work itself. Since shortly after its appearance, the *Logic* has been subject not only to a variety of interpretations but also to numerous critical attacks directed against its argumentative claims and its putatively scientific status.[2] Given its central role in the system, it is not unreasonable to contend that insofar as the *Logic* remains problematic, so too does the whole of Hegel's mature systematic philosophy.

In what follows I shall suggest a way of answering what are certainly the most immediate, and arguably the most crucial, interpretive and critical questions about the *Logic*, those concerning its beginning. But first I want to explain and defend my claim that it is the issue of the beginning of the *Logic* which deserves special attention. In so doing I shall also introduce the specific issues of *Logic* interpretation and critique that I plan to tackle.

For students of the *Logic*, the issue of its beginning takes priority—we most definitely need to begin at the beginning—for at least three reasons:

(1) According to Hegel, the salient distinguishing feature of systematic philosophy as science is its claim to rationally autonomous self-constitution or self-determination. The hallmark of the system's scientific character is the strict immanency of its genesis and development, its freedom from external determination in the constitution of its categories.[3] And as Hegel acknowledges, a claim to such autonomy and immanence can be supported only insofar as the system has, in some sense, a beginning which is itself devoid of external determination, to wit, a presuppositionless beginning.[4] But as Hegel also notes, the very possibility of such a beginning is questionable:

> . . . We can assume nothing and assert nothing dogmatically; nor can we accept the assertions and assumptions of others. And yet we must make a beginning: and a beginning, as primary and underived, makes an assumption, or rather is an assumption. It seems as if it were impossible to make a beginning at all. (*Encyclopedia Logic*: Paragraph 1, p. 3)

Thus, Hegel's larger claims about the distinctively scientific character of the system and his own views on the problem of making the kind of beginning the system requires focus our attention on the beginning of that work which begins the system proper. Understanding the overall scientific character of the system as self-constitutive requires us to confront the question of how a presuppositionless beginning can be made when any beginning seems to involve a presupposition.

(2) If the general question of how a presuppositionless science is to make its beginning were not enough to draw our attention to the opening of the *Logic*, the perplexing character of what Hegel has to say in the *Logic* about is beginning should give us pause. At the start of the *Logic*, Hegel tells us that it begins without presuppositions, and that it presupposes the *Phenomenology of Spirit* (*Logic*: pp. 70, 48, 60, 68). He tells us that the concept of science set forth in the *Logic* cannot be in any way predetermined, and that the *Phenomenology* is the deduction of this concept (*Logic*: pp. 43, 50, 68–69). Thus, an understanding of the beginning of the *Logic* is additionally crucial, for unless we can find a way to reconcile the

seemingly contradictory character of these claims, any further in-
terpretative conclusions about the meaning and the status of the
Logic must remain in suspension.

(3) Last, there is the problematic character of the actual opening section of the *Logic* itself. Some of Hegel's earliest and most
recent critics have contended that the character of the *Logic*'s opening development violates the strictures concerning immanency laid
down by Hegel. Dieter Henrich has specifically argued that the
movement from being through nothing to becoming can only be
rendered intelligible insofar as externally reflective operations are
brought to bear.[5] If this is in fact the case, then Hegel can only be
judged as having failed to meet his own specific demands and
assurances concerning the immanent character of the opening development of the *Logic* (*Logic*: p. 43). And if these demands are not
met here, then the scientific character of the *Logic* as a whole and
of the system is called seriously into question simply because the
claim to immanent self-constitution is inseparable from the system's
claim to be science.[6]

I wish to suggest that we can resolve the first and the third
issues by first tackling the second, by finding a way of reconciling
Hegel's seemingly conflicting claims about the *Phenomenology* as
the presupposition for a presuppositionless science. I shall now
turn specifically to that issue.

I. The Problem of Beginning and the Idea of Self-Sublation

If we are not to dismiss Hegel immediately on the grounds that he
engages in blatant self-contradiction when he claims that the *Logic*
has no presuppositions and that it presupposes the *Phenomenology*
we need to try to reconcile these claims by finding a way of distinguishing between the sense in which the *Phenomenology* is, and the
sense in which it is not a presupposition for that work. I am going
to argue that these senses can be sorted out if we can first make
sense of Hegel's crucial claim that the *Phenomenology* is a *self-
sublating mediation* for the logical science.[7]

How might the idea of a self-sublating mediation help us, and
how might the *Phenomenology* be understood as just such a creature? The notion of a self-sublating mediation may enable us to
reconcile the seemingly contradictory claims if we understand a
self-sublating mediation as a mediation—a presupposition—whose
own elimination *is* just that which is 'presupposed' for the beginning of science. Then what the science presupposes is just the

elimination of a presupposition. (So the science is presuppositionless in that it is made possible by the *elimination* of a presupposition, but begins with a presupposition in the sense that just this elimination is *presupposed*).

Before I proceed any further let me mention three questions which obviously arise at this juncture and which must be confronted. (1) What sort of a presupposition could be conceived as self-eliminating? (2) What sort of a presupposition might it be whose elimination would be relevant to a presuppositionless, self-determining science? (3) Even supposing that such a self-elimination could be effected, would not the science arising out of the elimination of this presupposition be only relatively presuppositionless? That is, would we not have to say that such a science might be presuppositionless relative to the presupposition eliminated, but not thoroughly presuppositionless? Clearly, the latter sense of presuppositionlessness is crucial to Hegel's notion of a radically self-determining science. In moving now to suggest how the *Phenomenology* may be understood as a self-sublating mediation, I'll be addressing these questions and also suggesting that the answers to the first and the second provide the grounds for dealing with the difficulty raised in the third. Following this I shall conclude with a consideration of how the problems Henrich raises may also be met through a proper understanding of the *Phenomenology* as a self-sublating mediation.

II. Understanding the *Phenomenology* as
Self-Sublating Mediation

We can understand the *Phenomenology* as a self-sublating mediation if we can appreciate how two conditions are met. First, its outcome must be radically negative in the sense that what is presupposed for the work's argument is negated in and by its outcome. Second, this sublation or negation must be immanently constituted: not externally imposed but engendered by the very subject matter introduced—presupposed—at the start. Put generally, we can understand the *Phenomenology* as a self-sublating mediation if it can be seen as beginning with a determinate thesis and culminating in its self-elimination.

Now, it is my contention that these two conditions for a self-sublating mediation can be met, *and* in such a way that the sublation in question is relevant for the beginning of a presuppositionless science just insofar as the topic of the *Phenomenology* is a thesis—a presupposition—*about how to begin philosophical science*. For, if the subject matter of the *Phenomenology* is a thesis about how to begin science, and if its outcome is a self-constituted rejection of this way of beginning, then perhaps, through this negative procedure of elimination the correct way of beginning science will have been made possible without being predetermined. To anticipate further, how then might looking at the *Phenomenology* as the self-elimination of a presupposition about how science is to begin enable us to resolve the apparently contradictory notion of a presuppositionless science having a presupposition by clarifying two different but related senses of presupposition? What is the specific presupposition about beginning science which comes to be eliminated by the *Phenomenology* and how is it relevant to the beginning of presuppositionless science? I want to answer these questions provisionally by outlining my reading of the *Phenomenology* as a self-sublating mediation. I shall then move to fill in the details.

The way of introducing I am sketching might be seen as constituting a presupposition for science in the sense that what science is seen to presuppose is a negative ground clearing: The *Phenomenology* shows that science presupposes—in the first sense of 'has as a preliminary or a prerequisite'—the elimination of a significant but erroneous notion concerning how science is to begin. At the same time though, this would not be a presupposition in the second sense of the term, the sense Hegel aims to avoid: Where a presupposition constitutes an external or a pre*determination* of the science (*Logic*: pp. 69, 43). More particularly, just this latter sense of presupposing—as predetermining—could be avoided if the *Phenomenology*'s negative function is more specifically one of eliminating just that which—somehow—*prevents* science from constituting or determining itself.

So, as regards the question previously raised about the seemingly relative character of a science which begins through the elimination of some presupposition: To stand as a presupposition for a presuppositionless science, the *Phenomenology* must not only function as the self-elimination of a presupposition about how science is to begin, it must also be the self-elimination of *that* presupposition about science which denies or precludes the possibility of a presuppositionless (self-determining) science. That is, the self-sublating mediation constituted by the *Phenomenology* can be seen as relevant to the beginning of a presuppositionless science if the presupposition about beginning science which the *Phenomenology* eliminates can be understood as that very notion about science which itself precludes the possibility of self-constitutive, autonomous science.

What I am suggesting is that the particular presupposition in the *Phenomenology* concerning how science is to begin which turns out to be self-eliminating, and which is relevant to the beginning of presuppositionless science, is a notion about the nature of cognition in general. In other words, it is a notion about what science must begin with which denies the possibility of autonomous science by holding that all cognition is ineluctably other-determined or predetermined. More specifically, the understanding of cognition which embodies this notion is just the view that regards the manner in which consciousness cognizes objects as definitive of all cognition. For, according to this view (*viz.*, the view that consciousness' mode of cognition can be presupposed for science) all cognition is always predetermined because all cognition is always cognition of that which is always already minimally determinate in virtue of being a given object for an awareness. Now, if this notion as to why it is that science cannot begin without presuppositions can be shown to be self-defeating—if it can be shown that consciousness cannot establish itself as exclusively definitive of cognitive possibilities—then, I submit, we *can* make sense of the idea that just this elimination is a 'presupposition' for a presuppositionless science. For this elimination will have shown that the understanding of cognition which purports to specify why a presuppositionless (self-determining) science is impossible, is arbitrary. And by having carried out this minimal and negative function the 'presupposition' in question—the *Phenomenology* as a whole—will have made a presuppositionless science possible without having determined anything in it and will thus be a presupposition (in the first sense) for a presuppositionless science (in the second sense).

So much by way of anticipation. How can these views be fleshed out and substantiated? Hegel points us in the direction of the view I am proposing—that the suspension of consciousness as a model for scientific cognition is what his science presupposes—at various places (*Logic*: pp. 49, 51, 60). To quote only one, he writes in the *Logic*:

> ... These views on the relation of subject and object to each other expresses the determinations which constitute the nature of our ordinary, phenomenal consciousness; but when these prejudices are carried out into the sphere of reason as if the same relation obtained there, as if this relation were something true in its own right, then they are errors the refu-

tation of which throughout every part of the spiritual and natural universe is *philosophy*, or rather, as they bar the entrance to philosophy, must be discarded at its portals (*Logic*: p. 45).

What Hegel is referring to here as that whose refutation is a prerequisite for science is what he refers to in the Introduction to the *Phenomenology* as the "natural assumption . . . in philosophy" (*Phenomenology*: p. 46). This is the foundational assumption, or presupposition, found in Descartes and throughout modern philosophy. It asserts that the beginning of science can be effected in and through a self-investigation by consciousness of the conditions of its cognition, a self-investigation which will allegedly culminate in the clarification and legitimation by consciousness of some specific features of its cognitive structure as definitive of scientific cognition. I have argued at length elsewhere for the interpretive claim that the *Phenomenology*, as the introduction to science, is nothing other than a thinking through of this foundational self-investigation—a thinking through of the claim that science must begin with consciousness.[8] So, I will now turn to the issue of just how the culmination of consciousness' self-investigation comprises a mediation which sublates itself and makes science possible.

III. Self-Sublation and Its Consequences

Hegel anticipates the negative outcome of the *Phenomenology* in the Preface and Introduction to the work, and he refers to it specifically in the *Logic*, as the deduced concept of science, when he points to the collapse of consciousness' own structure as resulting in the immediacy with which the *Logic* begins (*Phenomenology*: pp. 15–16, 49–50; *Logic*: pp. 49, 51, 68–69). How can that collapse be understood as the result of the thinking through of an attempt at vindicating the presupposition that it is in and through such a self-investigation that science must begin? More important, how can the self-refutation of just this presupposition specifically be connected to the possibility of a presuppositionless beginning?

The outcome of the *Phenomenology* as the collapse of consciousness' structure and the self-induced suspension of what is presupposed for us to follow through the development to this culmination can be understood, although not demonstrated, insofar as we consider what would be required for consciousness to successfully prove that its own structure is definitive of cognition.[9]

Minimally what consciousness must do to succeed in demonstrating the legitimacy of its mode of cognition—and the necessity
of presupposing consciousness in and for science—is to come to the
point of being able to simultaneously identify and differentiate
knowledge and object. Only at that point can correspondence—the
notion of knowledge inseparable from consciousness—be demonstrated as attainable.[10] But as Hegel shows at length in Chapter
VIII, and as he recapitulates in the *Logic*, at the very moment
when consciousness attains to such self-grounding, it is at once the
self-induced dissolution of the fixed opposition between subject and
object minimally constitutive of consciousness as such.[11] So, in
grounding itself as that which must be presupposed for scientific
cognition, consciousness suspends its determinate character and
thereby eliminates itself as a candidate for scientific cognition. For
the simultaneous identification and differentiation of knowledge
and object required to demonstrate correspondence, and thus to
vindicate consciousness, is a state of affairs in which the fixed
opposition definitive of consciousness as a cognitive structure renders itself into indeterminacy. Thus, we see that the attempt to
vindicate the presupposition that science can begin with a preliminary investigation of cognition culminating in a determinate principle for scientific cognition culminates rather in the self-refutation
of this presupposition about how science is to begin, for consciousness cannot attain the position of grounding its own structure without simultaneously sublating it.

How does this very culmination make a presuppositionless
science possible? The self-refutation in question is specifically relevant for the beginning of a presuppositionless science because
what has shown itself in the *Phenomenology* to be an illicit presupposition is not just any presupposition about cognition; rather, it is
that very assumption about cognition according to which all cognition must begin with a predetermined (given) determination. Thus,
the relevance of the elimination of consciousness—the importance
of the *Phenomenology* as presupposition—lies in the fact that consciousness instantiates that very conception of cognition which specifically holds that all cognition *must* begin with a presupposition,
and which purports to be able to show why this must be the case.
Understood according to or in terms of consciousness, knowing is
always, minimally and irreducibly, knowledge of an object: something which is always already *given* in its determinate character,
even if only in the minimal sense of being present to awareness.
According to consciousness, determinacy is always ineluctably pre-

determined. Thus, in asserting its own scientific character, consciousness claimed that cognition without presuppositions is impossible, because it held that its mode of cognition—for which some determination always is presupposed in always being given—is definitive of science.

So, given what consciousness instantiates, we can see that its suspension is specifically, indeed, preeminently relevant to the beginning of presuppositionless science. Hegel's science can make a claim to being more than just relatively presuppositionless because the suspension of consciousness is the suspension of nothing other than the structure of presupposing itself. To eliminate or suspend consciousness as a presupposition concerning science is to eliminate the structure of presupposing, for this suspension reveals as a prejudice and dismisses from scientific contention that view which holds that radical self-determination is impossible. Put differently, this elimination thoroughly undermines the authority of that view which holds that any determination of determinacy must involve some predetermination. In the latest jargon: this elimination deconstructs the fashionable postmodernist claim that all discourse is irreducibly constrained by contextuality.

In claiming to be the constitutive principle for philosophically scientific cognition, consciousness asserted the denial of the possibility of autonomous science (it asserted the supremacy of heteronomous contextuality) in a twofold way. First, by asserting its scientific primacy consciousness held that it (consciousness) must be presupposed for science. Second, given what it is as a cognitive structure, consciousness also denied the possibility of autonomous science by insisting that anything science comes to consider will itself involve a presupposition—a presupposed determinacy—because anything science considers must always already have the minimally determinate character of being an object. Thus, by articulating the self-sublation of the structure of presupposing itself, the *Phenomenology* renders the nature of presupposing perspicuous while revealing that the purported necessity of presupposing is itself non-demonstrable. For by showing how the demonstration of this necessity is at once the suspension of the (presupposed) structure in question, the *Phenomenology* reveals that in the last analysis this purported necessity cannot be anything other than an arbitrary assumption about cognition. Simultaneously, it shows how we can suspend that perspective according to which presupposing is necessary and unavoidable. For we come to see in a fundamental sense what presupposing minimally involves, and we come to discover that, and why, this manner of conceiving cognition need no longer be taken for granted as exclusively determinative of cognitive possibilities.

If this indicates in a general way how a presuppositionless science may be said to have a presupposition (in that it presupposes the self-elimination of the structure of presupposing) what can be said more concretely about this? How does the *Phenomenology*'s negative outcome nonetheless, and in its very negativity, function positively in regard to the beginning of a presuppositionless science? For one thing, in seeing that this presupposition eliminates itself, we (the observers of consciousness) come to see that a presuppositionless—radically self-determining or autonomous science—may be possible. It is important to note that nothing other than the possibility of such a science[12] can be or is provided for in the *Phenomenology* as a self-sublating presupposition for a presuppositionless science. The elimination of the structure of presupposing cannot itself constitute (in any determinate fashion) or require the beginning of presuppositionless science—if it did, this would be a predetermination and a heteronomous beginning. Nor can this suspension guarantee that the attempt to "take up what is there before us" (*Logic*: p. 69)—the indeterminacy resulting from the collapse of consciousness—will proceed in such a fashion that no external (pre)determinations will enter in. For any such guarantees for what purports to be a radically presuppositionless science could only be predeterminations themselves and, in any case, nothing determinate remains from what was presupposed in the *Phenomenology* to provide them. At this juncture, we might "resolve" "to consider thought as such" (*Logic*: p. 70), having been disabused of the preconception about cognition which seems to preclude such an endeavor. But as Hegel notes (*Logic*: pp. 69–70), nothing necessitates this move; it can be regarded as "arbitrary."

In addition to pointing to the general possibility of a presuppositionless science, the collapse of consciousness as the collapse of the structure of predetermination has indicated with what a presuppositionless science must begin: with nothing determinate whatsoever, i.e., with sheer indeterminacy (*Logic*: pp. 68–70). The self-induced collapse of consciousness (the structure of predetermination) at the moment of grounding the view that all considerations of determinacy must begin with a predetermination yields indeterminacy as the sole beginning point for science. Because indeterminacy results from the *Phenomenology*, it is part of the sense (the first) in which the *Logic* has a presupposition. But the beginning with indeterminacy does not obviate either the radically negative outcome of this self-sublating mediation or the crucial sense (the second) in which the *Logic* may be said to begin without presuppositions. For that which was presupposed in and for the *Phenomenology*—consciousness and its project—was something determinate, and in its rendering itself into indeterminacy nothing has been left behind as a referable object, that is, as something determinate which could function predeterminatively in the science. (How then determinacy arises out of indeterminacy is another matter.)[13]

Beyond these ways in which a presuppositionless science is made possible, the self-sublating mediation also shows us what it is that cannot be presupposed if such a presuppositionless science is to emerge from the consideration of indeterminacy. What cannot be presupposed is the notion that all determinacy is, and must be, minimally determinate in virtue of being regarded as an object for consciousness. This means that we know minimally how *not* to proceed if we make the resolve to think the indeterminate purely, as just what it is. We know that it cannot be done in the manner of consciousness. However, to know this is not a presupposition, simply because this negative knowledge is not necessary for science. This negative outcome does not constitute a predetermined method. For the negative knowledge is only vital for those who may happen to be in the habit of regarding consciousness' mode of condition as self-evidently definitive of all cognition, and are thus in need of being disabused of this notion. The fact that this habit is common throughout the history of Western philosophy—that in an important sense it constitutes this history—does not obviate my point. I will have something more to say about this in speaking to Henrich's objections.

In this way—without predetermining how the autonomous science will constitute itself (its 'method'), and without predetermining what it will constitute (its determinate content)—the *Phenomenology* functions as a presupposition for a presuppositionless science. The *Logic* has a presupposition in the sense that the *Phenomenology* comes before and does something that, historically, needs to be done: it eliminates from scientific purview the notion of cognition according to which cognizing must involve presupposing. The *Logic* does not have a presupposition in the sense Hegel claims it does not: its method, content, and scientific character are not predetermined just because what has come before (the *Logic*'s presupposition) has made possible a consideration free of such predetermining by articulating the self-elimination of the structure of predetermining.

IV. Henrich's Objections

We can also see how understanding the *Phenomenology* as a self-sublating mediation makes it possible to meet the criticisms against the strict immanency of the opening of the *Logic* which Dieter Henrich raises in his famous essay, *"Anfang und Methode der Logik."*

For Henrich, there is no question that the movement from being to nothing to becoming stands in need of a reconstructive—external—"proof" (p. 88). In fact, Henrich contends that we need to differentiate "the *science* of logic" from the "process of its logical thought-determinacies" and that the "science" only unfolds in a "retrospective grounding" which amounts to a "metalogic" (pp. 92–93). In respect to the beginning of the logic in particular, Henrich's claim is that the "logic of pure Being can only be explicated in general by a negative method [*nur via negationis*]" (p. 80). More specifically, this negative method consists in the negation [*Aufhebung*] of categories of reflection. When Hegel characterizes pure Being as the indeterminate immediate this shows the exclusion of reflection: "Thus *immediacy* is the negation of mediation and thus is as such mediated and determined through this concept" (p. 85). This shows that the "source" of the thought of immediacy is "transposed" [*verstellt*] to the logic of reflection. The upshot: "If . . . the nature of 'pure Being' can only be brought into view *via negationis* then the beginning of the *Logic* cannot be satisfactorily understood on its own terms." And, Henrich contends, Hegel "does not give us any other method [save *via negationis*] to explicate the thought of Being" (p. 86).

In fact then, Henrich presents a twofold critique. In addition to denying that the beginning of the logic of being can be understood without recourse to external reflection—in this instance, without recourse to the logic of reflection—he contends generally against Hegel that form and content are distinct in this work,[14] that that which makes it possible to explicate or ground or prove the argument lies outside of the development itself.

Both of these objections can be met just insofar as we have properly understood the nature of the *Phenomenology* as a self-sublating mediation.[15] As we saw, one dimension of that work's conclusion is to effect a negative lesson for anyone who would attempt to do science. We have learned that consciousness' mode of thought is precisely what is to be avoided for science. Whatever else a pure constitution or consideration of determinacy amounts to, it cannot be conducted in that manner.[16]

How does this relate to Henrich's claims about a *via negationis*, a reflective method? The connection comes into focus when one appreciates that it is just the structure of consciousness which can be alternatively described as the structure of reflection. What we find embodied in consciousness is a mode of conceiving determinacy in terms of a *fixed relation* of contrast or opposition. With consciousness determinacy is always minimally determinate in virtue of not being the other: the object is always minimally determinate as an object in virtue of not being awareness. Thus, consciousness is a structure whereby determinacy emerges out of a reflexive relation of opposition. Stripped of all other psychological and transcendental accoutrements, consciousness is the structure of mediation or of reflection. And if we focus on consciousness as minimally determining the determinacy of its object in virtue of the object's being an object—a *Gegen-stand* [that which stands over against]—them what we have with pure consciousness is the structure of constituting determinacy via reflection: through a process of relating which establishes determinacy by means of a distinguishing in which what is, is as 'other than' while yet 'for.' With consciousness, determinacy emerges via mediation. And just this structure collapses in pure knowing. So what Henrich sees as illicitly involved in the logic of being—the negation or exclusion of reflection or mediation—can be said to have come about licitly through the *Phenomenology* in its role as the consummate suspension of this structure. For the *Phenomenology*'s outcome in the collapse of consciousness not only establishes that whatever is to be thought purely (without presuppositions) is not to be thought in the manner of reflection, it also shows—in the way that Henrich's *ad hoc via negationis* cannot—why reflection is to be excluded. When seen from this perspective, Henrich's discovery of a need for the exclusion of reflection from the logic of being no longer amounts to a critique. Unbeknownst to Henrich, his analysis reinforces the preparatory role Hegel assigned to the *Phenomenology*.

How, more specifically, is Henrich's attack deflated? Henrich contends that the characterization of pure Being offered by Hegel and needed to make sense of the transition to nothing—Being's character as indeterminate immediacy—marks a negation of reflection and mediation and thus an illicit appeal to a later stage of the *Logic*. But it is easy to see that this characterization as negation of mediation or reflection is just the outcome of the collapse of consciousness.[17] Insofar as we take into account pure Being as the outcome of absolute knowing it immanently (legitimately) appears as the negation of the structure of reflection—which is to say, no longer as a determinate mediating structure but as *in*determinate *im*mediacy.[18]

Last, what about Henrich's larger critical claim, that the *Logic* is in fact only interpretable on the basis of a metalogic, which, if correct, would mean, against Hegel, that there is a distinction here between method and content? Such a reconstruction is only necessary as external and as destroying immanence insofar as we fail to see that the *via negationis* comes about through the self-sublating mediation. If we have followed the *Phenomenology* and understood the collapse of the structure of reflection, then we would not be predisposed to introduce the reflective approach to constituting determinacy into our thinking, and hence would not be *in need of* any metalogic which, according to Henrich, must be present to inform us what to do. An external, immanency-compromising *via negationis* as the method or metalogic of the *Logic* is needed only if we have failed to follow just that path Hegel offers to philosophical science.

So, if the *Phenomenology* is properly understood as self-sublating mediation, then we can say that Hegel has made a reasonable claim to having founded the kind of systematic philosophical science he sought: one which may offer us a system of autonomous reason in virtue of a beginning devoid of predetermining presuppositions. If this is the case, we can also suggest that further efforts to understand Hegel's system on its own terms are worthwhile, especially in an age in which many agree with Hegel in rejecting the primacy of consciousness but in which, unlike him, few offer anything as an alternative to the philosophy of consciousness save for what he prophetically decried in his own time as pious edification.

I have argued in Chapter 4 that making sense of Hegel's system as a philosophical science presupposes understanding the *Logic*, and that the most crucial interpretive problems and the most telling criticisms of that work can be met if we adopt—and continue to develop—the antifoundational approach to Hegel initiated in earlier chapters. By so doing we can begin to vindicate the crucial Hegelian claim about the nature of systematic philosophy: its self-grounding, self-determinative, presuppositionless or autonomous character. Insofar as the *Phenomenology* has functioned to critique foundationalism by showing that the subjectivist model of cognition cannot be legitimated, it also makes possible—mediates—a presuppositionless, self-grounding science, since it is just the subjectivist foundational model that holds that cognition must be construed as always grounded in a given—presupposed—determinacy. If the *Phenomenology* is right and this model cannot be legitimated as exclusively determinative of all possible thought, we have no basis for presupposing that a presuppositionless discourse cannot be achieved. Chapter 4 has also indicated something of a more positive nature about systematic philosophy, showing how we can not only appreciate, but also begin to actualize it possibility. The antifoundational outcome of the *Phenomenology* discloses the argumentative force of the *Logic*: the transitions Hegel lays out in the work can be seen as radically self-generated precisely if we do what the *Phenomenology* requires: Suspend our predilection to think in subjectivist terms and refuse to construe any determinacy as necessarily already given, predetermined. Just when we resist the temptation to do this we can engage in autonomous reasoning, in a consideration of the nature of determinacy which is radically self-determining in the sense that no external, no already given, presupposed determinacy enters in. And as self-determined, the discourse which ensues would also be self-grounding: what comes to be established would have its determinate character exclusively generated in the discourse and would need no further grounding.

In this way, Chapter 4 has linked the Hegelian critique of foundationalism with the vindication of one of philosophy's and foundationalism's goals: the establishment of a discourse which can give a full account of itself in that it is autonomous: what is asserted in it depends in its determinate character on nothing beyond itself. Thus, my earlier claims concerning Hegel's development of a philosophy which does justice to features of both foundationalism and antifoundationalism, while succumbing to the pitfalls of neither, have been further articulated. As I shall continue to reveal in subsequent chapters, reading Hegel as an antifoundationalist does not require us to impose a radically anachronistic interpretation which renounces Hegel's substantive claims about his system; it merely requires that we rethink the nature of these claims and the manner of their fulfillment. The picture of the "whole Hegel" promised in Chapter 1 continues to take on form and color.

Chapter 5, "Philosophy and Dialectical Method," addresses in greater detail some issues and claims raised in earlier chapters, and also further develops the positive, antifoundational reading of Hegel's system which those chapters have laid the groundwork for. I have contended that the *Phenomenology* functions as an immanent critique of the subjectivist model of cognition and that it culminates in this model's self-suspension. Chapter 5 works to further substantiate this reading by considering the nature and function of the dialectic in the *Phenomenology*. I have also asserted previously that Hegel's system needs to be rethought as nonmetaphysical and nonidealist, contending that while this system fulfills some of philosophy's traditional goals, it does so in a unique fashion which avoids some of the most serious contemporary criticisms of traditional philosophy. Chapter 5's overview of the argumentative character of the *Logic* and of the remainder of the system is designed to explain how this rethinking of Hegel is possible. All of these themes are brought together in this chapter's attempt to sort out the nature of Hegel's notorious dialectical method at various places in the system. (A theme addressed again, in relation to Marx, in Chapter 8.)

Chapter 5

Philosophy and Dialectical Method

> With the truth so dull and depressing, the only alternative is wild
> bursts of madness and filigree.
>
> —Hunter S. Thompson

The notion of dialectics is perhaps as old as the idea or practice of
philosophy itself. It did not originate with Hegel, but if he has
contributed something both original and significant to it, this can
be seen to lie, I believe, in his conception of a *systematic dialectic*. I
am going to try to explicate what systematic dialectic means for
him by focusing on the question: Does Hegel have a dialectical
method? I shall proceed in this manner because I feel that it is
crucial to an understanding of what Hegel means by 'dialectic' and
by 'dialectical philosophy' to see both why and how it is that he
does not have a dialectical method.

I shall try to show, by examining Hegel's sense of dialectic,
that he does not have a dialectical method insofar as one uses the
term 'method' in its traditional philosophical sense. That is, taking
'method' to denote a specific and specifiable set of rules of procedure as operational or cognitive principles for the consideration of
a given subject matter. Insofar as method is that which can—even
if only in principle—be justified, formulated or learned in abstraction from the subject matter to which it is to be applied, Hegel
does not have a method. Insofar as 'method' is taken to be a
significant term only in and through a contrast with some content
for which the method is designed and to which it is applied, Hegel
does not have a method. Insofar as a method constitutes a given

99

or theoretically derivable principle or set of principles *in terms of which* a subject matter is thought or considered, Hegel does not have a method. Insofar as one can speak of there being, in the sense just outlined, a phenomenological method, a scientific method, a transcendental method, an analytical method, a speculative method and so on, Hegel does not have a method.[1]

What I take to be the absence of any method—dialectical or otherwise—in this traditional sense in Hegel's philosophy does not indicate however that we cannot talk meaningfully about the issue of method in regard to his philosophical project. In fact, I hope that looking at Hegel in terms of the question of method will be a good method for illuminating what is significant, unusual and perhaps unique in his philosophy.

I shall consider the absence of method and the question of Hegel's understanding of dialectic in terms of the three major divisions of his philosophy. These divisions correspond to three of the four books he published: the *Phenomenology of Spirit* of 1807, the *Science of Logic*, and the *Encyclopedia of the Philosophical Sciences*. I shall attempt to isolate and consider as briefly as possible three different senses or understandings of dialectic to be found in each of these works: (1) In the *Phenomenology*: the dialectic of consciousness, or immanently critical dialectic; (2) in the *Science of Logic*: the dialectic of pure thought as such; (3) in the *Encyclopedia*: the dialectic of real philosophy.

Taken in their interconnection, and as a whole, these three dialectics constitute what I call Hegel's systematic dialectic. For each division or book, I shall attempt to explicate how each dialectic is peculiar or immanent to the subject matter. I shall also try to indicate how each dialectic operates, how each differs from the other and how each—taken in sequence—develops from or arises out of the other. In attempting to do all of this I shall at the same time be focusing on my contention that Hegel does not have a 'dialectical method.'

I. The *Phenomenology* of 1807: The Dialectic of Consciousness or Immanently Critical Dialectic

Hegel's consideration of method in regard to the *Phenomenology*, the presentation of what we might provisionally call his phenomenological method, is to be found in the Introduction to that work.[2] To sum up what he says on our topic there: The dialectical-phenomenological method of the *Phenomenology* is no method at all. This is the case according to him because the standpoint or position from which the phenomenologists consider their topic, consciousness, is one of *"reine zusehen"*: pure looking on or pure observation.[3] Looked at from the point of view of dialectic, what Hegel contends is that the dialectic found in the *Phenomenology* does not consist in a method of consideration. Rather, he holds, it is a dialectic in or of the subject matter itself: consciousness.[4] The 'method' of the *Phenomenology*, according to Hegel, consists finally in the fact that the phenomenologists, the on-lookers, neither have nor are in need of a method.[5] In other words, Hegel's claim is that it is just because consciousness is a self-determining self-constituting subject matter, that the observers of consciousness are in need of no 'method.'

If the alleged absence of method here means "pure observation," how is this possible? What does Hegel say to support his contention of a "pure observation?" Is it nothing more than a bold and unsupported claim to philosophically intuitive omniscience? A claim on Hegel's part, that is, to be in possession of a mode of 'absolute knowing' as an absolute method? Or is this standpoint of pure observation the result of a theoretically sophisticated preliminary reflection consisting in something like the epoches and reductions of contemporary phenomenology?[6] I think it is neither of these, although it bears far more resemblance to the latter than to the former. What then legitimates the claim that the phenomenologists do nothing, have no method?[7]

Hegel holds that the phenomenologists can sit back and observe because the dialectic of the *Phenomenology*, its manner and course of development, is not something distinct from its subject matter, consciousness. The phenomenologists need not do anything in the way of an application of criteria, a judging of the subject matter because consciousness, he claims, in and of itself generates a "sequence of shapes" of itself.[8] In short, what Hegel is maintaining is that we find a self-determining subject matter in the *Phenomenology*. We shall see that what this means for him is the following: That consciousness, as defined or presented, contains within itself a criterion or standard, and that consciousness' attempt to demonstrate the unconditional validity of its standard brings consciousness through a self-determined sequence of shapes of itself which are constituted through the critical self-application of the standard.[9]

But what then does *this* mean, and how is this self-constitutive or self-determinative process supposed to work? What is consciousness' standard and how does consciousness come to apply it to itself? According to Hegel, our phenomenological object is not merely or simply consciousness, but consciousness as a *knower*.[10] Furthermore, our object is that knowing consciousness which has been posited as engaged in a particular task or project. Our object here—consciousness as knower—is an epistemic structure which is engaged in the attempt to arrive at, to determine and demonstrate, the unconditional truth of its mode of knowing. To show, that is, that its manner of cognition is definitive of science.[11] According to Hegel, such a subject matter, as posited, will enable us to engage in sheer observation for two reasons:

(1) Consciousness as consciousness—as an entity which is what it is in being an 'awareness of' something other than itself—provides according to Hegel both a standard (or structure) of knowledge and a criterion of *true* knowledge or true knowing.[12] Consciousness, just in being consciousness, is minimally and irreducibly an awareness or consciousness of something other than or distinguishable from itself as awareness—some object. Thus, consciousness in and of itself, Hegel holds, contains or manifests a claim concerning what true knowledge or true knowing consists in: 'Knowledge,' according to consciousness, is the knowledge *of* an object; and 'true knowing,' according to consciousness, consists in the knowing of an object as this object is "in-itself," outside of or over against consciousness as the knower of it. Hegel's point is that because consciousness also gives a criterion of *true* knowing, the phenomenologists will not need to bring in any criteria of their own in considering consciousness.[13]

(2) This fact however is clearly not enough to constitute a self-determining subject matter which we need only observe. Even if it is given by definition or posit that consciousness qua consciousness itself determines a structure of knowing and contains a criterion of true knowledge or true knowing, something more is required in order for Hegel to be able to hold that consciousness itself generates a sequence of shapes, that consciousness itself is immanently dialectical or self-determining.[14] The second aspect which is required in order for the *Phenomenology* to have a self-determining subject matter is also posited by Hegel in the Introduction. (Why he posits this second feature, beyond its being required in order that the *Phenomenology* can have a self-determining subject matter, I shall consider below.[15]) Hegel tells us that the consciousness which we shall consider is not merely a

consciousness attempting to know the truth. In addition, it is a consciousness which is further concerned with coming to establish that its own mode or structure of knowing is true and valid as such.[16] That is to say, this particular consciousness is a consciousness which is concerned with the epistemological-transcendental task of demonstrating that the structure of knowledge which it defines in being consciousness is unconditionally true and valid. In this way, the consciousness in the *Phenomenology* is further posited as being engaged in the task of its own self-legitimation as structure of cognition.[17] Because consciousness' task is one of self-legitimation, the grounding of the validity of its mode of knowing must be immanent, i.e., effected by consciousness itself. Only if consciousness can bring off the job itself, by showing that it is in fact capable of attaining to knowledge of the in-itself, can it be said that its structure of cognition is not merely presupposed as valid by or for this consciousness but is rather valid unconditionally. In this sense the consciousness found in the *Phenomenology* is posited by Hegel as demanding its own immanent self-grounding through a self-investigation, and the phenomenologists are, according to Hegel, liberated from the tasks of supplying and applying criteria for the consideration of this subject matter and thus can engage in the simple observation of it.[18]

What then is the immanent dialectic of the *Phenomenology*? How will the self-constituting dialectic of the consciousness engaged in the search for its *own* truth, for the truth of its structure of knowledge, operate? What specifically is the truth criterion given by consciousness? In what manner will consciousness apply this to itself? How will this self-application come to constitute a finite series of "shapes of consciousness," immanently generated by consciousness, which culminates in "absolute knowing" as what Hegel calls the "ultimate and absolute truth" of consciousness?[19]

(1) What is consciousness' truth criterion? Since consciousness as consciousness is a mode of awareness whose type of cognition consists in knowing an object which is over against itself, 'true knowing' for consciousness will consist in the correspondence or approximation of its knowledge *of* the object with the object as it is in-itself. Thus consciousness' knowledge will have to be at one with, identical to the object, in order for the knowing to be true. But at the same time this knowledge must still be a knowledge *of* the object. Even as corresponding to it, the knowledge must be distinct from that which it is the knowledge of in order for this to be a true *knowing* according to consciousness' own implicit definition of knowledge. Thus, on the basis of what consciousness is as a knower, 'true

knowing' is defined as the correspondence or *identity in difference* of knowledge and object.[20]

(2) How does consciousness come to apply this criterion to itself, and how does this self-application generate the dialectic of the *Phenomenology* in constituting a series of shapes of consciousness culminating in "absolute knowing?" As consciousness is posited by Hegel as being engaged in the attempt to discover that specific mode of its relation to the object which will satisfy its truth criterion, consciousness will be engaged in the attempt not merely of knowing the object, but furthermore of *knowing its own knowing* as true. Thus, consciousness will take its purportedly true knowing of the object—the oneness of its knowledge with the object in-itself—as a further object of knowledge in order to determine if identity in difference is in fact manifested.[21]

Given this, we find then that the 'dialectical engine' of the *Phenomenology*, the generation of the shapes of consciousness by consciousness itself, arises in the following way: Until consciousness comes to the point of positing as the object in-itself *nothing but its own structure of knowing*, consciousness will continually fail in its attempt to specify a relation of knowledge to object which satisfies its own truth criterion. Surveying the *Phenomenology* as a whole, this means that consciousness will constitute and run through a series of self-transformational failures—"inversions of consciousness"—until it attains to what Hegel calls absolute knowing as a pure knowing of knowing.[22] Why? Why is it that consciousness will fail to find the identity in difference which it is looking for until it takes its own structure of knowing as its object and thus is engaged in a pure knowing of knowing?

Consciousness has an idea of the object which it takes to be true, which it believes to be in full correspondence with the object as it is in-itself. But consciousness must test this knowledge, i.e., compare it with the object, in order to see if it does correspond to it. Put differently, in order to test its knowledge, consciousness must thematize its *knowing,* that is, it must come to focus on the relation of its (purportedly true) knowledge to the object in itself. What this means is that in testing, consciousness comes to make what we might call the epistemic move: It focuses automatically on its idea of the object in-itself—its original immediate notion concerning what this object is—in its status as *knowledge of* the object. In order to effect the comparison, consciousness makes this knowledge of the object into an object of knowledge. It becomes in effect a second object which will be compared with consciousness' original idea of what the object in-itself is.

It is in doing this that the immanent dialectic of consciousness emerges. For in testing its knowledge consciousness comes to discover that the object qua known—its purportedly true knowledge of the object in-itself—is, although different from what it first took the object in-itself to be, not at the same time identical with it. This discrepancy arises from out of the very nature of the project consciousness is engaged in because in consciousness' making its knowledge of the object into an object of knowledge, what consciousness has to compare with the object in-itself is not *simply* knowledge, not simply this idea of the in-itself, but rather the object or its idea of the object *as known once again* by consciousness. It is the epistemic move, in other words, which necessarily gives rise to the discrepancy.

So, in making its knowledge of the object into a second object in order to test this knowledge, consciousness comes to automatically posit this, its *knowledge of* the object—that which it has necessarily come to thematize in order to make the test and what Hegel calls the "being for consciousness of the in-itself"—as the true in-itself.[23] And consciousness thus discovers in making the comparison that what it took the object to be in-itself is not what it truly is *as known.* In objectifying its original idea of the in-itself in order to test it, consciousness comes to take this—the in-itself as known by consciousness, or the in-itself as for consciousness—as the true object, the true in-itself.[24]

Consciousness thus systematically falsifies its original idea concerning the in-itself in its in-itselfness through the very attempt to show this idea to be true, and simultaneously produces a new candidate for testing (and thus a new "shape of consciousness"). This developmental process—the dialectic of consciousness whereby new notions of the object arise through consciousness' testing of its purportedly true knowledge of the object—will continue until consciousness posits the structure of its own knowing of the object as the object in-itself. Only at that point will identity in difference appear. For, when consciousness' own structure of knowing is posited as the in-itself, then consciousness' *knowledge of* this—the *being for consciousness* of this in-itself—consists in the being for consciousness *of* 'being for consciousness.' Here, in consciousness' knowing of its own mode of knowing, in what Hegel calls "absolute knowing," the identity in difference of the object as known and the object in-itself is at last achieved. Identity is manifested here because the object in-itself and the knowledge of it are of the same form: the form or structure of consciousness' knowing. And yet, because both the object in-itself and the knowing of it are of the form of the 'knowing *of*,' difference is also manifested.[25]

This dialectic is *immanent* because both the mode of its self-development and the criteriological or methodological principle in terms of which it takes place are given in or with consciousness—the subject matter—when its task is posited as the self-legitimation of its mode of knowing. In addition, it is an immanently *critical* dialectic because the final self-grounding of consciousness' mode of knowing in absolute knowing is at the same time the dissolution of consciousness as a structure of knowledge.[26] Given the nature of consciousness as indicated above, we can see why this must be the case. For, when knowledge and its object are at once both simultaneously identical to and different from one another, the *fixed difference* between knowledge and object which is presupposed by and definitive of consciousness is eliminated. That is, according to the principle or understanding of knowing being grounded in it, absolute knowing is not a knowing, just because in absolute knowing there is nothing determinate, distinguishable and identifiable either as knowledge or as the object of knowledge. The two poles which defined consciousness as a structure of knowledge and a principle of cognition come in absolute knowing to be indistinguishable from one another. For in a sheer identity in difference, nothing remains which can be said to be either identical to or different from anything else. Thus in absolute knowing the structure in terms of which absolute knowing subsists and is articulable as a determinate something and as a knowing eliminates itself.

Thus, in Hegel's words, absolute knowing "thereby ceases in and of itself to be a knowing" and collapses into an "*undifferentiated unity.*"[27] And this final *critical* outcome of the dialectic of consciousness is, just as the path of development which lead up to it, *immanent* or self-constituting because the definitive structure or understanding of cognition violated here—and thereby eliminated as a candidate for the absolute principal of all cognition as such—is consciousness' *own* principle and not one externally imposed upon it by the phenomenologists who observe the attempt at the self-grounding of this principle.

II.   The *Science of Logic*: The Dialectic of Pure Thought As Such

What is the significance of the outcome of the *Phenomenology*—absolute knowing and its collapse—for the *Science of Logic*? Hegel holds that the concept of Science with which logic begins has been "deduced" by the *Phenomenology* in absolute knowing.[28] Does the *Phenomenology* come in absolute knowing to deduce and determine a methodological principle for the *Logic*? Does the outcome of the *Phenomenology* constitute the method for the *Logic* by yielding an operational truth criterion, a determinate principle or structure through which the logical determinacies are determined and in which, as the principle of their constitution, the criterion of their validity lies? If this is the case, what are we to make of Hegel's claims: (1) that method and content are one in this logic; (2) that neither the nature, validity nor method of logical science can be given at its beginning but rather arise in it; (3) that the *Logic* has a presuppositionless beginning?[29]

The answer to these questions—which might be summed up as the question, "how can the *Phenomenology* be, as Hegel claims, the presupposition for a presuppositionless science?"—is to be found in grasping how it is that the *Phenomenology* can lead to the beginning point of science without predetermining either the validity or the method of this science.[30] My contention is that the *Phenomenology* yields a 'method' for the *Logic* only in a radically negative sense, and that it is the 'presupposition' for the *Logic* because it indicates *why* this science must begin without presuppositions. That is, because it indicates why the *Logic* must begin in and with the radical indeterminateness which according to Hegel is the final outcome of the collapse of the structure of absolute knowing and with nothing else.[31]

The *Phenomenology* serves an 'introductory' function for the *Logic* because it indicates the necessity of beginning, in an attempt at a pure philosophical science, without any presupposed or assumed methodological principle. This negative conclusion is arrived at through the *Phenomenology* because that work constitutes the consideration of the attempt to ground a determinate presupposition concerning the nature of cognition—consciousness' structure of knowledge—as *the* valid methodological principle for cognition *überhaupt*.[32] We—the phenomenological observers of consciousness— saw that when consciousness came in absolute knowing to complete its self-legitimation, to, in effect, legitimate the presupposing of consciousness' structure as a principle of cognition through a radical self-grounding, this had the consequence of collapsing the structure being grounded and eliminating absolute knowing as a knowing. Yielding, as final residue, nothing but an "unanalysable" "completely empty being" or "pure indeterminateness," something which according to Hegel neither contains any determinacy within itself nor in relation to anything else and is yet the concept of science with which logic is to begin.[33]

The *Phenomenology* can thus be understood to be Hegel's 'discourse on method' as a critique of method. That is, as a critique of the notion that one can begin in philosophy by either assuming or postulating some determinate methodological principle or principles as a guide, rule or truth criterion for the constitution of philosophical discourse. The critical outcome of the *Phenomenology* vis-à-vis method is this: There are no determinate self-grounding or self-legitimating principles, no self-evident assumptions with which one can begin. In this way, one is brought to a moment of decision as a choice between alternatives. One can give up the traditional aim of philosophy to constitute itself as self-legitimating discourse, the aim to be scientific in a radical sense. By so doing, one thereby resigns oneself to beginning in philosophy with some presupposition which can never be anything more than that, and which can claim no final legitimatable superiority over any other presupposition with which someone else begins. Philosophy, if this alternative is accepted, must then give up the claim to be able to speak critically to the question of truth, and must acknowledge that in the last analysis there are as many 'truths' as there are particular standpoints or cognitive interests.

The other alternative is that taken up by Hegel. We shall see that despite his rejection of the possibility of beginning in philosophy with a determinate 'principle of principles' as an absolute foundation, that this does not lead him to embrace an uncritical relativism. The conclusion of the *Phenomenology*—that philosophy cannot begin with a determinate self-grounding truth principle—leads him rather to make an attempt at a self-grounding philosophy that does not begin with any determinacy or determinate principle whatsoever.

The first step in this process is found in the *Logic* which begins in the thinking of the "pure indeterminateness" which results from the collapse of absolute knowing. The *Phenomenology* then, as the deduction of the Concept of Science, does not constitute a method for the *Logic* in that it establishes neither a determinate subject matter for scientific-logical consideration, nor a structure, rule or principle in terms of which the process of logical cognition is to proceed. The *Phenomenology*, owing to its radically negative outcome, does not predetermine what the science will be, how its 'dialectic' will operate, in what its 'scientific' character, in a positive sense, will consist, or whether such a pure science is possible at all and what it will mean. The negative idea or ideal—which idea or ideal the *Phenomenology* does give—is that a thoroughly immanent and self-determining science can have no such predeterminations or guarantees, and the alleged character of the *Phenomenology* as the "presupposition" for "presuppositionless" science is that it has shown why this must be the case.

Having asserted that the *Phenomenology* plays no *positive* role in the *Logic*, I must now show, by considering the dialectic which is involved in the move from the *Phenomenology* to the *Logic*, how it plays a negative role. Or, dialectically speaking, how its negative role is just its positive one. The *Phenomenology* does, in a sense, play a positive role in the constitution of the beginning of the science, in three ways. The first, which I have already considered, consists in the fact that the *Phenomenology* shows why such a science must begin without any method or methodological presuppositions, without any rule or principles for its development and constitution. The second positive function the *Phenomenology* plays is that it indicates specifically what the attempt at science must begin with: indeterminateness.

The third sense in which the *Phenomenology* has a positive function for the *Logic* is the sense in which it constitutes a *negative methodology* for the *Logic*. I shall consider this in some detail because what it means is clearly crucial to my contention that Hegel does not have any 'method' in the traditional sense. My claim is that the *Phenomenology* serves to indicate a negative methodology for the *Logic* in that, although it does not tell us how to proceed in the science because it gives no determinate principles or rules for logical cognition, it does tell us how *not* to proceed. The *Phenomenology* does this because it indicates specifically what *cannot* be presupposed if the *Logic* is to be a pure science; if, that is, its dialectic is to be an immanent and self-constitutive one.

In the *Phenomenology*, determinacy was always considered within the context of the structure of consciousness and determined in its determinacy in relation to consciousness as the knowing subject. But if the "ultimate and absolute truth" of consciousness, arrived at by consciousness in its self-grounding, consists in the self-elimination of this structure into indeterminateness, this indicates specifically that the constitution of the logic can neither have this structure as its subject matter nor be carried out in terms of the model or paradigm defined by consciousness' cognition of objects. Hegel tells us the "pure science presupposes liberation from the opposition of consciousness," i.e., from the subject/object model of cognition, and that when "the determinations which constitute the nature of our ordinary phenomenal consciousness . . . are carried out into the sphere of reason as if the same relation obtained there, as if this relation were something true in its own self, then they are errors the refutation of which through every part of the spiritual universe is *philosophy*, or rather, as they bar the entrance to philosophy, must be discarded at its portals."[34] Specifically, this means that in attempting to do pure logic—in attempting to think the indeterminate—we cannot presuppose or assume that it is already determinate simply in virtue of the fact that 'it' is an 'object.' We must not assume that the indeterminate is, even as indeterminate, already determinate in its indeterminacy just because it will now stand over against (be *gegenständlich* to) a thinking subject. Put differently, the givenness of 'our' human mode of cognition, the fact that we are finite thinking subjects, cannot be presupposed as having any constitutive primacy in an attempt to think without presuppositions. The 'givenness' of this our mode of cognition may be self-evident, as some philosophers claim, but the legitimacy of presupposing this mode of cognition as absolute, as constituting the 'bottom line' in terms of which all philosophical cognition must either be carried out or assessed in its validity has been rendered null and void by the *Phenomenology*. For that work has shown that when this structure of cognition is no longer simply presupposed, but is rather brought to its self-grounding, it transcends itself.

So, we cannot take consciousness' structure of cognition— according to which whatever is being cognized is always already determinate as being other than the awareness which thinks it, is always already determinate as an *object* in some sense, whether externally given or self-given—as the methodological model in a purportedly pure logic. For to do so would be to invest the allegedly thoroughly indeterminate indeterminateness with a determinate character by contrasting it, as object, with a predetermined determinacy (thought or the thinking subject) which is its other.[35]

The *Phenomenology* thus constitutes a negative methodology for the *Logic* simply because it tells us how indeterminateness is not to be thought.[36] To engage in logical cognition according to the model of consciousness would be to posit or hold indeterminateness as *stable*, as fixed or determinate in its indeterminateness *and thus as already contrastable with the determinate* because a thinking subject has focused on it as an object, and is 'holding' it as 'present' to the mind. As I hope to show, the negative methodology indicated by the *Phenomenology* will function in the opening of the *Logic* insofar as, in the thinking of indeterminateness, this is not done.

That this is the case, I would like to demonstrate by considering the opening of the *Logic*, and the 'move' from being, to nothing, to becoming. As we have seen, the claim that the *Logic* presents a pure and immanent dialectic rests in part on the claim that—as opposed to the *Phenomenology*—there is no operative and presupposed structure or principle taken as the 'method,' as the determinacy in terms of which the indeterminate is determined.[37] From a different angle, the claim is that what we find here is pure and presuppositionless thought—thought which is, at the starting point as yet thoroughly indeterminate and not even contrastable with being—engaged in self-determination. In short, the claim is that indeterminateness, insofar as it does come to be determined in logic, is determined only in and through itself. What I shall show—by reflectively examining the move from being, to nothing, to becoming—is how this self-determination of indeterminacy operates. I shall attempt to do this by showing how the contrast in and through which pure indeterminateness comes to be provisionally determined is an internal and immanent contrast because—as the *Phenomenology* demands—nothing is being presupposed here as already determinate.

Hegel tells us that the *Logic* begins with the thinking of indeterminateness at that which has resulted from absolute knowing.[38] Looked at reflectively, what we find in the opening moments of the logic of being is this: Insofar as we rid ourselves "of all other reflections and opinions whatsoever" and "take up *what is there before us*" we discover that thinking indeterminateness in and as indeterminate demands, requires or leads us to the thinking of a contrast.[39] (Or, we discover that this thinking *is* the thinking of a contrast.) Indeterminateness as first thought, in being thought as indeterminate, or in its indeterminacy, is thought as determinate in its indeterminacy; as *being*. But, insofar as no determinacy is invested in indeterminateness simply because it is being *thought as* indeterminate (simply because of the subjective act of focusing on it) we can see that as thought, this determinacy *of* indeterminateness—being—is no different from *utterly* indeterminate indeterminateness: *nothing*. Or, making the same point non-reflectively: Thinking "empty being," thinking the utterly and thoroughly indeterminate *as* indeterminate in its indeterminacy, *is* the thinking of nothing.

To proceed a step further, to becoming: Thinking indeterminateness as indeterminate in its indeterminacy demands or leads to the thinking of a contrast between the determinate and the indeterminate. To think indeterminateness as indeterminate demands or is the thinking of a contrast between the minimally determinate (i.e., indeterminateness first thought as being of the determinacy of indeterminateness) and the indeterminate (i.e., the utterly indeterminate indeterminateness, nothing). But since nothing here is predetermined, since we can presuppose no determinacy either as given or as resulting from the objectifying act of thinking, this thinking of the contrast is the thinking of a disappearing or vanishing contrast: *becoming*. (The "truth" of being and nothing is the "movement of the immediate vanishing of the one in the other: *becoming*; a movement in which both are distinguished, but by a difference which has equally immediately resolved itself."[40])

To move ahead in the logic of being, keeping the focus on the as yet still unstable contrast: we find that this contrast, arising out of the thinking of indeterminateness and requisite for it, seems minimally fixable as a contrast between being, now understood as something, and an other. What is—being—is what it is not because it is not nothing, but because as something it is not an other. But, in order to support this contrast, the other (that which gives being its determinacy through its contrast with it) must itself be determinate. Simplifying, and moving on to the outcome of the logic of being and thus to the transition to the logic of essence: This other can only be itself determinate, and thus contrastable with being, in virtue of *its* contrast with an other. But, since no determinacy can be presupposed, this other can only be itself. For: being as something was only determinate in virtue of its contrast with an other. But the other can only be itself determinate in virtue of its contrast with an other. But the only other to which it can be contrasted is being/something. Conclusion: Being is determinate as the other of the other, but since the other is only a determinate other as the other of being, being is only as the other of itself. And thus we find the thesis of the logic of essence: Being is determinate in virtue of an *internal* or *self*-contrasting; or, being is in and through positing its other. Being is essence which is what it is as a structure which contrasts itself with itself. The other, which, through its contrast with being renders being determinate is only an aspect or feature *of* being, a quasi-other. The logic of essence then unfolds, with the focus still on contrast, but now understood as a self-contrasting and as a search for the determining pole or side, the ground or essence of the contrast.

Being no longer disappears in or *becomes* its other (as being became nothing and then becoming in the logic of being). Rather, in the logic of essence, being *appears* or is determined in virtue of its contrasting and contrasted other. But again, if no determinacy is presupposed as determinate—that is, if we do not do what the *Phenomenology* as negative methodology demands that we do not do—where and what is the determinacy of the *determining* side of this relation, where being is thought as self-contrasting relation? If being here is determinate as a *result* of a *self*-contrasting, and if no determinacy is presupposed as given, where and what is the determinacy of the 'self' which contrasts itself with itself and is allegedly first constituted in its determinacy as a result of this contrasting? The logic of essence, as the search for the essential, determining side of this contrasting completes itself in the thinking of a *reciprocal contrast*: Insofar as no determinacy is illicitly pre-supposed as determinate, it turns out that there is *no* essential or grounding side of the essence/appearance relation. As no determinacy is presupposed, but can only arise in and through the contrasting, there is no primordial or determining side. Each side of the relation is determinate as what it is as the other of its other; each, as the other of its other is the other of itself *and it just itself* therein. This yields the thesis of the logic of the concept: Being, in being nothing but the other of itself, is itself. Put differently: When we undertake to think being in its determinacy as not already so given (for to think being as somehow already determinate would be to begin with, or to introduce, a presupposition) we find that self-subsistent, self-identical being is nothing but sheer self-differenti-ating, sheer self-contrasting or self-negation. This is the truth of being purely as thought. That is, it is the truth of being insofar as we do not explicitly or implicitly presuppose that it is determinate already in virtue of being taken as an object of thought.[41]

To sum up: If no determinacy is presupposed in pure logic, but is rather allowed to arise in and of itself, then the contrast requisite for the thinking of being will be evanescent until being is thought of in its being, in its determinacy, as self-negation, as the negation of negation. To once again omit much and leap ahead to the conclusion of the logic of pure thought: Being, as determined in and through pure thought alone, can only complete or fulfill itself as pure self-determining insofar as thought takes up the idea of an other—a determinacy—which can be thought, initially, as not at all of the character of a pure self-determining thought determinacy. That is, as a determinacy which is 'outside' of or external to thought in the sense that its determinacy does not derive or is not constituted through its being thought. This 'other,' as we shall see, is the idea of nature.

III. The *Encyclopedia*: The Dialectic of Real Philosophy

Hegel's philosophical project does not end with logic. But if the *Phenomenology* has shown that it is illicit, in philosophy, to presuppose any given determinacy as the 'determinacy in terms of which' we engage in philosophical consideration, and if the *Logic* as the domain of pure thought determinacies *is* pure because no determinacies other than pure thought determinacies have played a role in its constitution, how, on this basis, can this philosophy go on to say anything concerning what lies outside of this domain? That is, how is a philosophy of the real possible? One way to explain this—the way in which Hegel's *Realphilosophie* is traditionally interpreted—would be to say that this philosophy of the real is founded on the thesis that *nothing* 'lies outside' of pure thought, on the thesis that being or the real is identical to thought.

I shall first explain why this view is mistaken before going on to give an account of what Hegel's real philosophy actually is (not a metaphysical idealism) and how its dialectic can be understood to operate.

As we have seen, the *Logic*'s claim to purity itself rests, in part, on the claim that the model of consciousness' cognition of objects has been suspended and is not operative in it.[42] But this means that logic's purity has been bought at a great price. It means that logic as the domain of pure thought can have, as such, *no extension beyond itself*.[43] Were Hegel to claim that the *Logic* constitutes a 'method,' either in the sense that it is implicitly *about* the real as such (an ontology) or in the sense that it constitutes the necessary categories in terms of which the real is to be thought (a transcendental logic), this would be to once again—*and in his own terms illicitly*—reinstate or presuppose without justification just that model of cognition which has come to self-suspension in the *Phenomenology*. This would be the case because both these notions—ontology and transcendental logic—presuppose, implicitly if not explicitly, the structure of consciousness' cognition of objects as valid and paradigmatic. Ontology implicitly presupposes a difference between thought and being (or the real) only in order to deny the fundamentality of this difference and to claim that being qua being, the real in its truth, can be constituted or discovered in philosophical thought. Transcendental logic explicitly presupposes this model in its claim to set forth the necessary categories in terms of and through which being or the real can be cognized by the thinking subject.

If the *Logic*, then, is not an 'absolute method' *eo ipso* applicable to any subject matter, if its foundational thesis is *neither* that thought and being are identical *nor* that they are different but, rather, that from the standpoint of a philosophy which aims to be pure and presuppositionless, neither their identity nor their difference can be assumed, how on the basis of this logic can a consideration of the real come to be constituted and what role does the *Logic* play in this constitution?

Just as the completion of the *Phenomenology* constituted the foundation of the *Logic*, so too we need to grasp how the outcome of the *Logic* constitutes the foundation for systematic real philosophy. That is, for the consideration in and by thought of topics in some sense—as yet unspecified—'external' to pure thought. The key aspect, both in regard to the transition from logic to real philosophy as well as in regard to the role which logic plays in real philosophy, is something which I shall call *categorial self-transformation*.

We shall have to see what 'real dialectic' is, how it is constituted, and how it differs from the dialectic of pure thought. Important in our examination will be understanding why it is constituted neither through the articulation of an assumed identity of 'thought' and 'reality' nor through the application of a given pre-determined method, specified in the logic, to a content but rather by the self-transformation of the dialectic of pure thought, through categorial self-transformation.

The notion of a real dialectic is that of a dialectic which ensues when, from the standpoint of pure thought—logic—one attempts to consider in thought (to think) the idea of what is *other* than pure thought. (Why it is that this dialectic emerges immanently from the prior dialectic shall be considered below.) In this way, a new dialectic emerges as the dialectic (in thought, in systematic philosophical thinking) of the relation between pure thought as pure thought and its new topic, the idea of what is other than itself, other than pure thought as such.

The move from logic to real philosophy (from, textually speaking, the logic of the *Encyclopedia*, volume one, to the philosophy of nature, volume two) does not consist in the application of pure thought categories as such to something conceived as lying 'outside' of thought in the literal or ordinary sense. This is still systematic philosophy—still 'pure thinking'—because the new subject matter, the topic to be considered in real philosophy, is said to be immanently derived, and is not constituted as the topic for thought via abstraction from the real as we might conceive it to be *in re*. But, if real philosophy first comes to be constituted in and through thought's immanent consideration of 'its other,' if the 'real' as nature is initially defined in that manner, is this not tantamount to the assertion that the real is essentially identical to thought? Where the real would be a 'manifestation' or an 'appearance' of the underlying 'true' reality, thought.[44] Or, alternatively expressed, does this not amount to the assertion that reality in its truth is nothing but thought or mind in its self-externality? This appears, at first glance, to be the meaning of such remarks as the following "Nature has yielded itself as the Idea in the form of otherness . . . "[45]

As a matter of fact however, the foundation of Hegel's real philosophy is not grounded in the postulation of an essential identity of thought (or mind) and reality. Rather, its foundation lies in the necessary recognition *by* thought of its *limits qua* pure thought. In, that is, an acknowledgment and affirmation of the radical *non*-identity of thought and reality, an acknowledgment by philosophical thought that insofar as it is to think about reality it must initially acknowledge the radical otherness of the real *vis-à-vis* itself *and then think the idea of such a radical other*. (Why thinking this other must mean—for systematic philosophy—the thinking of *thought* as other than itself we shall see below.) According to Hegel, the greatest danger found in the attempt to develop a *philosophy* of the real in, initially, a philosophy of nature, lies in the prediliction to engage in idealism. That is, in the tendency to transform in thought what is other than thought into either a 'thought thing' or a 'thought-like thing':

> We want to know the nature that really is, not something which is not, but instead of leaving it alone and accepting it as it is in its truth, instead of taking it as given, we make something completely different out of it. By thinking things, we transform them into something universal; things are singular however and the lion in general does not exist. We make them into something subjective, produced by us, belonging to us, and of course peculiar to us men; for the things of nature do not think and are neither representations nor thought. . . . [W]hat we have started on may well seem impossible from the start. . . . Our aim is to grasp and comprehend nature however, to make it ours so that it is not something beyond and alien to us. This is where the difficulty comes in. How are we as subjects to get over into the object? If we venture the leap

over this gap, and, while failing to find our footing, think that we have found nature, we shall turn that which is something other than what we are into something other than what it is.[46]

So, according to Hegel there is something like a necessary contradiction in the very idea of a *thinking* of nature. As a pure thinking of, a pure philosophy of nature, Hegel's philosophy does not only begin, as we can see, with an awareness of this seeming contradiction, but also can be understood to consist—in its dialectic—in a thinking through of it—of the seeming contradiction which Hegel will claim is necessarily immanent in thought's thinking of what is other than itself. There is a seeming contradiction here, for if this other is radically other, and if we are not to lapse into idealism, how then are we to think it, to say something about it in an allegedly pure philosophy?

It is my contention that Hegel's philosophy of reality, in its initial appearance as a philosophy of nature, can be understood in general as a consideration by thought of the contradiction—or dialectic—involved in thought's thinking what is other than itself. In this sense it does not consist in the *thinking of* nature in the sense that we, as thinking consciousnesses ordinarily conceive nature as an object, given in its determinacy, for thinking. Rather, it is a thinking only of the *idea* of nature. As 'pure,' this is a philosophical consideration which cannot, and does not, presuppose as valid the cognitive structure of thinking awarenesses which would enable it, if presupposed, to 'look at' nature and derive its determinacy via abstraction. But nonetheless it claims to avoid idealism insofar as for it, for pure philosophical cognition, 'nature' is conceived neither as being nothing but thought nor as being somehow thought-like. And yet, we shall have to see how it is the case that, if for this philosophy of nature nature is not thought, it is nonetheless spoken of as being thought in its otherness or in its self-externality.

So what does it mean to say that nature here is "the Idea in its otherness" or is the self-externality of thought? We have already seen that, for Hegel, this does not mean that the real or nature as such *are* nothing but idea or thought. What then is being asserted is, I believe, this: If we are to consider, to purely and simply *think* the real or nature, this can be done in systematic philosophy in such a way that we do not transform our topic into a 'thought thing'—in such a way that does not lead to metaphysical idealism—if we conceive or define the subject matter to be considered as being 'other than thought.' But, since this is still presuppositionless and systematic philosophy, and because therefore we cannot assume on our part as philosophers the legitimate capacity to 'know' nature as an object such that we could derive its determinacy as 'other than thought' *from* nature 'itself,' then what is other than thought here can only be conceived in and through thought's *contrasting itself with itself.* The dialectic of real philosophy thus begins in and is constituted by thought's thinking itself as other than or as external to itself. (Why 'other than' shall mean 'external to' we shall see below.) The contrast requisite for the determination of determinacy here, the contrast necessary for the thinking about what is other than thought cannot, if this is to be a pure thinking of reality and nature, be said to arise *outside* of thought. In systematic philosophy the determinacies of reality and nature cannot be derived from 'reality' and 'nature' as they are 'given,' for, if they were, the systematic philosopher would then have to lay claim to the capacity to be able to 'know' the 'object' as it is 'in-itself.' In that case, the question of the justification of such a claim would immediately arise and we would once again be back in the scenario of the *Phenomenology*.

In regard to the question of method and the constitution of this new dialectic we again find, as in the case of the relation of the dialectic of the *Phenomenology* to that of the *Logic*, that the preceding dialectic plays a *negative role* in the constitution of the subsequent one. This negative operation—which can be seen to consist in the self-contrasting of thought with itself—is as follows: The coming to completion of the self-constitution of the domain of pure thought categories—logic—demands the consideration in and by thought of what is radically other than itself, other than pure thought. And, if we can correctly categorize pure thought determinacies as determinacies determined in, by and through thought alone, then what stands to be considered in and by thought in constituting its limit as pure thought is the thought or idea of a determinacy or a range of determinacies whose determinacy is *not* determined by thought alone.

So, in constituting real philosophy all one does is to *think the idea* of a determinacy which is not determined by thought, i.e., which is not determined in the way pure thought determinacies were determined. The thinking taking place can be said to consist in the self-contrasting or self-externalizing of thought in the following way: Just as pure thought determinacies, in the logic of being, evidenced a lack of self-sufficiency or self-stability, a decisive instability of determinacy and a tendency even in their determinacy to collapse into one another (or of each to become, in its being thought, the other) so the initial salient feature or determinacy of the idea of a range of determinacies which are radically other than pure thought determinacies will lie in the fact that it will consist in, or 'support,' determinacies as *independent* and *self-sufficient* in their determinacy, as *external to* one another. (Figuratively speaking, this range of determinacy will be such that it can *hold* determinacies as *standing next to* one another *in* it.) And these determinacies, unlike, (or as the 'other' of) pure thought determinacies, will be thought of as determined in their determinacy independently, or externally, of one another. Hegel's name for such a range of determinacy is *space*. In addition, just as the initial *mode of relation* of pure thought determinacies in the logic consisted in the transformation of one determinacy into the other, so the initial mode of the relation of real determinacies—of determinacies which are here being thought as *not being* thought determinacies—will consist in their *externality* one to another—as *points* in space. (It should be noted that just as in my presentation of the dialectics of the *Phenomenology* and the *Logic*, this is a simplification which necessarily omits much.)

Thus, in making the move from logic to real philosophy, we do not find that the system of thought determinacies or categories which makes up the logic is applied, as it stands, to some given or found determinacy which is said to be determinate, or to be known in its determinacy, prior to the application. Nor do we find that the determinacy of the real is constituted by an appeal to an *analogous resemblance* between logic and the real, a resemblance which would in some way allegedly legitimate the *application* of logical categories. Rather, what we find is a *self-transformation* of those pure thought categories, a self-transformation which arises in and through a self-contrasting. And thus nature in systematic dialectical philosophy is determined as 'thought in its self-externality' or as 'thought in its otherness.' For, to think thought as other to itself is: (1) to think the idea of determinacy as not determined by thought, which is to think a range of determinacies as not determined vis-à-vis their immediate interrelation with one another (as the determinacies were thought in the logic of being); and (2) to think these determinacies as capable of subsisting in their determinancy as independent of one another (which pure thought determinacies in the logic of being were not capable of).

So, you can see that the function of logic in real philosophy is not to provide a 'method' as a model, that is as a given thought structure which comes as such to be applied as a predetermined organizational 'framework' into which some 'contents' are plugged and consequently given a logical ordering or structure.[47] For the initial determinacies of reality—the determinacies of nature—are specifically thought as *not being* of the character of logical determinacies, either in the Hegelian or the traditional sense. Most definitely, they are not thought as being concrete constants which can replace the abstract variables of a logical system while leaving the relation framework of this system untouched. For these determinacies of nature are not at all thought as being in a 'logical' relation one to another. If the most general feature of logical determinacies is their 'internality,' that is, their immanent inter-connection and interdevelopment relation with one another, then the most general feature of the determinacies of the philosophy of nature, as arising through thought's contrasting itself with itself and thereby constituting 'nature' as 'thought in its otherness,' is externality. Nature, as conceived in this systematic real philosophy, is 'external' or 'externality' in a three-fold sense: (1) It is thought and defined as external to—other than—thought; (2) In and of it-self it is in its most basic determinacy externality, or space; (3) The determinacies 'in' or 'of' nature as externality, as space are thought of as *determined* as what they are externally to or outside of one another, and as *standing* external to one another, as, initially, points in space.

So, 'nature' here is thought of not only as not being identical to thought in some essential way, it is also not thought as being 'like' thought in some manner. Here, perhaps uniquely in philoso-phy it is not claimed that we can think about the real because thought and the real have some structure, some *logos*, in common. Rather, according to Hegel, what is required in order for philoso-phy to think the real is, first, a self-consideration by thought which does not already presuppose the contrast of thought and reality or their identity, and second, that thought comes to transform itself, and to thereby think what is other than itself. Thought must come to transform itself—to consider its other—systematically speaking, in order to realize its own limitations, and thereby to bring the process of its immanent self-consideration to a close. (In this sense there is no external necessity for the subsequent development of real philosophy.) In that Hegel's philosophy of reality is grounded in a genuine and thoroughgoing recognition of the otherness of nature and reality to thought, and in that it constitutes itself as a thinking of them by taking this otherness as its basis and thus acknowledging the limitations of pure thought, it must be recog-nized that however we wish to categorize—or criticize—his systematic philosophy, it is most definitely not an absolute idealistic meta-physics.

To sum up: Hegel's 'dialectical method' consists not merely in the absence of a method in the traditional sense, but also in the disavowal and critique of the idea of a philosophical method as an *a priori* set of rules for the consideration of a subject matter. For Hegel, there is no creature which can be specified and legitimated as a 'dialectical *method.*' The very notion of an *a priori* dialectic is contrary to Hegel's view of a proper and systematic philosophical dialectic, since for him the necessary introduction to systematic philosophy must consist in the immanent critique of the assumption that it is possible and legitimate to specify some determinate principle which can define, determine and set the limiting conditions of philosophical thought. There are as many different dialectics and 'dialectical methods' as there are specifiable topics of thought and specifiable standpoints from which these topics can be considered. The particular Hegelian dialectic and standpoint, both in regard to philosophical thought as such and in regard to what can be considered in philosophical thinking, is one which arises when one specifically makes the attempt to think without presuppositions.

Chapter 5 has addressed a variety of issues critical to fleshing out the interpretation of Hegel as a nonfoundational systematic philosopher. Themes introduced in earlier chapters have been further developed, new aspects of the character of systematic philosophy have been discussed, and an overview of the whole system in its interconnectedness has been presented.

The unifying chord of Chapter 5 is the consideration of what Hegel insists is the distinctive scientific feature of his system: its self-determinative character, the strict immanence of development which he calls dialectic. I have argued here that we can make sense of the system as autonomously self-determinative if, first of all, we properly understand its origin in the *Phenomenology* as an immanent critique of the foundationalist model of cognition and notion of philosophical science. This by now familiar theme is further developed by focusing on how the *Phenomenology* can itself be understood as meeting the requirement of immanent development. I have shown that if the consciousness considered in the *Phenomenology* is understood as foundational, we can make sense of the work as immanently developmental because no other assumptions are required for its argument *and* because the work then culminates in the self-elimination of its founding assumption. (It is this same self-suspension of foundational consciousness which we saw in Chapter 4 as making an immanently self-developmental *Logic* possible.) In explaining the distinctive self-developmental character of the *Phenomenology* I have also addressed questions remaining from Chapter 1 concerning the argument of the *Phenomenology*, and how it might be scientific without presupposing science.

Chapter 5 has also further explicated the nature of the self-developmental character of the *Logic* by further indicating just how the self-suspension of foundational subjectivity both makes possible a presuppositionless beginning while at the same time providing a negative methodology which enables us to reconstruct the argument of the *Logic*. On this basis I have traced out the development of the 3 'logics' of the *Logic*, showing how each follows from the previous and how the *Logic* culminates in a move into *Realphilosophie*. Crucial here has been showing that if we do adopt the antifoundational view, we can understand the *Logic* both as actually having an argument and as fulfilling the claims Hegel makes for it.

Chapter 5 also indicates further how the antifoundational interpretation introduces a Hegel who overcomes the problems of foundationalism while still committed to a notion of philosophical truth which avoids the inconsistencies and the relativism of antifoundationalism. Again, the key for this interpretation is the suspension of the fondationalist model. Reading the system in this light discloses a mode of philosophical discourse which is not metaphysically idealistic, because it is not a descriptive account of things as they are given; not absolutist, because it does not preclude the possibility of such descriptive accounts; and self-limiting, because its range has been so circumscribed.

This latter trio of themes is taken up in the next chapter which considers a traditional, and enduring, criticism of Hegel's systematic philosophy: that it erroneously, and blasphemously, purports to offer us a mode of divine, absolute knowledge. Refuting this charge provides an opportunity to examine further various positive features of the system as a whole and the philosophy of religion in particular. Additionally, it brings up a consideration of an issue of special concern for current antifoundationalism in its attack on the possibility of philosophy: the nature of our finitude. I argue in Chapter 6 that Hegel not only acknowledges our finitude, but also that this acknowledgment is a feature of self-determining systematic philosophy (and does not require abandoning the system's claim to philosophical truth), and that his conception of finitude is superior to current antifoundationalist accounts in various ways.

Chapter 6

ON THE PRESUMED BLASPHEMY OF
HEGELIAN ABSOLUTISM

The squirming facts are not to exceed the squamous mind.
—Wallace Stevens

A common accusation brought against Hegel is that he is guilty
of blasphemy as his philosophical system involves a human
claim to divine powers.[1] This issue is of more than strictly historical significance, since contemporary antifoundational
postmodernists indict not only Hegel, but the whole philosophical tradition on the grounds that philosophy's claim to offer objective knowledge of the truth is blasphemous in that it
abrogates the inescapable finitude of human knowing. We are
told that traditional philosophy must but cannot successfully lay
claim to what Hilary Putnam perspicuously calls the "God's eye
point of view."[2] The goal of this chapter is to show that the
charge against Hegel cannot be substantiated. While addressing
the question of philosophical blasphemy as it pertains to Hegel, I
will comment from time to time about the larger accusation,
suggesting that Hegel's manner of developing a systematic philosophy can provide a framework for defending philosophy as a
whole from postmodernist attacks.

Before examining the evidence and mounting a defense I want
to first explain the nature and significance of this charge.

I. The Nature of the Charge

There are at least two senses in which Hegel can be accused of blasphemy:

The first (hereafter, B1) is *epistemic* and concerns his systematic philosophy as a whole. According to B1, Hegel must claim a divine position, even if only implicitly, given what his system alleges about how it is established and what kind of knowledge it offers.

The second sense (B2) is *substantive*; it concerns the specifics of what the system says about God and focuses on the philosophy of religion in particular. According to B2, the knowledge of God Hegel propounds is blasphemous not only in presenting God as thoroughly knowable by human minds, but also in blurring, if not collapsing, the distinction between humanity and God. This collapse has purportedly taken place in that Hegel has construed divine nature in human terms while correlatively construing human nature in divine terms. In Emil Fackenheim's opinion, Hegel's philosophy presents religion as "a divine self-activity in finite humanity; and in order so to grasp it *Hegelian thought must have done nothing less than rise above a self-active thought confined to human finitude in order to become a self-active thought which is infinite and divine.*"[3] A central objective of this essay will be to show that Hegel's thought is "a self-active thought confined to human finitude."

At the basis of both charges is the issue of the nature of the human and the divine; more specifically, of the nature of the finite and the infinite as these terms pertain to knowledge and mind. This issue is, of course, a central and recurrent topic in Hegel's systematic philosophy. According to Fackenheim, the "struggle" between the infinite and the finite "and the struggle to resolve the struggle—is in the end the sole theme . . . of the whole Hegelian philosophy."[4] As we shall see, the question of the relation of the infinite and the finite concerns not only the philosophy of religion but also the very nature and status of systematic philosophy.[5] In fact, according to Hegel it is especially important for the philosophy of religion that we first understand properly the nature of systematic philosophy, for " . . . it very frequently happens when philosophy in general and philosophizing about God in particular are criticized, that finite thoughts, relationships of limitedness, and categories and forms of the finite are introduced in the service of this discourse. Opposition that draws upon such finite forms is directed against philosophy generally and especially against the highest kind, the philosophy of religion in particular."[6] This makes it essential that we consider B1—going "back to the alphabet of philosophy itself"—before turning to the philosophy of religion.[7]

II. The Significance of the Charges

If one must purport to possess divine powers either in order to enter the system or to establish its claims, the consequences are obviously devastating philosophically. The truth of the system would then rest on assertions which appear to be manifestly false insofar as we hold to the usual meaning of the term "divine," where it denotes a greater and other than human being, infinite in various respects, but necessarily transcendent; always irreducibly other than human in spite of possible manifestations in a finite guise.

It is important to observe that the force of the charges is not dependent on the piety of the accuser. One need not believe in a divinity or in a divine mind in order to conclude that neither Hegel nor anyone else is capable of attaining or approximating to a model of it. So Hegel can be accused of blasphemy on strictly philosophical grounds of a purely secular nature.

III. The First Charge

The basis for B1 lies in the claims that Hegel makes concerning the *kind* of philosophical knowledge or truth the system affords, absolute knowledge or truth, and the *manner* in which it comes to afford it, by means of absolute knowing. According to Hegel the system is absolute in that it is all-encompassing and fully justified; it expresses universal, necessary, unconditional, eternal, infinite, and absolute truth.[8] Additionally, he contends that it has this status because of its beginning in an absolute knowing which is the culmination of the *Phenomenology*, the acknowledged introduction to the system. Unpacking either of these claims would appear to provide a strong basis for B1.

Consider simply the idea that the system is absolute in virtue of being all-encompassing and fully justified.[9] To possess such features the system would have to be self-grounding, since nothing which has a basis or foundation outside of itself could be demonstratively complete and fully legitimated. But the demand for self-grounding would seem to require a kind of philosophical activity which is divine. How so?

If the system rests on nothing outside of itself, the activity which produces it must be self-generating or self-determining in a radical sense: both form (or method) and content must have a common source, and they must arise without predetermination.[10] But such purported activity of creative self-generation in the absence of prior determination could seemingly be undertaken only by a divine mind, a mind capable of constituting, from out of nothing, both itself as cognizer and its objects of cognition in and through one and the same act. The apparent necessity for *divine* cognition occurs for the following reasons. First, the act must be one of pure knowing which is fully self-constitutive of the knower. Otherwise something external and given—the form or method of knowing— would stand prior to or outside of the system, unfounded. Second, this activity must be simultaneously constitutive of the objects of knowledge. Otherwise that which comes to be known would have an external, given foundation, and would be to that extent derivative, conditioned, and unfounded. Our human knowing, however, seems to be unavoidably finite, not self-constitutive because rooted in contextual conditions which are always given prior to the knowing activity.

The bases for thinking that Hegel claims this kind of absolute knowing lie not only in the general claims about the system which I have considered so far but also in the fact that the *Phenomenology* culminates in something called "absolute knowing." And since Hegel tells us that the *Logic* and the system presuppose this absolute knowing as the deduced concept of science, the evidence for finding Hegel guilty of B1 appears incontrovertible, until we consider the nature of his absolute knowing and the manner in which it functions in and for the system.

IV. The Defense Against B1

I am going to argue not only that absolute knowing is not a blasphemous claim to divine knowing but that it is in fact a rejection of the human pretension to divine knowing. In addition, I aim to show that just as such—as an affirmation of the finite character of our knowing—absolute knowing functions as the beginning point for Hegel's systematic philosophy.

When we look at the details of Hegel's account of absolute knowing as the beginning point of science it is clear that no claim to divine knowing is being made simply because no knowing at all is involved. Hegel is quite explicit and unequivocal about the fact that absolute knowing, in its role as the deduced concept of science, is no knowing at all. According to him absolute knowing ceases as a knowing in its absoluteness; this self-cessation is the collapse of the determinate structure of consciousness and this collapse constitutes the beginning of science by yielding a radical indeterminacy which cannot be further characterized.[11] But divine knowing would seemingly be totally or absolutely determinate, both as regards the structure of the relationship between knower and objects, and as regards the concreteness of detail and the scope of what is known. So, whatever else we might say about absolute knowing, it fails to fit what could reasonably be regarded as the conditions of divine knowing. This absolute knowing which "ceases itself to be knowledge" and which is "distinctionless" is certainly not recognizable as the omniscient knowing of a divine being.[12]

While this defense accords with Hegel's own claims both about the role of absolute knowing as the deduced concept of science and with his view of the relation of the *Phenomenology* to the system, it would seem to conflict with his notions about the overall character of the system as noted above. If Hegel's absolute knowing is not blasphemous because it is not a form, state, or condition of knowing at all, how can it function as the beginning of the system? Put more specifically, if the system is *not* based on a claim to divine knowledge, how can it make a claim to the radical self-grounding and consequent self-determination upon which its general claim to absoluteness rests? To answer this question we must first appreciate how the outcome of absolute knowing functions as a *rejection* of the possibility of our attaining divine knowledge.

In the absolute knowing with which the *Phenomenology* culminates, consciousness finally comes to attain what it has sought all along, a demonstration of the fact that its purported knowledge of the object is knowledge of it in its objectivity, as it exists apart from consciousness. In anticipation of many contemporary critics of foundationalism and the philosophy of subjectivity, Hegel shows in absolute knowing why it is that such foundational knowledge proves aporetic. What absolute knowing reveals, simply, is that consciousness can come to the point of *knowing that* its knowledge of the object corresponds to the object as it is in-itself, only insofar as two conditions are fulfilled. (1) The known object must be nothing but consciousness' own mode of knowing—so that what is known and the knowing of it are *identical* in content. By having its own activity of knowing as its object, the very activity whereby consciousness constitutes its own being is at once also constitutive—creative—of its domain of objectivity. Failing such apparently divine activity (whereby an other to mind comes into being solely in and through this mind and without recourse to an already given material), consciousness cannot be certain that the object as object is what it takes it to be and thus cannot establish its capacity to know truly.

Something else is required for consciousness' success: (2) At the same time as identity is achieved—and in the manner of a divine mind which is fully certain of its objects as what they are while remaining distinct from the world of objects created—consciousness' knowing and its object of knowledge must be *distinct*. Identity of the knowledge and object is required for the certainty of correspondence consciousness seeks, but at the very same time distinction must be preserved because without a distinction between its knowledge and the object, consciousness' knowing ceases altogether. Establishing the truth of its knowledge requires the identity; ensuring the objectivity of its knowledge requires that the distinction also be maintained simultaneously with the identity.

So, the success of the consciousness in the *Phenomenology* which seeks to establish the unconditional truth of its mode of knowing requires that consciousness strive to reach the divine capacity of a mind which is at one and the same time certain of its knowledge of its objects, because they are at one with the activity which knows them (in the manner of a God who sustains objectivity in its being) while simultaneously remaining distinct as a knower from this domain of self-constituted objectivity (in the manner of a transcendent creator God who is also radically other than the divine creation). But what occurs, according to Hegel, when consciousness reaches a fulfillment of these conditions, when consciousness reaches absolute knowing? Hegel's presentation of absolute knowing is a radical critique of finite mind's blasphemous pretension to know absolutely because it shows both that consciousness cannot successfully attain to such a state of divine knowing and why consciousness cannot do so. He shows that consciousness' mode of knowing is *inescapably* finite by allowing consciousness to disclose that the conditions which it must attain to in order to achieve absoluteness cannot be attained as long as consciousness remains consciousness: Consciousness cannot remain a consciousness while simultaneously being in a cognitive state of identity and difference with its object, since to be a consciousness and to speak of conscious knowing minimally require the *preservation* of a fixed distinction between knowing and the object. But the required state of *simultaneous* identity and difference is one in which no such distinction is maintained. So by revealing how the very conditions for a successful demonstration of its ability to know absolutely require the self-suspension of consciousness as a knowing entity, Hegel provides a thoroughly immanent critique of foundationalism and subjectivity. And since the critique is immanent, and does not require a claim to know absolutely that absolute knowing is not possible, it avoids the self-referential inconsistency which plagues contemporary antifoundational postmodernism. Thus, rather than being the ultimate philosophical blasphemy, Hegel's presentation of absolute knowing is the consummate critique of it.

If this is what absolute knowing reveals, how can it possibly function as the beginning of an absolute system? Here we need to focus our attention on the fact that the collapse of consciousness is a "determinate negation;"[13] it has not only negative but positive results, or more precisely, its negative results, when fully comprehended, have an equally positive dimension. How so?

The disclosure of the inescapable finitude of consciousness makes possible a transformation of the conception of knowing; consciousness' negative revelation about itself as knower shows that, since cognition *cannot* be *successfully* defined in the manner of consciousness (in that consciousness' manner of knowing turns out to be one in which certainty of the truth can never be attained) it *need* not be *exclusively* defined in that manner either. Discovering that consciousness' mode of knowing cannot lead to certain knowledge of the truth can liberate us, even as conscious begins. It can do so insofar as we avoid the temptation to draw an exclusively negative conclusion about knowing from consciousness' failure. To do so would be to conclude, in the current postmodernist fashion, that since consciousness cannot ground its knowing, no genuine knowledge is possible at all.[14] Such a conclusion is simply the (self-referentially inconsistent) philosophical blasphemy of absolutizing our finitude in its finitude, because it takes an admittedly finite mode of knowing and claims to know unequivocally—that is, *absolutely*—that knowing can only be understood in that manner. This position fails to recognize the positive self-understanding which absolute knowing affords us in virtue of the totalizing manner in which consciousness reveals its finitude.

In absolute knowing the finitude of consciousness is disclosed as radical and ultimate because we finally discover that, conceived epistemologically, consciousness is itself a construct or posit which has no ultimate foundations.[15] The ultimate finitude of consciousness is that consciousness cannot even establish the certain truth of its own nature as consciousness. But if this is so, if the ego or subjectivity is no more primal than anything else, and if knowing conceived according to its nature cannot be shown to afford truth, then, Hegel positively concludes, we no longer need remain committed to understanding truth exclusively in its terms. The positive outcome of absolute knowing as a thoroughgoing revelation of the finitude of consciousness is the possibility of radically reconceptualizing the nature of knowing. What we must now see is how this reconceptualization can lead to a system which can claim absoluteness, in virtue of being self-grounding, without abrogating finitude. What I want to show is that the very 'absoluteness' of the Hegelian system is predicated upon its thorough recognition and respectful 'inclusion' of finitude, not, as popularly claimed, on a blasphemous denial and transcendence of it.

If the inadequacy of finite thinking, its inability to know the truth, lay in construing truth as a given, as that which is always minimally predetermined as an other to an awareness, and if this mode of understanding truth and cognition is, epistemologically speaking, a groundless posit, then we are also given an indication of how to conceptualize truth in a manner which is *not* constrained by this limitation. The positive lesson of the sublation of consciousness is this: do not regard the topic of philosophical consideration as necessarily always predetermined in virtue of the fact that, in the parlance of consciousness, it "stands as an object" for a thinking awareness. Put differently, the positive lesson of the *Phenomenology* is that we do not need to assume that objectivity as regards knowledge (the certainty and universality of what we know) must be construed as something which is founded in a given object. So for Hegel, philosophy presupposes the rejection of the dogma of the given, the rejection of the assumption that our ordinary way of knowing, wherein we seek to describe given objects, is absolute and philosophically primal.

This recognition of what consciousness' finitude (its inability to know the truth) consists in—always construing the truth as a given determinacy—makes possible the thinking activity of systematic philosophy. This activity is quasi-divine because it consists in a kind of limited and conditioned creativity consistent with self-grounding: through our rejection of the inadequacy of consciousness' model of predetermination it becomes possible for us to conceive of determinacy in a manner free from predetermination, since we no longer assume that whatever is determinate must be construed as given in its determinacy.[16] (As I shall indicate below, however, this by no means indicates a *total* abandonment by the system of the notion or the role of the given.) Liberated from the assumption that whatever is determinate is always determinate in virtue of its presence to awareness, and armed with the discovery that this assumption is what—minimally—has always predetermined what we conceive, we may then embark on a consideration of determinacy which is, in principle, self-grounding (and thus absolute in Hegel's sense) because it is based on no external predeterminations (save the 'predetermination' of rejecting consciousness as a model for philosophical cognition.)[17]

Yet this systematic consideration of determinacy is only quasidivine and not blasphemous.[18] For one thing, it is not blasphemous because, as Hegel asserts again and again, the very possibility of coming to engage in this self-determinative or self-constitutive thinking is conditioned, mediated; its presupposes the "liberation" from the opposition of consciousness which follows from the recognition of the thoroughgoing finitude of consciousness.[19] It is also not blasphemous because the nature of what self-determination *is* here is also conditioned, mediated: the system is constituted via 'self-determination' in virtue of the fact that determinacies are *not* constituted in the manner of consciousness. Hence this systematic self-determination is not self-determination in the divine manner. Presumably, God's self-determination is not mediated, and thus is not limited and conditioned as Hegel insists the self-determination of systematic philosophy is. Certainly the self-determination of an omniscient and omnipotent God would not be 'in virtue' of anything.

Yet in spite of being conditioned, mediated in these ways, it is clear that the system might make a claim to being absolute in Hegel's sense: it is self-grounding because—and insofar as—no predeterminations function constitutively in its conceptualizing, and thus its ground lies within itself in the sense that it presupposes nothing determinate.[20] But it is not absolute in the divine sense that it presupposes nothing at all. The system is self-grounding, absolute to the extent to which, in it, determinacy comes to be constituted out of indeterminacy in a manner such that no external determination enters into this process.[21] But this is radically different from the thoroughly *un*mediated and *un*conditioned self-constitutive activity of God which is not mere self-determination from out of (a mediated) indeterminacy but, so we are told, literally self-creation from out of nothing. The prevalent error of seeing Hegel's enterprise as blasphemous holds only so long as we see consciousness' mode of knowing as the only possible one. When we do that we cannot avoid misunderstanding the basis of the system's claim to absoluteness—"constituted without prior determination"—as meaning "constituted out of nothing," because we identify being determinate with being some *thing*, an object for a consciousness. The root of the false charge of blasphemy against the system is the genuinely blasphemous assumption that our merely finite way of knowing is the only possible way.

So, for Hegel, a thoroughgoing appreciation of the (to use current postmodernist jargon) 'inescapable contextuality of subjectivity,' an appreciation of the fact that (to use Hegelian jargon) 'consciousness is always tied to and conditioned by a given which can never be thoroughly grasped as it is objectively, in-itself, but only subjectively, as it is for consciousness,' need not lead to the postmodernist wholesale rejection of the possibility of objective truth. Properly, it leads only to a rejection of the model of truth in question, consciousness' correspondence model. For this is a model whose fundamental incoherence has been revealed through the *Phenomenology*'s demonstration that it defines truth in such a way (as knowledge of a given object as it is in-itself) that truth cannot be obtained. The strong conclusion which postmodernists wish to draw from the (by now commonplace) rejection of the possibility of establishing correspondence—that the very concept of objective truth must be rejected—only follows if it can be shown that the only conceivable understanding of truth is in terms of consciousness' model. But to make that unequivocal assertion is to absolutize consciousness, and not to reject it, as postmodernists claim to be doing. Additionally, to make that assertion is to tacitly lay claim to absolute, totalizing knowledge, the very kind of knowledge which postmodernists claim to abjure.

V. The Second Charge

B2 can be broken down into two parts: Hegel is guilty of substantive blasphemy (1) because in the system knowledge *of* God is claimed; (2) because in what the system claims *about* God's nature there is an approximation of the human to the divine and the divine to the human.[22]

Much that Hegel says apparently supports these charges. Hegel explicitly claims that knowledge of God is possible;[23] he acknowledges that his account of God is formulated in human terms;[24] he speaks of "the unity of divine and human nature" and holds that "... humanity has attained the certainty of unity with God, that the human is the immediately present God."[25] Now it might appear that in order to count these remarks as damning evidence of B2, we must read them in the mode of consciousness, as descriptive claims concerning a given transcendent object. And if, as argued, the system is predicated upon the rejection of the possibility of our attaining philosophically objective knowledge[26] of such objects, that would be to misread these remarks.[27]

But that defense seems to lead to a much more serious charge of blasphemy. The rejection of consciousness in absolute knowing precludes the system's describing a world of transcendent objects, (including a transcendent God) and it precludes postulating the identity of philosophical mind with such a transcendent God.[28] But what are we to make of the substantive claims about spirit and God? Must we not come to conclude that while Hegel has perhaps not claimed to have knowledge of a transcendent God, and while he has not postulated a naive identity philosophy, he has done something worse? Namely, eliminated such a transcendent God by reducing God to his system while elevating his system to God? This revised charge of blasphemy holds that, rather than having tried to bridge the gap between us and God, Hegel has done away with it.

There is considerable evidence for this. The central Hegelian notion of spirit may be said to render God human while it elevates humanity to the divine, both implicitly and explicitly. Throughout the philosophy of religion, we find God presented and explained in human and cognitive terms, as spirit, just as we find divine capacities attributed to humanity, insofar as it attains to spirit.[29] In addition, both the philosophy of religion and the *Encyclopedia* articulate the nature of spirit in human (albeit Hegelian-philosophical) terms, for spirit involves the concept, reason, and freedom: The essential structure of spirit is that of the concept: it is something which posits itself as different, but in such a way that this difference is sublated, so that spirit is with itself in otherness.[30] The activity whereby spirit is what it is is the activity of reason. Spirit as rational is self-determining, and as rational self-determination, is freedom.[31] And even as understood in terms of the concept, reason, and freedom, spirit is also to be equated with the divine. For, while "human beings are themselves spirit"[32] "the spirit that has entered into itself" "the concept that has only *itself* as its purpose . . . is God himself. . . . Spirit now has as its final purpose its concept, its concrete essence itself; it eternally realizes and objectifies its purpose, and is free in it—indeed it is freedom itself. . . . "[33] In a nutshell, the argument of the philosophy of religion is that we and God are spirit,[34] and it attempts to show how this correct understanding can be found expressed inchoately in religion.

VI. The Defense Against B2

Hegel has a twofold defense against B2. The first part of the defense again concerns the nature of the system and the mediation between the finite and the infinite which it has effected. This will pertain to the second feature of B2, the charge that the system is blasphemous because it collapses God into itself in various ways. I will try to show here that the senses in which the system and spirit can be regarded as infinite or absolute are not the divine senses of those terms. The second part of the defense also concerns the proper understanding of the infinite and the finite, and takes shape, again as with the defense against B1, by way of turning the charge of blasphemy back on the accusers. The defense here addresses the first feature of B2, the concern that the system's claimed knowledge of God is blasphemous.

    According to Hegel it is a cardinal error to understand infinity as utterly beyond and separate from the finite, but this is just what is presupposed even in the revised charge of collapsing the finite and the infinite, for a collapse assumes an original unmediated opposition. Thus, to bring the charge is to think undialectically, at the level of finite thought which fixes its categories into rigidly opposed determinations.[35] According to B2, the distinction between ourselves as finite and the divine infinite has disappeared because Hegel's concept of spirit has effectively eliminated the divine altogether as a transcendent object. But for Hegel, the whole possibility of the system is based on the dialectical *preservation* of a distinction which, as the mediation of the finite and the infinite, effects a reconciliation of them, not an identification, or a collapse, or an elimination of either. What is the nature of this reconciliation? The key idea for Hegel is that there cannot be an abstract opposition of the finite and the infinite, as though the infinite is infinite in simply *not* being the finite and vice versa. As applied to the system, this means that it is truly infinite, or absolute, only in and through a mediated relation with the finite, that is, one which does not deny the reality of the finite as finite, but recognizes it as what it is so that this very act of recognition is part of the infinite system's self-constitution. We have already seen how this recognition and reconciliation work in regard to the system's beginning in and through an acknowledgement of the genuine finitude of consciousness. Let us see more specifically how this recognition and reconciliation of the finite plays out in the rest of the system.

VII. The System's Recognition of Finitude

While Hegel has rejected finite consciousness, as a basis for philosophical cognition, and while he has thus ensured that the system does not purport to describe a transcendent world of objects (including an objective divinity), this is not at the price of denying that world of given objectivity in its givenness via an attempt to reduce it to itself, as the revised charge assumes. Hegel's system is misunderstood when seen as involving a claim to be infinite in the divine sense of being a literally all-encompassing, totalizing abrogation of finitude and givenness. To comprehend the other systematically is not to deny or to reduce the other to the system, it is rather, as we shall see, an attempt to conceive in thought what is radically other than thought without transforming that other into a derivative of thought.[36]

On what grounds can these claims be substantiated? For one thing, such a abrogation would require Hegel to forget his own dicta about the relation of the finite and the infinite. The system's attaining to infinity would be in and through an utter transcendence or reduction of the finite, one which would be fundamentally undialectical and unHegelian because it would leave finitude behind, in a onesided manner as something false, rather than incorporating it. But "[t]he real infinite, far from being a mere transcendence of the finite, always involves the absorption of the finite into its own fuller nature."[37] The system does not eliminate or abandon finitude (in this instance, the given world and our conscious relation to it as something given) because the systematic refusal to take a descriptive stance toward that world is part of an acknowledgement of the genuine and unavoidable limitations inseparable from *any* attempt to describe the given. Thus, in the system, finitude is accepted without being absolutized because this system is not offered as a substitute for finite, descriptive knowledge; and as all descriptive claims are abjured, the system also limits itself. Insofar as it offers absolute knowledge, this knowledge is not the divine variety which is presumably unconditional descriptive knowledge of the given universe.[38]

Additionally, not only does finitude fail to be eliminated in the system, it is also acknowledged and incorporated by it because—as we saw—the manner in which it attains infinity as self-determination is mediated by and predicated upon the recognition of the finitude of consciousness. By abandoning a descriptive stance *and* by then engaging in self-determination on the basis of not determining determinacy in the manner of consciousness, the system both recognizes finite mind as finite and goes beyond it, yet in such a way that this going beyond is not a denial of that finitude but precisely a recognition of it in and as finite. Just what makes finite mind finite has been disclosed and acknowledged as genuine in its finitude: consciousness as knower always confronts objects as given in their determinacy and is finite because it cannot demonstrate that what it takes them to be is what they are in-themselves. And, in and through that disclosure and acknowledgement, a way of thinking which differs from the finite (in not purporting to be or to compete with descriptive knowledge) has been made possible.[39]

There are two other ways in which the system can be seen as not blasphemous because thoroughly conditioned by finitude even while being infinite as self-determining. The first pertains to the role of the finite in the system's self-constitution; the second concerns the nature of spirit.

As we know, Hegel claims that the system is absolute as self-determining, yet he acknowledges the important role in it of finite determinations. Seeing how the finite enters into the system provides further evidence for the idea that the system accepts the reality of the finite (albeit in a manner different from consciousness which accepts the finite by taking the given as the source of its knowledge).[40]

How is the role of the finite to be understood and reconciled with the idea of the system as infinite because self-grounding?

The finite enters in without compromising the self-determining character of the system because the system in its self-constitutive self-determination engenders a process of categorial self-transformation which involves the recognition and conceptualizing of an other to thought.[41] This occurs in the system in the move from the sheer self-determination of thought, in the logic, to the conditioned self-determination of the *Realphilosophie*, in the philosophies of nature and spirit. In this move something finite—radically other than pure thought—is conceived, and the nature of what this is is conceptualized by systematic thought in conformity with the concept. So systematic self-constitutive thought comes on its own to acknowledge and to think the idea of what is other than itself, thereby effecting a move in its self-development through the self-limitation involved in incorporating the category of finitude within itself. On the one hand, self-determination is preserved, the infinite character of the system is not compromised, in that the *content* of the categories of *Realphilosophie* is provided by the transformation of pure thought categories which is engendered by thinking the *idea* of what is other than thought; thus the system limits *itself*, for the determination of the finite here is not derived by descriptive observation in the manner of consciousness.[42] On the other hand, because the *determinacy* of the finite is determined *as* 'other than thought' this self-limitation is nonetheless a genuine limitation to pure thought since it establishes the necessity for thought of thinking something as having the character of not being determined by thought. (What 'determined by thought' means has been established in the logic. Just what it means more specifically to be determined as 'other than thought' cannot be pursued here.[43])

In addition, this 'incorporation' of finitude is also not a reduction of finitude which denies its genuinely finite character by reducing it to the system, for Hegel recognizes that we need descriptive contents supplied by consciousness in order to help formulate the categories generated.[44] This would not be the case if philosophical mind were infinite in the manner of God, if our given character as finite consciousness had been transcended utterly.

If we think through the process of categorial self-determination as one of self-transformation in which finitude is recognized and incorporated, we find further evidence that the system recognizes finitude and thereby also limits itself, that is, establishes its own finite character. This occurs when we take into account *how* spirit emerges in the system and *what* it is.

The process of categorial self-transformation which leads us to the idea of nature continues as one in which that category, initially thought as what is fixed in its determinacy (i.e., as *not* self-determining) is gradually transformed. (As non-descriptive the transformation must not be understood as historical-evolutionary but as formal-categorical.) In broad terms the transformation takes place in that the activity of (what was in the logic) the sheer self-determination of thought gradually reappears, but transformed in its character, as what is called spirit. The topic is no longer the pure or sheer self-determination exhibited in logic, but an activity of determination located *in* and conditioned *by* what is conceptualized as the domain of the given, of finitude. The system's progression from nature through absolute spirit shows that what is finite, given, and not self-determining is necessary in its givenness as that in and through which spirit comes to constitute itself as self-determining.

So, conceptually speaking, finitude emerges in the system as that which arises out of the system's larger process of categorical self-determination. Thus the system remains self-grounding. But in what the system conceptualizes *as* the determinate character of the finite—its givenness as an other to thought—the system also recognizes the finite as *genuinely* and radically other than itself as self-determinative systematic thought. In this way the finite is not reduced to a mere adjunct or derivative of thought: In systematic philosophy the determinate characteristic of the finite is not established by purportedly cognizing a given object. (As Hegel saw, and as the history of philosophy shows, that approach leads to one or another version of idealism. Taking as paradigmatic the issue of how what is can be known by consciousness [or described by language] requires reading attributes and characteristics of consciousness [or language] into the domain of objectivity.)

Additionally, when we see *what* spirit is as self-determining we can see again that it is conditioned by finitude and cannot be characterized as divine in a blasphemous sense. Spirit's process of self-constitutive self-determination is not divine simply because it involves acting transformatively on the given, finite world in order to create in it the conditions for its own freedom. This vision of a gradual fulfillment of self-determination through action on a given world indicates clearly that spirit is God-like, but not divine in the blasphemous sense: "This struggling with the finite, the overcoming of limitation, constitutes the stamp of the divine in the human spirit. . . . " True religion has just this aspect central to spirit: recognizing but refusing to accept as absolute the given, finite character of the world.[45]

But does not this whole business of mediating and reconciling the finite and the infinite in an attempt to undercut the possibility of blasphemy still lead to blasphemy by eliminating the intelligibility of the notion of a transcendent infinite? Hegel has a defense against this move. For one thing, the system does not attempt to do away utterly with such a notion. It accords religion, as that which grasps the truth in pictorial, representative, finite form, an important role both in leading to spirit's discovery of its truth and in the world which is transformed by spirit's attainment of freedom.[46] Still, philosophical truth is given priority over religious truth,[47] and is not the philosophical truth about the infinite blasphemous in denying the radical transcendence of God?

Hegel's last defense is to indicate that the very conception of the infinite which postulates God as radically transcendent is itself blasphemous, in the following way.[48] Any discussion of God, he argues, even that which holds that we can know *that* God is but not *what* he is, claims that God is knowable. So in any talk of God we must allow that God is knowable.[49] Thus, if we wish to talk of God, the question becomes: in what way are we best to conceive of the nature of the divine? Those who bring the charge of blasphemy hold that God must be conceived as radically transcendent, non-finite, and other than human. But to conceive of God in such an apparently pious manner is to apply finite categories to God,[50] since to insist that God only be thought of in this manner is just to define God in exclusively human terms as nothing more than what is other than the human, the finite. "If God has the finite only over against himself, then he himself is finite and limited."[51] "[I]f the divine idea is grasped in the forms of finitude, then it is not posited as it is in and for itself. . . . To cognize the truth of something means to know and define it according to the truth, in the form of this idea in general."[52] God is rendered finite by the seemingly pious insistence that God be thought of only as a negation of the finite.[53] This limits, finitizes, God by way of making God a being who is only an abstract opposition to the finite.[54]

So we have seen that Hegel is not guilty of the charges of blasphemy. His system is not based on a claim to divine absolute knowing, but rather on a rejection of the possibility of such knowing. The system itself is only conditionally—not divinely—absolute or infinite: its character as self-grounding is conditioned by the suspension of consciousness' claim to absoluteness, a condition which limits the system's claim as knowledge by precluding descriptive truth from its purview. Both in the philosophical process which establishes the system and in what the system asserts, finitude is acknowledged and accepted in a variety of ways. In addition, we have seen that the systematic recognition of the finitude of philosophy and of the human spirit does not require the nihilistic rejection of the possibility of our knowing objective truth. Rather, when we see that the prospects for that truth lie not in attempting to describe what is, but in conceiving of how things should be, we can also recognize the *limits of finitude itself* and avoid the postmodern predilection for falling into incoherence through a tendentiously pseudo-pious absolutizing of finitude.

႙

Chapter 6 has further developed and explicated my assertion that rethinking Hegel's philosophy as antifoundational nonetheless enables us to hold onto a whole Hegel, an antifoundationalist who is still committed to a strong sense of philosophical truth. This claim has been articulated by unpacking Hegel's notorious notion of the system as absolute—its purported offering of self-determining, self-grounding, and in these senses, unconditional, absolute, truth—in antifoundational terms. Chapter 6 works to render intelligible the seemingly oxymoronic notion of nonfoundational absolute truth by showing how Hegel demonstrates that the absolute truth philosophy has sought can only be attained through a recognition and inclusion of finitude.

Chapter 6 has considered three central junctures—and three modes—in which Hegel's system acknowledges finitude: The whole enterprise is initiated by such an acknowledgement in that the system's beginning in the *Logic* is based on the disclosure of the ineluctable finitude of consciousness (its inability to attain self-grounding). But, unlike contemporary antifoundationalists, Hegel sees that this negative feature has a positive prospect: It opens up the possibility of a different conception of truth, one which does not conceive truth in terms of a given and hence is neither necessarily susceptible to the failings of the subjectivist model nor in competition with it. And thus, Hegel's system is not absolute in the sense of totalizing—abrogating all truth claims to itself. For it does not purport to replace finite knowing either by claiming to offer a more perfect version of its truth or by holding that such truth must be dismissed altogether. Rather, it is antifoundationalism which is guilty of a false absolutization in refusing to allow for the possibility of any other mode of knowing save the subjectivist model whose limitations it has recognized.

So, the very possibility of the system's mode of articulating philosophical truth is predicated upon recognizing the finite character of subjective knowing, and on the basis of this recognition, considering an alternative. Additionally, Chapter 6 has argued that the system itself recognizes finitude in the process of presenting this alternative. For self-determinative thought to constitute itself, it must think a radical other—recognize, in thought, the given precisely in its ineluctable, sheer otherness as given—and thus acknowledge its own limits as pure thought. So, what is other than thought comes to be thought—the system conceptualizes the real—but not in the descriptive mode of finite knowing which claims to grasp the real as it is in fact given. Chapter 6 has shown why Hegel's account of the real is not a version of metaphysical idealism, for the system does not deny a given world, or possible knowledge of it, and it does not collapse such a world into itself. Unlike other modes of philosophical thought which attempt to say something in thought about the given as given, systematic *Realphilosophie* thinks the other in its nature as radically other to thought. Thus this account presupposes neither that thought and the given are identical nor even that they have any features in common. Because this account does not purport to be of the real as something given, it further acknowledges its own limitation and the conditional legitimacy of nonphilosophical accounts of the real. Lastly, Chapter 6 has pointed to how the system acknowledges finitude and the given in its account of spirit: Systematic philosophy's own self-development leads it to conceptualize conscious agents acting in the world of the given, and its account of human agency is one which again acknowledges, without absolutizing, the finite character of human subjectivity. Chapter 6 has shown that the traditional understanding of Hegel as propounding an impossible, blasphemous, absolute philosophy must ignore the system's own considered treatment of various aspects of finitude.

Part One of *Philosophy Without Foundations* has made a case for the contemporary relevance of Hegel by indicating how his philosophy can be rethought in nonfoundational terms. At various junctures in Part One, I have contended that Hegel's philosophy should be rethought today both because its critique of foundationalism is superior and because, unlike contemporary antifoundationalism, it offers something other than and superior to the self-referentially suspect attempts to replace philosophy with relativistic or nihilist glorifications of finitude which cannot coherently capture the nature of finitude itself. Part Two, "The Transcendence of Contemporary Philosophy," works to develop and further substantiate this latter theme by considering various contemporary alternatives to Hegelian systematic philosophy. Chapter 7, "Hegel and Hermeneutics," takes up the theme of finitude discussed in Chapter 6. It focuses on Hans-Georg Gadamer, arguing that despite his appreciative dialogue with Hegel, Gadamer does not succeed in giving coherent expression to his insights about finitude.

PART TWO

❧

The Transcendence of
Contemporary Philosophy

Chapter 7

HEGEL AND HERMENEUTICS

> We must have a new mythology, but this mythology must be in the
> service of the ideas, it must be a mythology of reason.
>
> —Hegel

Three of the major schools of contemporary continental thought—
critical theory, poststructuralism and philosophical hermeneutics—
are alike, despite the manifold differences which distinguish them,
in criticizing and rejecting the traditional aim of modern philosophy: our Cartesian legacy as defined by the ideal of an autonomous,
fully transparent, self-legitimating standpoint of reason as a standpoint attainable by the reflective ego, consciousness or thinking
self.[1] To a degree, this common point also marks the importance, for
them, of Hegel. All can be said to be involved in a love/hate relationship with him. Both the negative and positive impact of Hegel
on critical theory is clearly acknowledged, at least by Habermas.[2]
More intriguing is the self-understanding of Hegel's influence on
poststructuralism as expressed by Foucault: " . . . our age, whether
through logic or epistemology, whether through Marx or through
Nietzsche, is attempting to flee Hegel. . . . But truly to escape Hegel
involves an exact appreciation of the price we have to pay to detach
ourselves from him. It assumes that we are aware of the extent to
which Hegel, insidiously perhaps, is close to us; it implies a knowledge, in that which permits us to think against Hegel, of that which
remains Hegelian. We have to determine the extent to which our
anti-Hegelianism is possibly one of his tricks directed against us, at
the end of which he stands, motionless, waiting for us."[3]

I have quoted Foucault on Hegel because I think one of the
points on which poststructuralism and hermeneutics are closest

consists in their shared self-understandings of the complexity and the ambiguous character of their respective relations to Hegel.[4] Foucault's remarks might just as well have been expressed by Gadamer. In fact, Gadamer tells us: "Concisely stated, the issue here is whether or not the comprehensive mediation of every conceivable path of thought, which Hegel undertook, might not of necessity give the lie to every attempt to break out of the circle of reflection in which thought thinks itself. In the end, is even the position which Heidegger tries to establish in opposition to Hegel trapped within the sphere of the inner infinity of reflection?"[5] Indeed, of all contemporary thinkers who take Hegel seriously and are yet critical of him, Gadamer is the most sensitive and appreciative, the most alert to Hegel's nuances and the most willing to acknowledge both the importance of Hegel's influence and the continuing challenge which Hegel presents to his own philosophical position. In Gadamer's words: " . . . it is of central importance for the hermeneutic problem that it should come to grips with Hegel."[6]

In what follows, I shall (1) reflect on the complex ambiguity of the Gadamer-Hegel relationship, indicating the points on which they are in disagreement, the points where they come close to one another, and the points where there is an unresolved tension in their relation. In addition, and in the course of this task, I shall indicate (2) what I think it means, and why it is important, for hermeneutics to overcome Hegel.

Central to understanding the importance and the complexity of the Gadamer-Hegel relationship are three interrelated issues: (1) the rejection of subjectivity, (2) the issue of finitude and (3) the problem of the circle of reflection. My central thesis is that on all these points of impact between Gadamer and Hegel there exists an underlying ambiguity in Gadamer's position on Hegel.

(1) Amongst interpreters of Hegel, Gadamer has a highly sophisticated appreciation of the fact that Hegel's completion of transcendental idealism is effected in and through a critique of egological subjectivity and the epistemology founded on it. "For it is Hegel who explicitly carried the dialectic mind or spirit beyond the forms of subjective spirit, beyond consciousness and self-consciousness."[7] Yet what is initially unclear in Gadamer is the degree to which Hegel carries out such a critique and the extent to which his critique is effective, for Gadamer also notes critically that Hegel's project proclaims itself as having "free self-consciousness."[8] Did Hegel fully overcome subjectivity? Or did he only produce its ultimate or penultimate transformation into an absolute

subjectivity? Does an absolute consciousness which is neither consciousness per se nor self-consciousness but is in essence still a
consciousness pervade in Hegel's thought?[9] It seems to me that
this is the point that Gadamer is getting at, and that his interpretation of Hegel gives an affirmative answer to the last two questions. The point of difference seems to be that the "free self-consciousness" which Hegel affirms is not an individual, finite self-
consciousness, but rather the self-consciousness of spirit, and that
what Gadamer is critical of is not the notion of spirit per se but
rather the idea of such a self-conscious spirit as being capable of
full and unconditioned self-transparency, i.e., as being the
progenitor of an absolute knowledge.[10]

Reading Gadamer in this way, it is clear that for him Hegel's
rejection of subjectivity is incomplete. It is only a rejection of its
primitive or egological forms, such that the basic structure of the ego
or consciousness remains dominant. "Precisely this elevation [of the
"empirical 'I' to the transcendental 'I' "] is what Hegel claims to have
accomplished through the *Phenomenology*. . . . Hegel demonstrated
that the I is spirit."[11] Thus what Gadamer sees as purification is not
at all a thoroughgoing rejection; the knowing subject qua individual,
finite consciousness has its limited character recognized, but not
acknowledged as final. Rather, the urge of reflection for totality and
complete transparency drove Hegel's philosophy on to proclaim the
false triumph of an infinite ego (spirit) which, rather than accepting
its finitude as defined by the limiting conditions of an other, swallows or subsumes the other into itself: "Absolute knowing is thus the
result of a purification in the sense that the truth of Fichte's concept
of the transcendental 'I' emerges, not merely as being a subject, but
rather as reason and spirit and, accordingly, as all of reality."[12] So,
despite the fact that "Hegel's concept of spirit . . . transcends the subjective form of self-consciousness . . . " the ultimate structure of consciousness remains dominant, for "[T]he light in which all truth is
seen is cast from consciousness's becoming clear about itself."[13]

Thus, in regard to subjectivity what initially appears to be an
ambiguity in Gadamer's reading of Hegel can be resolved by paying
closer attention to Gadamer's texts: He thinks that a variety of
modes of subjective consciousness are overcome by Hegel, but the
basic form of consciousness prevails and is absolutized. Nonetheless, subjectivity is important because it is intimately related to the
issues (2) of finitude and (3) of reflection. In addition, all three are
ultimately crucial because of the fact that, in their interconnection
one with another, they define the focal point of hermeneutics'

confrontation with Hegel and because it is around them and around this confrontation that the even more basic issue of the foundation and legitimacy of hermeneutics revolves. That is to say: The confrontation between Hegel and hermeneutics on subjectivity, finitude, and reflection is directly connected not only with hermeneutics' attempts to overcome Hegel, but also with the question of the foundations of hermeneutics itself. As I shall suggest, these are different ways of approaching the same issue. Thus the question as to whether or not hermeneutics has succeeded in founding itself philosophically is intimately tied to the question as to whether or not it has succeeded in overcoming Hegel.

Determining the precise nature and limits of subjectivity is crucial in this respect simply because the keystone of hermeneutics itself, as well as its critique of Hegel, lies in its affirmation of the primacy of finitude, as defined in part by the notion that the thinking subject cannot attain to the full self-transparency of an absolute knowing. For hermeneutics this is a *fundamentum inconcussum*, and the rejection of Hegel hinges on it: "In its uniqueness, finitude and historicity, however, human *Dasein* would preferably be recognized not as an instance of an *eidos*, but rather as itself the most real factor of all."[14]

But, despite his rejection of what he sees as Hegel's transcendence of *Dasein* in its uniqueness and finitude, it is with good reason that Gadamer speaks of Hegel's dialectic as "a continual source of irritation."[15] For the deeper complexity of the issue of subjectivity, reflected in Gadamer's understanding of Hegel, and especially as regards the matters of finitude and reflection, concerns the manner in which one is to go about establishing the finitude of consciousness or subjectivity, and hence concerns the question of the foundations of hermeneutics itself. The problem consists in doing this in a way which is philosophically adequate, but which does not lead, just in virtue of this adequacy, to the transcendence into an absolute consciousness. The decisive foundational question for hermeneutics, one which prevails despite its rejection of the perceived Hegelian notion of absolute subjectivity concerns the following: How is one to bring finitude—the self-evident awareness of the limited character of all human subjectivity—to *philosophical* legitimacy? This metaquestion, which delineates the deeper level of the Hegel-Gadamer relation, is connected with the problem of reflection, for the preeminent method of philosophical discourse is that of reflective thought. How is the pre-philosophical experience or awareness of finitude to be articulated in such a way that, despite reflection's demand for an accounting of the conditions of the possibility of the *philosophical* knowing of this fact, such an accounting does not become "trapped within the sphere of the inner infinity of reflection"?[16] How does one articulate finitude in such a way that the very possibility of such an articulation does not testify to the infinite power and capacity of the reflecting philosophical subject and such that reason remains "aware that human knowledge is limited and will remain limited, even if it is conscious of its own limit?"[17]

It is evidence both of the depths of Gadamer's philosophical understanding and of the extent of his openness that he is aware of this situation and the reflective-Hegelian objections which it presents to his own position. Where does he stand in regard to reflection's demand for a full accounting of the 'position from which' he makes his philosophical claims? And where does he see the locus for a philosophically adequate articulation of finitude? I think we shall see that Gadamer's position on the former question is marked by an inner tension or ambiguity which is not ultimately resolved, but which is broken off by his decision to reject reflection by stepping outside of its circle. An assessment of the extent to which hermeneutics overcomes Hegel must focus on this move. Furthermore, we shall see that both his rejection of reflection and his delineation of the nature of finitude are mediated by his complex dialogue with Hegel.

The crux of the tension within hermeneutics in regard to reflection, and the problematic character of reflection for it, lies in the need for a balanced or self-limiting reflection. Insofar as it articulates finitude philosophically, rather than as a dogmatic article of faith, hermeneutics must make use of and is a version of the philosophy of reflection.[18] As such, Gadamer by no means straightforwardly denies the demand for a reflective or philosophical grounding of the conditions of its own possibility: "It is a question of recognizing in it [hermeneutics] an experience of truth that must not only be justified philosophically, but which is itself a mode of philosophizing."[19] Reflection cannot be fully renounced, for it is in and through reflection—and historically in Kant's philosophy—that we reach, if not the awareness of our finitude, at least a philosophical articulation of those conditions which define it: Reflective self-understanding is that activity in and through which we come to an awareness of our situatedness. In addition, hermeneutics' claim to universality requires that it ground itself and legitimize this claim: "the hermeneutic problematic . . . must establish its own universality."[20] Yet reflection is dangerous, for it demands 'validation everywhere' and offers itself as a "power" to afford this validation which is "false."[21] Nonetheless, it cannot deny the question of its own possibility: "Anyone who takes seriously the finitude of human existence and constructs no . . . 'transcendental ego' to which everything can be traced back, will not be able to escape the question of how his own thinking as transcendental is empirically possible."[22] It would seem then that the very rejection of the infinite capacity for reflective grounding which hermeneutics demands forces it to pay even greater attention to the question of its own foundation. A self-limiting philosophy of reflection must pay special attention to this issue, and in a hermeneutics which does so Gadamer seems to see the truth of the claims of philosophy of reflection properly realized: "Hermeneutics achieves its actual productivity only when it musters sufficient self-reflection to reflect simultaneously about its own critical endeavors, that is, about its own limitations and the relativity of its own position. Hermeneutical reflection that does that seems to me to come closer to the real ideal of knowledge, because it also makes us aware of the illusion of reflection."[23]

But the decisive question concerns whether or not and how this self-limitation of reflection—which, if it were a *self*-limitation would ground hermeneutics' assertions concerning finitude and thus substantiate its rejection of Hegel in a twofold way—can be achieved. How is the self-limiting reflection of hermeneutics, understood as an expression of its own relativity, to be effected in a way that is not self-defeating? In confronting the issue of hermeneutics' rejection of reflection, Gadamer notes that reflective arguments against hermeneutics are "formally correct" in that they "demonstrate the inner contradictions of all relativist views." Yet they "have something about them that suggests that they are attempting to bowl one over. However cogent they seem, they still miss the main point. In making use of them, one is proved right, yet they do not express any superior insight of any value." They are "sophistic" and "in fact they tell us nothing."[24] This invective, which is not directed against Hegel, marks the point where the intimations of a reflectively adequate self-limiting philosophy of reflection are broken off, the point where Gadamer, in a highly self-reflective way, consciously steps outside of the circle of reflection. Thus, through his own self-reflection, Gadamer comes to realize that reflection cannot be limited from within: "Polemics against an absolute thinker has itself no starting point. The Archimedean point from where Hegel's philosophy could be toppled can never be found through reflection. This is precisely the formal quality of reflective philosophy, that there cannot be a position that is not drawn into the reflective movement of consciousness coming to itself."[25]

Gadamer appreciates what it is, from the standpoint of reflection, that is unacceptable in his own thought: "To be sure it is 'obvious' that finitude is a privative determination of thought and as such presupposes its opposite, transcendence. . . . Who will deny that? I contend however, that we have learned once and for all from Kant that such 'obvious' ways of thought can mediate no possible knowledge to us finite beings. Dependence on possible experience and demonstration by means of it remain the alpha and omega of all responsible thought."[26] And thus: "It seems to me that it is essential for taking finitude seriously . . . that . . . experience renounce all dialectical supplementation."[27] We come then to the bottom line vis-à-vis reflection: it must be broken with. But even this break deepens the ambiguous character of hermeneutics' relation with Hegel: One the one hand, Hegel is acknowledged as articulating a successful critique of egological subjectivism (by implication, this is also a critique of the transcendental philosophy of his predecessors, and hence a critique of Kant); on the other hand, hermeneutics returns to Kant's philosophy as the *locus classicus* for its assertion of finitude and its denunciation of the powers of reflection. Once again though, Gadamer is to be given credit for his appreciation of the untenability of this position as viewed from the standpoint of reflection: " . . . this critique of idealism [Kant's and Heidegger's] was faced then as now, with the comprehensive claim of the transcendental position. Inasmuch as philosophical reflection did not want to leave unconsidered any possible area of thought . . .— and, since Hegel, this was the claim of transcendental philosophy— it had already included every possible objection within the total reflection of the mind."[28] And testifying to the strength of the reflective position in Hegel, he notes: "It is necessary to recognize the compulsive power of reflective philosophy and admit that Hegel's critics never succeeded in breaking its magic spell. We shall be able to detach the problem of an historical hermeneutics from the hybrid consequences of speculative idealism if we refuse to be satisfied with the irrationalistic reduction of it, but preserve the truth of Hegel's thought . . . we are concerned to conceive a reality which is beyond the omnipotence of reflection. This was precisely the point against which the criticism of Hegel was directed and where the principle of reflective philosophy proved superior to all its critics."[29]

Does Gadamer succeed in 'breaking the magic spell' of Hegelian reflection? Does he feel that he has succeeded in doing this and in overcoming Hegel? Reflecting what I believe is Gadamer's own position, I think we have to answer: yes and no. No in that, and as I think Gadamer himself appreciates, his rejection of reflection is a step outside of the circle rather than a genuine breaking of it. A step outside because, from the standpoint of reflective philosophy, he seems not to have come up with an articulation of finitude which will satisfy the insistent demand of reflection for a reflective accounting or grounding of the legitimacy of the position from which the primacy of finitude is asserted. The qualified answer of yes to the question is evidenced by Gadamer's unquestioned belief that this reflective demand is fundamentally illegitimate, at least in part because to meet it must lead, in his eyes, to a renunciation of the primary datum of finitude. Insofar as finitude remains the "alpha and omega" of hermeneutics, and insofar as Gadamer is correct in holding that no reflectively adequate philosophy of reflection can succeed in limiting itself, then it is clear for him that hermeneutics constitutes a superior philosophical position vis-à-vis Hegel despite its inability to mount that mode of a critique of infinite reflection which reflective philosophy would acknowledge: a reflective, that is, a thoroughly immanent one.[30]

Given his acknowledgement of the fact that Hegel proves superior to the critiques of his position implicit in Kant and explicit in Heidegger, I think we can see in Gadamer's own efforts to articulate the fundamental character of finitude a development mediated by his understanding of and confrontation with Hegel.[31] I will no argue this point in detail, but I believe that Gadamer's so-called "linguistic turn"—his emphasis on language rather than *Dasein* as the primary datum of finitude—stems from his realization that the attempt to present finitude in terms of the subject, along the lines of the *Critique of Pure Reason* and *Being and Time*, relocates one within the reflective and problematic format of Hegelian philosophy. Thus, Gadamer turns to the experience and phenomenon of language because of his realization of the inadequacy of the Kantian and Heideggerian critiques of reflective idealism, and in order to effect his own conception of a "reality which is beyond the omnipotence of reflection."[32]

I will omit a consideration of whether or not language, as it is conceived by either the later Heidegger or Gadamer, suffices to meet Hegelian objections. I want to return instead to the theme of the complexity and ambiguity of the Gadamer-Hegel relationship by first of all noting the points where Gadamer emphasizes his closeness to Hegel.

I noted earlier that Gadamer's rejection, despite their "formal correctness," of reflective arguments against hermeneutics is not directed by him against Hegel. In fact, Gadamer himself is quite explicit about the closeness of his project with Hegel's. It seems to me that there are two central and related points of contact here: (1) Gadamer acknowledges, as we saw, the importance of Hegel's critique of egological subjectivity, and remarking on the necessity of 'coming to grips' with Hegel he writes: " . . . Hegel's whole philosophy of the mind claims to achieve the total fusion of history with the present. It is concerned not with a reflective formalism, but with the same thing as we are. Hegel has thought through the historical dimension in which the problem of hermeneutics is rooted."[33] Clearly, Hegel's emphasis on history, and especially on the necessity of historical consciousness for philosophy is a central point where the Hegelian and hermeneutic projects meet. Again, the crucial point of difference is the perceived Hegelian claim to absoluteness, specifically his claim to have achieved an absolute historical consciousness: "Hegel's application to history, insofar as he saw it as part of the absolute self-consciousness of philosophy, does not do justice to the human consciousness."[34] In Chapter 1 I have indicated how Hegel's awareness of his historical locatedness can be reconciled with his claim to have attained the truth.[35]

The second point of contact concerns the earlier noted issues of the idea of a self-limiting (non-absolute) philosophy of reflection and the proper manner in which finitude is to be philosophically grounded. As mentioned, Gadamer's position on these matters is especially sensitive for, (a) he is aware of the difficulties involved in establishing finitude in a philosophical satisfactory way and (b) he is also aware that Hegel's philosophy not only provides a critique of subjectivism but also presents, in its further development, a serious challenge to attempts to locate finitude primarily in a notion of subjectivity or *Dasein*. Gadamer's position on Hegel here is complex for, although unquestionably critical of what he sees as Hegel's absolutism, he nonetheless sees the parallels between his notion of language and Hegel's concept of spirit: " . . . despite his speculative dialectical transcendence of the Kantian concept of finitude. . . . (Hegel's) concept of spirit is still the basis of every critique of subjective spirit. . . . This concept of spirit that transcends the subjectivity of the ego has its counterpart in the phenomenon of language. . . . " But " . . . in contrast to the concept of spirit . . . the phenomenon of language has the merit of being appropriate to our finitude."[36]

To summarize the Gadamer-Hegel relationship: For Gadamer, the positive aspects of Hegel's thought are: (1) The definitive critique of egological subjectivity (including the notion of a dialectics of experience.);[37] (2) The emphasis on history; (3) The development of 'spirit' as a notion which transcends subjectivity and which points towards the phenomenon of language. In each of these cases, however, the breaking point lies in Hegel's insistent pushing of reflection on to completion, a drive which is seen as transforming his philosophy into absolutism in its ultimate desire to overcome all otherness and to attain certain self-knowledge in a reflective consciousness which transcends all experience.[38] In short, from Gadamer's point of view it is the reflective desire for radical justification—'validation everywhere' and for completion, the lust to grasp totality, which brings Hegel to reject finitude despite his anticipations of the hermeneutic position.[39]

But when we recollect how systematic philosophy manages to articulate a self-limiting philosophy of reflection which acknowledges without absolutizing finitude, we can better see the flaws of this hermeneutic position. In the last analysis, Gadamer asks us to acknowledge a given—the finitude of *Dasein*—as *philosophically* primal and, consequently, as foundationally determinative for all philosophical considerations. (As we saw, hermeneutics insists on its universality and its primacy.) So, rather than rejecting foundationalism as the search for some absolute, determining ground for all possible thought, Gadamerian hermeneutics merely seeks to offer a revised, non-Cartesian, account of subjectivity, as the foundational candidate. Even if we move to language (or to a Heideggerian Being of beings) as something beyond all subjectivity, we are still in the position of philosophically postulating a given as the absolute determinative ground for thought: hermeneutics insists that what it discloses about finitude must be acknowledged. Thus, the framework of the subjectivist model of truth (and foundationalism's pretensions to absolutism) remains in force even if there is no explicit talk of the subject, and even if talk of subjectivity is rejected for something which purportedly transcends and grounds the subject. As we have seen Hegel show, to begin with *any* notion of a determinate given is to remain within the framework of foundational subjectivity. The difference that hermeneutics makes—the slight step beyond Cartesianism—is simply that now the determinative, foundational absolute is postulated as something ineluctable, rather than as transparent. So, hermeneutics, as one version of contemporary antifoundationalism, fails to significantly distinguish itself from foundationalism. Like foundationalism, it claims universality for its assertions, while refusing to enter into the traditional foundational process of reflective justification. And like foundationalism, it remains wedded to the subjectivist model of truth. One can assert again and again, as defenders of anti-foundationalism do, that the substantive content of their thought, *what* they assert, is a renunciation of foundational absolutism, an affirmation of finitude. But both the manner of their assertions and what they offer as primal truth belie these postulations of humility. As a version of antifoundationalism, hermeneutics is Cartesianism in sheep's clothing.

Chapter 7 has suggested that Gadamer's effort to conceive a 'reality beyond reflection' has gone awry. As we have seen, the traditional Hegel he engages is a straw man. Gadamer is in good company in misconstruing Hegel's system as totalizing, in failing to see that Hegel does not overcome all otherness, and in failing to see how Hegel combines the possibility of radical self-legitimation with an awareness and acknowledgement of limitations of thought. Like hermeneutics, Marxist philosophy purports to offer a radical alternative to traditional philosophy and to do so through a confrontation with the failures of Hegelianism. Chapter 8 will disclose how Marx's efforts in these directions fail. Additionally, Chapter 8 furthers the account of the nature of Hegelian nonfoundational systematic philosophy by addressing the important question: if systematic philosophy must abjure presenting a descriptive account of the given, what is it?

Chapter 8

THE CRITIQUE OF MARX AND MARXIST THOUGHT

Hegel has no problems to formulate. He has only dialectics.
—Karl Marx

Karl Marx is one of the most famous, influential, and genuinely important critics of Hegel. Before I move on to the substance of this chapter, to a consideration of why I believe that Marx's critique of Hegel is fundamentally wrong, let me first comment on why I nonetheless feel that this critique is of central philosophical importance.

One aspect of the importance of what Marx has to say about Hegel simply has to do with the stature of Marx in the intellectual community. Marx's thought commands considerable respect, attention, and numerous adherents, both in the larger intellectual world and in the narrower confines of philosophy.[1] In the world of ideas, Marx is a heavyweight, and what he has to say about Hegel is, and should be, taken seriously.

For philosophers in particular though, Marx's critique of Hegel has a special significance. This is not only the case because Marx and Hegel offer sweeping and comprehensive, but divergent, philosophical accounts of the human condition and of the nature and prospects for the good life. Particular differences in their views of man and the world aside, Marx's critique of Hegel is especially important to philosophers because it is the focal point for a major confrontation on metaphilosophical issues of continuing relevance. For Marx's critique is at the center of an *Auseinandersetzung* between what are closely related but nonetheless sharply contrasting views on the nature and limits of philosophy itself and on the

159

proper understanding both of the relation between philosophical theory and reality and of the relation between the philosopher and the world of his age, issues which have always concerned philosophers and which are the subject of much philosophical discussion today.

But beyond this the importance of Marx's *Hegelkritik* is even greater, especially for philosophical students of Hegel and Marx who are particularly interested in questions about the nature and legitimacy of systematic-dialectical philosophy and the possibility of critical theory. This is the case, because unlike many other critics past and present, Marx does not dismiss the legitimacy of systematic-dialectical philosophy as such. He does not condemn Hegel's whole approach, Hegel's whole idea of a philosophical science, as irredeemably perverse and hopelessly wrongheaded.[2] Refusing to regard Hegel as a "dead dog," Marx defended Hegel against what he saw as all too prevalent unjust attacks. He forthrightly described himself as a "pupil of that mighty thinker," consistently acknowledging his indebtedness to Hegel.[3] And not only did he speak of setting Hegel aright, Marx even went so far as to conceive his own philosophy as a corrected continuation and development, an *Aufhebung*, one might say, of Hegel's.[4]

So, far from being a critic who would reject, or even simply correct Hegel, Marx seems to have understood and justified his own position in Hegelian systematic terms, as the proper, dialectically generated refinement and furtherance of Hegel's. Given this self-understanding of his position then, we can say that the overall status of Marx's philosophy, and specifically its claim to being dialectically scientific, rests at least in part on the rightness of Marx's *Hegelkritik*.

Thus, the deeper philosophical significance of Marx's critique of Hegel is twofold. On the one hand, it deserves attention from anyone interested in the general topic of the proper nature and limits of philosophical theory. This is especially the case today, when so much philosophical effort is being exercised in attempts to demonstrate the aporetic character of the Western philosophical tradition to which Marx and Hegel belong.[5] On the other hand, this critique and the reconceptualization of dialectical philosophy that Marx develops in conjunction with it compels attention for some, as it is of decisive importance to students of Hegel and Marx concerned with questions about the status, the overall character and legitimacy, of systematic-dialectical philosophical theory. For what is finally at stake in this critique are the claims of this theory's two major proponents to have raised philosophy to the level of a science.

What, briefly, are the essential features of Marx's critique? How does it lead to what is allegedly a correct reconceptualization of the nature and limits of dialectical philosophy? Further, how does his critique lead to what Marx sees as a necessary and radical transformation of the relation between philosophical theory and reality and thus also to a transformation of the tasks of the philosopher, both theoretical and practical?

The leitmotif of Marx's critique of Hegel is a familiar one, and it is not original to Marx.[6] It amounts to the charge that Hegel propounds a patently metaphysical, idealistic, and pantheistic system: a system in which thought or the Absolute Idea is literally and erroneously postulated as the true essence of reality and the moving subject behind history, such that empirical actualities are regarded as the mere appearances, the products or manifestations of this Idea.[7] For Marx, however, Hegel's purported lapse into the idealistic fallacy is not a genetic flaw or an unavoidable consequence of the systematic-dialectical approach to theory which he originated. Hegel's mistake, according to Marx, is not attributable to the very nature of systematic philosophy, but rather to the particular and erroneous fashion in which Hegel understood and developed dialectics. What is wrong with Hegel's philosophy is so to speak, essentially a matter of its content as opposed to its form, although, as we shall see, correcting the error of content does have serious implications for the nature and form of dialectical philosophy.[8]

In any case, perceiving Hegel's mistake as attributable not to dialectical thought per se, but rather to a misconstrual of the proper nature of dialectics, the substance of Marx's critique is directed against what he construes as the "mystification" dialectic suffers in Hegel's hands: "With him it is standing on its head. It must be inverted in order to discover the rational kernel within the mystical shell."[9] As this mystification consists in regarding empirical actuality as a manifestation of the Absolute Idea the demystifying inversion amounts to establishing the proper priority of the material over the ideal, of reality over thought. It finally amounts to transforming what Marx takes to be a dialectical idealism into a dialectical materialism. Rather than construing dialectics fundamentally as a process or activity of thinking, dialectic for Marx must rather be seen as a process or activity in and of reality itself.[10]

Continuing this corrective inversion, seeing dialectics as a process which is discovered in reality, we come to realize then that the motor of dialectic is properly understood not as thought or the Absolute Idea, but rather as human makers and actors: as a process taking place in and of this world and by humans, the dialectic consists in humanity's historical self-realization and self-creation through the continual and continually creative development, enhancement, and transformation of those productive capacities that define our species being.[11] Thinking through this material, dialectical, historical process to completion, we finally come to see that it will inevitably culminate, as a consequence of human action, in a state where these capacities are capable of full realization.[12]

There are significant consequences to this effort at a critical reconceptualization of the character of dialectics and dialectical philosophy, according to which the idea or philosophy, now properly understood, is "nothing but the material world reflected in the mind of man and translated into forms of thought" (rather than the other way around, which was Hegel's error).[13] These consequences do not pertain only to the content and substantive features of Hegel's and Marx's dialectical conceptualizations of reality. In addition, they concern their metaphilosophies, their respective understandings of the nature, limits and potential of systematic-dialectical philosophy, as well as their views on the relation between philosophical theory and reality and their positions on the tasks of the philosopher, both worldly and philosophical. As we shall see, what is finally at stake here in general is the question of the nature and possibility of a critical philosophy or theory.

From the Preface to the *Philosophy of Right* we know the views of the mature Hegel on these latter topics: philosophy cannot give 'instruction,' it cannot provide us with a recipe for making the world what it ought to be, and it must remain silent as to the future course of history. The task of the philosopher is not to direct action, but to provide comprehension and understanding of the real to the extent to which it is rational.[14]

Marx's view, as encapsulated in the XI Thesis on Feuerbach, could not be in sharper contrast: "The philosophers have only interpreted the world, in various ways; the point is to change it."[15] Now as Marx develops and refines this position in his philosophical project what we see emerging is a vision of the philosopher's task as involving more than just world-transforming action. What Marx presents is not merely a call for philosophers' engagement in and with the world; he also calls for, and comes to offer, a radical reformation of the character and objectives of philosophy itself and of the tasks of the philosopher as a theorist.

For as a consideration of Marx's subsequent writings and career reveals, his claim is not at all that the work of philosophy is done and that philosophers should stop philosophizing and *just* act. Rather, Marx himself continues to philosophize, and in so doing redefines the nature of philosophy itself in that he conceives a properly and thoroughly demystified systematic-dialectical philosophy as constituting not merely a call for but also a *theory* of world-transformative action as revolutionary praxis.

How so? Corrected and taken beyond Hegel, systematic-dialectical philosophy, now distinctively labeled "critique," is to provide a theory of the overcoming of philosophy; it is to present a theory of the final transformation of philosophy qua theory into actuality through revolutionary praxis, a praxis which is itself understood specifically as action guided by theory.[16] What this means is that the job of the philosopher is not merely to provide an account of the manner and extent to which the real is rational. In addition, and more importantly, his task is twofold: to make the real rational through action, and to comprehend in philosophical, systematic-dialectical theory the character, legitimacy and necessity of this action. Put differently, the job of the philosopher, revealed by and consequent upon the demystification of dialectics, is to provide a dialectically scientific—a necessary and comprehensive—account of the empirically discoverable dialectical process by which the opposition between all philosophical theory and reality is inevitably to be overcome in and through human action.[17]

So, the special and new goal of systematic-dialectical philosophy as now understood by Marx is to give a theory of the realization of theory, a theory of how, through dialectics, philosophy is to become real and of how the real is to become rational or philosophical.[18] Thus, Marx's attempt to demystify dialectics reconceptualizes the very nature and limits of dialectical philosophy. First of all, it postulates a dialectically necessary relation between theory as a whole, including systematic-dialectical philosophy, and reality. (It conceives them as at present in an opposition in need of overcoming.) Secondly, it calls for a new or further systematic-dialectical theory to comprehend the past origins, the present state, the future movement, and the ultimate resolution of this dialectical opposition.[19]

It is just such a theory—one that claims to comprehend in dialectical terms the necessity of its own overcoming and realization qua theory—which can then finally claim to stand as a philosophical science of praxis in the strong sense that Hegel regards as beyond the limits of philosophy: in the sense of a theory comprehending the necessity of and both predicting and legitimating certain courses of action.[20] For on the basis of its purported comprehension of the dialectical relationship between itself as theory and reality, this transformed and expanded systematic-dialectical philosophy can claim to speak of the future in more than a hypothetical or tentative fashion, and it can not merely suggest, but ordain, certain courses of action. That is, for Marx, systematic-dialectical theory offers us a *science* of praxis in that the nature and legitimacy of certain future actions can be philosophically demonstrated by first establishing that they follow as a consequence of thinking through the dialectic. Dialectics, according to Marx, is a process in and of reality, discoverable by thought; thought, having uncovered the basic workings of dialectic, can then further disclose, through dialectical reasoning, at least the general features of the dialectic's future unfolding in reality. Having disclosed this movement, theory can announce that course of action seen as in accordance with and as necessitated by the lager movement of the dialectic, thus establishing a science of praxis. Since the developmental dynamic of dialectics pertains not merely to theory, or reality, but also to the relation between the two—as demystified dialectics encompasses the emerging necessary synthesis of the ideal and the real, of the conceptual and the material—demystified dialectical theory can claim to reveal in theory what must subsequently come to be in reality.

It is important to note that this thoroughgoing reconceptualization of the nature, limits, and objectives of systematic-dialectical philosophy and the demystifying corrective inversion of dialectics involved in it seem, at least in part, to be justified by Marx in dialectical, Hegelian terms. For, according to Marx, thinking dialectically beyond Hegel entails thinking dialectically about the relation between Hegel's completed system and the contemporary world.[21] Thinking dialectically about Hegel reveals the dialectical character of Hegel's errors, as well as it reveals the need and the basis for going beyond him.[22] Thus, in provisional defense of Marx as a critic of Hegel, one might present his move beyond Hegel as one that is seemingly in agreement with Hegel's own notion of an immanent dialectical critique.[23]

What I shall now attempt to show is that in working to develop further and to transform radically the nature and limits of systematic-dialectical philosophy in the ways I have indicated, Marx has misconstrued the proper character of this philosophy and illicitly transgressed what Hegel happened to have correctly understood as the necessary limits of dialectical theory. Put in another way, what I aim to indicate is that in finally assessing Marx's claim that his is the true dialectical philosophy, we need to attend not only to Marx's explicit critique of Hegel but also equally to what I shall present as Hegel's implicit critique of Marx. In laying out Hegel's critique of Marx, I shall work to show explicitly what the limits of systematic-dialectical philosophy are through a consideration of Hegel's views on that philosophical standpoint or theoretical assumption which he sees as in need of rejection if philosophy is to be a science. I shall then claim that Marx reverts to this pre- or extra-philosophical standpoint in what he offers as his demystification of dialectics, arguing that Marx's claim that dialectics must correctly be seen as something which is first found in reality only subsequently to emerge in philosophical thinking represents not a demystification, but in fact a mystification of dialectics. Put differently, I shall argue that Marx's purported demystifying inversion of dialectics is a fundamental conceptual error, analogous to the error Marx himself diagnoses as the fetishism of commodities. I shall then argue on these grounds that Marx is also in error in attempting to develop a philosophy—a systematic-dialectical science—of praxis. Here I shall attempt to show that a proper construal of the nature and limits of systematic-dialectical philosophy precludes the attempt to construe a dialectical relation between theory and reality in Marx's sense of such a relation: namely, as a relation which can lead to an action predicting and legitimating science. Put differently, I shall argue that the limits of philosophy as sketched by Hegel in the Preface to the *Philosophy of Right* follow from the character of systematic philosophy as science and are not merely attributable to the pragmatic conservatism of a prominent Prussian philosopher and state employee. Finally, I shall consider the implications of this critique of Marx for the question of the possibility and nature of a critical philosophy.

In order to see how Marx comes to transgress the nature and limits of systematic-dialectical theory we need first of all to consider those features of such a philosophical theory that can be said to comprise its philosophically scientific character. Secondly, and of greater import, we also need to see what minimal conditions must be met such that a theory or philosophy can claim to possess these features and thus present itself as having attained the status of philosophical science. The latter is especially important because my claim is that Marx violates these conditions and thus obviates his claim that his theory is scientific in a dialectical sense and because it is the proper continuation of dialectical philosophy.

According to Hegel, systematic-dialectical philosophy is scientific thought or philosophy par excellence in that it expresses philosophical truth.[24] More specifically, it is philosophical science because it articulates what is rationally universal and necessary in a manner that is both unconditional and complete.[25] Furthermore, this philosophy can lay claim to such unconditional universality and necessity, and to completeness for what it articulates, only insofar as this philosophy is fully and exclusively self-grounding.[26]

What this idea of self-grounding means is that this philosophy's claim to be scientific rests initially *and minimally* on the claim that nothing external to the system enters into its constitution in a determinative manner. In addition, this feature of being self-grounding itself rests further on, or amounts to, this philosophy's claim to being exclusively founded in pure and autonomous reason.[27] The connection between being self-grounding and being founded in pure and autonomous reason is this: only a mode of thought founded and developed in and through reason's radical *self*-constitution can lay claim to being a mode of thought which is genuinely and exclusively self-grounding, and thus capable of unconditionally articulating what is rationally universal and necessary. For to be self-grounding is, minimally, to be devoid or free from anything arbitrary, assumed, or merely postulated, i.e., anything requiring further legitimation or grounding. Thus, to be scientific, this philosophical discourse must be free from anything determined or justified extra-systemically or extra-rationally. And such freedom as it pertains to the nature and content of systematic philosophy—freedom from external determination—can only be attained insofar as reason is autonomous in its operations, insofar as reason is not externally or other-conditioned or determined. Thus, systematic philosophy is only fully justified or grounded and systematic philosophy can only be a science if reason is, or can be brought to be, autonomous and if reason alone can be said to have determined the form and content of the system. I trust that it is obvious from these brief remarks that, while self-groundedness is not a sufficient condition for all the attributes of scientific philosophy, it is certainly a necessary one.

Now for Hegel, what is crucial if philosophy is to become a science in this sense, a necessary pre-condition for science, is first showing that such a standpoint of autonomous reason is attainable. And according to him this requires a prior exercise of thought in which it is systematically demonstrated that reason possesses the potential for radical autonomy and is thus in the position of generating a self-grounding science because it has been shown that reason need not necessarily be conditioned in its operations by anything external to or other than itself. Such a prior demonstration of reason's potential for autonomy involves indicating what such external conditioning amounts to or consists in and in further revealing how and why it is that the factors that constitute such conditioning—the factors which may be said to render reason heteronomous in its operations—are not endemic to these operations.

Put differently, coming to the standpoint of science requires first showing that what Hegel calls the prevailing "natural assumption . . . in philosophy"—according to which reason is always construed as in some manner necessarily conditioned—is itself an arbitrary assumption about the character of reason.[28] Revealing the arbitrary character of the assumption that reason must always be heteronomous—allegedly always conditioned by some factor or factors—is a vital condition for science because, failing such a demonstration, this philosophy's claim to autonomy would itself be, or appear, merely arbitrary: the claim to autonomy would only be a "bare assurance" unless it can be shown how it is that the contending position on reason is not a sufficient condition for science.[29] Showing that reason can come to an awareness of and can reveal as unfounded that assumption about its own nature that allegedly establishes its necessary conditionality—its heteronomy—amounts only to an indication of the *prima facie* possibility of an autonomous self-constitution and self-development of reason.

More specifically, what particular assumption concerning the character of reason as necessarily conditioned must be revealed as an unfounded and how, in brief, does Hegel work to do this? The governing "natural" assumption that can be said to define the necessarily heteronomous character of reason, and that is deconstructed in the *Phenomenology of Spirit*, is this: it is that preconception or understanding of reason which construes reason as always unavoidably conditioned in its operations by some given. (The *Phenomenology* is thus an attack on what Sellars calls the "myth of the given."[30]) In this prevailing assumption about the character of reason, reason is always seen as heteronomous because, according to Hegel, reason is here identified with consciousness; the conditions of all possible thought are identified with the conditions of human subjectivity. So reason is construed as necessarily conditioned—as less than autonomous, less than genuinely self-determining or self-constitutive—in that it is assumed that the operations of reason must and can only be construed in terms of that model or mode of thought in which whatever comes to be known or thought *is* always, in some sense, a *Gegenstand*, something whose determinate and knowable character is always in one way or another given to conscious awareness. And if reason can be identified with consciousness, then reason cannot be autonomous, for whatever it might come to establish or claim will always be ineluctably other-determined: it will be in some way

founded in that whose determinate character is, as a 'given,' predetermined. But, as Hegel puts it speaking of consciousness:

> These views on the relation of subject and object to each other
> express the determinations which constitute the nature of our
> ordinary, phenomenal consciousness; but when these preju-
> dices are carried out into the sphere of reason as if the same
> relation obtained there, as if this relation were something true
> in its own self, then they are errors the refutation of which
> throughout every part of the spiritual and natural universe is
> *philosophy*, or rather, as they bar the entrance to philosophy,
> must be discarded at its portals (*Logic*: p. 45).

As we have seen the *Phenomenology* comes to indicate that
this is an arbitrary assumption about reason. While the rejection of
the standpoint and structure of consciousness allows systematic
philosophy at least a plausible claim to autonomous self-grounding,
it does so only at the price of establishing certain limits for this
philosophy. These are limits of such a character that they cannot
be transgressed if systematic-dialectical philosophy is to retain its
claim to being science and which must be, and are, transgressed in
Marx's attempted revision and extension of systematic-dialectical
theory.

If the rejection of the standpoint of consciousness as a necessary model for philosophical thought helps to establish the scientific character of systematic philosophy as self-grounding by making it possible for reason to engage in a genuinely autonomous
process of self-constitution, it does so at the price of establishing a
certain kind of limitation or closure for this system as a dialectically scientific one. Insofar as part of the system's claim to autonomy rests on the claim that the categories generated in it are
autonomously produced by reason alone, and as this claim to autonomy is itself based on the rejection of the form of consciousness
as a determinative model for the constitution of systematic categories, this then requires that the scientific character of the system
preclude an attempt within systematic-dialectical philosophy, to
construe its relation to reality, *in the sense that* "reality" is conceived extra-systemically, or from the standpoint of consciousness:
namely, as something that we find given in its determinacy for
thought.

What does this mean, and how does it relate to Marx? To
claim that the system cannot conceive reality from the standpoint
of consciousness is not to say that systematic philosophy cannot

speak of reality, even as an other to thought. Nor is it to say that
the system cannot speak of consciousness, or of reality as a datum
for consciousness. The system can and does do all of these things.
It is to say that insofar as systematic-dialectical philosophy conceptualizes the real, and these and other features of it, this philosophy
cannot constitute the real—as a category of systematic philosophy—in the manner of consciousness, i.e., as a category given in its
determinacy.[31] Put more specifically, systematic-dialectical philosophy cannot appeal to any aspects or features of the real apprehended as a datum for consciousness, either as foundationally
constitutive for its conception of the real or as evidence for the
philosophical truth of its conception of the real. It cannot do this
simply because, were it either to derive or to attempt to ground its
categories in such a manner—by reference to what is given to conscious awareness—it would surrender to the primacy of the given
and thus to a mode of thinking whose rejection as authoritative in
and for the system is crucial to its claim to being scientific.

That the real is not to be conceptualized within the system in
this manner is clear not only from Hegel's remarks about what
conditions must be met and what position must be rejected if philosophy is to be science. It is also clear from what he has to say
about the move in the system from logic to *Realphilosophie*: "The
logical idea does not thereby come into possession of a content
foreign to it: but by its own native action is specialized and developed to nature and mind" (*Encyclopedia Logic*: Paragraph 43). "Nature has yielded itself as the idea in the form of otherness (*Philosophy of Nature*: Paragraph 247).

So, to do what Hegel precisely claims he is not doing in systematic-dialectical philosophy—to look to and at the real as a given
object (*Gegenstand*) and as a determinative and not merely illustrative source for the categories and determinacies of systematic
philosophy—would be to resort to the pre- and extra-scientific standpoint of consciousness. And because it would necessarily involve
bringing into the system merely given and not systematically and
autonomously generated determinacies, it would invalidate the
system's claim to being self-grounding and hence its claim to being
philosophical science.

Thus, while systematic-dialectical thought can conceptualize
the real and can even come to conceptualize its relation to the real,
as philosophical theory and its own emergence in history—conceptual actions which are part of its working to completeness—these
notions or categories ("the real," "philosophy," "history," and so
forth) must be understood as categories of systematic philosophy.

That is, not as categories whose determinate character and validity are established in virtue of the claim that they agree with, are 'true' or 'correct' descriptions of the real, history, etc., as we happen to apprehend them phenomenally, as given data for conscious thought. (Correlatively, the activities of conceptualizing the real and of conceptualizing the relation of philosophy to the real must be undertaken 'systematically': without constitutive reference to the real as a datum for consciousness.) In a word, then, systematic-dialectical philosophy does not 'describe' reality. According to Hegel:

> The Idea is the Truth: for Truth is the correspondence of objectivity with the notion—not of course the correspondence of external things with my conception, for these are only *correct* conceptions held by me, the individual person. In the Idea we have nothing to do with the individual, nor with figurate conceptions, nor with external things (*Encyclopedia Logic*: Paragraph 213).

This then is the fulcrum of the difference between Hegel's and Marx's views, both as to the proper 'method' of doing systematic-dialectical philosophy as well as on the issue of how systematic-dialectical philosophy or theory 'relates' to reality. And the difference between them on these points has serious consequences for an assessment both of the nature and status of their philosophies and for the notion of a systematic-dialectical science of praxis.

First, as regards an assessment of the status of a philosophy that constitutes and presents its categories in the manner systematic philosophy must reject, in the mode of consciousness, as descriptions: as we can see, and as Hegel claims, to construe the truth of philosophical categories in this way, and to proceed in philosophy in this manner, is to operate in the mode of pictorial/metaphysical thought:

> We must in the first place understand clearly what we mean by Truth. In common life truth means the agreement of an object with our conception of it. We thus presuppose an object to which our conception must conform. In the philosophical sense of the word, on the other hand, truth may be described, in general abstract terms, as the agreement of a thought content with itself. This meaning is quite different from the one given above (*Encyclopedia Logic*: Paragraph 24, Addition).

And in metaphysics, he writes:

> ... the predicates by which the object is determined are supplied from the resources of picture thought, and are applied in a mechanical way. Whereas, if we are to have genuine cognition, the object must characterize its own self, and not derive its predicates from without (*Encyclopedia Logic*: Paragraph 28, Addition).

What Hegel's rejection of a foundational as well as referential basis for his philosophy indicates is that it is wrong—as Marx and others do—to regard Hegel's philosophy as metaphysically idealistic.[32] This is not to deny that various things Hegel says suggest this sort of a reading. More significantly, this is not to deny that Hegel presents his system as, in some sense, an account of what is 'true' in reality.[33] As I shall argue below, what I see as the critical force of this system involves this latter claim. But as I shall also indicate, such critical force hinges on the system's not being, or not being read as, an idealistic metaphysics. In any case, to contend that Marx begins to go awry in his *Hegelkritik* by seeing Hegel's philosophy as an idealistic metaphysics is, for the moment, to say two things:

(1) This system is not metaphysically idealistic (or permits of a nonmetaphysical, nonidealistic reading) because it does not claim to be an account of the real as it is phenomenally given, because it is not meant to be a 'correction' of what we know about reality from the standpoint of consciousness. How so? How can this claim be made for Hegel, given the tradition of Marx's misreading? As we can now see, to hold that it is such a correction would involve making in systematic philosophy a comparison between its account of the real and what is purportedly a phenomenal account of the real. But just such a comparison, if offered as a test to determine which account is true in the sense of truth as correspondence—the sense of truth I have just quoted Hegel as rejecting—would necessitate a return to the standpoint of consciousness and the importation into the purview of systematic philosophy of extra-systemic determinations.

(2) More generally, this system is not metaphysically idealistic, nor is it an identity philosophy, because any metaphysical idealism or identity philosophy presupposes as a primal given the opposition between thought and the materially or empirically given in order to deny the primacy of such given in favor of the primacy of thought. The opposition between thought and the given must be

taken as a given in order to be denied or corrected: the thesis of the primacy of thought or of the identity of thought and the given cannot be maintained without the opposition. The alleged truth of any idealism or identity philosophy thus presupposes the opposition and is unintelligible without it. But as we have seen, for Hegel a precondition for systematic philosophy is the suspension in it of the opposition of consciousness, of just that opposition between thinking awareness and the given which must be presupposed and which cannot ultimately be eliminated if any metaphysical idealism or identity philosophy is to remain coherent.

Given these features of systematic-dialectical philosophy, and given that in criticizing Hegel's metaphysical idealism, Marx was attacking a straw man, how do things stand with Marx? Precisely because of what he offers as the corrective, demystifying inversion—the turn to material reality as an empirically given foundational datum—we can see that Marx's version of systematic-dialectical philosophy invalidates any possible claim to be scientific in a systematic-dialectical sense of what this means. By incorporating what he claims and insists are empirically given data, correct or true descriptions of reality as we find it, Marx's version of systematic philosophy sacrifices any claim to being self-grounding, and with it any legitimate claim for the necessity and completeness of the dialectic it postulates.[34] (Whether Marx regarded it to be scientific in some other sense is questionable. Whether it might be scientific in some other sense cannot concern us here.)[35]

Additionally, we can also see that it is in fact Marx and not Hegel who propounds a mystified idealism, albeit an idealism that flies the flag of materialistic realism. Marx's dialectical theory is a version of idealism because it takes what is properly understood as a feature of the relation of categories or determinacies in systematic philosophy—the necessity of the dialectical interrelatedness and progressive co-determination of its categories, the dialectical necessity that establishes the system's claim to completeness for what it considers—and reads it into reality and history as an allegedly empirically discoverable feature of both. In fact, this amounts surreptitiously, and under the guise of what is purportedly an empiricistic realism, to doing just what Marx claims Hegel is doing: imposing the rulership of ideas or philosophy over reality.

To put the point in another way Marx's empiricistic-materialistic misconstrual of dialectics is analogous, as an error, to what Marx diagnoses as the fetishism of commodities. Speaking of the "commodity form and its relation," Marx writes:

It is nothing but the definite social relation between men themselves which assumes here, for them, the fantastic form of a relation between things. In order, therefore, to find an analogy, we must take flight into the misty realm of religion. There the products of the human brain appear as autonomous figures endowed with a life of their own, which enter into relations both with each other and with the human race. So it is in the world of commodities with the products of men's hands. I call this the fetishism which attaches itself to the products of labor as soon as they are produced as commodities, and it is therefore inseparable from the production of commodities (*Capital*: 1, p. 165).

I would suggest that in order to find a further analogy we must take flight, not now into the misty realm of religion, but into the equally misty realm of Marx's metaphysics. There a product of human thought—dialectics—'appears as an autonomous figure endowed with a life of its own.' An 'autonomous figure' that 'enters into relations both with itself' (dialectics according to Marx is a cosmic process, a feature both of theory and reality and of the relation of the two) and that also enters into relations with the human race. For dialectics according to Marx is also, as found in reality, a feature of human historical relations and activities. 'So it is in the world' of Marx's dialectics with this 'product of thought.' *I* call this the *fetishism of dialectics*, which attaches itself to a product of thought as soon as it is read as a real thing. It is therefore inseparable, as I have suggested, from the production of an empirically founded systematic-dialectical philosophy.

What can we say then, finally, about the notion of a systematically dialectical science of praxis? What are we to make of Marx's claim that demystifying Hegel, and thus thinking through the dialectic between systematic-dialectical theory qua theory and reality as an empirical datum, can enable and lead us to offer a recipe for action? Can we have a theory of praxis that, on the basis of the theory's comprehension of the dialectic, is capable generally of predicting and legitimating courses of human action? Put differently, what are we to make of Marx's claim that his version of systematic-dialectical theory permits us to assume the throne of philosopher kingship? Or, taking a critical stance, just why, as I have suggested, does the proper understanding of the nature and limits of systematic-dialectical philosophy preclude such a science of praxis? How can we come to see that Hegel's views on the limits of systematic-dialectical philosophy and the worldly role of the philosopher follow from the nature of systematic-dialectical philosophy?

It is here that we need to consider and assess Hegel's claim about the 'truth' of the system *vis-à-vis* reality, now regarding 'reality' not as a categorical determination of systematic philosophy, but as an empirically given datum. Just as I have suggested that it is Marx's systematic-dialectical philosophy, and not Hegel's, that is idealistically metaphysical, I believe that it is also Hegel's systematic-dialectical philosophy that presents itself—potentially—as a truly legitimate critical philosophy.

How so? I believe that the motivation for Hegel's attempt to develop a philosophy grounded in and exclusively generated out of autonomous reason did not arise merely out of a desire to raise philosophy to the level of a science. Beyond this strictly theoretical motivation, I believe that Hegel saw that any possible worldly role for philosophy—any role that is, for a critical philosophy that can claim that reality as we find it given ought to conform to reality as we rationally conceive it—hinged on first establishing that reason has a right to claim authority over the given.[36] More specifically, Hegel felt a critical, worldly role for philosophy presupposed showing, against Hume and even against Kant, that reason need not submit, in what it conceptualizes, to the authority of any given. That is, if Hume, Kant—and Heidegger—are correct, if it is true that reason is and must always be in some way either externally or internally determined by a given which resists final penetration by reason, then the theoretical and pragmatic legitimacy of reason's claim to take a critical stance *vis-à-vis* the given is undercut. If they are correct, anything reason might claim to establish on its own as rational is and must always be arbitrary and finally unfounded, because necessarily other-determined. So, if they are correct, then a consequence of reason's heteronomy is its impotence as a critical force; reason must surrender to the authority of the given. Thus, indicating that there is a legitimate critical role for reason in the world of human events requires something like a *Phenomenology*, a systematic demonstration that reason need not necessarily be determined in its operations and discoveries by some allegedly ineluctable given.

But such a demonstration has the consequence of ordaining a limited role for philosophy and the philosopher in the world of the given. For, as the philosophical account of the real as rational requires that extra-systemic, given determinancies be eliminated from the system, this further means that if the completed account of the real as rational is to have any critical force *vis-à-*

vis the given status quo, it can only have this force extra-systemically.

Put more straightforwardly, in systematic-dialectical philosophy one cannot claim to speak in systematic-dialectical terms (with the force of unconditional, rational universality and necessity) as to whether reality as it is given, or as we think it might be, is or is not rational. Hence, one cannot claim, as Marx does, to scientifically and systematically-dialectically predict or give advice as to how the world will be made rational. Why does the critical dimension of systematic-dialectical philosophy fall outside of systematic-dialectical philosophy strictly so-called? The critical dimension must fall outside simply because, in speaking as systematic philosophers, we cannot make descriptive truth claims, the sort of claims necessary for making predictions or for legitimating certain actions. We cannot do this because it ultimately undercuts not only the scientific status of the system, but also its claim to be what autonomous reason conceptualizes. To do so would undercut any legitimacy the system might have as a critical device.

So, *as* systematic-dialectical philosophers, we must remain silent about whether the world or society does or does not accord with the demands of reason as articulated by this philosophy. Or if we choose to address these questions and if we choose to claim that the world already does or that it should accord with reason, we must be careful to offer these judgments as opinions: as unavoidably involving empirical claims that are subject to challenge by non-philosophers and which are subject to challenge in a different way than the claims of systematic philosophy are. In short, if we wish systematic philosophy to have a rightful worldly impact, we must not seek to take on the role of philosopher kings.

If I am correct on these matters, it indicates that what Marx presents as the truly 'critical' philosophy cannot finally have any legitimate force as critical *philosophy*. This is simply because: (1) By incorporating empirically given data it stands open to philosophically irresolvable challenges concerning its correctness; and more seriously, (2) by incorporating empirically given data as a foundation for its claims concerning the manner in which the real should be made rational, it obviates any possible claim to be speaking for autonomous reason. By acknowledging the authority of the given over what reason might establish on its own, it surrenders the basis for reason's rightful claim to critical authority and thus fundamentally and irreparably undercuts its own critical legitimacy.

The irony of this, of course, is that Marx's philosophy has given birth to so many philosopher kings, both those who genuinely

rule and those who are pretenders to the throne. This might reinforce for us Hegel's skepticism about the worldly impact of philosophy, a skepticism I have tried to show as in agreement with his
systematic philosophy. For appreciating its limits can also lead to
an appreciation of the fact that, in a world that might in some
ways approximate to a world of rational freedom, one cannot and
does not want to try to coerce people to be rational. In any case,
appreciating the limits I have spoken of can help us see how Hegel's
philosophical caution, his somewhat pessimistic philosophical resignation can be explained as truly philosophical in character.

Not all contemporary philosophy abjuring Hegel is cast in the
antifoundational mold. The various schools of Marxist thought are
as adamant in their rejection of Hegel as are today's antifoundationalists. However, their criticisms are made in the name of a
mode of dialectical theorizing which purports to succeed in articulating philosophical truth where Hegel failed, because of their correction of Hegel's errors. Chapter 8 has presented a Hegelian
response to the central Marxist contention that Hegel's is a failed
idealistic philosophy.

In describing Hegel's nonfoundational systematic philosophy
in earlier chapters I asserted that it is not, as traditionally understood, a metaphysical idealism, in that it does not purport to describe the given, and that it is nonabsolutist (a philosophy of finitude) in being self-limiting. But if it does not describe the world we
inhabit, what is this philosophy about? In Chapter 1 I contended
that it has a critical dimension. These features of Hegel's philosophy have been brought together in Chapter 8's consideration of the
Marxist critique. I have argued here that a consideration of the
salient features of systematic self-determining philosophy indicates
not only that this philosophy is self-limiting, but also that this self-
limitation must be respected if a genuine critical philosophy is
to be afforded, showing how Hegel, and not Marx, respects these
limits.

We have seen already from earlier chapters (especially Chapters 5 and 6) how nonfoundational systematic philosophy limits
itself at various places in its self-constitution, and in so doing precludes the traditional idealistic, absolutist reading in which the
system swallows up everything by reducing all otherness to itself.
Chapter 8 has now addressed these issues in regard to the system
as a whole, showing why systematic philosophy as a totality must
be strictly self-limiting. The crux of the matter is this: Hegel insists

that the essence of the system is its autonomous, immanent, self-determination. What I have shown here is that such self-determination requires radical self-closure. In order to be self-determining, nothing from without can enter in a determinative fashion into the system: it cannot base itself on anything given without sacrificing the autonomy necessary for its scientific character. But then the system cannot be taken to describe reality as given. Insofar as it affords unconditional, necessary, truth, it does so precisely by abandoning any heteronomous determination by what we might find given. Thus, Marxists (and critical theorists) who argue that a critical philosophy must be grounded in empirical science (or in some or another descriptive account of the human condition) are fundamentally mistaken. Such a foundation necessitates that something given is taken as determinative for reason, thus undermining any critical force such a philosophy may wish to have in regard to the given: It is precisely the heteronomy of the given over reason that any critical philosophy challenges, hence any purportedly critical philosophy undercuts its own critical force by seeking a foundation in anything given, for it thereby recognizes the legitimate authority of the given over critical reason. Additionally, if we wish to understand the nature of autonomy, we proceed in a self-contradictory fashion if we *first* accord the given heteronomy over reason in our considerations. It is only through the radical rejection of the claims of the given (first articulated through *Phenomenology*) that the possibility emerges of a revolutionary, critical philosophy which can comprehend the true character of autonomy because it is itself autonomous. So Hegel's rejection of the framework of givenness, of the foundational model, is necessary not only to attain philosophically objective truth. It is also called for insofar as a critical philosophy of freedom—a philosophy of modernity—is possible. And, by showing how rationally justifiable truth and autonomy coincide, Hegel indicates the justice of modernity's claims to the primacy of autonomy and the rightfulness of a rational determination of the nature of autonomy. But as Chapter 8 has shown, this precludes the possibility of a theory of praxis and the sort of philosopher kingship which Marxists claim and critical theorists long for.

Marx claimed to have overcome philosophy (and the pretensions of modern, bourgeois, society) through a new mode of theorizing called critique or praxis. A central theme of antifoundational postmodernists is also the death of philosophy. While earlier chapters have examined antifoundationalism's difficulties in providing a coherent articulation of the rejection of foundationalism and an affirmation of finitude, Chapter 9, "The Dead End of

Postmodernism," considers and criticizes Rorty's version of the postmodernist claim to have overcome philosophy. It defends an alternative view of the history of philosophy in which past philosophers are regarded as living participants in an ongoing enterprise, and further develops the notion of an antifoundational philosophy which is not the death, but the continuation of the philosophical tradition.

Chapter 9

THE DEAD END OF POSTMODERNISM

The point of living is getting ready to stay dead.
—William Faulkner

Who is not made better and wiser by occasional intercourse with the tomb?
—George Blair

Like other humans, philosophers relate to their departed ancestors in a wide variety of ways. At one extreme is a perspective suggested by Quine's joke that there are two kinds of people interested in philosophy: those interested in philosophy, and those interested in the history of philosophy. On this view of the past physically non-living philosophers are also philosophically irrelevant for the living, dead on all counts.[1] At another extreme are those historical scholars who live philosophically in a dead past, concerned only with getting dead right just what Plotinus, or Spinoza, or Marx, or other dead philosophers thought. Still others of us have a more complex—or perhaps casual—relationship with the departed. Like Odysseus, Roderick Usher, or Norman Bates, we move from the living to the (seemingly) dead and back again, not quite ignoring the difference, but not paying too much attention to it either, at least in that we do not operate with the foregone conclusion that physical decomposition is a sure indication of philosophical decease. (It may be that we believe we've found a way to engage in a dialogue with the departed even though we must keep up both sides of the conversation ourselves.)

179

As everything in philosophy seems to be related to something (if not to everything) else in philosophy, these three ways of construing a relation to thinkers who are dead and buried in the corporeal sense reflect different understandings of the status of the philosophical enterprise. I want to sketch out what they are and suggest that recent developments in philosophy indicate that there is a fourth approach, that of the zombie philosophers who have risen from the tomb like Madeline Usher to stalk the living and bring down the Fall of the House of Philosophy.

What overviews of philosophy are reflected by the three ways of relating to dead philosophers I've mentioned so far?

Quine's joke suggests a view which seems to be born out elsewhere in his work: that philosophy as conceived by the great dead philosophers, as a distinctive enterprise which is unique in attempting to assume thoroughgoing responsibility for its discourse, is dead. Philosophy has been 'naturalized.' What once passed under its name is now something to be thought of as more or less continuous with science. This intimates that, generally, those not on the scene physically are irrelevant. So, what do we do with dead philosophers? We could simply bulldoze the philosophical boneyards and erect some labs. Or, since Quine allows for the history of philosophy—albeit as something distinct from real philosophy—perhaps we should approach the dead in the manner of the real estate developers in the movie *Poltergeist*: preserve the tombstones but move them around any way we want, ignoring what's buried under them since just what the stones mark is no longer of importance to the living.

On this last point at least the outlook of the historical scholars is antithetical to the naturalizers: the historians' view is that the living need to be dead serious about what the stones mark. Yet this divergence in regard to caring about the dead buries over a basic agreement between the naturalizers and the historians. For both, the dead *are* dead and getting deader all the time. Hidden in the form of respect which the historians show for the dead is a tacit judgement about the philosophical lifelessness of those they study. For one can only be concerned centrally with getting *just* right what the physically dead have said—consumed with the importance of determining what the historical X really meant—if one believes that these figures are in fact philosophically dead. A philosopher's overwhelming attention to an elusive historical accuracy is only meaningful when that about which she aims to be accurate is assessed as fixed and final, and as such, unproblematically accessible. The texts of the dead generally are fixed and final, as is the context of their production. So directing attention to these things exclusively, to the corpse left behind, as what's most important indicates conviction about its terminal condition, as well as a philosophical naivete—or unconcern—about the questionable possibility (and the value) of determining what these texts 'really' mean. (The naivete in question stems from the scholars' insistence that, in claiming to be able to present what X really meant, they are somehow free from interpretive judgements shaped by contemporary philosophical interests. As the historian M. I. Finley puts it, we ought to beware of those who claim that their presentations of the past are free of interpretive theories, for they are merely operating with a theory which they are unaware of.)[2]

But while the historians are as willing as the naturalizers to sign death certificates, their attitude about the remains is strikingly different. Rather than leaving the dead to rot in their graves the scholars are committed to embalming. To mummify (or exhume), to reconstruct and lovingly preserve the features just as they once were is their goal. And looking more closely, we may find further agreement with the naturalizers here: to devote one's *philosophical* life to embalming the thoughts of dead philosophers would seem to indicate a conviction that whatever their overall project was, it can no longer be carried on. So where the naturalizers see themselves as having moved on to something else—science—the embalmers move back to something that once was. Both reject the possibility of the philosophical tradition as alive in the present.

The third attitude toward the dead is based on the assumption that physical decay does not necessarily indicate philosophical demise. It's an approach marked by ambiguity and a seemingly irreverent casualness towards the corpses of the departed. Marked by ambiguity, for we do not assume either that *all* dead philosophers might still be alive (or live again), or even that every part of the corpus of their works is worth attending to. Like Dr. Frankenstein some of us like to pick and choose: a heart from Hume, a liver from Leibniz, etc. Further marking our irreverence toward the dead as dead is our refusal to take the dead bodies of their texts as of paramount significance; we deflect the scholar's charge of anachronism—'that's not what X meant!'—because, refusing to regard X the philosopher as dead, we don't care all that much what the genuinely dead X (the person who really is rotting in the grave) might have meant. Unlike the historians, we do not see these texts as frozen in rigor mortis, nor do we assume that our approach to them is neutral. Thus, our sometimes casual irreverence about the remains of the departed is just what marks our conviction about and respect for the departed as those who remain alive philosophically; whether we agree or disagree with them we regard their enterprise—our enterprise—as ongoing. Our common objective is not, finally, getting right what they said, or what we might say, but rather, just *getting it right.*

Recent work in philosophy suggests another way of thinking about and dealing with those philosophers who are no longer here to speak for themselves, what I call the approach of the zombie philosophers. Those I have in mind generally are the postmodernists, especially the deconstructionists; and in particular, on this occasion, one who has reflected most systematically on the theory and practice of zombie philosophy, Richard Rorty. What does it mean to speak of zombies, and how can a philosophical movement be characterized in zombie terms?

As I hope we all know from a healthy diet of horror movies, and perhaps most recently from Michael Jackson's classic video *Thriller*, zombies are, in philosophical terms, walking contradictions: they are the *living dead.* The factual soil from which they crawl is Haitian voodoo, where a zombie is the mindless corpse of a dead person brought back to life. "Emptied of the soul, the carcass may be sold for food; the walking corpse, dead in features and mechanical in action, may be hired out as a drudge."[3] As creatures of the cinematic imagination, zombies have undergone interesting transformations. In some manifestations they escape sheer robothood to take on a life, and powers, of their own. The *locus classicus* for this zombie variation is George Romero's *Night of the Living Dead,* where, in a brilliant dialectical twist, the living dead eat the flesh of the living and transform them into zombies.

So, the notion of zombies incorporates both the living reanimating the dead as soulless slaves and the living dead consuming the life of the living in such a way that they—the living—become, not dead, but alive in death or dead in life. I will suggest that the zombie philosophers are a synthesis—or melange—of both those Haitian and Romerian concepts of zombies. Our zombie philosopher *is*, philosophically, a zombie, one of the living dead, and one who sustains this state of living death only by killing off and consuming both the living and the dead. As in the original Haitian voodoo tales, the zombie philosopher brings the (physically) dead back to a living death to serve as soulless or mindless slaves to his wishes. And as in *The Night of the Living Dead,* he works to turn the living into the living dead. In fact, both of these necrophilic tasks are combined by the zombie philosopher, for he enlists the dead he has rendered into zombies in his own zombie mission of stalking new ghouls among the still living.

What is the philosophical voodoo chant which creates zombie philosophy? Bringing zombie philosophy to life is the currently fashionable postmodern contention that truth with a capital T is unattainable and that, as a consequence, philosophy in the traditional sense, as a distinctive enterprise capable of grasping the Truth, must be carted to the morgue. What is philosophically alive about zombie philosophy—what literally gives it life—is just its act of effecting the philosophical death of the departed and their whole tradition. Physically dead philosophers are resurrected to a philosophical death; this act creates and sustains zombie philosophy. It's the basis of the larger postmodernist mission of showing just how and why it is that philosophy past and present is and must be forever devoid of life. But it is not only their peculiar use of dead philosophers which earns postmodernists the name of zombies. Further examination of the postmodernist philosophical condition reveals a deeper basis for the appellation. On the one hand, postmodernists themselves are not philosophically alive. They announce this, for central to their mission is the claim that they are not really doing philosophy. Philosophy is impossible; it's dead, and our age needs to notice the rotting corpse, entomb it, and get on to something else; on the other hand, they're not quite philosophically dead either. They present their message, they strive to effect the death of philosophy, philosophically, and they sustain their theoretical careers in and through consuming both living and dead philosophers who suggest otherwise. Thus, philosophically speaking, as neither alive or dead, they are living dead, in a word, zombies. In order to flesh out these claims, let's examine the preeminent zombie philosopher, Richard Rorty.

Rorty's crowning of himself as the voodoo high priest of the zombie philosophers is clearly evidenced in *Contingency, Irony, and Solidarity*, but the roots of his transformation from a living philosopher to a philosopher of the living dead go back to *Philosophy And The Mirror Of Nature*. In that work Rorty called our attention to a central theme of zombie philosophy: the discovery (which he attributes to his zombie forbearers Nietzsche and Heidegger) that the philosophical tradition has culminated in its own self-elimination. This sweeping diagnosis of an inevitable suicide is based on the still radical but arguably less problematic claim that the search for Truth has itself led to the discovery that there is no permanent neutral framework, no final ground in God, nature, or language to which we can refer as something which anchors our beliefs about ourselves and our world as anything more than happenstance fabrications.

This latter claim need not lead to the former zombie conclusion; it is not self-evident that a rejection of foundationalism must entail an abandonment of philosophy as concerned with objective truth. (It may only require us to reconceptualize the nature of objective truth.)[4] But for the zombie philosophers, only truth as somehow grounded or founded in a given is worthy of the name, and the disclosure of the myth of the given demands the zombie task of 'revealing' the death of philosophy. The act of revelation involves resurrecting the physically dead in order to pronounce and diagnose their philosophical death. Once dragged from their crypts to live again in philosophical death, their corpses are paraded about as exemplars of the unavoidable putrefaction of all philosophical endeavors. This display of rotting flesh is meant to create more dead philosophers by bringing those still living philosophers to recognize their terminal condition, thus enlisting them in the dance of death. *Contingency* reveals Rorty masterfully at work on this ghoulish project. Central there is his notion of "irony"; I shall now dissect it to reveal the tell-tale zombie heart beating beneath this innocent linguistic floorboard.

According to Rorty, ironist theorists (and he lists Hegel, Nietzsche, Heidegger, and Derrida as exemplars) are "the philosophers who define their achievement by their relation to their predecessors rather than by their relation to the truth."[5] So, already we find something morbid and parasitical at the core of the view Rorty espouses. One succeeds as an ironist exclusively in terms of a relation to one's predecessors, and this relation is minimally defined by contrast to a relation which seeks truth. What is the relation which the ironist seeks, and what is the goal of entering into it? We'll see that the relation is funereal and that the goal is the traditional one behind creating zombies.

The relation the ironist takes to her predecessors is what Rorty calls "redescription" and for the ironist, *everything* is redescription: Redescription is what's left to do when one realizes that Truth—a final, authoritative description—is a chimera. If the goal of truth as description must be abandoned, then, according to Rorty, what is left, short of abandoning the arena of philosophy altogether, is some treatment of the past which recognizes that it is dead.[6]

Inspecting Rorty's view of the goal of redescription further reveals its zombiesque soul. As the dead philosophers threaten to enslave us, we must enslave them. One redescribes, he announces, in order to be free of the dead, to "break the spell" cast by the philosophical tradition. "The ironist wants to find philosophy's secret, true, magical name—a name whose use will make philosophy one's servant rather than one's master."[7] So rooted in the notion that the only option is to redescribe is a fundamental conviction that *all* that is possible for philosophy now is a relation to a dead past. For to hold that we can only redescribe our predecessors— where to redescribe is to enslave—rather than enlisting them in a shared, ongoing enterprise, presupposes that no dialogue is possible, that they have no say in what is going on, that they and their enterprise are, in short, dead. More precisely, what's involved in redescription?

In Rorty's account—according to his redescription—what Nietzsche did to Hegel, what Heidegger did to Nietzsche, what Derrida has done to Heidegger (and seemingly what Rorty is doing to all of them) is to reveal how each in turn has failed to do what he claimed, to escape from the dead past of philosophy to something radically new. It is just by revealing that failure of the predecessor that each in succession seeks to effect an escape for himself. Each has proclaimed himself alive in and through his rejection of dead forbearers, a rejection which consists in showing how and why these forbearers are *still* philosophers and thus dead. Yet each of these efforts to attain life by transforming predecessors into zombies—mindless robots whose only living purpose lies in the service they render in being revealed as dead, so that it's their death as disclosed by the zombie master which gives him life—each of these efforts in turn succumbs to the same treatment. For—at the heart of ironist/zombie theory—lies the paradox of the living dead, of those who would attain and sustain philosophical life through the death of philosophy.

The paradox, of course, is that a rejection of the enterprise needs to be philosophical if it is to be successful. (As Rorty appreciates, no theorist/philosopher is endangered by the ironist poets and novelists.) Yet, if the rejective redescription is philosophical, the redescriber enslaves herself at the same time, or leaves herself open to being redescribed—made into a zombie—by someone else. According to Rorty this difficulty, "how to avoid being *aufgehoben*,"[8] is the central problem for irony theory. Every ironist theorist strives "to write something which will make it impossible to be redescribed except in one's own terms."[9] However, one can only avoid redescription either by attaining a "final vocabulary" or a uniquely private one. But final vocabularies are the stuff of philosophy, and uniquely private vocabularies are the creations of art, not theory. So in the ironists' view, properly redescribed, the philosophical world is finally an unending night of the living dead. Zombies are everywhere; they threaten one from the dead past, the living present, and the unborn future: one needs to make zombies of one's predecessors; only thereby can one avoid enslavement by them; but this selfsame act of attaining autonomy by making zombies of one's predecessors opens one to redescription, to being rendered a zombie by others.

What's problematic about zombie philosophy? Perhaps the most striking thing about it is the question of why anyone engages in it at all, since, as we've seen, if its basic premises are accepted, there is no escaping from it, and as Odysseus discovered on his visit to Hades, being undead affords little peace: one is trapped in a curious condition in which one is neither philosophizing nor not philosophizing. While the inability to escape—the zombie philosophers' entrapment in the zombie state—discloses what nonzombies see as the underlying conceptual problem with zombie philosophy, it is also that which earns postmodernists the ultimate zombie status of being philosophically undead. As Rorty acknowledges, irony theory presupposes a view of philosophy which calls for but which is incapable of successful philosophical demonstration. The ironist/postmodern attempt at total philosophical destruction must fail because only a final vocabulary would effect it. But final vocabularies are the stuff of philosophy. Thus, the very conditions which would have to be met to reach the zombies' goal of killing philosophy—attaining final authoritative truth about the nature and the (im)possibility of truth—would also constitute a rebirth of it. The ultimate paradox confronting the zombies is that the total death of philosophy would be its rebirth. Thus, for them, philosophy can neither die nor live. All that's left is the zombie state of living death where philosophy is neither alive nor dead. Zombie philosophy is not alive, because Truth cannot be attained. But it's not dead either, since that very claim is and can only be a philosophical assertion.

This curious condition of zombie philosophy—the manner in which the purportedly dead past of the philosophical tradition itself crawls from attempted entombment by the zombies to stalk them—is revealed in other ways. Consider what zombie philosophy announces as its positive goal: total liberation from the dead past, the attainment of something radically new, something which is *not* philosophy. Yet zombie philosophy is fundamentally incapable of effecting such a break. We have been promised this 'new thinking' which would be 'beyond philosophy' and radically other than it since Nietzsche. But zombie philosophy—postmodernism in its various forms—remains incapable of moving beyond its stock in trade of critiques of foundationalism, the logocentric subject, totalizing discourse etc.; all of which we have now heard *ad nauseam*. All its talk of the radically new remains just that, talk about something new which fails to present anything radically new. Why is this? I'd like to offer a suggestion as to why zombie philosophy cannot escape from being haunted and possessed by the very tradition whose death it proclaims and from which it seeks liberation.

The zombie philosophers cannot effect the sought for liberation from the past, in part, because without it they literally have nothing to say. And this ironic enslavement arises from the fact that, in the terminology of one dead philosopher, theirs remains an *abstract* negation of the past.[10] Which is to say that the problematic nature of their critique of philosophy condemns them to fall prey to the very errors they aim to denounce and to transcend. I want to illustrate this in a couple of ways before considering just what is problematic about their critique.

Consider for a moment simply the idea of attaining to a mode of discourse which is radically new, where it is presupposed that that must minimally mean 'nonphilosophical.' This very presupposition, without which postmodernism cannot claim to be post anything, prevents it from attaining anything new by tying it to that from which it aims to escape. Because it seeks total liberation, it cannot effect any genuine liberation at all. How so?

Postmodernism's goal is based on the idea of a *thoroughgoing* rejection of the traditional philosophical project. But any rejection of this all-encompassing form cannot avoid assuming a stance which is itself totalizing, i.e., philosophical. Postmodernism's wholesale rejection of the past succumbs, in a negative fashion, to the major crime which it condemns the past of having committed in a positive fashion: promulgating a discourse which is 'totalizing'—authoritarian and insensitive to difference. And postmodernism practices what it denounces *while it is in the very act of attacking authoritarian discourse and proclaiming difference.*

Postmodernism is guilty of the authoritarianism it condemns, since its wholesale condemnation of past and present philosophy recognizes no alternatives to itself as worthy of serious attention. Crucial to what is purportedly "post" in postmodernism is the deconstructive move which denies that other texts/discourses can ever succeed in saying what they mean. Their only legitimate status is as objects for the deconstructive exercise, corpses ripe for zombiehood. Thus the self-styled new thinking which purports to reject philosophical authoritarianism does so by postulating a theory which presents itself as the new—sole—authority. Similarly, its championing of difference as that which the tradition purportedly abrogates is a scam. It fails to conceptualize this difference except in terms of the tradition, as what is other than the tradition, namely, as itself. But what postmodernism *is* as other than the tradition has amounted to nothing more than the now commonplace attacks on the tradition.[11] As a theory, postmodernism has yet to get beyond its deconstructive assaults on the past to conceptualize 'difference' in positive terms, as something more than what the tradition denies or suppresses. (And if the point is that 'difference' cannot be conceptualized or grasped in theory, or *is* what cannot be grasped or conceptualized—the ineffable—this does not conflict substantively with claims made by various traditional philosophers. It amounts to nothing more than the traditional observation that not everything can be comprehended theoretically.) So what it is, postmodernism is only parasitically, in virtue of what it opposes. Thus, the 'difference' it purports to articulate is merely negative, and as merely negative fails to amount to the genuine, radical, difference being sought: one that is not a variation on traditional themes. In sum, postmodernism fails to attain or to make 'difference' possible. It does not allow for difference, and is thus just another version of the authoritarianism it attacks, because it denies the legitimacy of other, different, modes of discourse. It does not attain difference (as that which the tradition allegedly missed or suppressed) since it construes difference as what it is, and what it is, it is solely in terms of opposing the tradition.

Postmodernism's disclosure of itself as nothing more than a negative echo of the modernism it abjures shows, in another way, why it earns the name of zombie philosophy: the dead philosophers come back to enslave the living who would turn them into zombies; postmodernism transforms itself into an inverted mirror image (a merely abstract negation) of that which it aims to reject. And it is not a failure of effort or imagination which prevents this new thinking from emerging; it is rather the inadequacy of its conception of the limitations of the past which both leads and blinds postmodernism to its own repetition of the tropes it claims to be rejecting. The root of this inadequacy may be seen if we consider another instance of postmodernism falling victim to the totalizing view it aims to criticize. As noted above, the origin of the zombie project and the foundation of its criticism of the tradition is the conviction that Truth is unobtainable, a conviction based on the failure of the foundational project. (In a nutshell, the failure consists in our being unable to demonstrate that how we take things to be is how they are, independently of our description of them.) This has led to the zombie reconceptualization of obtainable truth as a personal and subjective redescription in opposition to the tradition's unattainable truth as objective description. But by insisting that the only alternative conception of truth lies in a *redescribing* which must be idiosyncratic and hence private and nonobjective, zombie philosophy again reveals its entrapment by what it aims to reject, while at the same time disclosing the problematic character of its critique of the philosophical tradition.

For redescribing is simply an inverted form, an abstract negation, of describing. In the traditional descriptive model, either the subject or the object is taken to be the determinative ground of truth. Redescription differs from that model not through an abandonment of the notion of a privileged ground for truth, but by its relocation of the privileged determiner in the text (or in language, or in Being beyond presence), rather than in the object or subject. This view denies the possibility of attaining descriptive correspondence, for the text, language, or Being are said to be incapable of being rendered transparent (or of being brought to presence for thought). But it remains committed to the traditional conceptual framework which construes truth in terms of an oppositional relation and which sees truth as grounded in something given. The commitment remains, since the sweeping denial of the possibility of obtaining objective truth can work only if we presuppose that truth must be construed in descriptive terms, as the representation of a given other (even while we deny the possibility of accessing that given). Correspondingly, the notion of a privileged determining ground for truth in a given other remains, for according to postmodernists, it is the text, or language, or Being (as entities which are prior to and always other than us) which is determinative of what we say or think (even if we cannot determine the manner in which this determination occurs). So even in its denial of our capacity to attain it, postmodernism still understands objective truth as correspondence; and even in its purportedly liberating rejection of the authority of given foundations for thought and action, it still conceives of something given as that which rules over us.

Thus, the foundation of zombie philosophy—its critique and reconceptionalization of truth—fails on two counts. For one thing, as we've seen, the reconceptualization fails to escape from the essential structure of the notion of truth being criticized. It endorses this structure (through conceiving redescription as a variation on it) and—more seriously—by denying other alternatives it unavoidably makes a descriptive truth claim. One can only unequivocally assert that subjective redescription is the best we can do as an alternative to objective description insofar as one has, or claims to have, objective knowledge of the conditions of the possibility of truth *überhaupt*. Postmodernism's whole critique of the tradition is based upon theories—of the text, of language, of Being beyond presence—which refer to and describe conditions which are said to make reference and description impossible.

Are there any positive lessons to be learned from zombie philosophy's inability to escape from the tradition? I want to briefly suggest that there are, that the failure of zombie philosophy points the way to a move beyond the tradition which is not merely negative, but positive, and which can succeed in actually getting beyond the tradition in ways in which postmodernism has not.

We have seen how deeply committed zombie philosophy is to what it opposes, even as it attempts to negate and go beyond it. More specifically, we've seen that in its attack on the tradition, postmodernism has remained unquestioningly committed to the oppositional, correspondence model of truth, and that this commitment haunts the zombie philosophers and brings them to engage in a form of philosophizing which unintentionally mimics that which it opposes. This unfortunate situation points specifically to the underlying incoherence of the model of objective truth in question. The tradition has failed to show that descriptive truth is attainable, and postmodernism, in its attempt to demonstrate that descriptive truth is unobtainable, presupposes its own capacity to afford this truth. A model of truth according to which it turns out that truth is neither demonstrably obtainable nor demonstrably unobtainable is fatally flawed. Zombie philosophers wish to conclude broadly that the whole philosophical enterprise, as concerned with truth, is impossible, or pointless. A more reasonable, minimal, conclusion would be that, not philosophy, and not truth, but the operative model of truth is questionable. What we need then is a new conception of truth, based on a recognition of what is problematic about the old one. How might a new conception take shape? Again, we need to look at the specifics of what has failed.

Modernism's and postmodernism's failures reveal that what is most fundamentally problematic is always construing truth in terms of that which is given and determinate prior to the act of conceiving or knowing it. That assumption about truth sets up an unbridgeable gulf between knowing and its object, since something about the object, as given, *always* falls beyond or outside of what can be grasped with certainty in the act of knowing.[12] And postmodernism's peculiar failure—its falling victim to what it alleges is problematic about the model in the totalizing critique which aims to get beyond objective truth entirely—suggests that a more effective escape may lie in not attempting a total negation of the conception of truth as knowable, but in a determinate negation of this particular model of truth. A determinate negation would be this: if the problem lies in construing 'knowing the truth' in terms of 'representing a given determinate object,' let us specifically begin by not construing our subject matter as already having a given determinate content, but as indeterminate. Correlatively, let us abandon the schema of *re*presentation. Let us not assume in our cognizing of this subject matter that it is always already minimally determinate (not only in terms of a given content but also) simply in virtue of being an other, an 'object for a consciousness,' and thus present for representation.

Making the specific rejections suggested would effect a determinate negation of the old model because, rather than attempting to abandon the conception of objective, knowable truth wholesale and in an unequivocal manner, we instead abandon as necessary foundational presuppositions just the two features of the traditional understanding of truth which make it problematic: the tradition's (and postmodernism's) unquestioned assumptions that cognition always begins with a given determinate object, and that knowing consists in a determinate relation to such an object. Put differently, we would begin by specifically and deliberately not assuming that the structure of subjectivity or consciousness—the ordinary manner in which we construe knowing—is unconditionally determinative for philosophical cognition. (Of course, to refuse to begin by taking that traditional assumption for granted would not preclude a subsequent consideration of it, after the nature of philosophical cognition is established.)

Further consideration of what gets rejected also enables us to see what remains from the traditional notion of truth. What is not abandoned, and what now becomes realizable are philosophy's traditional goals of attaining certain truth in an unconditional, self-legitimating fashion. Yet we shall see that the manner in which these goals become realizable entails a transformation of the traditional understanding of what they consist in.

Insofar as we begin our consideration in such a way that there is not already a subject matter construed as an 'object,' standing determinate prior to and outside of cognition itself, then the act of cognition would be thoroughly constitutive of the subject matter in its determinacy. And insofar as the always hitherto presupposed determinate difference between cognition and its object has been rejected as a model, cognition here may begin in just as indeterminate a fashion as its subject matter. That is, the act of cognition would also be constitutive of the character of cognition as determinate. The initial dual indeterminacy of cognition and its subject matter follow from the determinate negation discussed above. For precisely what has been rejected is the model which always construes cognition as necessarily involving a minimal predetermination, i.e., the predetermination (1) that the subject matter of cognition must always be something already given in its determinacy, and (2) the predetermination that cognition involves a relation between such an object and a knower. The abandonment of these predeterminations, which makes it possible that now neither cognition nor its subject matter would possess any already given determinacy, also makes it possible to attain the two of the tradition's goals mentioned above.

First, the certainty of truth long sought for by the tradition and denied by postmodernism would be afforded in that what comes to be known and the knowing 'of' it are no longer separated by an unbridgeable gulf. Since any determinate distinction between cognition and its subject matter is missing, and since neither possesses any pregiven determinacy, the insoluble problem of attaining certain truth by establishing correspondence between knowledge and its object fails to arise. As lacking in determinacy, the subject matter would not bring anything already given to the act of cognition which would be ungraspable by cognition. Correlatively, as equally lacking in predetermination, the cognitive act would not bring anything determinate to distort or antecedently determine what is cognized. Thus, any and all emerging determinacy would arise from the activity itself and thus the possibility of failing to establish this determinacy just as what it is would be absent. (How determinacy might arise out of indeterminacy is another question.[13])

Further reflection on the conditions which make it possible for certain truth to be attained reveals how another of philosophy's traditional goals (also denied by postmodernism) can be reached. Philosophy has long sought to be that mode of discourse which is distinctive from others in assuming thoroughgoing responsibility for itself; it has aimed to attain a radical self-legitimation by establishing its mode of discourse as thoroughly self-constitutive, and hence unconditioned and autonomous, because lacking in any ground or foundation outside of itself. Insofar as cognition and its subject matter here lack any already given determinacy, any determinacy arrived at could arise exclusively from the activity in question in a transparent fashion, since conditioned by nothing antecedently determined. There would then be no external grounds or foundations for what this mode of discourse comes to establish, and as constituted without foundations, it would be self-grounding. As dependent in its determinate character on nothing outside of itself, responsibility for what comes to be determined in this discourse would fall exclusively to the discourse itself, and in this sense it would be self-legitimating.[14]

But while specifically rejecting the tradition's assumption about cognition and truth allows for a self-grounding mode of discourse which affords certain truth, further consideration of how this can come to pass through a determinate negation shows that others of the tradition's goals are, and must be abandoned.

For one thing, the certain truth established is the truth of self-constitutive discourse, a discourse made possible specifically by rejecting the idea that certain truth concerning the given can be known. Thus, the truth—the determinacies—established by this discourse cannot be construed as descriptive of the given. So, the price of attaining the tradition's goal of certain truth established in a self-grounding discourse is that we must abandon the tradition's belief that such discourse can tell us anything *a priori* about a given world. (By abandoning the notion that the proper subject matter of philosophy is somehow already always given in its determinacy, it becomes possible for philosophy to be demonstrably truth-affording, autonomous, and self-constitutive; but sacrificing the anchor in the given also means that we cannot assume any necessary connections between this discourse and the given.) We must abandon the tradition's guiding belief, going back to Parmenides, that the conditions of logos are the conditions of being. With this abandonment, of course, we also abandon the conditions for the possibility of both realist and idealist metaphysics, as well as the notion that philosophy is foundational—in the sense of determining the necessary conditions—of other modes of discourse which do concern themselves with cognition of the given as it is given. Thus, this mode of discourse, even while it can claim certain truth and self-legitimacy for its own domain, represents a radical break from the tradition. It is limited in the scope of its claims, and is neither totalizing nor authoritarian in the manner criticized by postmodernists.

While it could claim to speak authoritatively in a limited domain—in regard to the nature and range of what is determined or constituted without predeterminations—this discourse only attains this authority by recognizing that certain truth pertains only to what is self-constitutive. Thus, any claim to authority this philosophical discourse might make would be to speak authoritatively only over the domain of that which can be conceived autonomously, i.e., without externally determinative predeterminations. In more traditional jargon its claim to authority would be restricted thus: this discourse would speak only about that which unconditioned thought or autonomous reason can establish. In addition, as nondescriptive, the discourse could only have a normative authority: not authority concerning what is (understood as what is given) but authority concerning what ought to be according to reason. Thus, it would not incorporate within itself other modes of discourse which recognize the authority of the given, nor would it supplant them or deny their right to speak of the given, except insofar as in so doing, they claim to articulate unconditional truth. The right of this discourse to deny the name of unconditional truth to modes of discourse which recognize the given as their starting point follows from the revelation that discourses which presuppose a foundation in the given cannot even establish that certain truth concerning the nature of the given is attainable. As we have seen, they undermine their own presumption to afford truth in the philosophical sense of the term.

So, while this discourse is genuinely pluralistic in that, unlike postmodernism, it does not deny altogether the legitimacy of modes of discourse other than itself, it is not relativistic, for it does not hold that all discourses are equally true (or untrue) but rather than only one mode of discourse can attain demonstrable truth. Of course the *acknowledgment* of any normative authority for this discourse would presuppose a belief in the rightful authority of truth; a belief in the consummately modernist philosophical conviction that what is, is not justifiable simply because it is; a belief in the subversive notion that the given world ought to accord, insofar as is possible, with the demands of reason. So, while it would not replace them, or deny altogether the legitimacy of modes of discourse which purport to describe the given, this discourse would demand the acknowledgment that these modes of discourse are inescapably limited; their limitedness being founded in the relative character of any attempt to describe the given. And the legitimacy of the normative authority of this philosophical discourse (*vis-à-vis* descriptive modes of discourse) would follow from the problematic character of acknowledging any final normative authority for what is given over what reason can establish on its own. Since any claim to know the given must be relative and conditional, the very notion that what is (construed on the basis of a description of the given) has legitimate normativity is insupportable, simply because we have no conclusive means for determining "what is." Since the very idea of normativity presupposes the ability to claim a rightful distinction between (at least some) cases, it follows that any consistent normativity must acknowledge the rightful authority of reason over the given, on the already mentioned grounds that accounts of the given are inescapably relative and hence incapable of establishing any but a finally arbitrary ground for distinguishing between cases. The rightful authority of reason over the given follows, since relativity and normativity are logically incompatible. If we have no grounds for objectively distinguishing between cases we also have no nonarbitrary grounds for preferring one to the other, and if we have no nonarbitrary grounds for preference we have no norms, for to speak of a norm is, by definition, to speak of that which is not arbitrary. But we have no grounds for objectively distinguishing between different descriptive accounts of the given. Hence no account of the given can provide a basis for legitimate normativity.

And while the absence of constitutive predeterminations opens the possibility of a discourse which could be complete (in the sense that all of its determinations would be internally engendered and not dependent in and as what they are on anything 'outside,' on anything already given as determinate), it would not be totalizing (in the sense of claiming that these determinations are capable of grasping or accounting for that which we might indeed find given). So rather than committing what postmodernists regard as the inevitable blasphemy of any philosophy which lays claim to objective truth—promulgating a totalizing, authoritarian discourse which refuses to recognize that which is different and 'other'—this approach presupposes a recognition of radical otherness—of irreducible givenness as that which cannot be grasped by philosophical thought—just in its beginning in and through the determinate rejection of the model of truth and cognition which erroneously assumes that given otherness can be truly known. And thus, rather than abrogating finitude, as postmodernism claims philosophical pretensions to know the truth must, this mode of discourse begins in and through a recognition of the inevitably finite character of all claims to know the given. Unlike postmodernism however, it refuses to absolutize this mode of knowing in its finitude.

In its denial of objective truth and of the possibility of philosophy, postmodernism fetishes and absolutizes a radical otherness or difference as an other that can never be known—except, of course, by postmodernism, which somehow knows this other, zombie fashion, in its unknowability. The approach I am suggesting does not require this self-referentially inconsistent claim, and while it recognizes the given as genuinely other than itself—by its refusal to attempt to describe it, or to supplant modes of discourse which do—it does not transform otherness, the given, the irreducibly different, into a new transhuman authority which must be bowed before. If truth construed in terms of 'determination given in an other' cannot be attained, then truth construed in terms of self-determination—in terms of autonomy, most broadly and fundamentally conceived—becomes an option worth pondering.

Chapter 9 has argued that the most radical of the antifoundationalist claims—to have overcome philosophy and replaced it with something new—is without substantiation, despite the continuing appeal of postmodernist orthodoxy. I have contended that postmodernism, especially in its Rortian version, can be helpfully thought of as a version of zombie philosophy: it is philosophically neither alive nor dead, but undead, and has as its goal the recruiting of new zombies from among dead as well as living philosophers. Zombie philosophers are not alive, for their message is that philosophy is something impossible and dead; it is not what they do, for they know that objective truth is unattainable. But they are not philosophically dead either, they have not left philosophy behind for something else. For they make philosophical arguments to effect the death of philosophy, and they continually rob the graveyards of philosophy's history, resurrecting the dead to zombiehood in order to substantiate their morbid contentions. This chapter has diagnosed the central flaw in the zombie position: disclosing that truth cannot be construed in foundational terms and in accordance with the correspondence model does not show that there cannot be another conception of truth, one capable of a radical legitimation. Once again we can see that, when carefully examined, antifoundationalism remains committed to the foundational notions it claims to transcend: Only if truth must be conceived foundationally can we hold that no other mode of truth is possible. But antifoundationalism cannot claim this, for it purports to show that foundationalism, which asserts that its model of truth is universally valid, cannot succeed in such an endeavor. Thus antifoundationalism must fail in its efforts to bring philosophy to an end by showing that the search for objective truth cannot possibly attain its goal. Every attempt to bring an end to philosophy recreates it, even if only implicitly, since the very weapon used to destroy philosophy is, and must be, philosophical argumentation itself.

However, Chapter 9 has done more than reassert the familiar charge of self-referential inconsistency. In addition it has argued that postmodernists have not made, and cannot make, good on their claim to offer something new, a new, nonphilosophical mode of thought. The flaw has been seen to lie in the indiscriminate, totalizing character of their critique of philosophical truth: even in purporting to reject it, their commitment to the foundational model—their inability to think beyond it—is revealed in what postmoderns offer as an alleged substitute. Rather than escaping from the past, postmodernism is disclosed here as a feeble echo, a ghost of the foundational past it strives so earnestly to do away with.

Beyond this, Chapter 9 has further disclosed how a systematic philosophy in the Hegelian mold *can* afford a discourse which succeeds where postmodernism fails, in being nontotalizing, nonauthoritarian, and respectful of difference—while still avoiding relativism by means of a new conception of objectivity found in the irreducibly modernist notion of self-determination. The history of foundationalism and antifoundationalism shows that construing truth as founded in a *given* determinacy has proved aporetic; the specific alternative is to conceive truth in terms of self-determination. Chapter 9 has further indicated just how self-determination may be attained insofar as neither the object nor subject of cognition are taken as determinate givens. And it has also argued that conceiving truth as self-determination makes possible the realization of two of philosophy's traditional goals: the attainment of truth which is certain and self-grounding. As not grounded in any given, the truth of systematic philosophy is critical, in that it articulates how things ought to be when conceived from the standpoint of autonomous reason. Correlatively, as not grounded in any given, it does not challenge accounts of the given (except insofar as they claim demonstrable universal validity) and is consequently not totalizing. Thus, while systematic philosophy affords unconditional, nonrelative, truth (for as radically self-determining, the truth of this discourse is not relative to or conditioned by any givens), it does so in a manner which avoids the pitfalls of absolutism antifoundationalists abhor. It does so in part just because it recognizes, and differentiates itself from, the radical otherness of the given and those other modes of discourse which begin with what is given.

Chapter 10 considers yet another contemporary attempt to avoid the problems of foundationalism and the epistemological gambit, that of Donald Davidson. Comparing his work with Kant's, I argue that Davidson can be seen as part of the transcendental project which seeks to sidestep certain foundational difficulties while still arriving at foundationalist conclusions. Although Davidson avoids certain pitfalls that Kant succumbed to, I contend that he is still wedded to foundationalist assumptions and does not succeed in his attempt to legitimate knowledge.

Chapter 10

THE RENEWED APPEAL TO
TRANSCENDENTAL ARGUMENTS

We are in for a sequentiality of improbable possibles.

—James Joyce

In recent years philosophers from both the continental and analytic traditions have subjected what has come to be known as foundationalism to a sustained barrage of attacks. Not the least of what is controversial about these attacks is that they seem to render suspect not only a good part of the philosophical tradition, but also the idea or ideal of epistemic and metaphysical objectivity associated with it.[1] Denying that there is anything like an undistorted or neutral cognitive standpoint—a foundational, God's eye, view from nowhere—antifoundationalists have asserted the perspectival, embedded, or located character of all cognition.[2] Their claims about the impossibility of attaining a foundational standpoint—put positively, their assertion that knowledge conditions are unavoidably opaque—and their consequent claim concerning the embeddedness of knowledge are usually accompanied by a rejection of metaphysical and epistemological realism. We are counseled to abandon the notion that we can meaningfully lay claim to manifestly objective knowledge of a real world of mind independent objects.

Donald Davidson, however, is a prominent exception to the widespread tendency of coupling a rejection of foundationalism with a dismissal of the twin realisms. While he holds that knowledge cannot have foundations, while he rejects the idea of epistemic confrontation and scheme/content dualism, he has nonetheless endorsed a view of the knowing situation which involves the idea of correspondence.[3] In addition, he has argued for the realistic conception of a reality which supersedes the subjective and which is objectively knowable in the straightforward, traditional, and nonrelative sense most antifoundationalists reject.[4] Yet at least part of his argument here (toward these foundationalist ends of correspondence and realism) hinges upon demonstrating the untenability of certain foundationalist notions (chiefly confrontation and scheme/content dualism). So, it would seem that Davidson wants to abandon at least part of the central conceptual apparatus of traditional foundationalism while at the same time—or even in and through this abandonment—endorsing some of the conclusions it sought to establish.

What makes Davidson's position especially interesting—and perhaps puzzling—is the fact that he makes use of transcendental arguments to achieve these ends.[5] This may seem puzzling because the transcendental approach in philosophy is usually associated both with scheme/content dualism and with a full-blown, foundationalist program. Thus, locating Davidson within the scheme defined by the traditional relationship between foundationalism, transcendental argumentation, and the idea of a conceptual scheme seems difficult. Can the transcendental approach be separated from scheme/content dualism and foundationalism? More importantly, can one salvage correspondence and present a successful philosophical defense of realism while abandoning this dualism and the idea of epistemic confrontation? I want to explore Davidson's transcendental philosophy with these—and especially the latter—questions in mind. In what immediately follows I will try to sort out and assess his transcendental procedure by first considering his relation to the preeminent transcendental philosopher. First I will take up the similarities, then the differences between Kant's and Davidson's transcendental approaches.

Transcendental philosophy has been closely associated both with the foundationalist conception of knowledge discussed above and with the foundationalist endeavor itself. In much of the literature which discusses foundationalism, Kant is given pride of place with Descartes as a paradigmatic foundationalist philosopher. While Davidson rejects both the idea that knowledge has foundations and the understanding of knowledge based on a conceptual scheme, the attempt to articulate the foundations of knowledge in terms of a conceptual scheme is central to Kant's transcendental project.[6] How then can we locate Davidson in this tradition?

We can begin by appreciating the extent to which both Kant's and Davidson's transcendental approaches share, in certain important respects, comparable motivations and goals. Speaking broadly, both turn to transcendental approaches in attempts to arrive in an indirect fashion at realist conclusions about the objectivity of knowledge and reality while avoiding the difficulties to which a more direct route to these conclusions seems to lead. What I see as integral to their common transcendental approach is the idea that we can establish the legitimacy of our subjective claims to knowledge of objectivity by a process of reasoning which avoids appealing to some conception of a directly discoverable evidentiary connection between what are taken to be the separate domains of subjectivity and objectivity.[7] In adopting the indirect-transcendental approach to realism[8] both renounce the confrontationalist vision of a connecting bridge linking subjectivity and objectivity; both also reject the idea of a standpoint that transcends subjectivity, yet both seek to do so without totally collapsing or eliminating the distinction between subjectivity and objectivity. Although they go about it in significantly different ways, each of their transcendental attempts to preserve objectivity and demonstrate its accessibility without breaching subjectivity involves reconceiving the subjective domain in such a way that objectivity comes to be seen as somehow necessarily 'present' or 'manifest' within subjectivity, so that no confrontational bridge is needed. Rather than conceiving subjective and objective either as radically separate domains which need to be tied together, or as finally indistinguishable, these transcendental thinkers attempt to reveal that, and how, subjectivity and objectivity are at one and the same time distinct yet inseparable. Before seeing how this transcendental gambit is meant to work, what, more specifically, is the problem with confrontationalist epistemology which it is designed to avoid?

The central difficulty which the transcendental approach aims to meet can be put in various ways. For example, one might point out that every attempt to establish a connecting bridge between subjectivity and objectivity fails, indeed must fail, because the specification of the linking medium as tying (or leading) into the subjective immediately erects a barrier to the objective. Everything we can compare our subjective notions with is, in virtue of being comparable, itself something subjective and hence no longer serviceable for establishing a *real* comparison. To phrase the difficulty in the linguistic mode Davidson favors: Every attempt to present the facts to which language corresponds calls for a specification of facts in language. If the question is not begged—if it is not assumed that language fits the facts—then the purportedly evidentiary specification of facts in language is really no evidence at all for language's accessibility to the facts.[9] The 'fit' has not been shown. Confrontationalist epistemologies confront a major problem: Objectivity must be brought within subjectivity in order for the confrontational comparison to take place, but once objectivity is brought within, its evidentiary status is compromised. Thus, conceptualizing the project of demonstrating how we have objective knowledge of a real (trans-subjective) world in terms of a subjectivity's capacity for coming into contact with what is conceived as lying radically beyond its domain seems to reinforce our entrapment in that domain.[10]

Thus the very effort to show that how we take things to be is how they are by describing some apparatus or procedure which ties together what are originally conceived as separate domains not only fails to demonstrate the correspondence of subjectivity and objectivity; additionally, it reinforces our isolatedness in subjectivity by undermining any naive confidence we might have had about the accessibility of objectivity. Trying to show how the separate domains of subjectivity and objectivity can be tied together results in a startling realization: The chasm between these domains cannot be bridged. Rather than dispelling skeptical and solipsistic doubts, confrontationalist epistemologies would seem to put them on a more secure footing.

The transcendental approach may be thought of as an attempt to turn this problem into its own resolution. It strives to make a virtue out of the inescapability of subjectivity by trying to get us to rethink the idea that subjectivity can properly be understood as something within which we are trapped, forever cut off from an objectivity lying beyond. The broad program of the transcendental approach is fittingly captured in Kant's notion of a Copernican revolution, for it involves a radical alteration or inversion of perspective in which an attempt is made to turn the situation which seems to call for skepticism (unbridgeable subjectivity) against skepticism itself. I call the transcendental approach an indirect one because, rather than asserting that there is a bridge, it involves an attempt to show that, properly understood, subjectivity and objectivity are such that a bridge between them is unnecessary.

So at the heart of the transcendental enterprise is a process of reconceptualization. Transcendental thinkers ask us to interiorize objectivity at least in the sense of seeing that objectivity thought of as a radically separate inaccessible domain does not make sense. How does the transcendental procedure of reconceptualization and interiorization work? With an eye to answering this question I will now discuss the procedure more specifically, but still in general terms as one common to Kant and Davidson. Then I will move on to a discussion of details which will bring out the considerable differences in their approaches.

In both Kant and Davidson, the transcendental procedure involves two stages: (1) Objectivity is subjectivized or interiorized; (2) It is argued that the distinction between objectivity *as subjectivized* (how things appear, how we describe them in language) and some *radically other* objectivity (some conception of objectivity which might be inaccessible from the domain of subjectivity) is unintelligible or incoherent.

In speaking of the subjectification of objectivity, (step one) what I have in mind is a conceptual reorientation through which talk of our access to objectivity is brought within or recast in terms of what can be found within subjectivity, understood as that domain to which we are held to have unproblematic access. In the transcendental enterprise generally, "subjectivity"—however otherwise defined—is just that domain whose workings are held to be privileged or to possess a kind of epistemic primacy because of our purportedly unmediated access to it. In psychological terms the subjective domain is that of the thinking subject: mind, ego, consciousness, the understanding. If we make the linguistic turn and concentrate on language as our starting point we may avoid using these terms. The focus of attention remains the same, however. For in either case there is a basic sense among those concerned that we must look to a domain of epistemic primacy in order to clarify all else. In other words, it seems to be generally agreed—and this whether the theory employs psychological or linguistic terms—that all philosophically respectable talk of cognition presupposes a domain of epistemic primacy.[11] That domain is commonly and, I suspect, not infelicitously, called the subjective domain.

Once we are brought then to understand how objectivity is in some sense a feature of subjectivity, we can take the second step. This involves getting us to see that this conception of objectivity (as accessible because wedded to subjectivity) is the only intelligible conception of objectivity. To make this point both Kant and Davidson mount an attack on the meaningfulness of the idea of an objectivity which is radically other in the sense of lying beyond all grasp by subjectivity. So, the second step involves a movement from interiorized or subjectified objectivity (the conceptualization, articulated in step one, of objectivity in terms of what takes place or is found within subjectivity) to the 'objectification' of this whole interiorized or subjectified domain.

What I mean here in speaking of the second step as a process of objectification—the objectification of subjectivity—needs to be carefully stated. The second, objectifying (or reobjectifying step) is *not* an attempt to move back outside of the domain of subjectivity in question. It is *not* an attempt to *show how* objectivity as subjectively conceived really does correspond to something else lying outside. Such a move would constitute a return to the confrontationalist epistemology of bridge building. But on the other hand, the second step also does not involve an attempt to thoroughly reduce objectivity to subjectivity. The transcendental thinker as an objectivist and a realist cannot be seen as holding that there is nothing other than subjectivity. Both Berkeleyan and absolute idealism must be avoided. What he wants to show is that objectivity is other than subjectivity without being something so radically other as to be thoroughly beyond and completely inaccessible from it.

How can this procedure be reconstructed more specifically (and what are its problems)? Looking at the first step—the subjectification of objectivity, the conceptualization of objectivity in terms of subjectivity—more closely, it involves first the specification of what are taken to be some unchallengeably given, obvious features of our human subjectivity. We begin with some aspects of the domain of subjectivity whose basic nature is, or seems to be, immediately accessible to us, with some feature or features of the life world which are unproblematically present.

In the case of Kant the domain of subjectivity is defined as consciousness, and our attention its drawn to the unassailable fact that conscious experience is by and large not random or chaotic but spatially, temporally, and causally organized in such a way that it manifests overall coherence or intelligibility. In the case of Davidson the domain of subjectivity is defined as language, and attention is drawn to the fact that we use language as a medium of communication, that, by and large, we understand others and they us.[12]

Once such sweeping and unassailable features of our life world have been laid out we are then asked to consider how these phenomena are to be explained or accounted for. And both—despite their different construals of the subjective domain—present accessible objectivity as a necessary explanatory condition for those given unassailable features of subjectivity whose explanation is being sought. What is found to be given in subjectivity is held to be explicable only insofar as objectivity is accessible. And further, for both, addressing the accessibility of objectivity involves thinking of objectivity either as something established (Kant) or always already manifest (Davidson) within the domain of subjectivity. In the case of Kant, objectivity is seen as accessible because it is to be understood as partially constituted by subjectivity. In the case of Davidson, objectivity is seen as accessible in that our access to it is construed in terms of an operation present within subjectivity. Kant asks us to understand objectivity as a product of a synthesizing transcendental ego. Davidson asks us to understand objectivity as necessarily immanent within language as understandable. In both cases objectivity is subjectivized in the sense that a procedure said to be inseparable from subjectivity—the constitution of the unity of consciousness, the determination of linguistic meaning—is explained as an activity which can be accounted for only on the condition of the involvement of objectivity in it. In both cases objectivity is subjectivized in the sense of coming to be viewed in and through its role as a necessary component of relations established and holding within the domain of subjectivity. What we find is that the accessibility of objectivity—and by implication the very nature of objectivity as accessible—is tied to a constitutive activity (synthesis, meaning determination) which establishes the essential nature of subjectivity.

How do these reconceptualizations of objectivity in terms of a relation established within the domain of subjectivity take shape? What, more specifically, is step one?

Kant's contention is that experience as we find it given must be explained by reference to the activity of a transcendental ego which synthesizes the sensibly given manifold according to rules. My experience and that which it is experience of are construed as correlative byproducts of this ego's activity. The question of whether things as I know them correspond to things as they are is resolved by conceiving both sides of the relation as resulting from the common synthesizing action. The certainty we can have about what we know stems from the invariability of the scheme—the categories or rules—as applied to a content given in sensible intuition. Objective certainty is not a matter of getting beyond the subjective but of the alleged necessity of carrying out the synthesizing process according to rules, a necessity said to be required insofar as we are to explain experience as we find it given.

For Davidson too the issue of objectivity—and more specifically an account of truth as a correspondence relation established within the domain of the subjective—is central to his account of the conditions of the possibility of the linguistic phenomenon he wants to explain.[13] Just as our ability to know things as they are is basic to the Kantian explanation of experience, so is it basic to Davidson's account of how it is possible for us to understand language.

Davidson's contention is that our ability to understand the utterances of a language can best be explained by reference to a Tarski-style theory of truth. In terms of such a theory, one's ability to understand an utterance is tied to one's knowledge of its truth conditions. Generally, understanding a language means being able to specify truth conditions according to a rule or formula. Thus, as with Kant, explaining a given feature of our life world is tied to presenting objectivity as accessible. In this instance our ability to understand is tied to our ability to determine under what conditions a statement is true or false. And also, as with Kant, this accessibility itself is specified in terms of a relation of correspondence internal to the domain of subjectivity. Following Tarski's formula, knowledge of truth conditions is a linguistic matter: To know the truth conditions for an utterance S is to be able to assert S is true if and only if p, where p is itself a statement, either in the same or another language. Access to objectivity is described in terms of an activity internal to the domain of subjectivity: translation.[14]

So both Kant and Davidson make access to objectivity a condition of subjectivity, and both aim to avoid confrontationalist bridge building by construing access in terms of a correspondence relation established within subjectivity. Yet despite the general parallels between the Kantian and Davidsonian transcendental projects considered so far, there are considerable—one might even say radical—differences in their approaches. These differences pertain not only to how each defines the domain of subjectivity but also to the ways in which they go about construing objectivity from within that domain. I want to consider what I see as the essential difference in the ways they carry out what I have called the first step of subjectivizing objectivity. I'll suggest that Davidson's procedure can be thought of as designed to avoid problems with the Kantian approach. After briefly considering what these problems are and how Davidson attempts to avoid them, I'll then assess how he carries out the second step, which I have not discussed in terms of Kant. Here, Davidson's arguments to show why an objectivity inaccessible to subjectivity is incoherent will receive special attention.

The crux of the difference between the ways in which Kant and Davidson subjectivize lies in the fact that Kant is concerned with the transcendental psychology or mechanics, with the architecture and dynamics of the actual connective relation between subjectivity and objectivity, while Davidson is not. For Kant, the issue of *how* a fit between subjectivity and objectivity is established is crucial, while for Davidson, avoiding this issue is crucial.

Unlike Davidson, Kant attempts to give a precise explanation of the manner in which objectivity is accessible from within subjectivity. His way of attempting to avoid the problem of bridging separate domains is to postulate the transcendental ego as concurrently constitutive of both domains.[15] But this approach, as Davidson sees, cannot really avoid the traditional epistemological confrontational problems. Rather than getting around the problem of contact and confrontation between two domains, it now emerges twice, both internally and externally. For even if experience and its objects are the correlative products of a synthesis, the question remains how what come together in subjectivity are predisposed to being synthesized: How is it that scheme (the transcendental categories) and content (the sensibility given) happen to fit? Insofar as the activity of synthesis is an operation carried out on something *given* to subjectivity, the question of linking separate domains remains, even if it has been raised at a different level. Instead of asking how knowledge and object correspond, we now need to inquire how it is that spontaneity and receptivity are coordinated. In addition, the mechanics of Kant's internalization of objectivity leads to the re-emergence of an unknowable objectivity beyond: in accounting for our knowledge of things this is reduced to knowledge of things as they appear. So knowledge is something relative to our scheme. It is knowledge of phenomena, not of things-in-themselves from which we remain cut off.

The avoidance of these problems is essential to Davidson. That is why he eschews any consideration of transcendental mechanics. For Davidson there can be no talk of how any evidentiary contact or connection, any mediation between subjectivity—language—and objectivity—the world—is effected. "The moral is obvious. Since we can't swear intermediaries to truthfulness, we should allow no intermediaries between our beliefs and their objects in the world.[16] While Davidson does speak of "the causal relations between our beliefs and speech and the world,"[17] he is careful to insist that such relations carry no epistemological burden. As a self-described coherentist and antifoundationalist,[18] for him the very idea that we can make sense of evidentiary connections, or construe our knowledge of the world as something that can be justified or guaranteed by an appeal to some notion of how knowledge and the world join up, is anathema. "What we must guard against," he writes, "are epistemic intermediaries."[19]

Davidson's refusal to address the question of the means and methods whereby we make contact with objectivity is, as we'd expect, manifest in the contrast between his and Kant's subjectification of objectivity. Davidson's account of our access to the objective in terms of an intralinguistic relationship is not at all constructivist in the manner of Kant. In fact, while truth is characterized in terms of a linguistic relation, nothing at all is said about *how* we come to know the truth conditions for a statement.[20] Our ability to know objectively is wedded to linguistic capability;[21] to be an objective knower is to be in a position of being able to provide T sentences.[22] (Or, one's knowledge is manifest in one's ability to translate.) But nothing is said in an extralinguistic vein about how one comes to be in that position. There is no talk of how language ties to things—"nothing can reveal how a speaker's words have been mapped on to objects"[23]—and Davidson is adamant in his rejection of that approach. There can be no justification for our holding a sentence true "outside of other sentences held true. . . ."[24] I think the implication here is that coming to learn how to use a language and coming to know the world are inseparable, and I will return to this point later.

In any case, it seems that, for Davidson, knowledge of the world as expressible in language functions as part of the explanans in his account of language as a medium of communication. Our general ability to know and describe what there is, is—at this juncture—taken for granted. Thus more is required for Davidson to complete his transcendental project as a defense of realism. How can the idea of correspondence be saved if there is to be no construal of a link, no cogent story respecting that which establishes or guarantees correspondence? How can we be assured that the world as described in language is not just "our own picture of things"? What assurance do we have that "what we take there to be is pretty much what there is?"[25] On what basis can Davidson claim that "by studying the most general aspects of language we will be studying the most general aspects of reality?"[26] Davidson's refusal to address the question of the contact between language and the world—however well founded—seems to leave us all the more confined within subjectivity, in no position to answer the questions just posed.

I want to suggest that Davidson attempts to answer them and to complete the transcendental procedure by arguing in a manner which, initially at least, seems to involve reinforcing our understanding of the extent to which we are 'trapped' within subjectivity, unable to step beyond or outside of language. In his rejection of attempts to construe contacts between subjectivity and objectivity, Davidson is, in a sense, more radically subjectivist than Kant. But his position, I think, is that it is just a radical or thoroughgoing subjectivism—a subjectivism without limits—that leads to a satisfactory objectivism. Or as he puts it, "coherence yields correspondence."[27] I would summarize his argumentative position metaphorically in this way: Understanding the dimensions of our purported entrapment within subjectivity—within language—is accompanied by the revelation that we are effectively cut off from nothing. For we cannot help coming to the realization that the borders of the trap are unavoidably unspecifiable or untouchable from within.

Davidson moves in this direction, taking the second step of the transcendental procedure by attempting to reveal the conceptual untenability of an inaccessible objectivity, in essays such as "On the Very Idea of a Conceptual Scheme" and "A Coherence Theory of Truth and Knowledge." What he offers us here are transcendental arguments which have a general form. They are designed to show that our inability to effect an epistemological escape from language—evident from the fact that every articulation of what language refers to, every specification of the facts is *in* language[28]—does not provide evidence of our entrapment. Rather, this manifest inability calls into question the intelligibility of the perspective from which we can meaningfully regard language as a trap, as something from which we should like to escape. Davidson's general point is that we can come to regard objectivity as generally accessible because no attempt to articulate the conditions of its general *in*accessibility can succeed. Failure to demonstrate inaccessibility is unavoidable—skepticism and relativism fail—because we cannot provide a meaningful formulation of the notion that we are trapped within language. Every attempt to do so requires an effort to articulate what lies outside this trap in order to specify and substantiate its entrapping or limiting powers. But making this effort requires us to draw what is purportedly outside within the domain of the intelligible and the communicable. To show the inaccessibility of objectivity from language we need to be able to specify in language just what it is about objectivity that lies beyond us, but doing this can only manifest its accessibility.

One way in which Davidson makes this point is by considering the notion of language as a conceptual scheme. According to the conceptual schemer's view, language is something which sets a limiting or distorting condition on what we can know: As a scheme, it stands as an intermediary between us and the given. So this is one way of understanding language as a perspectival trap. Yet to sort out this view of language, Davidson argues, we must do something we cannot: make sense of an alternative conceptual scheme. The supposition that there is at least one alternative scheme—in Davidson's terms, an untranslatable language—is a necessary condition of the intelligibility of the idea that we are operating within the constraints of a conceptual scheme that does not do justice to things as they are. Only if there is an alternative view can one claim that one's own is *a* view, just a perspective.[29] But every attempt to make sense of such alternatives requires us to grasp a view which is correct—true relative to the scheme—but not translatable into our own. And as truth is inseparable from translatability, this cannot be done. To understand or make sense of a different conceptual scheme is, unavoidably, to make it our own. Thus the idea of language as a potentially distortive or alternative medium between us and the world simply cannot be cashed out, given Davidson's understanding of the necessary conditions for interpretation.

Davidson argues to a similar conclusion in "A Coherence Theory of Truth and Knowledge."[30] Again, the position under consideration is one which denies that objectivity is accessible in language. In this case we are asked to reflect on the possibility that our (or someone else's) subjective conception of things—the world as described in language—is globally mistaken. Davidson contends that reflecting on this possibility leads us to preclude it because we finally realize that the notion of global error is unintelligible. Only that which we can understand is intelligible, and for Davidson the conditions for understanding are linguistic: To understand is to be able to interpret and articulate in language. But we have no means for understanding such error or rendering it intelligible. It cannot be coherently expressed in language, since general agreement about things, which is impossible here in an imagined case of global error, is a precondition for understanding (expression). Thus, coming to understand a view as massively wrong is impossible since understanding presupposes general agreement about truth.

So, arguments to show our entrapment in language, arguments designed to show why language may not get things right or may fail to correspond to things as they are, are self-defeating. From this, Davidson draws a strong positive conclusion. Although we cannot oversee any connection between language and the world, a consideration of the conditions of subjectivity—linguistic communication—permits us to reason to the general correctness of such a connection, to the notion that things as described in language are

pretty much as they are. "My main point is that our basic methodology for interpreting the words of others necessarily makes it the
case that most of the time the simplest sentences which speakers
hold true are true."[31] Is Davidson entitled to draw such a strong
conclusion, to argue from coherence to correspondence? Do
Davidson's transcendental arguments to realism succeed?

I think not. It's one thing to contend that mutual understanding requires general agreement about the truth (or perhaps about
some basic truths). I do not want to quibble with the notion that we
must have—or think we have—a basis of agreement if we are to
disagree. But what, or how much, follows from this? Davidson, of
course, does not simply contend that objective truth *is* what we
agree on, he does not hold the view that agreement *constitutes*
truth. That would be a relativist version of coherence theory, one
denying the objectivist notion that truth is out there, independent
of what we might think or say. "And certainly agreement, no matter how widespread, does not guarantee truth."[32] Rather than holding that our view of the world is by and large true because we
agree on it, or that "truth" means agreement, he contends that we
agree on it because it is by and large true. His view is that agreement is indicative, not constitutive of correctness. We just could
not be massively wrong and find as much agreement as is needed
for communication. But just what grounds has he given us for
reasoning from the fact of widespread agreement to confidence that
the things we agree on are the case? Having precluded any possibility of comparing the things we agree on with the facts 'out there,'
he resorts to the aforementioned arguments. How much do they
establish? I want to argue that they do not establish what he thinks
they do, that Davidson does not succeed in showing that agreement indicates correctness, or as he puts it, that coherence yields
correspondence.

Where Davidson does succeed with them is in giving us one
way of seeing why there cannot be successful conclusive arguments
designed to demonstrate our entrapment in language. He has shown
that there are real difficulties with certain versions of relativism
and skepticism. If relativism requires the *articulation* of an alternative conceptual scheme which is radically other than our own, if
skepticism must *demonstrate*—give a true account of—massive error, then, as Davidson suggests, these positions are self-defeating.
But I wonder about two things: (1) Are the demands Davidson puts
on the relativist and the skeptic reasonable and such that the
failure to meet them conclusively defeats these positions? In a moment I will suggest how a relativist and a skeptic might respond in

a somewhat Davidsonian manner to Davidson's arguments. (2) I wonder whether pointing out difficulties with the entrapment position really establishes Davidson's strong conclusions.

(1) In response to Davidson, a relativist might contend that the most he has done is to indicate that relativism cannot be conclusively established by reasoned argument, but not that the conditions a relativist suggests may obtain cannot obtain. The reason that this is a difference that makes a difference pertains to the difference between the negative positions of a weak relativism or skepticism and Davidson's strong realistic position. The skeptic or relativist has less to do to make her point. For, to argue that coherence, or anything else, yields correspondence and grounds realism one needs to eliminate the very *possibility* of relativism or global error. (Which of course, is what Davidson tries to do.) Realism requires the positive demonstration that the conditions for realism can be said to hold with certainty, (where the "with certainty" proviso demands the defeat of skepticism and relativism), whereas relativism and skepticism, at least in their weak versions, only require showing that there is a possibility that the conditions for relativism and skepticism may hold. In short, the relativist and skeptic only have to give us reasons to doubt realism in order to make their cases, while the realist must prove that relativism and skepticism are impossible.

How does this pertain to Davidson? While showing why we might not be able to prove that there are alternative conceptual schemes, Davidson has not established that there may not be alternative conceptual schemes. Yes—our relativist says—maybe every attempt to present, to articulate, an alternative conceptual scheme requires that we translate it into our own. But it does not follow that we can rule out conclusively the possibility of an alternative conceptual scheme. For there may be a view which we have translated, but massively misunderstood, that is mistranslated, without knowing it. Unbeknowst to us, our translation may be in error. You cannot demonstrate that such mistranslation is impossible; at best what you've shown is that we wouldn't be able to *recognize* the misunderstanding/mistranslation. For even if translation requires agreement about truth conditions, it might be the case that I have unwittingly misconstrued what you regard as truth conditions. After all, I can no more confront my beliefs about truth conditions with yours than I can confront my beliefs with objects. The most I can do is confront my beliefs about truth conditions with my beliefs about your beliefs about truth conditions. So it does not follow from what you may be said to have shown—our inability to recognize massive mistranslation—that we have correctly translated and understood and thus that some alternative conceptual scheme cannot possibly exist. While translation may require construing understanding as present, as having occurred, translation cannot guarantee genuine, correct understanding.

Moreover, given the understanding of translation Davidson operates with, it is hard to see how my being able to translate a conceptual scheme *could* prove it is not a radical alternative. I say this because Davidson's view of translation just does not allow for the possibility of our going radically wrong in translating and realizing it. But without the possibility of our recognizing such error (mistranslation), we are not really entitled to assume that our (seeming) ability to translate could guarantee that there are no radically alternative conceptual schemes. Unless it is conceivable that the error can be recognized, we are not entitled to rule out its possibility in the unequivocal Davidsonian fashion which seeks to buttress correspondence by eliminating any possibility of our language being radically off in its account of things. Again, there is a difference between showing why we could not discover this error and showing why it could not possibly be the case, and the latter is not entailed by the former, barring assumptions I'll discuss below. So while Davidson may succeed in showing why relativism cannot be demonstrated—a weak claim—he has not established the stronger claim of demonstrating correspondence.[33] (What I am suggesting is that translation understood à la Davidson—as a process which always necessarily carries with it a guarantee of large scale success—is translation understood in such a way as to rule out large scale failure. Maybe this is the only adequate account of translation. But, in any case, if such failure is precluded from the realm of possibilities from the start, then the idea of a 'largely *correct* translation'—which idea seems crucial to Davidson's argument against alternative conceptual schemes—loses the contrast which gives it force.)

A skeptic might respond in a similar fashion to Davidson's argument about global error. Yes, I may not be able to understand (to interpret and express) some view as massively wrong (or I may not be able to grasp, that is to say, to articulate, its massive erroneousness as such), since understanding requires interpretation which presupposes agreement. But this shows not that I cannot or may not be wrong, it only shows that I could never recognize this error. And, as a matter of fact, this is just the possibility Descartes' evil genius points to: My (or our) error may be so systematic and consistent—so coherent—that we take it, and cannot help taking it, for the truth. Rather than showing that such a situation is impossible, Davidson has helped to explain how such colossal blindness might be possible by clarifying our inability to recognize it for what it is. Coherence not only fails to yield correspondence, it is equally compatible with noncorrespondence.

So I do not see that Davidson has succeeded in moving from coherence to correspondence, in arguing from a consideration of the subjective conditions of communication to the claim that objectivity as we talk about it is necessarily pretty much as it is. "In sharing a language," he writes, "in whatever sense this is required for communication, we share a picture of the world that must, in its large features, be true."[34] "Must" is simply too conclusive. Showing that we cannot conceive (express in language) an alternative conceptual scheme, or discover massive error (correctly interpret a view as massively mistaken) does not preclude these possibilities—that the world may be quite other than we describe it. Our inability to describe the world as other than we do describe it does not show that it may not be other—unless we further assume that the limits of objective possibility are defined by what is subjectively possible. But insofar as this assumption is not fleshed out in, and into, a Fichtean or Schellingean idealism, this is simply to introduce correspondence by a kind of fiat. Insofar as one holds *both* that we cannot transcend language to view its connection with the world *and* that we can be certain that the world is by and large as we describe it, one tends towards collapsing the distinction between language and objectivity. In Davidson's case, this seems to amount to holding either that the limits of language are the limits of the knowable world (which smacks of Kant and conceptual scheming, and suggests an unknowable residue beyond) or that the limits of language are the limits of the world as such, a position which smacks of the logico-linguistic mysticism of the early Wittgenstein. And taking into account his adamant rejection of conceptual scheming, it would seem that Davidson does tend in the latter direction. "But if we do say this, then we should realize that we have abandoned not only the ordinary notion of a language, but we have erased the boundary between knowing a language and knowing our way around in the world generally."[35]

In the end, Davidson's commitment to correspondence and to a metaphysical realism which holds that ontological gems can be minded from a study of language[36] seems puzzling, since he has gone to such great lengths to undermine the framework of assumptions usually associated with both these positions. What he seems to fail to see is that correspondence is an irreducibly contrastive concept. By this I mean that it does not pass muster as a coherent philosophical notion (with epistemological and metaphysical consequences) unless it is possible for us to see *both* how success *and* how failure to correspond can be made out. Davidson argues that traditional—confrontational—notions concerning the successful demonstration of correspondence cannot work. He also argues, against relativism and skepticism, that failure to correspond also cannot be demonstrated. Yet despite this twofold attack on it, he thinks correspondence—in the traditional sense he accepts as not demonstrable via confrontation—remains to be saved.

To conclude: Davidson attempts to harvest ontological and epistemological fruit from the idea that, unless we get things mostly right, we cannot make sense of getting things wrong. More particularly, he wants to dismiss the possibility that, for the most part, we might be getting things wrong. I want to insist that there is a parallel here. It does not make sense to claim that language *must*, by and large, be "getting things right" unless we can make sense at least of the possibility of it by and large "getting things wrong," which Davidson denies. The sense of getting things right connected to correspondence and realism requires just the contrast—the possibility of getting things wrong—rejected by Davidson. In his attacks on relativism and skepticism Davidson has gone a long way towards explaining why failure to correspond cannot be made out. He needs to let the other shoe drop. Correspondence is a relation, and if we can neither see that the relata correspond nor that they fail to, then it has become an empty notion, a wheel which turns but moves nothing.

≥●

Foundationalism's traditional goals were to show how objective knowledge of a real world is possible and to thereby defeat skepticism. As Hegel—and Davidson—clearly see, attaining these ends by demonstrating that and how our purported knowledge of such a world corresponds to that given world is impossible. But while this realization leads Hegel to thoroughly abandon the subjectivist, correspondence model of truth and knowledge, Davidson, like Kant, tries to avoid bridging the unbridgeable gulf between subjectivity and objectivity by means of a mode of transcendental argumentation. Chapter 10 has argued that these projects cannot succeed, that, as earlier chapters have contended, the foundationalist model must be thoroughly abandoned.

I have indicated here that definitive of the transcendental approach to foundationalism is the contention that certain conditions unquestionably manifest within the subjective domain can only be rendered intelligible on the condition that a real, and knowable, objective domain exists. Specifically, Davidson's version of transcendental argumentation holds that the intelligibility or coherence of language is possible only insofar as we have access to the truth, and that this truth must be construed in the mode of correspondence. The latter is the case, he has argued, because we can make no sense of the notion of an inaccessible domain beyond the grasp of language. In an argument reminiscent of Hegel's criticism of Kant's thing-in-itself, Davidson holds that every attempt to demonstrate that access to objectivity is impossible fails because it cannot avoid presupposing successful reference to that domain. So, Davidson's position is not that we can access objects epistemologically, but that we can finally make no sense of objects, or of talk of objects, as inaccessible. I have shown that this position does not vindicate correspondence and foundationalism, because the skeptic need not fall into Davidson's trap: Skepticism does not need to demonstrate that an inaccessible domain exists. It merely needs to indicate that we *could* be wrong in our beliefs about the domain of the given, not that we need to *know* that we are wrong. The former state of affairs is compatible with the conditions of intelligibility and communication on which Davidson rests his case. Davidson has moved in a quasi-Hegelian direction by abandoning epistemology and raising questions about the nature of intelligibility itself. But what we have seen is that, in so doing, he still presupposes the framework of givenness and cannot avoid its problems.

Chapter 11, "The Problematic Role of God in Modern Epistemology," provides a detailed analysis and an independent criticism (along Hegelian lines) of the foundational project and its subjectivist model of truth. Opening with a formal consideration of the nature of the project and its demands, I argue that foundationalism cannot succeed because it literally requires a divine mind. Chapter 11 moves on to indicate how a variety of modern foundationalists have attempted to incorporate such a mind in their projects, and how each has failed.

Chapter 11

THE PROBLEMATIC ROLE OF GOD
IN MODERN EPISTEMOLOGY[1]

All history is modern history.

—Wallace Stevens

Since Hegel, more and more philosophers have come to conclude that, despite its basic appeal and initial plausibility, foundational epistemology is not merely a seriously flawed project but one whose successful completion is impossible in principle.[2] Antifoundationalism transcends many of the traditional boundaries between the continental and analytic camps, and its implications extend beyond epistemology and concern larger issues such as the objectivity of rational thought, the possibility of universal norms, and the future of philosophy.[3]

In any case, whatever overall position one takes on the question of the possibility of epistemology as a meaningful endeavor, a survey of its modern history from Descartes through Nietzsche indicates that fulfilling its basic aim of providing foundations for knowledge, through an articulation of the conditions definitive of legitimate knowing, has proved to be more difficult than most epistemologists expected. There are, of course, many different approaches to epistemology to be found in the modern era: various versions of rationalism and empiricism, as well as several varieties of critical or transcendental idealism. Nonetheless, one way of focusing on a common feature, and especially on a common *difficulty* which modern epistemologies share, is to take note of the explicit or implicit role

217

which God—or, more accurately put, which a conception of the divine mind—plays in various epistemologies. The central thesis of this chapter is that the use of God by various modern epistemologists is not accidental in that it arises from a fundamental difficulty endemic to epistemological projects. In fact, I shall argue in Part I that, historical considerations aside, implicit in the very idea of a successful epistemology is the conception of a mind which possesses divine attributes. In addition, and in connection with what I shall contend is a constitutive role for God in epistemology, I shall work in Part II to trace out a historical path of development in modern epistemology in terms of the manner and extent to which various epistemologists have made use of or reference to God in their projects, either explicitly or implicitly. Lastly, and in regard to contemporary skepticism about epistemology one of my aims throughout is to show that we can focus on what is fundamentally problematic about epistemology by taking into account how an idea of God or of a divine mind does emerge centrally in attempts to complete the epistemological project.[4]

Part I. The Objectivity Problem

What is the difficulty endemic to epistemology which can be said to require the involvement of a divine mind for its solution? To answer this question we must examine the motivating impulse which defines epistemology's nature and goals.

Epistemology's roots lie in a desire to attain certainty concerning knowledge, and the basis of this desire, as noted by Descartes (in the *Meditations*) and Locke (in *An Essay Concerning Human Understanding*) can be characterized as follows. If we are to be certain and secure when we go about the business of knowing, we must first engage in a *preliminary investigation* of the faculty or instrument of cognition (the mind or the understanding) so that, having established its very capacity to afford knowledge, and having acquainted ourselves with its nature and proper manner of functioning—having learned that and how it works—we may then make correct use of it. Basic here is the idea that we are (or believe we are) capable of knowledge, but that error is likely unless we first establish the proper method or methods for arriving at knowledge.

Insofar as one subscribes to this apparently reasonable view, an equally reasonable conception of the *basic structure of cognition* follows. Knowledge must be regarded as something which is distinct and distinguishable from an object, and the act of knowing must be seen to consist in a relation between knowledge and its object. This overall understanding of the structure of cognition follows from what I have described as epistemology's motivating impulse, for two reasons.

For one thing, only if knowing involves a relation such that knowledge is regarded as distinct and distinguishable from the object of knowledge, is there a basis for speaking of a standard against which our purported claims to know can be measured and found adequate (true) or wanting (false). Epistemology presupposes from the first that we can be right or wrong in our attempts to know, and that we can determine which, in at least some cases. And being able to do so requires an understanding of cognition as a relation in which one of the relata is a measure against which the other is measured. Furthermore, only if cognition has the afore-mentioned structure is it possible to conceive of a preliminary investigation which could establish that and how knowledge is possible in general. The ultimate goal of epistemology is to specify the general conditions under which the faculty or instrument succeeds and fails in providing knowledge. To do this, knowledge must be conceived as distinct and isolatable from its object, for only then can one undertake an examination both of the overall nature of its relation to the object and of the agency which establishes the relation. If the structure of cognition is not understood as a determinate relation with general features, each act of knowing would seemingly have to be regarded as an unanalysable, unique, event and it would not be possible to specify those general conditions of knowing which epistemology seeks: no methodological principles governing all legitimate cases could be articulated, no rules for the direction of the mind could be promulgated, no foundations of cognition could be laid down. So, the idea that we can sometimes ascertain when we have and have not grasped the truth, and the idea that there are discoverable general conditions which determine when our grasping succeeds and fails, both require the structure of cognition outlined.

Given this structure, a *general understanding of truth* also follows. Truth is what we attain when our purported knowledge corresponds to, mirrors, pictures, adequates, or re-presents the object as it is in-itself or in its objectivity.[5] Our knowledge must be identical in its determinate character to the object as it is prior to and apart from our conception of it; the objectivity of knowledge (or, if you will, the distinction between subjective and objective truth) lies in the avoidance of any coloring, distortion, or admixture to knowledge by the cognitive act; objectivity resides in the exclusive determination of the contents of knowledge (what it 'says' about the object as object) by that which it purports to be the knowledge of. A paramount task for epistemology lies in demonstrating that one or more modes of knowing can provide such knowledge of at least some of the domains of possible objects of knowledge. If this cannot be shown, then knowing must be construed as a knowing of things as they appear, as subjective in the pejorative sense. And if this turns out to be the case, we again have a situation where no general criteria, methodological conditions, or standards for cognition can be established.[6]

One last feature of the epistemological agenda needs to be considered before we examine epistemology's root difficulty. Knowing must involve a knower as the locus of knowledge. For the project to work there must be a cognitive agent for whom the relational event of knowing is present. Epistemologically understood, cognition is unthinkable without an awareness, an intentional entity—mind, understanding, consciousness, subjectivity—which is distinct from and can distinguish itself from its knowledge and the object of knowledge, while holding both present in its field of awareness. Again, the need for a structure which provides for this tripartite relating and distinguishing is required because the cognitive relation must itself be *present for* a knower if the knower is to be capable of distinguishing between truth and falsity. Not only a standard for judging knowledge claims, but a judge too is required. Additionally, the possibility of an epistemological investigation also presupposes that the knower can make, not only his knowing act, but also his own knowledge-enabling capacities or faculties an object of knowledge: the determination of the general conditions under which objective knowledge is possible requires that the epistemological investigator has access not merely to knowledge and object (to determine whether they correspond) but also to the conditions which make cognitive successful (or failure) possible. And finally, it must be the epistemologist's own faculties which are accessible to her (the mind must be a *"lumen naturale"* transparent to itself'; otherwise an infinite regress of investigations would ensue, rendering the project pointless from the start.[8]

So, given that cognition is an event of and for a conscious subject; given that the object of knowledge is regarded as something distinct from the knowledge of it; given that knowledge is certifiably true insofar as it corresponds to the object in its objectivity; and given that legitimate cognition consists in that mode (or modes) of relating knowledge to object in and through which truth is afforded, what is the fundamental difficulty with epistemology?

The most direct way of focusing on this difficulty is through considering what the epistemologist must accomplish in order to complete the project in light of the position from which this accomplishment must be effected. In order to demonstrate that a mode of knowing provides truth, the epistemologist must show that the knowing in question affords correspondence between purported knowledge, something directly and unproblematically accessible (usually taken to be an idea) and its object as it is in-itself.[9] To demonstrate that correspondence has been attained (and to specify the conditions which make it attainable) the epistemologist must claim to have knowledge of this correspondence: the epistemologist must be in the position of comparing the mind's purported knowledge of the object with the object. This correspondence-establishing comparison requires that the epistemologist can distinguish between knowledge and object—in order that a *genuine* comparative test takes place—while at the same time establishing the identity or sameness of their contents—in order to show a *successful*, correspondence-revealing comparison which demonstrates that the mode of knowing being examined is truth-affording.

If *objective* knowledge is to be spoken of, the difference between the purported knowledge and the object as standard must be maintained, for the epistemologist must be in the position of guaranteeing that a genuine test—one with a criterion given independently of that which is being tested—has taken place. The assurance of the objectivity of the standard against which the purported knowledge is to be measured requires a guarantee of its being determined independently of the mode of cognition undergoing the test: A ruler cannot be an objective measure of its own accuracy. Since the epistemologist must be able to certify that the standard is so determined, the difference between purported knowledge and object which insures this independent determination must be manifest to the epistemologist.

If the *truth* of the purported knowledge is to be spoken of, then the identity of knowledge and object must be equally manifest to the epistemologist, for only when knowledge and object are present as identical can their correspondence be certified. And arriving at correspondence requires the maintenance of difference and identity at one and the same time, for otherwise a question can arise as to whether the knowledge differentiated from the object is the same as the purported knowledge found to be identical. So, in sum: In order for the test to be objective, the difference between knowledge and object must be maintained; in order for the test to be a success, it must be eliminated.

Attaining to this state creates what I call the objectivity problem simply because the standpoint and locus of comparison—the instrument of the epistemological investigation—must be the same cognitive agency whose purported knowledge is undergoing testing, for the reason outlined above that knowledge and object must both be *for* the same knower if a comparison is to take place.[10] What is problematic is then the following: How, from the subjective domain[11] of this agency, is one to demonstrate correspondence between the purported knowledge and the objective standard, given that this standard must not only be different from the knowledge being tested, but must also be certified as determined independently of the subjective domain altogether?[12] If the test is to be genuine, assurance must be provided that the standard is so determined, that what the purported knowledge is being measured against is the object as it is in objectivity, and not just another subjective account of what the object purportedly is. But if the comparative test is to take place at all, the standard must be as accessible to the epistemological agent as the knowledge being compared to it; it must be present in the epistemologist's field of awareness just as the purported knowledge to be tested is. Yet once the standard is so accessed, it seems that the assurance of objectivity is lost, for what guarantee can there be that what is now present as standard is in fact the object as independently determined and not as determined by the agent? The standard must become known in order to be compared with the purported knowledge, but once it is so known it is no longer suitable as a genuine standard. In a nutshell, the problem seems to be that all that the epistemologist can compare to her purported knowledge of the object in a comparative test is another instance of purported knowledge.

This is an objectivity problem because the paramount goal of epistemology is to show that how things subjectively appear to us is not merely how things are 'for us' but also, at least in some specifiable instances, how they truly are in themselves, or in their objectivity. We want assurance that how we take things to be (or how we describe things in language) is 'how things really are,' at least where that signifies 'determined independently of arbitrary whim.' It should be noted that it makes no difference for the issues under consideration what ontological coloring the domain of objectivity takes; it can be construed as Moore's world of ordinary physical things (against which philosophical concepts are to be measured) or as Plato's world of ideas (against which the apparent world of physical things is to be measured) or as the empiricists' domain of sense data (against which complex ideas are to be measured). We can construe objectivity as material, as mental, as some hybrid of the two, or we can follow the pragmatists and abstain altogether from distinguishing knowledge and objective standard in an ontological fashion. A test still requires a meaningful distinction and the central problem remains as long as that distinction is drawn. Furthermore, as we shall see in more detail subsequently, it is irrelevant whether objectivity is understood in a literal sense, as a domain conceived as distinct from and contrasted with a subject, or whether the locus of objectivity is said to be found in subjectivity, or whether traditional distinctions pertaining to subjects and objects are qualified or denied altogether. As long as the epistemological project is to be undertaken the minimal distinction between purported knowledge and an objective standard, construed as determined independently of the knowledge candidate, must be maintained—just how this independent determination is more specifically conceived makes no relevant difference—and as long as it is maintained the objectivity problem arises.

What is needed for epistemology to succeed in its initial goal of demonstrating correspondence is an act of knowing by the epistemologist which is somehow or other not merely another subjective act. For the test to be genuine, objective, the agent must engage in a knowing which is not 'of' the agent in the sense that it must be a knowing by the agent of how things are apart from the field of awareness in which the purported knowledge is to be found. Yet, as we saw, for the comparative test to take place at all the standard must also be in that same field of awareness. In short, epistemology calls for a mind whose objects are both immanent and transcendent at once, a divine mind.

Part II. The Epistemologist Becomes Divine

To make this epistemological difficulty concrete, and to show how an appeal to God may be used to attempt to get out of it, let us consider Descartes' position in the *Mediations*. I want to pick up with Descartes after he has discovered his epistemological Archimedean point in the cogito; that is, after he has withdrawn into the solitary thinking ego through a process of methodological doubt which has led him to classify all the rest of his ideas as provisionally false. Where does Descartes stand at this point? That he has ideas of many things other than of his own mind, Descartes is certain. But he is uncertain as to whether these ideas are objectively true, namely, that there exist real things outside of his mind and that his ideas of these things correspond to them. Supposing that he may be dreaming or being deceived, Descartes intensifies the notion that the presence of an idea in the subjectively privileged domain of the mind does not guarantee the existence of its objective referent.

Descartes has come swiftly to (what he envisions as a temporary) position of skeptical solipsism in that he has adopted a manifestly subjective criterion, the mind's inability to doubt, as the preliminary identifying mark of an idea's truth. And he has found it possible to doubt everything except that he is a mind, that he exists as a thinking thing. That the cogito is Descartes' epistemological foundation point, the exemplary truth which his search for the truth about truth has uncovered, is not at all surprising, given the requirement that the epistemologist must have as his object an instance of purported knowing in which idea and object correspond. For the cogito is such that the mere act of thinking this idea suffices to manifest the existence of that object to which the idea refers. In thinking of one's existence as a thinking thing one perhaps comes as close as is humanly possible to approximating the divine power of bringing forth existence from out of nothing but thought. Whenever I conceive or think the idea, "I think," that there is something which thinks and hence that this idea is objectively true is immediately given by the mere act of thinking. When the mind's idea is of itself as a thinking thing it has no need to try to escape from the subjective domain to verify that there is some objective, independently determined thing to which this idea corresponds, for in this instance the cognitive (thinking) act itself immediately constitutes the objectivity in question (that thinking is), even if it does not create it *ex nihilo*. Just to think the idea of oneself as a thinking being is to establish or constitute the *truth* of that idea, since to think the idea of oneself as a thinking being, is *to be* a thinking being and *to be aware* of oneself as a thinking being, and hence also to be aware of the *correspondence* between this idea and this object: In pure self-reflection where the subject and object of reflection are manifested simultaneously in the act of reflection, idea, object and their correspondence are given at once. (Which is not to say that all that which makes this reflection possible is either constituted or made manifest by this act.)

So the cogito is serviceable not merely because it apparently meets Descartes' specific demand for resistance to doubt (and the evil genius). It can meet this specific requirement and has a more basic appeal because this object seemingly affords an instance of cognition in which the epistemological need to bridge subjectivity and objectivity can be met without reducing objectivity to subjectivity in the pejorative sense of that term, for in the case of the cogito the objective reality in question is simply the restricted domain of the thinking subject, as Descartes acknowledges in his analysis of the cogito. (Since there is no bridge, neither doubt nor the evil genius can block the path to certainty.)

Thus the cogito is paradigmatic for the special object the epistemologist seeks, but which is so hard to find: one which can be *known* in its correspondence with the idea of it. It is not accidental that postCartesian epistemological efforts take as their model the correspondence-affording situation which arises when the mind makes its own activity its object. It is not merely that seeking to legitimate cognition requires the epistemologist to have knowing as the topic of investigation. Looking at it in hindsight, and in terms of the problem of epistemology, what we find with the cogito is the first small step in a development in which, in an ever more expansive fashion, the character of objectivity itself comes to take on the features of the self-knowing mind. Descartes' successors gradually move to define the nature of the objectively real in terms of that particular object which seems to meet the basic epistemological need of being knowable in a certifiably true fashion. It is the special demands of epistemology which shape the ontologies of modernity. The need to move in this inflationary direction becomes apparent when we consider Descartes' confrontation with the objectivity problem.

Once having arrived at the cogito, Descartes' paramount difficulty, of course, concerns the existence of *other* things about which he has ideas; Descartes the dualist and realist will not claim that these things are given directly in and through the act of thinking these ideas. What Descartes needs if he is going to recapture the world bracketed by his epistemological doubt is a bridge which can be erected from the mind's resources alone and which can lead from the mind to the domain of objects outside his mind. The solution he offers is ingenious, given his dilemma. First of all he needs to establish that there really is a domain of such mind-external objects (that he is not dreaming or being deceived). But he must do this from within the subjective domain of the mind; he has no resources save the cogito. So he needs to find an idea in his mind like the cogito—in that merely thinking it will suffice to guarantee its truth, in the sense of establishing that the idea correctly refers to something real—but also different from the cogito—in that the existence of the object to which the idea refers is objective: the reality referred to must be mind-independent. Second, this bridge must not only connect, it must be crossable: he also needs a way of insuring that some of his other ideas are also true in that they correspond to objective realities. Descartes finds an answer to both of these needs in the idea of God. " . . . I must enquire whether there is a God . . . and if I find that there is a God, I must also inquire whether He may be a deceiver; for without a knowledge of these two truths I do not see that I can ever be certain of anything."[13]

I am not going to go through Descartes' proofs of the existence of God nor consider objections to them. Neither the precise nature of the proofs nor the problems with them concern the issues at hand in an essential way. What we do need to note is that the workability of his solution hinges ultimately on the genuine existence of a mind which can be known as capable of attaining what Descartes' mind cannot: a mind which has not only its own existence but also the existence of an objective world of knowable objects given in the idea of its own being. The divine world-creative mind of Christian thought is just such a mind: one which possesses the certainty of the correspondence between its ideas and their references because, *as a mind*, it is both self-caused and creates or constitutes these objects *ex nihilo*. As strictly self-caused, such a divine mind can entertain no questions about its apprehension of its own ideas or the working of its faculties; literally nothing conditions its knowing; there remains no conceptual space for doubt. And since it creates out of nothing but its own ideas (and by an unconditioned act) there remains no unknowable residue which can block correspondence between the ideas and the things.

This unconditioned character which permits of certain knowledge by God is captured in Descartes' important notion of divine perfection. And it is only because Descartes believes that he can and does know such a perfect God as more than an idea that he is able to reestablish the certainty of veridical contact between his mind and the world and avoid solipsism and the objectivity problem. He needs to know the truth of a God who, because he is the cause both of Descartes' ideas and of things in the world, guarantees for Descartes the correspondence between these ideas and those things.

For to begin with, that which I have just taken as a rule, that is to say, that all the things that we very clearly and very distinctly conceive of are true, is certain only because God is or exists, and that He is a Perfect Being, and that all that is in us issues from Him. . . . But if we did not know that all that is in us of reality and truth proceeds from a perfect and infinite Being, however clear and distinct were our ideas, we should not have any reason to assure ourselves that they had the perfection of being true.[14]

Only through claiming to know a mind which can do what his mind cannot can Descartes move to meet his difficulties. "And so I very clearly recognize that the certainty and truth of all knowledge depends alone on the knowledge of the true God, in so much that, before I knew Him, I could not have a perfect knowledge of any other thing."[15] Yet because *that* claim must remain suspect (among other reasons, because it fails to reach the cognitive standard of certainty established by the cogito), Descartes' project is bound to fail on its own terms. But, as the rest of my story will indicate, this failure does not prompt a rejection of the cognitive standard established by the cogito as that object which provides epistemological satisfaction. Rather, it leads to a reconceptualization of the nature of the knower and the known in order to meet that standard. Instead of rethinking knowledge in a nonepistemological fashion, subsequent epistemologists reconceive all of reality in accordance with epistemological demands.

The next epistemologist I want to consider is the Irishman Bishop Berkeley. Although Berkeley conceptualizes the nature of the mind's relation to objects in such a way that one of Descartes' problems is directly eliminated without an appeal to God, he too finds a need to refer to God in attempting to give an adequate account of knowledge, one which is capable of explicating both the truth and the objectivity of knowledge.

Descartes' rationalistic realism—his commitment to the mind-independence of worldly objects—led him into two difficulties: without a divine mind as a connecting bridge the mind cannot be certain either that the objects it conceives have a genuinely objective existence (are more than the mind's subjective fancies: solipsism), or that I know them as they truly are independently of my subjective conceptions of them (skepticism). Berkeley offers a solution to the second difficulty. "What I here make public has, after a long and scrupulous inquiry, seemed to me evidently true and not unuseful to be known; particularly to those who are tainted with Scepticism. . . ."[16] He does so through moving in the inflationary direction I mentioned above: he expands the domain of the mind, extending the parameters of what is immediately given to conscious awareness to *include* the domain of objects. If the mind, the knowing subject, is the locus of certainty, and if, as mind, it cannot get beyond what is immediately given, then why not redefine the nature of objectivity in terms of the immediately given and directly accessible, in terms of ideas?

> Some truths there are so near and obvious to the mind that a man need only open his eyes to see them. Such I take this important one to be, viz. that all the choir of heaven and furniture of the earth, in a word all those bodies which compose the mighty frame of the world, have not any substance without a mind; that their *being* is to be perceived or known. . . . [17]

If "to be is to be perceived," if the true being of things consists in *nothing but* their being objects for a mind, then the mind has immediate and incorrigible certainty of the correctness of what it conceives, for just what it thinks or perceives is immediately at one with what is. Ideas are not copies, they are the things themselves.[18]

This Berkeleyan move confronts nicely the problem of skepticism, for it eliminates the epistemologist's need to somehow get out of the mind or to appeal to a mind outside of the epistemologist's own mind, in order to be able to show that ideas in the mind are in agreement with objects 'out there.' However, this solution does not deal with the issue of the objective status of what the mind knows. Insofar as the being of objects consists in their being perceived, it would seem to follow that the very existence of objects is made dependent on my mind, and thus that objects are annihilated or destroyed whenever I am not perceiving them. Skepticism at one level disappears while the problem of solipsism remains. But if this is how things stand, then although I may be immediately certain of the correctness of my perceptions, this correctness is utterly one-sided and radically subjective, for my perceptions have no objective, mind-independent referents to which they may be said to correspond. Thus I have attained the *certainty* of the truth of what I know at the cost of the *objective reality* of what I know.

If to be is to be perceived, how is the objectivity of knowledge to be guaranteed? Although Berkeley avoids skepticism and establishes the truth of ideas by extending the domain of the mind he can only avoid the other horn of the epistemological dilemma, solipsism, by introducing God: as constantly all-perceiving, this divine mind establishes and insures the continued existence and the objective reality of the world. And as the cause of my perceptions, God also insures that what I perceive corresponds with that objective reality. Leibniz might be said to confront a similar situation in a similar way in the *Monadology*: As an awareness, nothing falls outside of a windowless monad's purview; the world is immanent, present in an unmediated fashion. Thus the gap between subjects and objects is overcome. This establishes subjective certainty and avoids skepticism. Objectivity is guaranteed (solipsism avoided) in a twofold fashion: There is a plurality of monads and our perceptions are coordinated by a divine monad who is the cause of the whole infinite series of monads. "The idea of things in us is nothing but the fact that God, the author alike of things and of mind, has impressed this power of thinking upon the mind, so that it can by its own operations produce what corresponds perfectly to the events which follow from things."[19] Note that as with Berkeley, only more so, objectivity itself comes to take on the character of the mind. In Berkeley's case, what is objectively real is defined in terms of its being *for* a mind. With Leibniz, objective material reality is literally constituted *out of* minds.

Having considered philosophers who appeal to a divine mind in their epistemological projects, I want to deal now with the notion that in the later period of modern epistemology the epistemological mind itself comes to be construed in such a manner that it comes closer and closer to approximating a divine mind. Let us look at Kant, Fichte, and Schelling.

On the face of it, it might seem strange to contend that Kant's transcendental epistemology involves a conceptualization of the knowing mind which approximates it to the divine. Establishing the fundamentally limited character of the understanding in the face of reason's pretensions to know in an unlimited, God-like fashion is central to Kant's project. In Book II of the transcendental dialectic of the first *Critique* he argues against the possibility of any rational proof of God's existence.[20] Clearly then, as someone awakened from his dogmatic slumbers by Hume's critique of rational metaphysics, Kant will not *appeal to* God to demonstrate how objective knowledge is possible. But although he accepts Hume's criticisms of the ways in which earlier philosophers had attempted to justify knowledge, Kant still aims to provide such a justification. I want to suggest that it is because Kant accepts Hume's criticisms while refusing to accept his skepticism that Kant is driven, in his attempt to justify knowledge, to rethink the nature of the mind in such a way that an important step is taken in approximating the epistemological to the divine mind.[21]

How is this? In arriving at skepticism, Hume had shown that while a passive-receptive mind can be certain of the character of its immediately present impressions, it can attain to no certain knowledge of the purportedly objective, ostensibly mind-external sources of these sense impressions. No appeal to God is possible, although we can understand how habit creates the subjective necessity of my belief in an objective world. Where Descartes and Berkeley felt confident in invoking God as a bridge who guarantees correspondence between ideas and things, thus providing for the objectivity of my knowledge, Hume will allow no such options and is content to accept the consequences for philosophy. Kant's way out of this, his self-styled Copernican revolution, is based in a reconception of the knowing mind which involves the attribution of quasi-divine powers to the mind. If *appealing to* God in the fashion of Descartes and Berkeley is ruled out, why not bring God within? With Kant, we find that the objective validity of knowledge is not a matter of the mind's capacity to have true or correct copies of thoroughly mind-transcendent objects impressed upon it. (We can have no knowledge of things-in-themselves.)[22] As we saw, earlier attempts to account for knowledge in that manner failed because the epistemological mind, without God, could not transcend itself to compare ideas with objects in order to certify their correspondence. But with Kant, objectivity is accounted for because the mind, albeit in a limited or restricted sense, is creative. With Kant, we take the first step towards transforming the epistemological mind into the divine mind in that he offers a reconceptualization of the mind as essentially active rather than passive, as something which does not find correspondence but which establishes or legislates it.[23]

> Thus the understanding is something more than a power of formulating rules through comparison of appearances; it is itself the lawgiver of nature. Save through it, nature, that is, synthetic unity of the manifold of appearances according to rules, would not exist at all (for appearances, as such, cannot exist outside us—they exist only in our sensibility). . . . [24]

According to Kant, "we can discover it [nature] only in the radical faculty of all our knowledge."[25] Attaining knowledge is not a matter of receiving impressions as copies of objects; it is an act of creative synthesis in which knowledge and objects are constituted in one and the same act by a transcendental ego. The objectivity of my knowledge is not a matter of (unattainable) access to some domain which thoroughly transcends subjectivity; it pertains instead to the universality and necessity of the rules of synthesis.[26] The model for this synthesis is Descartes' cogito. But now this is not simply an ego which makes itself present to itself through the thinking act. It is now an ego as an actor whose self-knowing act is nothing less than the constitutive formula for the organization of all objectivity. This self-knower is a lawgiver whose adjudicative code is its primal (self) constitutive thinking activity, which, as a unifying activity according to rules, extends beyond itself to objectivity. "The original and necessary consciousness of the identity of the self is thus at the same time a consciousness of an equally necessary unity of the synthesis of all appearances according to concepts. . . . " "It is only when we have . . . produced synthetic unity in the manifold of intuition that we are in a position to say that we know the object."[27] Correspondence between mind immanent ideas and mind transcendent objects does not need to be found; it is *established* or *constituted* because the conditions for the possibility of knowledge and the conditions for the possibility of objects of knowledge are identical.[28] We can be assured of the objective validity of our knowledge not because we know that there exists a God who created our minds and the world and who insures their correspondence, but because we *can* know that *our* minds, as synthetically active, function in a God-like manner to shape knowledge and the world at one and the same time according to the necessary constitutive principles. Correspondence between what we find in subjectivity and what is objective is assured because the act constitutive of the unity of consciousness is also the act which unifies the sensible manifold.

Now, although Kant works to account for objectively valid knowledge in this manner, the viability of his project is undermined, as his critics and successors immediately saw, by the presence in it of the notion of things-in-themselves. The problem of the thing-in-itself in Kant is the form in which the objectivity problem appears in his philosophy. Although Kant had brought the objective world into the domain of what the mind has certain access to by attributing object-formative powers to the mind, the success of his account as one which establishes knowledge as objective rests on two dubious claims.

For one thing, and as Kant clearly saw, solipsism is avoided only insofar as the material synthesized by the transcendental ego is itself given from without. Kant insists that this active ego is only

conditionally active.[29] "Material idealism" is avoided, according to
him, by the fact that the stuff the mind works on is not itself
created by the mind.[30] Our understanding is not "intuitive": it does
not give objects to itself merely by thinking them.[31] So, the nature
of the Kantian divinization of the human mind is that of a demiurge,
a God who imposes form on given material. What renders this
move epistemologically problematic is the issue of the intelligibility
of the theory which attempts to root the mind in objectivity by
preserving a passive dimension. In terms of the theory itself, we
seem to need to think of things-in-themselves as the sources of
what is given in the manifold of sensible intuition. For if they are
not, what is? "[T]hough we cannot *know* these objects as things in
themselves, we must yet be in a position to *think* them as things in
themselves; otherwise we should be landed in the absurd conclusion that there can be appearance without anything that appears."[32]
Unlike Hume, Kant cannot remain agnostic on this issue. Some
provision must be made for such an other-than-mind source, call it
what you will, if, in our desire to avoid solipsism, we are not to err
in the other direction by attributing full creative powers to the
mind. Yet claims about things-in-themselves as the ground or source
of appearances must remain problematic. The validity of the synthetic categories lies in their restricted application to what is given
in sensible intuition, but that validity can seemingly only be *accounted for* if we cash out the notion of such givenness, which
would seem to require applying a category—causality—beyond what
is given to the source of givenness.

For another thing, there is a related problem which does not
concern the internal coherence of the theory but the epistemically
questionable character of its status as knowledge. Earlier we saw
how Descartes, Berkeley, and Leibniz needed, as epistemologists,
to claim veridical knowledge of a transcendent God to complete
projects designed to show how knowledge is possible in the first
place. Now, with Kant we see that something like such a God has
been transposed within. (Rather than Descartes' proofs we have a
transcendental deduction.) But this does not obviate the problem of
the status of the epistemologist's knowledge of this quasi-divine
mind. How is knowledge of the transcendental ego possible? In
some sense this ego is not the directly accessible phenomenal self
of ordinary consciousness, although according to Kant it is a condition of the possibility of that self. But if it is a noumenal self, lying
behind appearances, we must again ask how, and in what sense, is
it knowable? The transcendental epistemologist must somehow claim
to know both a noumenal transcendental ego and a noumenal world

of things-in-themselves. (As I shall argue below, being able to 'think' these things does not meet the skeptic.) But how can the transcendental philosopher know these things-in-themselves as the two roots of possible knowledge? Only if things-in-themselves are knowable as that which provides material for synthesis, and only if the transcendental ego is knowable as capable of synthesizing is Kant's account of knowledge intelligible as one which guarantees objectivity and answers Hume's skepticism. For if the transcendental philosopher cannot attain to it, there will be no assurance of the fit between what is given to the transcendental ego and its categories, the fit between receptivity and spontaneity.[33] And establishing this fit at the transcendental level seems as problematic as ever as long as the ultimate source of what comes to be known is conceived as radically other than the mind, be it the phenomenal, noumenal, or some other mind. Postulating things-in-themselves avoids the problem of the mind's having to transcend itself at one level (of the understanding), only to reintroduce it at another, since the account can only work if these things-in-themselves are knowable in some sense. As Jacobi so aptly put it, without the thing-in-itself you cannot enter Kant's philosophy, with it, you cannot remain within Kant's philosophy.

Of course, the transcendental philosopher does not want to claim that his transcendental 'knowledge' of these matters is of the same form, or order, as ordinary knowledge of objects. Transcendental argumentation to the noumenal realm consists in claiming that, from certain conditions immediately and indubitably manifest in subjectivity, we can infer to the transcendental conditions of their possibility without having to claim direct access to such a domain. (See the "Refutation of Idealism.")[34] But without such access, skepticism is not defeated, for the skeptic (see Hume) has his own account of the conditions for what is found manifest in subjectivity (such as the subjective feeling of causal necessity). The necessity of our subjective belief in objectivity is not at issue between the skeptic and the Kantian. What the skeptic disputes is that this can be more than a belief, that we are entitled to *infer* to anything independent of that subjectivity in order to account for it. If—as the transcendental philosopher contends—we cannot have access to the domain of the given which is the (purportedly) ultimate source of the content of our knowledge, then we have nothing against which to compare the rival skeptical and transcendental accounts, and thus no *objective basis* (in the sense of something independent of what we find in subjectivity) for preferring one over the other. (There may be, as Kant intimates, a practical basis for preference.

As we shall see below, from Fichte on, a move to the practical to ground the cognitive comes to the fore.) If the transcendental philosopher cannot attain to—or refuses to try to attain to—knowledge of a domain which does transcend subjectivity, at least in the sense that such a domain can be certified as not having been determined by subjectivity, the objectivity of our known world may be nothing more than the objectivity of a dream world. Simply contending that we *must think* that there is such a domain of objectivity is not enough. The need to think that may simply be a curious feature of our subjectivity; it provides no guarantee that there is such a domain. But an objectivity which is no more than a subjective requirement of thought is useless, if the term is supposed to signify that I can be certain that how I take things to be has been measured, or at least constrained by, a standard given independently of human subjectivity.

So once again epistemology confronts the skepticism/solipsism, truth/objectivity, immanence/transcendence dilemma: Things-in-themselves are transcendent and cannot be spoken of at all. In this case we are back with Hume and the account of synthetic *a priori* judgements is a more complex and cumbersome version of his treatment of the subjective necessity of our mode of thought. Or, things-in-themselves are knowable and transcendental philosophy is possible. In which case things-in-themselves cannot fall outside of the mind and must be the products, if not of a subjective empirical mind then of an ultimate transcendental ego or cosmic creative mind.

Unwilling to resort to Humean skepticism about philosophy, Kant's immediate successors seize the latter alternative, realizing that as long as anything in the affair of knowing is conceived of as having its origin outside the mind, then the epistemological project of showing how knowledge and object correspond (or, after the transcendental move, of showing how spontaneity and receptivity are suitably fitted for synthesis) will be short-circuited.[35] In so doing they took another step toward fully attributing divine powers to the human mind.

In fact, with the development of postKantian epistemology in Fichte and Schelling, we find an explicit positing and expansion—now as the fundamental and final truth about mind and reality in general—of what Descartes had originally discovered in the cogito as that radically minimal truth in which epistemological certainty can be attained. The postKantians sought to avoid the objectivity problem which leaves one trapped within the subjective mind and unable to demonstrate correspondence by expanding the borders of the mind to enclose the totality of reality in its knowability.[36] Fichte tells us:

> So what then, in a couple of words, is the import of the *Science of Knowledge*? It is this: reason is absolutely independent; it exists only for itself; but for it, too, it is all that exists. So everything that is must be founded in itself, and explained solely from itself, and not from anything outside it, to which it could never get out without abrogating itself. . . . [37]

Fichte and Schelling worked out the notion implicit in Descartes that objects can be known in their correspondence with ideas insofar as ideas and objects alike are nothing other than the products of a fundamentally *active* mind whose activity is creative and is the ultimate source and the final unifying ground of ideas and objects. "The concept of action, which becomes possible only through the intellectual intuition of the self-active self, is the only concept which unites the two worlds that exist for us, the sensible and the intelligible."[38] When the domain of objects comes to be regarded as constituted both *by* the mind and *as* the mind in its objectivity or self-postulated otherness, the fundamental character of Descartes's cogito reaches its full articulation and the stage is set for the completion of epistemology. For Schelling the model of the self is Cartesian: the self " . . . is nothing distinct from its thinking; the thinking of the self and the self as such are absolutely one. . . . " Additionally, this self is "the highest principle of knowledge," "is pure act, pure doing" and as such it is "*a knowing that is simultaneously a producing of its object*."[39] And in Fichte, an unconditioned act lies behind everything, and the model of this act is again Cartesian self-knowing: "In this act, then, which . . . for the self is that which it constructs . . . the philosopher contemplates himself, scans his act directly, knows what he does, because he— *does* it."[40] From this active self, objectivity arises: "*In the self I oppose a divisible not-self to the divisible self*."[41] This is the penultimate stage of the approximation of the epistemological to the divine mind in that the conception of mind worked out here is one whose essence is pure, unrestricted, and autonomous (unconditioned) creative acting. "I *ought* in my thinking to set out from the pure self, and to think of the latter as absolutely self-active; not as determined by things, but as determining them."[42]

Yet, as with Kant, the mind postulated by these epistemologists to complete their projects is not the ordinary mind, and its knowability remains problematic. For Fichte, and even more clearly for Schelling, it is a mind we must postulate, but cannot ultimately know. The self I am is not fully active-determinative, but has a passive dimension. (As with Berkeley, objectivity is felt as a resistance to the whim of my subjective self.) But this objectivity as resistance to the self cannot be accounted for by things-in-themselves; that notion is incoherent. Thus, just as Kant distinguished the transcendental ego as the ultimate synthetic ground from our phenomenal ego, so do Fichte and Schelling distinguish their absolute theoretical egos, necessary postulates of thought, from the practical ego of experience.[43] (So, as with Descartes, Berkeley, and Leibniz, the divine mind is other than my mind, but now the distinction between them has been internalized as the distinction between the phenomenal and the transcendental egos.) For us, the true unity of subject and object is only achievable through willing.[44] If correspondence between subjective ideas and an objective reality cannot be known, perhaps it can be achieved through the will. Of course this will is limited and ultimate unity remains an ideal.[45] But this is a fateful move. The Schelling of 1809 anticipates the position of the last figure in this story, Nietzsche, when he asserts:

> In the final and highest instance there is no other being than Will. Will is primordial Being, and all predicates apply to it alone—groundlessness, eternity, independence of time, self-affirmation. All philosophy strives only to find this highest expression.[46]

To put it quite simply, only a mind as will seems capable of doing justice to the demands of epistemology because, as pure, unconditional willing activity, this mind is at once both continual postulation of the other and the overcoming of the difference. The being of pure will *is* corresponding, without the residue of unincorporated, unbridgeable otherness which shipwrecked earlier projects.

What is problematic in such a conception of mind as demanded by epistemology is that, as finally articulated it provides no indication of any determinate conditions for knowledge. It presents, as Hegel noted about Schelling, a night in which all cows are black.[47] And finally in Nietzsche's conception of knowing and being as sheer will to power—the notion of willing in order to will as the hidden truth about the nature of truth—one can see a fragmentation, a particularization of the cosmic divine active-willing mind of absolute idealism: There is no God, the idea of truth as correspondence is a lie, for each of us can be a god who creates truth and reality for ourselves through the willing act.[48] Thus, epistemology leads either to a failure to successfully show that truth as correspondence is demonstrably attainable (Descartes through Fichte), or to a conception of truth as totally monolithic undifferentiated identity in Schelling, or to a vision of truth as totally pluralizing differentiation in Nietzsche (and in his contemporary followers who fetishize *différance*). For only if there is either one cosmic mind which is at one with objectivity as a whole, or a plurality of minds each of which is at one with the reality they individually will, can correspondence seemingly be accounted for. We saw earlier that completing epistemology successfully by demonstrating correspondence of knowledge and object required attaining identity and difference at one and the same time. Schelling's resignation to sheer identity and Nietzsche's to sheer difference point to the impossibility of attaining both. In neither instance is the correspondence attained stable and susceptible to providing foundations for knowledge.

So, epistemology fails. It does so not because it must appeal to God, nor because a divinely active-creative mind cannot be conceived, either as a cosmic totality or a personal truth, but simply because by forcing us to conceive of a divine mind as the only mind capable of establishing correspondence, nothing remains behind which can enable us to speak in a determinate fashion of either knowledge or objects of knowledge. Neither the undifferentiated cosmic unity of Schelling's absolute nor the will to will of Neitzsche's will to power provides any basis for judging the truth or falsity of our ideas. As an attempt to provide such a basis, epistemology's historical failure is not accidental but indicative of the conceptual bankruptcy, not of any possible notion of objective truth, as Nietzsche and his descendants claim, but of the particular model of truth wedded to epistemology.

NOTES

Preface

1. "Recent Work on Hegel: The Rehabilitation of an Epistemologist," *Philosophy and Phenomenological Research* 52, no. 1 (March 1992): p. 177.

Introduction

1. Ludwig Wittgenstein, *Philosophical Investigations*, trans. G. E. M. Anscombe (New York: Macmillan, 1953), Section 133, p. 51.

2. On this point see especially Richard Rorty, *Consequences of Pragmatism* (Minneapolis: University of Minnesota Press, 1982), Chapters 2, 3 and p. 40.

3. For a general consideration of this development see Richard J. Bernstein, *Beyond Objectivism and Relativism* (Philadelphia: University of Pennsylvania Press, 1983); J. Rajchman and C. West, eds., *Post-Analytic Philosophy* (New York: Columbia University Press, 1985); K. Baynes, J. Bohman, and T. McCarthy, eds., *After Philosophy: End or Transformation* (Cambridge: MIT Press, 1987).

4. The major anglophone proponent of antifoundationalism is, of course, Richard Rorty, whose *Philosophy and the Mirror of Nature* (Princeton: Princeton University Press, 1979) is the first attempt at a systematic consideration of the issue on the part of an analytic philosopher. In *Reason, Truth and History* (Cambridge: Cambridge University Press, 1981), Hilary Putnam also adopts an antifoundational stance while being concerned with the questions about rationality and objectivity which antifoundationalism raises and which I shall discuss in connection with Hegel. In the Introduction (p. xi) he writes, "In short, I shall advance a view in which the mind does not simply 'copy' a world which admits of description by One True Theory. But my view is not a view in which the mind *makes up* the world, either. . . . If one must use metaphorical

language, let the metaphor be this: the mind and the world jointly make up the mind and the world. (Or, to make the metaphor even more Hegelian, the Universe makes up the Universe—with minds—collectively—playing a special role in the making up.)"

5. I will not attempt to present anything like a comprehensive survey of the various specific philosophers who may be said to make up the antifoundational movement, nor—especially—will I assess the many differences in background, approach, focus, style, and content which distinguish them. To speak of a group which includes thinkers as diverse as Quine, Heidegger, Davidson, and Gadamer is obviously to cast one's inclusionary net quite widely. I will soon address those points on which I think a common ground exists. Anyone wishing a more detailed overview should consult Rorty's *Mirror*, Bernstein's *Beyond Objectivism* (for book-length treatments) as well as the excellent brief overviews of the movement provided in *After Philosophy* and *Post-Analytic Philosophy*.

6. I have deliberately omitted the critical theorists of the Frankfurt School and their followers from this list. While they share many of the negative positions of the antifoundationalists, critical theorists agree with the philosophical tradition in holding that philosophy, or something like it, can still maintain a legitimate and authoritative critical position in regard to the status quo. In Chapter 1, "Reason and the Problem of Modernity," and in Chapter 8, "The Critique of Marx and Marxist Thought," I argue that it is Hegel, rather than Marx and his descendants, who develops a successful critical theory.

7. For the idea that foundational philosophy has historically culminated in its own self-destruction, see the work of Nietzsche and Heidegger. In *Contingency, Irony, and Solidarity* (Cambridge: Cambridge University Press, 1989), Rorty has also developed this thesis.

8. For considerations of Cartesianism see Rorty's *Mirror* and Bernstein's *Beyond Objectivism*. The Introduction to *After Philosophy* provides a nice contrastive overview of the foundationalist and antifoundationalist positions.

9. The phrase is Bernstein's: *Beyond Objectivism*, p. 16.

10. The phrases are Hilary Putnam's (*Reason, Truth and History*, p. 50) and Thomas Nagel's (*The View From Nowhere* [Oxford: Oxford University Press, 1986]). See also Rorty, *Consequences*, p. 161. Thomas Nagel writes: "The attempt is made to view the world not from a place within it, or from the vantage point of a special type of life and awareness, but from nowhere in particular and no form of life in particular at all. The object is to discount for the features of our prereflective outlook that make things appear as they do, and thereby to reach an understanding of things as they really are. We flee the subjective under pressure of an assumption that everything must be something not to any point of view, but in itself. To grasp this by detaching more and more from our point of view is the

unreachable ideal at which the pursuit of objectivity aims." "Subjective
and Objective," p. 41 in *Post-Analytic Philosophy*.

11. Having made the linguistic turn, analytic philosophy sought to complete the foundational project by focusing on language and the conditions
of its possibility. There is considerable skepticism about whether this version of foundationalism fares any better than earlier psychologistic approaches. In *Quine and Analytic Philosophy* (Cambridge: MIT Press,
1983), p. 186, George D. Romanos writes "... if Quine is right about
indeterminacy of translation ... there is no single right way to construe
the grammar and meaning of words in a language, even from within a
clearly defined theoretical perspective.... The idea of a fixed conceptual
scheme mediating between us and our theories of the world is as useless
and meaningless as the idea of a fully determinate extralinguistic reality
beyond all theoretical construction." In Chapter 10, "The Renewed Appeal
to Transcendental Arguments," I argue that Donald Davidson's attempt at
a compromise, his efforts to save the traditional foundational goals of
objectivism and realism while rejecting conceptual schemes and foundational epistemology, fails.

12. Ian Hacking speaks of "styles of reasoning" in "Styles of Scientific
Reasoning," in *Post-Analytic Philosophy*. For the analytic consideration of
the myth of the given, see Wilfred Sellars "Empiricism and the Philosophy
of Mind," p. 127 in his *Science, Perception, and Reality* (London: Routledge
and Kegan Paul, 1963).

13. Romanos brings out this point nicely. See p. 187 of *Quine*.

14. The expressions are Gadamer's and Rorty's. See Hans-Georg
Gadamer, *Philosophical Hermeneutics*, ed. and trans. D. Linge (California:
University of California Press, 1976), p. 172; Rorty, *Consequences*, p. xix.
On the same page Rorty writes "One can use language to criticize and
enlarge itself, as one can exercise one's body to develop and strengthen
and enlarge it, but one cannot see language-as-a-whole in relation to
something else to which it applies or for which it is a means to an end."
Also see Romanos, *Quine*, p. 53.

15. See Bernstein, *Beyond Objectivism*, pp. 129, 137, 143; Romanos,
Quine, pp. 96, 97. "The object of knowledge is always already
preinterpreted, situated in a scheme, part of a text, outside which there
are only other texts. On the other hand, the subject of knowledge belongs
to the very world it wishes to interpret.... Thus the idea of a knowing
subject disengaged from the body and the world makes no more sense
than the idea of self-transparence; there is no knowledge without a background, and that background can never be wholly objectified." *After Philosophy*, Introduction, p. 5.

16. I am using the notion of a framework of givenness in a broader sense
than usual, one which does not restrict it to an association with notions of
representation and the correspondence model of truth. In the view I am

developing, antifoundationalism—which rejects these notions—nonetheless remains committed to the idea of the inescapability of determinative
givens, and hence to the notion of the framework of givenness. Antifoundationalism differs from foundationalism in asserting that they are
ineluctable. The full ramifications and the pervasiveness of the assumption that all discourse and knowledge are necessarily conditioned by givens—and Hegel's attack on this assumption—is a central theme of this
book.

17. See Romanos, *Quine*, pp. 186–187; Bernstein, *Beyond Objectivism*, pp.
3–4.

18. Just what, if anything, remains for philosophy to do subsequent to the
abandonment of foundationalism is a controversial topic. Heidegger,
Derrida, and Rorty doubt whether anything which bears much of a connection with the philosophical tradition will remain. Other antifoundationalists, such as Quine and Davidson, seem to feel that little of
the technical analysis they favor will be affected. See Davidson, *Inquiries
into Truth and Interpretation* (Oxford: Oxford University Press, 1984). For
a general discussion of the issue see Rorty's *Consequences*, especially
Chapter 9, as well as *Beyond Objectivism*, and the essays in *After Philosophy. Philosophy Without Foundations* lays out an argument for a
nonfoundational systematic philosophy.

19. See Rorty's Introduction to *Consequences*, p. xix, and the other essays
in that volume for a consideration of the issue of antifoundationalism's
view of knowledge and whether it is offering a theory of knowledge. On
the issue of self-referential inconsistency, see Bernstein's *Beyond Objectivism*, Part One, and Putnam's *Reason*, especially Chapters 2 and 3.

20. See, for example, Hans-Georg Gadamer, *Truth and Method*, trans. G.
Barden and J. Cumming (New York: The Seabury Press, 1975), pp. 308–
309. I explicitly address this issue in Chapter 2, "Philosophy as Systematic
Science."

21. F. H. Jacobi, *Werke II*, eds., F. H. Jacobi and F. Koeppen (Leipzig:
Fleisher, 1812), p. 304. Ramsey is quoted in John Passmore, *A Hundred
Years of Philosophy* (Harmondsworth: Penguin Books, 1968), p. 362.

22. See, for example, Putnam, *Reason*, pp. 49–50, 55, 133; Romanos,
Quine, pp. 180, 185; Rorty, *Consequences*, p. 92. In "Belief and the Basis of
Meaning," Donald Davidson writes "Each interpretation and attribution of
attitude is a move within a holistic theory, a theory necessarily governed
by concern for consistency and general coherence with the truth, and it is
this that sets these theories apart from those that describe mindless objects, or describe objects as mindless." *Inquires into Truth and Interpretation*, p. 154.

23. " . . . [O]ur notion of rationality and of rational revisability are not
fixed by some immutable book of rules, nor are they written into our

transcendental natures, as Kant thought, for the very good reason that the whole idea of a transcendental nature, a nature that we have *noumenally*, apart from any way in which we can conceive of ourselves historically or biologically, is nonsensical." Putnam, *Reason*, p. 83.

24. The notions that knowledge needs to be considered intersubjectively rather than from the egological model, and that social context has a decisive bearing on the conditions of knowledge have their classical articulations in the work of Hegel, and have remained central features of the German wing of continental philosophy through Marx, the Frankfurt School, and its contemporary representatives Habermas, Apel, and Wellmer. Wittgenstein and Dewey are important sources for holism in the analytic tradition where the holistic and antifoundational approach has taken hold through Quine and Davidson and, in the philosophy of science, through Kuhn, Feyerabend, and Hacking.

25. Putnam, *Reason*, p. 84. He also asserts there that "most of what we regard as *a priori* truth is of a contextual and relative character . . ."

26. See "Questions of Method: An Interview with Michel Foucault," especially pp. 102, 104, in *After Philosophy*.

27. See "Subjective and Objective," by Thomas Nagel, p. 32 in *Post-Analytic Philosophy* for a characterization of the traditional hierarchical outlook.

28. Putnam, *Reason*, p. 50. See Rorty, *Consequences*, p. xxxix. On pluralism generally, see Nelson Goodman, *Ways of Worldmaking* (Indianapolis: Hackett, 1978). Feyerabend is an especially articulate defender of pluralism.

29. "Although the quest for certainty and the search for absolute constraints continues to haunt philosophy, there is a sense in which 'absolutism,' to use William James's phrase, is no longer a 'live' option. The dominant temper of our age is fallibilistic." Bernstein, *Beyond Objectivism*, p. 12. See also Putnam, *Reason*, p. 83.

30. In the continental antifoundational tradition the call to abandon the philosophical belief in a Platonic True World and to focus our attention on the here and now in its given particularity has been commonplace since Kierkegaard and is echoed in Heidegger and Gadamer. In analytic philosophy such a move is commonly associated with Wittgenstein. More recently Donald Davidson has written: "In giving up the dualism of scheme and world, we do not give up the world, but reestablish unmediated touch with the familiar objects whose antics make out sentences and opinions true or false." "On the Very Idea of a Conceptual Scheme," p. 198, in *Inquiries*. See also Part Three and Part Four of Bernstein, *Beyond Objectivism*; Putnam, "After Empiricism," p. 29; and Rorty, "Solidarity or Objectivity," in *Post-Analytic Philosophy*, p. 15.

31. Rorty, *Mirror*, Chapter VIII. He adopts a more Nietzschean outlook in *Contingency*.

32. Rorty, *Mirror*, p. 389. See also *Consequences*, p. 166. Similar themes are prominent, informally, in Gadamer, and in Habermas. See "What is Universal Pragmatics," in Habermas' *Communication and the Evolution of Society* (Boston: Beacon Press, 1979). Among postfoundationalists who regard such moves as an attempt to establish a new authority, see Jean-François Lyotard, *The Postmodern Condition: A Report on Knowledge*, trans. Geoff Bennington and Brian Massumi (Minneapolis: University of Minnesota Press, 1984).

33. See Rorty, *Consequences*, pp. 173–174.

34. Bernstein, *Beyond Objectivism*, p. 19. See Rorty, "Solidarity or Objectivity," in *Post-Analytic Philosophy*; Chapter 9 of *Consequences*, "Pragmatism, Relativism, and Irritationalism;" and Davidson, pp. xviii and xix of the Introduction to *Inquiries*.

35. Putnam writes: "Just as the methodological solipsist can become a *real* solipsist, the cultural relativist can become a cultural imperialist. He can say, 'Well then, truth—the only notion of truth I can understand—is defined by the norms of *my* culture.' ('After all,' he can add, 'which norms should I rely on? The norms of *somebody else's* culture?')" "Why Reason Can't Be Naturalized," *After Philosophy*, p. 232.

36. "Philosophy may in no way interfere with the actual use of language; it can in the end only describe it.

For it cannot give it any foundation either.

It leaves everything as it is."

Wittgenstein, *Philosophical Investigations*, Section 124, p. 49.

37. Putnam writes: "Hegel already denounced the idea of an 'Archimedean point' from which epistemology could judge all of our scientific, legal, moral, religious, etc., beliefs (and set up standards for all of the special subjects)." "Why Reason Can't Be Naturalized," *After Philosophy*, p. 223.

38. Stanley Rosen, *G. W. F. Hegel: An Introduction to the Science of Wisdom* (New Haven: Yale University Press, 1974), p. 130.

39. *Hegel's Logic: Being Part One of the Encyclopedia of the Philosophical Sciences*, trans. William Wallace (Oxford: Oxford University Press, 1975) Paragraph 60, p. 93. Hereafter referred to as the *Encyclopedia Logic*.

40. This view of a non-foundational systematic philosophy grounded in Hegel is also articulated in the work of Richard Dein Winfield. See: *The Just Economy* (New York: Routledge, 1988); *Reason and Justice* (Albany: SUNY Press, 1988); *Overcoming Foundations* (New York: Columbia University Press, 1989); and *Freedom and Modernity* (Albany: SUNY Press, 1991).

Chapter 1, "Reason and the Problem of Modernity"

1. The major expositors of this point of view are to be found in Herbert Marcuse, *Reason and Revolution* (London: Oxford University Press, 1955); Joachim Ritter, *Hegel and the French Revolution* (Cambridge: MIT Press, 1982); Ernst Bloch, *Subjekt/Objekt* (Frankfurt am Main: Suhrkamp, 1971); Jürgen Habermas, *Theorie und Praxis* (Berlin: Luchterhand, 1963). Other, more conservative readings of Hegel are legion. For a recent appraisal which attempts a synthesis of the left and right schools of Hegel interpretation, see Michael Allen Gillespie, *Hegel, Heidegger and the Ground of History* (Chicago: University of Chicago Press, 1984).

2. In speaking of the French Revolution as a "world-historical event," as announcing "our world, our age" as the age of the "will free to will itself," the age of the "rulership of philosophy" (pp. 535, 524, 527), Hegel writes the following in his *Lectures on the History of Philosophy*: "In the thought of right there now arose a state of mind [*Verfassung*], and on this foundation everything should now be based. For as long as the sun had stood in the firmament and planets circled about it this had not been seen, that man stands on his head, that is, on thinking, and constructs actuality according to it. Anaxagoras was the first to say that nous rules the world, but now for the first time man came to know that thinking should rule spiritual actuality. This was then a magnificent sunrise. All thinking beings have joined in celebration of this epoch. A noble emotion has ruled in this time, an enthusiasm of spirit has transfigured the world, as though a real reconciliation of the divine with the world has just occurred. (G. W. F. Hegel, *Werke,* vol. 12 [Frankfurt am Main: Suhrkamp, 1970], p. 529.)

A third development distinctive of the modern world and also of concern to Hegel—the rise of the modern capitalist economy—will not be considered here. See my introduction to the essays in *Hegel on Economics and Freedom* (Macon, GA: Mercer University Press, 1987), and *The Just Economy,* by Richard Dein Winfield.

3. It should be noted that Hegel's views on the French Revolution, on modern scientific thought, and on the capitalist economy were by no means uncritical. The *locus classicus* for Hegel's critical perspective on the French revolution is to be found in Chapter VI, "Absolute Freedom and Terror," in the *Phenomenology of Spirit,* trans. A. V. Miller (Oxford: Oxford University Press, 1977). Also see Ritter's *Hegel and the French Revolution.*

4. The *locus classicus* for a consideration of the modern problem of legitimation and of antimodernism is Hans Blumenberg, *The Legitimacy of the Modern Age* (Cambridge: MIT Press, 1983). See also Jürgen Habermas, *Legitimation Crisis* (Boston: Beacon Press, 1975), and Leo Strauss,

Natural Right and History (Chicago: University of Chicago Press, 1953). On the specific issue of the epistemic legitimacy of modern natural science, see Michael Foster, "The Christian Doctrine of Creation and the Rise of Modern Natural Science" and Francis Oakley, "Christian Theology and the Newtonian Science: the Rise of the Concept of Laws of Nature," both in *Creation: The Impact of an Idea*, eds. O'Connor and Oakley (New York: Charles Scribner's Sons, 1969).

5. The most recent and comprehensive statement of this point of view as it applies to issues of cognition is to be found in Rorty's *Mirror*. As it applies to issues of conduct and action, see Alasdair MacIntyre, *After Virtue* 2nd ed. (South Bend: Notre Dame University Press, 1984).

6. In addition to Rorty and MacIntyre, see also Wittgenstein, *Philosophical Investigations*, and Gadamer, *Truth and Method*. For the particular view that modern natural science lacks, and must lack adequate, philosophically rational foundations see especially Paul K. Feyerabend, *Against Method* (London: Verso Editions, 1978).

7. It is important to note at this juncture that not all of those who have criticized the traditional ideal of autonomous reason and the foundational project can be classified as anti- or postmoderns (in the sense of these terms as used in this book.) As I shall show, Hegel rejects foundationalism but not modernity. In a similar vein, Feyerabend and Habermas fall into the Hegelian tradition discussed here. Neither of them are unequivocally critical either of modern science or of the modern idea of freedom. And both aim for philosophy to maintain a critical edge and explicitly see philosophy as furthering the modern tradition of freedom. See Habermas, *Knowledge and Human Interests* (Boston: Beacon Press, 1971), and *The Theory of Communicative Action* (Boston: Beacon Press, 1984); Feyerabend, *Science in a Free Society* (London: Verso Editions, 1978), and "Two Models of Epistemic Change: Mill and Hegel," in *Problems of Empiricism* (Cambridge: Cambridge University Press, 1981). For Rorty's consideration of recent analytic philosophy as turning away from its earlier foundational impetus, see "Epistemological Behaviorism and the Detranscendentalization of Analytic Philosophy," in *Hermeneutics and Praxis*, ed. Robert Hollinger (South Bend: University of Notre Dame Press, 1985), which focuses especially on Sellars and Quine as implicit but not fully self-conscious antifoundationalists. Rorty's pursuit of this topic continues in *Mirror* and *Consequences*. For Rorty on Davidson: "Pragmatism, Davidson and Truth," pp. 333–355 in *Truth and Interpretation: Perspectives on the Philosophy of Donald Davidson*, ed. Ernest Lepore (London: Basil Blackwell, 1986). An interesting historical account of analytic philosophy which presents it as self-deconstructive is to be found in Romanos, *Quine*.

8. See the references to Hegel in the following: Foucault, "The Discourse on Language," in *The Archeology of Knowledge* (New York: Harper & Row, 1976); Gadamer, *Truth and Method, Hegel's Dialectic: Five Hermeneutical*

Studies, (New Haven: Yale University Press, 1976), and *Reason in the Age of Science* (Cambridge: MIT Press, 1982); Habermas, *Knowledge and Human Interests* and *Theorie und Praxis*.

Rorty, MacIntyre, and Sellars too, are hard to pin down as regards their assessments of what is positive in Hegel. At several places in *Mirror*, Rorty speaks tantalizingly of Hegel in positive terms, but, neither in that work nor in *Consequences* does he develop an overall assessment of the pluses and minuses of Hegel's philosophy. MacIntyre's treatment is also equivocal. See *After Virtue*, which he identifies as a work in "philosophical history" of the type "propounded by writers such as Hegel" (p. 3); yet he rejects what he sees as Hegel's absolutism (p. 270).

9. See Rorty, *Mirror*, pp. 165 and 167. On p. 192 he speaks of the "Hegelian . . . project of deconstruction . . . " and see note #59 to "Pragmatism, Davidson and Truth," in *Truth and Interpretation*, p. 354. See Gadamer's essay "Hegel and Heidegger," in *Hegel's Dialectic*. For Habermas's view, see *Knowledge and Human Interests*, Chapter 1, "Hegel's Critique of Kant: Radicalization or Abolition of the Theory of Knowledge."

10. Feyerabend's *Against Method*, Rorty's *Mirror*, MacIntyre's *A Short History of Ethics* (New York: Macmillan & Co., 1966) and *After Virtue* are all either explicit or implicit testimonies to the importance of the history of philosophy, and of history itself, for contemporary philosophy. On the contextual embeddedness of knowledge, see, in addition to the above, Habermas's *Knowledge and Human Interests*; on morality, Feyerabend's *Science in a Free Society*, MacIntyre's *Short History* and *After Virtue*. On the holist and historicist turn in philosophy of science following Kuhn, see Ian Hacking, *Representing and Intervening* (Cambridge: Cambridge University Press, 1983); Andrew Pickering, *Constructing Quarks: A Sociological History of Particle Physics* (Chicago: University of Chicago Press, 1984); and Robert Ackermann, *Data, Instruments and Theory: A Dialectical Approach to Understanding Science* (Princeton: Princeton University Press, 1985).

In the Preface of the *Philosophy of Right*, Hegel writes: "To comprehend what is, this is the task of philosophy, because what is, is reason. Whatever happens, every individual is a child of his time; so philosophy too is its own time apprehended in thoughts. It is just as absurd to fancy that a philosophy can transcend its contemporary world as it is to fancy that an individual can overleap his own age, jump over Rhodes." *Hegel's Philosophy of Right*, trans. T. M. Knox (Oxford: Oxford University Press, 1967), p. 11.

11. "The true shape in which the truth exists can only be the scientific system of such truth. To help bring philosophy closer to the form of Science, to the goal where it can lay aside the title '*love* of knowing' and be *actual* knowing—that is what I have set myself to do. The inner necessity that knowing should be Science lies in its nature, and only the systematic

exposition of philosophy itself provides it." The *Phenomenology*, Preface, p. 3. MacIntyre writes: "Hence this kind of historicism, unlike Hegel's involves a form of fallibilism; it is a kind of historicism which excludes all claims to absolute knowledge." (*After Virtue*, Postscript to the 2nd edition, p. 270). Rorty, like other postmoderns, tends to see Hegel from two sides. He likes to speak favorably of others' critiques of Hegel. See "Epistemological Behaviorism and the Detranscendentalization of Analytic Philosophy," *Mirror*, pp. 5, 135, 362, n. 8. And he remains elusive in *Consequences*. See, amongst other places, p. xlvii, pp. 16, 94–95.

12. "Henceforth, the principle of the independence of Reason, or of its absolute self-subsistence, is made a general principle of philosophy, as well as a foregone conclusion of the time." *Encyclopedia Logic*, Paragraph 60, p. 93.

13. For a contemporary attack on the "myth of the given," see Sellars, "Empiricism and the Philosophy of Mind," in *Science, Perception and Reality*. In this essay Sellars mentions Hegel's attack on givenness (p. 127), calls his own work "Meditationis Hegeliennes" (p. 148), but holds that Hegel is not free of the "framework of givenness" (p. 127). One of the points to be considered subsequently, albeit briefly in this Chapter is that it is just the "framework of givenness" which Hegel decisively and thoroughly criticizes and rejects in the *Phenomenology*. See my essay "Understanding Hegel Today," in the *Journal of the History of Philosophy* 19:3 (July 1981), as well as Chapters 4 and 5.

14. The *locus classicus* for viewing modern science as a rejection of Aristotle and Aristotelianism is, of course, Bacon. For a more balanced view see E. A. Burtt, *The Metaphysical Foundations of Modern Science* (London: Routledge & Kegan Paul, 1924). For a consideration of Galileo as someone who rejects both Aristotle and common sense, see Feyerabend, *Against Method*, and Stillman Drake, *Galileo* (Toronto: University of Toronto Press, 1990).

15. The *locus classicus* here is, of course, Descartes' *Meditations on First Philosophy* and the *Discourse on Method*. For his statement of the need for a philosophical foundations of the new science, see the opening paragraphs of the *Meditations* and p. 86., (vol. 1) of the *Discourse* in *The Philosophical Works of Descartes*, trans. Haldane and Ross (Cambridge: Cambridge University Press, 1931). See also Kant, Preface to the first edition of the *Critique of Pure Reason*, trans. Norman Kemp Smith (New York: Macmillan, 1929), p. 8.

16. For the view, from an historical perspective, that modern natural science still lacks an adequate philosophical foundation, see the essays by Foster and Oakley in *Creation: The Impact of an Idea*, and Feyerabend, *Against Method*.

17. Speaking of modern science as a rebellion against tradition which asserts the individual's right to freedom of thought, the historian of sci-

ence I. B. Cohen writes: "Traditionally, knowledge had been based on faith and insight, on reason and revelation. The new science discarded all of these as ways of understanding nature. . . . The consequences were as revolutionary as the doctrine itself. For not only did the new method found knowledge on a wholly new basis, but it implied that men and women no longer had to believe what was said by eminent authorities. . . . What counted, therefore, in the new science of the seventeenth century was not the qualifications of learning of any author or reporter but rather his veracity in reporting, his true understanding of the method of science. . . . Knowledge thus took on a democratic rather than a hierarchical character and no longer depended so much on the insight of a chosen few as on the application of a proper method, accessible to anyone with sufficient wit to grasp the new principles. . . . " I. B. Cohen, *Revolution in Science* (Cambridge: Harvard University Press 1985), p. 79. For a thorough critique of the philosophical tradition which attempts to provide foundations for knowledge, see Rorty's *Mirror*.

18. See the "Declaration of the Rights of Man," in *Readings in European History*, vol. 2, ed. J. H. Robinson (Boston: Ginn & Co., 1906), pp. 409–411.

19. For the view that a philosophical science of morality and politics can be founded in an analysis of desire, see Hobbes' *De Homine* and *Leviathan*; in natural sentiments, see Hume's *A Treatise of Human Nature* and *An Enquiry Concerning the Principles of Morals*; in innate rules, see Kant's *Foundations of the Metaphysics of Morals* and *Critique of Practical Reason*. And for a devastating critique of the whole project of moral and political foundational philosophy, see MacIntyre's *After Virtue*.

20. For a developed consideration of the claim that Hegel's philosophical project commences with a rejection of foundationalism see Chapters 4 and 5. See also Richard D. Winfield, "Conceiving Reality Without Foundations: Hegel's Neglected Strategy for *Realphilosophie*," *The Owl of Minerva* 15:2 (Spring 1984).

21. See pp. 5–9 of the Introduction to the *Prolegomena to Any Future Metaphysics*, trans. Carus (Indianapolis: Bobbs Merrill, 1950). Hume's negative, solipsistic, and skeptical conclusions parallel the undesired conclusions to the same effect which follow from Descartes' attempt at foundationalism in the *Mediations*, assuming his proofs of the existence of God fail. See Chapter 11.

22. For Hume's advocacy of skepticism as regards knowledge, see *An Enquiry Concerning Human Understanding* in *Essential Works of David Hume*, ed. Ralph Cohen (New York: Bantam Books, 1965), pp. 157f. and 162. That according to Hume, custom and habit must prevail in matters of morality, see *A Treatise of Human Nature*, Book III, "Of Morals," ed. Selby-Bigge (Oxford: The Clarendon Press, 1888), p. 486. That civil society and its notion of justice derive from and are based on convention, see *A Treatise*, Book III, pp. 543, 550. That Hume was no advocate of modernity

or revolution, see *A Treatise*, pp. 552, 553, 556, 563. And that morality can have no final rational grounding, see *A Treatise*, pp. 267, 413, 457.

23. For a more detailed consideration of Hegel's rejection of the foundational project, see Chapters 4 and 5.

24. See Hume, *An Enquiry*, pp. 166–167. Hegel writes: "Even Hume's skepticism does not deny that the characteristics of universality and necessity are found in cognition. And even in Kant this remains a presupposition after all; it may be said, to use the ordinary phraseology of the sciences, that Kant did not more than offer another *explanation* of the fact." *Encyclopedia Logic*, Paragraph 40, p. 65.

25. For a defense of the idea that the circularity of the critical project is not merely benign, but in fact a demonstration of the truth of its claims, one might attempt to argue that the very need to presuppose what must be demonstrated indicates that what are being presupposed are inescapable fundamental principles for thought. For an argument along these lines, see Rudiger Bubner, "Kant, Transcendental Argument and the Problem of Deduction," *The Review of Metaphysics* 28:3 (March 1975).

26. See Heidegger, *Discourse on Thinking*, trans. J. M. Anderson and E. H. Freund (New York: Harper and Row, 1966), and "The Turning," in *The Question Concerning Technology and Other Essays*, trans. W. Lovitt (New York: Harper and Row, 1977).

27. Hegel summarizes and considers these assumptions, as well as the inadequacies of the critical project and his intention to engage in a metacritical consideration of epistemology and transcendental philosophy in the Introduction to the *Phenomenology*.

28. "In common with Empiricism the Critical Philosophy assumes that experience affords the sole foundation for cognitions: which however it does not allow to rank as truths, but only as knowledge of phenomena." (*Encyclopedia Logic*, Paragraph 40, p. 65) For Hegel's view that the nature of the given—whether an externally given object or an internally given idea or principle—is a matter of indifference as regards a critical consideration of foundational epistemology and transcendental philosophy, see the Introduction to the *Phenomenology*, p. 53.

29. See Hume, *An Enquiry*, pp. 63–64, and *A Treatise*, p. 415; Kant, *Critique of Pure Reason*, p. 174, B 166–167, and *Groundwork of the Metaphysics of Morals*, trans. Paton (New York: Harper and Row, 1964), pp. 79, 92–93.

30. See *Critique of Pure Reason*, pp. 298–300, B 352–354.

31. Of course, to include Fichte here one must add that it is what reason must posit for itself in order to constitute itself as consciousness and as moral will.

32. For Habermas' critique of Gadamer's hermeneutical antifoundationalist position and his defense of reason see *Philosophische Rundschau* XIV, Beiheft 5 (1967): pp. 149–180. Gadamer responds in "On the Scope and Function of Hermeneutical Reflection," in *Philosophical Hermeneutics*.

33. On the possibility of Nietzschean nihilism as an alternative, assuming the failure of foundationalism, see MacIntyre, *After Virtue*, Chapter 9 and Chapter 18.

34. See *Hegel's Science of Logic*, trans. A. V. Miller (London: George Allen & Unwin, Ltd., 1969), pp. 45, 49, 51, 63, where he speaks of rejecting the form of consciousness as a prerequisite for his systematic science. Hereafter referred to as the *Logic*.

35. For Hegel's general consideration of the problems, paradoxes, and inadequacies of the critical philosophy, see, in addition to the Introduction to the *Logic*, the Introduction to the *Phenomenology*, the "Second Attitude of Thought to Objectivity," in the *Encyclopedia Logic*, Paragraphs 37–60, pp. 60–94, and the *Lectures on the History of Philosophy*, Vol. 3, *Recent German Philosophy*, trans. Haldane and Simpson (New York: Humanities Press, 1974), p. 409ff.

This is a paradoxical point about the nature of critical-transcendental philosophy which is certainly well recognized by Wittgenstein in the *Tractatus*: "My propositions serve as elucidations in the following way: anyone who understands me eventually recognizes them as nonsensical, when he has used them—as steps—to climb up beyond them. (He must, so to speak, throw away the ladder after he has climbed up it.)" *Tractatus Logico-Philosophicus*, trans. D. F. Pears and B. F. McGuinness [London: Routledge & Kegan Paul, 1961]; 6.54.

36. That Hegel regards the self-sublation of consciousness as the outcome of the *Phenomenology* and the beginning of the system of reason, see the *Logic*, pp. 49, 51 and 60. A standard interpretation of the logic and system is that they are based on and generated out of a superpurified transcendental consciousness or ego of some kind. For why this cannot be the case, according to Hegel, see p. 76 of the *Logic*, where he explicitly rejects the notion that philosophical science can begin with the ego. Note also the remarks in the logic of the concept, pp. 582–587, where he goes to considerable length to make clear that his logical science is neither based on nor developed out of the structure of consciousness. Of course, these remarks only show that the standard interpretation conflicts with Hegel's self-understanding, not that the model of consciousness is not implicitly present.

37. I am grateful to David Baird for the useful bit of terminology, "referential skyhook," suggesting as it does a position, itself located nowhere, which links represented and representation.

38. For a consideration of the idea that the *Phenomenology* articulates this discovery, see Chapter 3, "Hegel's *Phenomenology* as Introduction to Systematic Philosophy," and Chapter 4, "Beginning Philosophy Without 'Beginnings.'" Also see p. 45 of the *Logic* where Hegel speaks of the overcoming of consciousness as something which must be undertaken prior to the beginning of philosophical science.

39. See Chapter 5, "Philosophy and Dialectical Method," for a detailed consideration of this issue.

40. On this point, see the three "Attitudes of Thought to Objectivity," Paragraphs 26–78, pp. 47–112, in the *Encyclopedia Logic* and pp. 50, 51, 64 in the *Logic*.

41. In fact, if it can be shown that the system does contain such references, used constitutively and not merely illustratively, then this would, of course, amount to a critique of its autonomous and scientific character. I would suggest that there are various places in the system Hegel developed, perhaps most obviously in the *Philosophy of Right*, where Hegel can be so criticized: according to his own criteria for systematic philosophy. In this regard, see the essay, "Hegel's Challenge to the Modern Economy," by Richard D. Winfield, in *Hegel On Economics and Freedom*, and "Hegel: A Non-Metaphysical View," by Klaus Hartmann, in *Hegel: A Collection of Critical Essays*, ed. A. MacIntyre (New York: Doubleday & Co., 1972).

42. It is on this point of transcendental philosophy and Hegel's continuation of it that the interpretation of Hegel's systematic philosophy being presented here parts company with that of Hartmann's mentioned above and also that of Alan White's in *Absolute Knowledge: Hegel and the Problem of Metaphysics*, (Ohio: Ohio University Press, 1983).

43. It should be noted once again, given the prevalence of readings which take the opposite point of view, that Hegel is quite explicit as to the fact that the thought determinacies or categories of his system are not generated from out of some form of reflection which is based on any version of the model of consciousness or the subject. In addition to the references given in note 40, see also the *Logic*, pp. 75, 583, 586.

44. Hegel is acutely aware of the problems and pitfalls which arise when one attempts, philosophically, to conceive reality—as opposed to cognizing it—as what is other than thought. (For Hegel, cognizing reality is a matter for empirical science.) See the Introduction to the *Philosophy of Nature*, especially Paragraph 246; Addition, p. 196ff., in volume 1 of *Hegel's Philosophy of Nature*, 3 vols., trans. M. J. Petry (London: George Allen & Unwin, Ltd., 1970).

45. That this self-restriction of what systematic philosophy can do does not necessarily lead to the conclusion that Hegel—or, more significantly, systematic philosophy—advocates quietistic resignation to the status quo for the philosopher as citizen (or for the non-philosopher), see the *Encyclopedia Logic*, Paragraph 213, p. 274ff., especially the Addition.

46. See the essays in *Hegel On Economics and Freedom* and also "Freedom As Interaction: Hegel's Resolution to the Dilemma of Liberal Theory," by R. D. Winfield, in *Hegel's Philosophy of Action*, eds. L. S. Stepelevich and Lamb (Atlantic Highlands, NJ: Humanities Press, 1983).

47. "The freedom of the will itself, is the principle and the substantial basis of all right, it is itself absolute, in and for itself eternal right, and is the highest right, insofar as other particular rights stand next to it; it is thereby that by means of which man is man, thus the fundamental principle of spirit." Hegel, *Lectures on the Philosophy of History, Werke*, vol. 12: p. 524–525.

48. See MacIntyre's *After Virtue*, especially Chapters 4, 5, and 6. "My own conclusion is very clear. It is that . . . we still, in spite of the efforts of three centuries of moral philosophy and one of sociology, lack any coherent rationally defensible statement of a liberal individualist point of view . . . " *After Virtue*, p. 259.

49. See my introductory essay and that by Richard D. Winfield in *Hegel On Economics and Freedom*. From the point of view of the systematic philosophy being presented here, one must include among those givens which cannot support a rational and adequate conception of freedom the latest to be introduced in a long line of foundational candidates for freedom: the linguistic-communicative principles appealed to by Habermas and Apel. For a brief critique of Apel's attempt at a "transcendental deduction" of such principles in his *Transformation der Philosophie*, see my review of the same in the *Graduate Faculty Philosophy Journal* 6:2 (Fall 1977).

50. " . . . the truth is plain: there are no such rights, [human rights] and belief in them is one with belief in witches and unicorns." For " . . . every attempt to give good reasons for believing that there *are* such rights has failed." "Natural or human rights are fictions . . . " MacIntyre, *After Virtue*, pp. 69, 70.

51. To anticipate a possible objection to what I have said in regard to this reading of Hegel: one can of course, within the system, reconstruct history in a rational fashion. That is, as leading up to an historical situation whose conditions allow for freedom and even for the emergence of a philosophy of freedom. But this rational reconstruction of history does not commit the systematic philosopher to a metaphysical, transhistorical claim that history as a datum displays such necessary teleological development. For a reading of Hegel's philosophy of history in line with the view of Hegel presented in this essay, see George Dennis O'Brien, *Hegel On Reason and History* (Chicago: University of Chicago Press, 1975), and R. D. Winfield, "The Theory and Practice of the History of Freedom: The Right of History in Hegel's *Philosophy of Right*," in *History and System: Hegel's Philosophy of History*, ed. R. L. Perkins (Albany: SUNY Press, 1984).

52. "On Empirically Equivalent Systems of the World," *Erkenntnis* 9 (1975): p. 328.

53. For a detailed critique of Marx from the point of view of Hegel's systematic philosophy, see Chapter 8, "The Critique of Marx and Marxist Thought," and Klaus Hartmann's *Die Marxsche Theorie* (Berlin: Walter de Gruyter & Co., 1970).

54. See the Preface to the *Philosophy of Right*, p. 11ff.

Chapter 2, "Philosophy as Systematic Science"

1. For a consideration of the issues discussed here in the context of Hegel's system, see Chapter 1.

2. Rorty, *Mirror*, p. 394.

3. The issue of how these latter goals may be attained without a foundational philosophy is developed at some length in Chapter 1.

4. See Descartes' Third Meditation.

5. Gadamer, *Philosophical Hermeneutics*, p. 172.

6. See Rorty, "Epistemological Behaviorism and the Detranscendentalization of Analytic Philosophy," in *Hermeneutics and Praxis*, and *Mirror*, p. 371–372; Gadamer, *Philosophical Hermeneutics*, p. 36; *Truth and Method*, p. 309.

7. To hold that they are identical in terms of content, but also simultaneously distinct as 'knowledge' on the one hand and 'object' on the other will not suffice. To preserve that distinction, the nature of the difference must be articulated; there must be some determinate difference, either ontological or formal. But once such a determinate difference is established, the requisite moment of identity is lost: If knowledge and object are in some respect(s) different, the foundationalist can no longer be sure that knowledge corresponds to the object as it is objectively, independent of the knowing act. As long as some determinate difference is allowed, the foundationalist cannot claim that knowledge captures the object as it truly is as determined independently of the knowing act. He would only be entitled to claim that the knowledge in question is knowledge of things as they appear, not as they are in themselves. This is discussed at greater length in Chapter 11.

Chapter 3, "Hegel's *Phenomenology* as Introduction to Systematic Science"

1. "The Concept of pure science and its deduction is therefore presupposed in the present work insofar as the *Phenomenology of Spirit* is nothing other than the deduction of it." The *Logic*, p. 49, translation revised.

2. Wim van Dooren, *Hegel-Studien* 4 (1967); 7, (1972). J. N. Findlay, foreword, the *Phenomenology*, p. xiii: "Despite the sensitive work of Jean Hyppolite, we are far from having anything like a really full commentary on the *Phenomenology*." See also Howard Kainz, *Hegel's Phenomenology*, (Alabama: Alabama University Press, 1976), who asserts that no "true" or "refutable" commentary is possible.

3. Otto Pöggeler, "Die Komposition der Phänomenologie des Geistes," in *Materialien zu Hegels Phänomenologie des Geistes*, eds. H. F. Fulda and D. Henrich (Frankfurt am Main: Suhrkamp Verlag, 1973), pp. 382, 333–334, 371–372.

4. Pögeller, "Zur Deutung der Phänomenologie des Geistes" in *Hegels Idee einer Phänomenologie des Geistes* (Freiburg: Karl Alber, 1973), pp. 171, 181.

5. See Pögeller, "Zur Deutung . . . ," pp. 188–189. Also, Charles Taylor, *Hegel* (Cambridge: Cambridge University Press, 1975), p. 233, footnote; Malcom Clark, *Logic and System* (The Hague: Martinus Nijhoff, 1971), pp. 143–144; Emil Fackenheim, *The Religious Dimension in Hegel's Thought* (Boston Beacon Press, 1967), pp. 73–74. Also Rudolf Haym, *Hegel und seiner Zeit* (Hildesheim: Georg Olms, 1962); Theodor Haering, *Hegel, sein Wollen und sein Werk* (Aalen: Scientia Verlag, 1963); Werner Marx, *Hegel's Phenomenology of Spirit* (New York: Harper and Row, 1975).

6. Amongst the chief expositors of what I call the received view can be found the following: Malcom Clark, *Logic and System*; Werner Becker, *Hegels Phänomenologie des Geistes* (Stuttgart: 1971); Ernst Bloch, *Subjekt / Objekt*; Rudiger Bubner, "Problemgeschichte und systematischer Sinn der 'Phänomenologie' Hegels" in *Dialektic und Wissenschaft* (Frankfurt am Main: Suhrkamp Verlag, 1971); Emil Fackenheim, *The Religious Dimension in Hegel's Thought*, J. N. Findlay, *Hegel: A Re-examination* (Oxford: Oxford University Press, 1976); Hans Friedrich Fulda, *Das Problem einer Einleitung in Hegels Wissenchaft der Logik* (Frankfurt am Main: Klostermann, 1975); Hans-Georg Gadamer, *Hegel's Dialectic: Five Hermeneutical Studies*, Jürgen Habermas, *Knowledge and Human Interests*; Johannes Heinrichs, *Die Logik der Phänomenologie des Geistes* (Bonn: Bouvier Verlag, 1974); Jean Hyppolite, *Genesis and Structure of Hegel's Phenomenology* (Evanston: Northwestern University Press, 1974); Alexander Kojève, *Introduction to the Reading of Hegel* (New York: Basic Books, 1969); Quentin Lauer, *A Reading of Hegel's Phenomenology of Spirit* (New York: Fordham University Press, 1976); Georg Lukacs, *The Young Hegel* (Cambridge: MIT Press, 1976); Herbert Marcuse, *Hegels Ontologie und die Theorie der Geschichtlichkeit* (Frankfurt am Main: Kostermann, 1968); Werner Marx, *Hegel's Phenomenology*; Wolfgang Marx, *Hegels Theorie logische Vermittlung* (Stuttgart: Frommann-Holzboog, 1972); G. R. G. Mure, *The Philosophy of Hegel* (Oxford: Oxford University Press, 1965); Horst Henning Ottmann, *Das Scheitern einer*

Einleitung in Hegels Philosophie (Munich: Verlag Anton Pustet, 1973);
Otto Pögeller, *Hegels Idee einer Phänomenologie des Geistes*; Stanley
Rosen, *G. W. F. Hegel: An Introduction to the Science of Wisdom*; Charles
Taylor, *Hegel*; Karin Schrader-Klebert, *Das Problem des Anfangs in Hegels
Philosophie* (Munich: Oldenbourg Verlag, 1969); Manfred Wetzel,
Reflexion und Bestimmtheit in Hegels Wissenschaft der Logik (Hamburg:
Fundament Verlag Dr. Sasse, 1971).

7. See Taylor, *Hegel*, p. 138; Werner Marx, *Hegel's Phenomenology*, pp.
50, 84; Bloch, *Subjekt/Objekt*, pp. 59–60; Kainz, *Hegel's Phenomenology*, p.
12ff.

8. A somewhat dissenting voice is raised by Rudiger Bubner in his article "Problemgeschichte und systematischer Sinn der 'Phänomenologie'
Hegels." To my mind, Bubner correctly perceives that the function of the
Phenomenology was meant by Hegel to be a critical one. (See his page
39ff.) But he is nonetheless to be classified as a holder of the received view
since he holds that the outcome of the *Phenomenology* as critique is positive in the traditional sense in that it establishes the truth of knowing:
Consciousness discovers the essence of its truth as pure reflection, pp. 42–
43. Bubner holds that the function and the method of the *Phenomenology*
are critical, but that its outcome is positive and determinate. As I understand it, the outcome of the *Phenomenology* is also to be seen as a radically negative one. And it is also one which functions positively in its
radical negativity: the *Phenomenology* does not establish the truth of
knowing as reflection, it establishes the 'truth' of no mode of knowing at
all, and just this is its positive function of determining what
presuppositionless science must begin with. I discuss this at greater
length in Chapter 4, "Beginning Philosophy Without 'Beginnings.'"

9. On this point see especially Taylor, *Hegel*, pp. 136, 214; Lauer, *A
Reading*, pp. 19, 263ff., 267; Werner Marx, *Hegel's Phenomenology*, pp. 8,
33, 43; Gadamer, *Hegel's Dialectic*, p. 11; Kojeve, *Introduction*, pp. 31, 166;
Rosen, *G. W. F. Hegel*, pp. 40, 234, 240; Marcuse, *Hegels Ontologie*, pp.
349–350.

10. For those who hold that the *Phenomenology* fails as an argument, see
Ottman, *Das Scheitern*, especially pp. 145, 191ff., 200; Heinrichs, *Die
Logik*, pp. 53–54; Clark, *Logic and System*, pp. 31, 166; Schrader-Klebert,
Das Problem, pp. 35, 36, 46, 47.

11. See, for example, Taylor, *Hegel*, p. 214; Werner Marx, *Hegel's Phenomenology*, pp. xxiii, 49, 87, 99; Heinrichs, *Die Logik*, p. 66; Gadamer, *Hegel's
Dialectic*, pp. 10, 111; Kainz, *Hegel's Phenomenology*, p. 12; Hyppolite,
Genesis, p. 587; Ottmann, *Das Scheitern*, p. 133; Findlay, *Re-examination*,
p. 145.

12. Wetzel, *Reflexion*, pp. 2–4, 15, 21, 30; Werner Marx, *Hegel's Phenomenology*, pp. xxi, 11, 49, 99; Gadamer, *Hegel's Dialectic*, pp. 10, 111; Kojeve,
Introduction, p. 167; Heinrichs, *Die Logik*, pp. 58, 60, 75, 112, 487;

Hyppolite, *Genesis*, pp. 589, 590, 591, 599, 601, 603; Schrader-Klebert, *Das Problem*, pp. 11, 35, 62, 93, 95; Rosen, *G. W. F. Hegel*, pp. 41, 48, 111–114, 119, 196, 197, 235; Clark, *Logic and System*, p. 69; Taylor, *Hegel*, pp. 226, 299; Lukacs, *Young Hegel*, pp. 471, 515, 533; Marcuse, *Hegels Ontologie*, p. 355.

13. See the previous note and especially Wetzel, *Reflexion*, Wolfgang Marx, *Hegels Theorie*, Schrader-Klebert, *Das Problem*, Werner Marx, *Hegel's Phenomenology*, Taylor, *Hegel*. Dieter Henrich, in his article, "Anfang und Methode der Logik," in *Hegel im Kontext* (Frankfurt am Main: Suhrkamp Verlag, 1971) indicates that the notion that the *Logic* begins in or with reflection does not coincide with Hegel's self-understanding and claims concerning this beginning. I discuss Henrich's critical views extensively in Chapter 4.

14. For Hegel's assertion that the *Logic* begins without presuppositions: "Thus the beginning must be an *absolute*, or what is synonymous here, an *abstract* beginning; and so it *may not presuppose anything*, must not be mediated by anything nor have a ground; rather it is to be itself the ground of the entire science" (*Logic*, p. 70). That the *Phenomenology* is the presupposition for science: "In the Introduction it was remarked that the phenomenology of spirit is the science of consciousness, the exposition of it, and that consciousness has for result the *Concept* of science, i.e., pure knowing. Logic, then, has for its presupposition the science of manifested spirit, which contains and demonstrates the necessity, and so the truth, of the standpoint occupied by pure knowing and of its mediation" (*Logic*, p. 68, translation revised). (See also *Logic* pp. 60, 48, 49.) For Hegel's assertion that neither the Concept nor the method of science can be predetermined from outside the science: "Logic, on the contrary, cannot presuppose any of these forms of reflection and laws of thinking, for these constitute part of its own content and have first to be established within the science. But not only the account of scientific method, but even the Concept itself of the science as such belongs to its content, and in fact constitutes its final result: what logic is cannot be stated beforehand, rather does this knowledge of what it is first emerge as the final outcome and consummation of the whole exposition. . . . the Concept of logic has its genesis in the course of the exposition and cannot therefore be premised." *Logic*, p. 43, translation revised. Also see *Logic*, p. 53.

15. Pögeller explicitly notes the difficulties for interpretation raised by these remarks. See "Zur Deutung . . . ," in *Hegels Idee*, p. 244.

16. That Hegel regards absolute knowing and pure knowing to be one and the same, compare *Logic*, p. 48 with pp. 68–69. On p. 48, the concept is referred to as the truth of consciousness, the result of the *Phenomenology*, and is called absolute knowing. On pp. 68–69, the concept is again referred to as the truth of consciousness and the result of the *Phenomenology*, but here it is called pure knowing.

17. This last remark, taken in conjunction with Hegel's claim that into which this knowing vanishes is "unanalysable" (*Logic*, p. 75) also rules out that line of interpretation which holds that there is an implicit structure, functioning as a telos within the beginning point, and discoverable via reflection. A logical science which aims to begin, as Hegel's does, without any determinate content, subject matter, or method is certainly unusual. And whether or not any such science could ever be brought off is certainly a topic worthy of consideration. Just how such a science may proceed is discussed at length in Chapters 4, "Beginning Philosophy Without 'Beginnings,'" and 5, "Philosophy and Dialectical Method"; it is also considered in Chapter 9, "The Dead End of Postmodernism." What concerns us here is establishing the fact that Hegel did aim to produce just such a science. "The essential point of view is that what is involved is an altogether new concept of scientific procedure." *Logic*, p. 27.

18. For Hegel's specific denial that the beginning of the science can be made with the structure of the knowing self—the ego or self consciousness, see *Logic*, p. 75–78, and pp. 582–587, especially the remarks at 586–587.

Chapter 4, "Beginning Philosophy Without 'Beginnings'"

1. For example, Hegel observes the following in the Remark to Paragraph 2 of the *Philosophy of Right*: "What constitutes scientific procedure in philosophy is expounded in philosophical logic and is here presupposed" (p. 15). The 2nd Addition to Paragraph 24 of the *Encyclopedia Logic* states: "It will now be understood that Logic is the all-animating spirit of all the sciences, and its categories the spiritual hierarchy" (p. 40).

2. Dieter Henrich provides a summary of the critical objections in "Anfang und Methode der Logik." For a recent critique see Michael Rosen, *Hegel's Dialectic and Its Criticism* (Cambridge: Cambridge University Press, 1982).

3. "The essential point of view is that what is involved is an altogether new concept of scientific procedure. Philosophy, if it would be science, cannot, as I have remarked elsewhere, borrow its method from a subordinate science like mathematics, any more than it can remain satisfied with categorical assurances of inner intuition, or employ arguments based on grounds adduced by external reflection. On the contrary, it can be only the nature of the content itself which spontaneously develops itself in a scientific method of knowing, since it is at the same time the reflection of the content itself which first posits and generates its determinate character" (*Logic*, p. 27). "... [T]he character of the rational ... is to be unconditioned, self-contained, and thus to be self-determining" (*Encyclopedia Logic*, Paragraph 82, Addition, p. 120). "For reason is unconditioned only insofar as its character and quality are not due to an extraneous and

foreign content, only insofar as it is self-determining [*sich selbst bestimmt*] and thus, in point of content, is its own master" (*Encyclopedia Logic*, Paragraph 52, Addition, p. 86; *Werke*, Vol. 1, p. 137, translation revised). (Compare Paragraph 238, Addition, p. 294; Paragraph 9, Remark, p. 13; Paragraph 232, p. 289; Paragraph 4, p. 7; Paragraph 16, Remark, p. 22; Paragraph 17, pp. 22–23; Paragraph 77, pp. 110–111) " . . . I hold that Science exists solely in the self-movement of the Concept." *Phenomenology*, p. 44, translation revised.

4. "Thus the beginning must be an *absolute*, or what is synonymous here, an *abstract* beginning: and so it *may not presuppose anything*, must not be mediated by anything nor have a ground, rather it is to be itself the ground of the entire science." *Logic*, p. 70.

5. "Anfang und Methode der Logik," pp. 73–94.

6. See above, note #3.

7. "Here the beginning is made with being which is represented as having come to be through mediation, a mediation which is also a sublating of itself [*durch Vermittlung . . . welche zugleich Aufheben ihrer selbst ist*]; and there is presupposed pure knowing as the outcome of finite knowing, of consciousness." *Logic*, pp. 69–70; *Werke*, Vol. 5, p. 68.

8. See Chapters 1, 2 and 3.

9. Such a successful demonstration would seemingly substantiate the claim that an investigation by consciousness is the way to begin science and it would specify the determinate mode of consciousness' cognition definitive of scientific cognition. If successful, it would result in a substantive, determinate beginning point for science.

10. The impossibility of demonstrating such correspondence is a foregone conclusion for many contemporary philosophers from both the analytic and continental camps. For example, see Donald Davidson's essays "A Coherence Theory of Truth and Knowledge," and "Empirical Content," in *Truth and Interpretation*.

11. As soon as sheer identity in difference is attained, it is no longer possible to speak of knowledge in the only terms in which it can make sense for consciousness: for consciousness 'knowledge' always is and must be determinatively distinct from its object. The outcome of consciousness' attempt to show the unconditional legitimacy of its mode of knowing is the revelation that such a demonstration cannot be effected except insofar as the very mode of knowing purported to be unconditional is transcended.

12. Speaking of our beginning with the "pure knowing . . . [which has] sublated all reference to an other and to mediation . . . [and which thus] ceases itself to be knowledge," Hegel notes: "Here"—that is, from the vantage point of the completion of the *Phenomenology*—"the beginning is made with being which is represented as having come to be through

mediation, a mediation which is also a sublating of itself; and there is presupposed pure knowing as the outcome of finite knowing, of consciousness." *We* can see this as the mediated outcome of consciousness. But, in thinking through the self-cessation and the sublation, we also see that what was presupposed in the *Phenomenology*—the notion that a foundational self-investigation will lead to science—has eliminated itself, and the determinate agency required for thinking through this investigation—the structure of consciousness—has rendered itself indeterminate. Our seeing this makes it possible for us to then adopt the following stance: "But if no presupposition is to be made and the beginning itself is taken *immediately*"—and the aforementioned mediation (the *Phenomenology*) makes this possible—"then its only determination is that it is to be the beginning of logic, of thought as such. All that is present is simply the resolve, which can also be regarded as arbitrary, that we propose to consider thought as such." *Logic*, pp. 69–70.

13. See Chapter 5 for a specific consideration of this issue.

14. "What we are dealing with in logic is not a thinking *about* something which exists independently as a base for our thinking and apart from it, nor forms which are supposed to provide mere signs or distinguishing marks of truth; on the contrary, the necessary forms and self-determinations of thought are the content and the ultimate truth itself." *Logic*, p. 50.

15. Interestingly, Henrich mentions the *Phenomenology* as the "condition of the possibility of logic as *science*" in a footnote (#6, p. 83) but carries on no further discussion of it.

16. What the scientific procedure consists in more specifically, what its method unfolds itself as qua method, can only be seen in retrospect.

17. Speaking of what emerges from the *Phenomenology*—"pure knowing"—as that which is taken up in the *Logic* in its role as pure science, Hegel characterizes pure knowing as the cessation of mediation and reflection: "Pure knowing . . . has sublated all reference to an other and to mediation; it is without any distinction and as thus distinctionless ceases itself to be knowledge; what is present is only *simple immediacy*." And, against Henrich, Hegel notes that this characterization *is* an expression of reflection and thus can be considered as referring, not ahead (as Henrich would have it) to the logic of reflection, but back to that from which this beginning point has emerged: "Simple immediacy is itself an expression of reflection and contains a reference to its distinction from what is mediated. . . . Here the beginning is made with being which is represented as *having come to be through mediation, a mediation which is also a sublating of itself . . .* " *Logic*, p. 69, last emphasis added.

18. What about Henrich's contention that the *Logic* requires a method of proof, the *via negationis*? Henrich seems to claim that we as thinkers are involved in applying this method of excluding reflection. I would suggest, in at least partial agreement with Henrich, that a *reconstruction* of the

opening transitions would involve reference to the exclusion of reflection, but that even this would not require illicit appeal to a negated *logic* of reflection: The legitimacy of what Henrich claims to find (illicitly) present in his reconstruction is established through the self-sublating mediation, for, as noted, it is just the predilection to determine determinacy through a fixed—presupposed as given—structure of reflection which is sublated by the *Phenomenology*'s outcome in the collapse of consciousness in pure knowing. So, if a reconstruction finds 'reflection present as negated,' this is perfectly in accord with Hegel's claims about the beginning of the logic as arising out of the sublation of mediation. For the self-sublating mediation which the *Logic* presupposes is the sublation of the structure of mediation. (This outcome and this relationship between the *Phenomenology* and the *Logic* is also in accord with Hegel's claim that "What philosophy begins with must be either *mediated* or *immediate*, and it is easy to show that it can be neither the one nor the other; thus either way of beginning is refuted" [*Logic*, p. 67].) However, for the reason why such a reconstruction is not needed, see the next paragraph of this chapter.

Chapter 5, "Philosophy and Dialectical Method"

1. On this point, see also K. R. Dove, "Hegel's Phenomenological Method," the *Review of Metaphysics* 23, 4 (June, 1970).

2. *Phenomenology*, p. 46ff.

3. *Phenomenology*, p. 54; *Werke*, vol. 3, p. 77

4. *Phenomenology*, p. 55: "this *dialectical* movement which consciousness exercises on itself . . . "

5. "Consequently, we do not need to import criteria, or to make use of our own bright ideas and thoughts during the course of the inquiry; it is precisely when we leave these aside that we succeed in contemplating the matter in hand as it is *in and for itself.*" *Phenomenology*, p. 52ff., esp. p. 54.

6. On the Hegelian and Husserlian phenomenological methods, cf. K. R. Dove, "Die Epoche der Phänomenologie des Geistes," *Hegel-Studien*, Beiheft (Bonn: Bouvier Verlag, 1974).

7. Hegel does note (on p. 55) that there is an aspect of the dialectic which constitutes "something contributed by *us.*" Our contribution however, as Hegel's discussion shows, consists in observing and recording something which consciousness itself, because of its involvement in the dialectic, cannot see.

8. "But not only is a contribution by us superfluous . . . since what consciousness examines is its own self, all that is left for us is to simply look on." *Phenomenology*, pp. 49, 50; 54.

9. "Consciousness provides its own criterion from within itself, so that the investigation becomes a comparison of consciousness with itself." *Phenomenology*, p. 53. See also note 10.

10. "Yet it" (the presentation of knowledge as a phenomenon which constitutes the *Phenomenology*) "can be regarded as the path of the natural consciousness which presses forward to true knowledge." *Phenomenology*, p. 76, translation revised.

11. That consciousness is concerned in the *Phenomenology* with the philosophical problem of knowledge, i.e., with demonstrating the validity of its own mode of knowing, see p. 49, the passage which begins "Natural consciousness will show itself . . . " Also see pp. 52–53.

12. *Phenomenology*, pp. 53–54.

13. "But not only is a contribution by us superfluous, since Concept and object, the criterion and what is to be tested, are present in consciousness itself, but we are also spared the trouble of comparing the two and really *testing* them, so that, since what consciousness examines is its own self, all that is left for us to do is simply look on." *Phenomenology* p. 54, translation revised.

14. "*Inasmuch as the new true object issues from it*, this *dialectical* movement which consciousness exercises on itself, and which affects both its knowledge and its object, is precisely what is called *experience*" (*Phenomenology*, p. 55). One of the descriptions Hegel gave the *Phenomenology* is "the science of the *experience of consciousness*." *Phenomenology*, p. 56.

15. p. 104.

16. That the object of concern in the *Phenomenology* is the status of the structure of consciousness as definitive unconditionally of true knowing—science—is not stated explicitly in the Introduction by Hegel, although it is clear from the Preface. Also see the *Logic*, p. 45, where he distinguishes between "ordinary, phenomenal consciousness" and the "sphere of reason." It is also implied in the earlier sections of the Introduction to the *Phenomenology*, especially in the reflections by Hegel on the dilemma of attempting to introduce science—reflections which lead him to posit consciousness' search for the truth as our object.

17. In the *Logic*, p. 68, Hegel informs us that it is the "ultimate, absolute truth of *consciousness*" which is arrived at in absolute knowing by consciousness.

18. *Phenomenology*, p. 54. In this way the *Phenomenology*, as Hegel's 'introduction to science' has as its topic consciousness' attempt to introduce science.

19. *Logic*, p. 68.

20. "Thus in what consciousness affirms from within itself as the *being-in-itself* or the *True* we have the standard which consciousness itself sets up

by which to measure what it knows" (*Phenomenology*, p. 53). "Since both [knowledge and the object] are *for* the same consciousness, this consciousness itself is their comparison; it is for this same consciousness to know whether its knowledge of the object corresponds to the object or not." *Phenomenology*, p. 54.

21. See *Phenomenology*, p. 54, the passage beginning "The object, it is true seems only to be for consciousness in the way that consciousness knows it . . . "

22. *Phenomenology*, p. 55, translation revised.

23. *Phenomenology*, p. 55, translation revised. " . . . *das Für-das Bewusstseins des ersten Ansich, das zweite Gegenstand selbst werden soll* . . . " *Werke*, vol. 3, p. 79.

24. *Phenomenology*, p. 55.

25. When consciousness takes its own structure of knowledge as its object, the essential difference definitive of this structure—the difference between consciousness as knowing awareness and its object—is both found in the object and preserved in the knowing of it. And thus the simultaneous identity in difference demanded by consciousness is attained to.

26. *Logic*, pp. 68–70; see also p. 60, p. 49, pp. 44–45.

27. *Logic*, p. 69, (translation revised), p. 74.

28. "The Concept of pure science and its deduction is therefore presupposed in the present work in so far as the *Phenomenology of Spirit* is nothing other than the deduction of it." *Logic*, p. 49. See also p. 48, pp. 68–69, p. 60, p. 45.

29. *Logic*, pp. 43–45, p. 68, p. 70, pp. 74–75.

30. "But in the Introduction, the Concept of logic was itself stated to be the result of a preceding science, and so here, too, it is a *presupposition*" (*Logic*, p. 60, translation revised). "Logic, then, has for its presupposition the science of manifested spirit . . . " *Logic*, p. 68.

31. Hegel tells us that "the phenomenology of spirit . . . has for result the *Concept* of science, i.e., pure knowing," that "Pure knowing . . . has sublated all reference to an other and to mediation, it is without distinction and as thus distinctionless, ceases itself to be knowledge," that "its only determination is that it is to be the beginning of logic, of thought as such," that it "cannot possess any determination relatively to anything else" and "cannot contain within itself any determination, any content," that it is "this pure indeterminateness." *Logic*, p. 68, translation revised, p. 69, p. 70, p. 72.

32. Hegel was of the opinion that the uncritical assumption of such a principle of cognition was the major failing of his predecessors. See the *Logic*, pp. 44–45, pp. 50–51, p. 63.

33. *Logic*, pp. 75, 72.

34. *Logic*, pp. 49, 45. That consciousness—the structure of the subject, the ego—is that which is to be overcome in order to begin this science, and that an exposition of the logical science and its categories in terms of that structure is, from Hegel's standpoint, illicit: "But the logical form of the Concept is independent of its non-spiritual and *also of its spiritual shapes.* The necessary premonition on this point has already been given in the introduction. It is a point that must not wait to be established within logic itself but must be established before that science is begun," that is, as I have argued, in the *Phenomenology* (*Logic*, p. 586, translation revised, emphasis added). This remark is from "The Notion in General," where Hegel is discussing the inadequacies of Kantian transcendental philosophy. The hallmark of this inadequacy lies in its unreflective assumption of the primacy and paradigmatic character of the structure of the ego or consciousness. Something fatal, in Hegel's eyes, for a philosophy which calls itself critical.

35. It would also be illicit to read the *Logic* as though some difference, or some identity in difference or some subject/object structure were preserved in indeterminateness. Hegel explicitly rules this out: " . . . if pure being is to be considered as the unity into which knowing has collapsed at the point of its union with the object, then knowing itself has vanished in that unity, *leaving behind no difference from the unity and hence nothing by which the latter could be determined. Nor is there anything else present, any content which could be used to make the beginning more determinate.*" *Logic* p. 73, emphasis added.

36. *Logic*, p. 70; see also the Preface to the *Phenomenology*, pp. 20, 32.

37. Hegel does note that an "arbitrary resolve" is required in order to begin the process of logical thought. (*Logic*, p. 70.) This seems to me to be in consonance with his idea that the *Phenomenology* is a self-sublating mediation, and with the consequent claim that nothing of a determinate nature remains or is carried over into logic from the *Phenomenology*. If indeterminateness is radically indeterminate and if there are no presuppositions guiding or leading us on, then we must simply decide, or resolve, to think the indeterminate.

38. The beginning of the logic is made "in the element of thought that is free and for itself" in "pure knowing" which is the "ultimate, absolute truth of consciousness" and the "result" as "*Concept* of science" of the *Phenomenology,* (*Logic*, p. 68, translation revised). One starts from "this determination of pure knowledge" and "ridding oneself of all other reflections and opinions whatsoever" one "consider(s)" or "take(s) up" "*what is there before us*" (*Logic*, p. 69). This is pure knowing as "concentrated" into a "unity" which has "sublated all reference to an other and to mediation; it is without any distinction" and "ceases itself to be knowledge" owing to the absence of distinction (*Logic*, p. 69). It is "*simple immediacy,*" but as

this it is an "expression of reflection and contains a reference to its distinction from what is mediated"; it is, in its "true expression," *"pure being"*; it is "merely *immediacy* itself" or "this pure indeterminateness." *Logic*, pp. 69, 70, 72.

39. *Logic*, p. 69.

40. *Logic*, p. 83. Thinking indeterminateness as indeterminate, as in no way predetermined, requires, or is, the thinking of a contrast or a difference: Indeterminateness can only be thought as indeterminate insofar as it is contrasted with the determinate. But since no determinacy is given and none can be presupposed, the contrast or difference which one thinks in thinking the indeterminate is a vanishing or disappearing contrast.

41. This is the 'truth of being' where being is understood solely as a determinacy of pure systematic logic, which is another way of saying that it is the truth of being when we do not implicitly or explicitly presuppose that 'being' can be thought in its determinacy through being contrasted with thought or the thinking subject (or through being identified with either thought or the thinking subject). It is important to keep in mind that the logic is not 'about being,' it is not an ontology which is 'about' something which exists independently, through which a distinct subject matter is conceived or cognized. Clearly, when Hegel speaks in the *Logic* of both thought and being he is using these terms in a manner radically different from their ordinary use in philosophy. See *Logic*, p. 50, pp. 72–73, p. 78.

42. I say "in part" here because the suspension of consciousness' model of cognition can in no way guarantee that logic is pure and presupposition-less, that some other methodological presupposition cannot, does not, or will not become operative.

43. The *Logic*'s claim to being a radically self-grounding science demands radical self-inclusiveness. That no externally determined determinacies can either come into play in it or act as guides for its self-development has the consequence that this domain of logical determinacies cannot, simply as given, as constituted, be held to 'refer to' or to 'pick out' anything outside of the logic.

44. The validity of either constituting—or understanding—the relation of the logic to its 'other' in terms of an essence/appearance or ground/grounded relation is ruled out through the immanent critique of these relations in the *Logic*. See in particular p. 592.

45. *Philosophy of Nature*, Paragraph 247, p. 205. This is volume 2 of the *Encyclopedia of the Philosophical Sciences*.

46. *Philosophy of Nature*, Paragraph 246, Addition, p. 198.

47. Thus Hegel avoids the epistemological dilemmas which arise from attempts to justify such an application. He has no need to claim either

that reality must correspond to logic/thought (as the allegedly truer reality) or that the logical framework is legitimate because it is in some manner derived from reality.

Chapter 6, "On the Presumed Blasphemy of Hegelian Absolutism"

1. The major articulation of this charge is made by Emil Fackenheim. "Hegelian thought, then, can achieve its . . . goals only if it is not finite and human but rather infinite and divine" (*Religious Dimension*, p. 162). Stanley Rosen is more blunt: Hegel is "[l]ike other geniuses" in "confusing himself with God. . . . " *G. W. F. Hegel*, p. 130.

2. Putnam, *Reason*, p. 50.

3. Fackenheim, *Religious Dimension*, p. 58, emphasis in original.

4. *Religious Dimension*, p. 73.

5. Although B2 concerns the issue of the nature and relation of the finite and infinite as construed in the philosophy of religion, the treatment there cannot be considered in isolation from B1, where the issue pertains to the nature of the system as a whole, any more than the latter could successfully be considered in isolation from the former. To rest content with an isolated consideration in a system which alleges that the truth is the whole would be fatal from the start. For example, an assessment of the character of Hegel's claims in the philosophy of religion concerning the knowability and the nature of the divine would be question-begging were this to be undertaken without considering the nature of the kind of knowledge which this system claims to afford.

6. *Lectures on the Philosophy of Religion*, One Volume Edition, *The Lectures of 1827*, ed. Peter C. Hodgson (California: University of California Press, 1988), p. 96. Hereafter referred to as *Lectures*.

7. *Lectures*, p. 99.

8. See the *Encyclopedia of the Philosophical Sciences*, Part One, *Encyclopedia Logic*, Part Two, the *Philosophy of Nature*, Part Three, the *Philosophy of Mind*, trans. William Wallace (Oxford: Oxford University Press, 1971). See Paragraph 213, p. 274ff.; Paragraph 9, p. 13ff.; Paragraph 12, p. 16ff.; Paragraph 14, p. 19ff.; Paragraph 17, p. 22ff.; Paragraph 41, Addition, p. 66ff.; Paragraph 52, Addition, p. 86; Paragraph 77, p. 110ff.; Paragraph 232, p. 289; Paragraph 238, Addition, p. 294; (The 'Additions' to the *Encyclopedia* were not prepared by Hegel but by the editors, based on student lecture notes.) Also see the *Logic*, p. 27, and the *Phenomenology*, p. 44.

9. It can also be argued that the other features mentioned require self-grounding. See Chapter 8, "The Critique of Marx and Marxist Thought."

10. Hegel, of course, claims both of these features for his system. According to him, in "the standpoint of *philosophy*" "thinking" "does not have the concrete 'over there,' but rather is itself essentially concrete, and thus it is comprehension, meaning that the concept determines itself in its totality and as idea. It is free reason, which has being on its own account, that develops the content in accord with is necessity, and justifies the content of truth." *Lectures*, p. 487.

11. See the *Logic*, pp. 49, 53, 60, 68–75. As this indeterminacy results from the collapse of consciousness, we are left neither with a determinate object of knowledge nor with a determinate mode of relating to an object, unless we choose to lapse back into the mode of consciousness which has just sublated itself in absolute knowing. Thus, the *Phenomenology* yields neither a determinate form nor a determinate content, and insofar as knowing presupposes these determinacies, we are left with no knowing at all. See Chapters 3 and 4.

12. The *Logic*, p. 69.

13. See the *Logic*, p. 54.

14. By 'genuine knowledge' I mean objective knowledge whose truth is certain.

15. This, of course, is from the standpoint of the "we." For an extended discussion of how the *Phenomenology* functions as yielding the beginning point of science see Chapters 3, 4, and 5.

16. How could merely abandoning that assumption offer the prospects for a mode of philosophical consideration free from predetermination? The plausibility of this lies in appreciating that the consciousness sublated is itself the structure of predetermination in general. See Chapter 4.

17. For Hegel, attaining to this level of self-determination is the fulfillment of knowledge and freedom. "Free mind or Spirit is, as we have seen, in conformity with its concept perfect unity of subjectivity and objectivity, of form and content, consequently absolute totality and therefore infinite, eternal" (*Philosophy of Mind*, Paragraph 441, Addition, p. 181ff., translation revised). And this is something we can attain to even as conscious beings: "In the scientific domain we are not dealing with what is in feeling, but exclusively with what is outside it—and indeed is set forth for thought as an object for consciousness, more explicitly for the thinking consciousness, in such a way that it has attained the form of thought." *Lectures*, p. 116.

18. According to Hegel, Spirit which is "the perfect unity of subjectivity and objectivity, of form and content" is "absolute totality and therefore infinite, eternal" and "[f]or this reason we must declare spirit to be the *likeness* of God, the divinity of man." *Philosophy of Mind*, Paragraph 441, Addition, pp. 181–182, emphasis added, translation revised.

19. *Logic*, p. 49.

20. "The witness of spirit in its highest form is that of philosophy, according to which the concept develops the truth purely as such from itself without presuppositions." *Lectures*, p. 398. For an extended discussion of how this procedure might be understood see Chapter 4.

21. But if we are finite, if we always engage in thought under given conditions, must we not assume that they determine what we come to think? I shall argue below that Hegel's philosophy does not involve a denial, but a recognition of this possibility.

22. That God is reduced to the human: after identifying God with Spirit, Hegel writes: "In order not to be one-sided, spirit must encompass finitude within itself, and finitude in general means nothing more than a process of self-distinguishing. Consciousness is precisely the mode of finitude of spirit: distinction is present here. One thing is on one side, another on the other side ... Spirit must have consciousness, distinction, otherwise it is not spirit. ... It must have this character of finitude within itself—that may seem blasphemous" (*Lectures*, p. 405, cf. p. 406). "The transition [to the consummate religion] is the spirit that has entered into itself: it is the concept that has only *itself* as its purpose—this inwardly subsisting mode [of being] whose purpose is only itself, is God himself." *Lectures*, p. 410. (Material in square brackets is added by the editors.)

23. "Besides, in philosophy of religion we have as our object God himself, *absolute reason*. Since we know God [who is] absolute reason, and investigate this reason, we behave cognitively." *Lectures*, p. 96

24. "The divine idea is the pure concept, without any limitation. The idea includes the fact that the concept determines itself and thereby posits itself as what is self-differentiated." *Lectures*, p. 420.

25. The quotations are from pp. 469 and 468 in the *Lectures*. Hegel also writes ". . . in philosophy of religion we have as our object God himself, *absolute reason*. Since we know God [who is] absolute reason, and investigate this reason we cognize it, we behave cognitively. Absolute spirit is knowledge, the determinate rational knowledge of its own self. Therefore when we occupy ourselves with this object it is immediately the case that we are dealing with and investigating rational cognition, and this cognition is itself rational conceptual inquiry and knowledge" (*Lectures*, p. 96). On God's knowability see also the *Logic*, p. 50. See also the *Philosophy of Mind*, Paragraph 441, Addition, p. 181ff.; Paragraph 442, p. 183ff.; Paragraph 564, p. 297ff.

26. By "philosophically objective knowledge" I mean knowledge whose universal and necessary truth can be established. This is discussed in Chapter 9.

27. Absolute knowing has shown that we finite beings cannot attain to certain truth insofar as we remain committed to the idea of finding truth in the domain of objectivity. Thus, whatever the nature of God the system

affords when it speaks of God, it cannot be construed as descriptive knowledge of God as a transcendent other.

28. To know its identity with its object is just what consciousness failed to do in absolute knowing.

29. Hegel writes "in relation to the idea of God itself . . . it is the concept itself that sets up these distinctions and attains to itself through them, becoming for the first time idea in this way . . . " (*Lectures*, p. 413). "The divine idea is the pure concept, without any limitation. The idea includes the fact that the concept determines itself and thereby posits itself as what is self-differentiated" (*Lectures*, p. 420). "The fact of the matter is that humanity is immortal only through cognitive knowledge, for only in the activity of thinking is its soul pure and free rather than mortal and animallike. Cognition and thought are the root of human life, of human immortality as a totality within itself." *Lectures*, p. 446.

30. "Spirit is essence—but only insofar as it has returned to itself from out of itself, only insofar as it is that actual being which returns and is home with itself, that being which posits itself from itself as at home with itself. This positing produces the distinctive determinations of its activity, and these distinctive determinations are the forms through which spirit has to move" (*Lectures*, p. 410). "Spirit is the process of self-differentiating, the positing of distinctions" (*Lectures*, p. 453). But " . . . the self-positing and sublating of otherness is love or spirit." *Lectures*, p. 454.

31. "This freedom, which has the impulse and determinacy to realize itself, is rationality." *Lectures*, p. 482.

32. *Lectures*, p. 425, note #93.

33. *Lectures*, p. 410.

34. "According to the philosophical concept God is *spirit*, concrete; and if we inquire more precisely what spirit is, it turns out that the basic concept of spirit is the one whose development constitutes the entire doctrine of religion. If we ask our consciousness for a provisional account of what spirit is, the answer is that spirit is a self-manifesting, a being for spirit" (*Lectures*, p. 90). "God is the one who as living spirit distinguishes himself from himself, posits an other and in this other remains identical with himself, has in this other his identity with himself. This is the truth." *Lectures*, p. 453.

35. *Encyclopedia Logic*, Paragraph 45, Addition, p. 73.

36. See the Remark and Addition to Paragraph 246, p. 196ff., of the *Philosophy of Nature*.

37. *Encyclopedia Logic*, Paragraph 45, Addition, p. 73.

38. Hegel's remarks in the Introductions to the *Encyclopedia Logic* and the *Philosophy of Nature* make it clear that he sees systematic philosophi-

cal knowledge and the descriptive knowledge of the given offered by the
empirical sciences as different modes of knowing which are not in competition with one another.

39. "For the nonspeculative thinking of the understanding, distinction
remains as distinction, e.g., the antithesis of finite and infinite." *Lectures*,
p. 422.

40. It is important to note that the systematic rejection of the model of
consciousness for philosophy also precludes understanding the system as
offering transcendental categories which are determined in light of their
intended application to some external, given content. (As though the application to the given content constituted the manner in which finitude
entered the system.) See Chapters 8 and 5. This view of Klaus
Hartmann's must be rejected for the following reasons: it returns us to the
abandoned level of consciousness and to the unreconciled opposition of
finitude and infinite; it requires abandoning any claims the system could
make to completeness and self-grounding (since the given other would be
requisite for the truth of the categories); and it would be a step backwards
to the framework of the Kantian approach Hegel unequivocally rejects
(see the *Encyclopedia Logic*, Paragraph 45, Addition, p. 73.)

41. For an extended discussion of this see Chapter 5.

42. See Chapter 5.

43. See Chapter 5.

44. See the *Philosophy of Nature*, Paragraph 246 and Remark, p. 196ff.

45. *Philosophy of Mind*. Paragraph 441, Addition, p. 182. See also *Lectures*, p. 460; *Philosophy of Mind*, Paragraph 416, Addition, p. 157; Paragraph 417, Addition, pp. 157–158; Paragraph 424, Addition, p. 165;
Paragraph 437, Addition, 177ff.

46. See the discussion of religion in the *Philosophy of Mind*, Paragraphs
564 through 570, pp. 297–302. Religion is important for " . . . the witness
of spirit can be present in manifold and various ways; it is not required
that for all of humanity the truth be brought forth in a philosophical way"
(*Lectures*, p. 398). And "religion is consciousness of freedom and truth"; it
has the same object as philosophy, yet it is not philosophy, rather it is "the
manner or mode by which all human beings become conscious of truth for
themselves." Religion is vital because in it truth appears in "the form of
immediate sensible intuition and external existence for humankind" (*Lectures*, pp. 76, 106, 455). (Cf. *Lectures*, p. 144.) In religion "the consciousness of the absolute idea that we have in philosophy in the form of
thinking is to be brought forth not for the standpoint of philosophical
speculation . . . but in the form of *certainty*. The necessity . . . is not first
apprehended by means of thinking; rather it is a certainty for humanity."
Lectures, p. 454. Also see *Lectures*, p. 426, note #93.

47. "The witness of spirit in its highest form is that of philosophy, according to which the concept develops the truth purely as such from itself without presuppositions" (*Lectures*, p. 398). Philosophy goes beyond positivity and even revealed religion is in the form of positivity (pp. 396, 402). "But, even though representation grasps the content in its own forms, the content still belongs to thinking. We are considering the idea in its universality, as it is defined in and through pure thinking. This idea is the one truth and the whole truth; therefore everything particular that is comprehended as true must be comprehended according to the form of this idea." *Lectures*, p. 428.

48. The correct—philosophical—conception of God does not deny finitude but includes it: "Finitude must be posited in God himself, not as something insurmountable, absolute, independent, but above all as this process of distinguishing that we have in spirit and in consciousness—a distinguishing that, because it is a transitory moment, . . . is also eternally self-sublating." *Lectures*, p. 406.

49. See *Lectures*, p. 88ff.

50. Of course, within the bounds of religion there is no problem with this. "Religion has its reality as consciousness," but, the "*elevation to God*" is "a passing over from finite things, from the things of the world or from the finitude of consciousness . . . to the infinite. . . . " *Lectures*, pp. 202, 162.

51. *Lectures*, p. 406. "For the understanding holds fast to the categories of thought, persisting with them as utterly independent of each other, remaining distinct, external to each other, and fixed. . . . But for the concept it is equally true that these distinctions are sublated. Precisely because they are distinctions, they remain finite, and the understanding persists in finitude. Indeed, even in the case of the infinite, it has the infinite on one side and finitude on the other. But the truth of the matter is that neither the finite nor the infinite standing over against it has any truth; rather both are merely transitional." *Lectures*, p. 423.

52. *Lectures*, p. 428.

53. *Lectures*, p. 428.

54. "God, after all, is the universal that is determined within itself in manifold ways. In the form of representation, however, God is in this simple manner in which we have God on one side and the world on the other." *Lectures*, pp. 148–149.

Chapter 7, "Hegel and Hermeneutics"

1. See Gadamer, *Philosophical Hermeneutics*, the essay "Man and Language," pp. 61–62 for his discussion of this Cartesian legacy as providing "the background for all of modern thought."

2. Habermas, *Knowledge and Human Interests.*

3. Foucault, *The Archeology of Knowledge*, "The Discourse on Language," p. 235.

4. The simplest way of putting this point is to say that they all—including Marx and Richard Rorty—wish to break off reading the *Phenomenology* at some point or another prior to absolute knowing.

5. Gadamer, *Hegel's Dialectic*, the essay "Hegel and Heidegger," pp. 101–102.

6. Gadamer, *Truth and Method*, pp. 309–310.

7. *Hegel's Dialectic*, "Hegel and Heidegger," p. 104.

8. *Hegel's Dialectic*, "Hegel and Heidegger," p. 107.

9. See Chapters 3, 4, and 5 for a refutation of this reading of Hegel.

10. "The hermeneutical consciousness does not compete with that self-transparency that Hegel took to constitute absolute knowledge and the highest mode of being." *Philosophical Hermeneutics*, "On The Problem Of Self-Understanding," p. 55.

11. *Hegel's Dialectic*, "The Idea of Hegel's Logic," p. 77. Cf. also p. 11, "Hegel and the Dialectic of the Ancient Philosophers."

12. *Hegel's Dialectic*, p. 78.

13. *Hegel's Dialectic*, p. 78.

14. *Philosophical Hermeneutics*, "The Phenomenological Movement," p. 135. Also: " . . . understanding is not suitably conceived at all as a consciousness of something, since the whole process of understanding itself enters into an event, is brought about by it and is permeated by it" (*Philosophical Hermeneutics*, "The Philosophical Foundations of the Twentieth Century," p. 125). But "For Hegel, it is necessary, of course, that the movement of consciousness, experience should lead to a self-knowledge that no longer has anything different or alien to itself. . . . [for Hegel] the dialectic of experience must end with the overcoming of all experience, which is attained in absolute knowledge, i.e., in the complete identity of consciousness and object." (*Truth and Method*, pp. 318–319). And: "Real experience is that in which man becomes aware of his finiteness." *Truth and Method*, p. 320.

15. *Hegel's Dialectic*, p. 3.

16. *Hegel's Dialectic*, "Hegel and Heidegger," p. 102.

17. *Philosophical Hermeneutics*, "Semantics and Hermeneutics," p. 94.

18. Despite Gadamer's emphasis on the reflective dimension of hermeneutics and on the continuity of hermeneutics with the reflective

tradition, he does intimate that the only true expression of finitude is to be attained in religious experience: "The real concept of self-understanding . . . is not to be conceived in terms of the model of perfected self-consciousness, but rather in terms of religious experience." *Philosophical Hermeneutics*, "The Nature of Things and the Language of Things," p. 80.

19. *Truth and Method*, p. xiii.

20. *Philosophical Hermeneutics*, "On the Scope and Function of Hermeneutical Reflection," p. 37. On the universality of hermeneutics: "Hermeneutic reflection, however, is universal in its possible application" (*Philosophical Hermeneutics*, p. 93). "The phenomenon of understanding not only pervades all human relation to the world. It also has an independent validity within science and resists any attempt to reduce it into a method of science" (*Truth and Method*, p. xii). "It is important to realize that this phenomenon [the hermeneutical problematic] is not secondary in human existence, and hermeneutics is not to be viewed as a mere subordinate discipline within the arena of *Geisteswissenschaften*." *Philosophical Hermeneutics*, p. 19.

21. *Philosophical Hermeneutics*, p. 33–34.

22. *Philosophical Hermeneutics*, "On the Scope and Function of Hermeneutical Reflection," p. 36.

23. *Philosophical Hermeneutics*, "Semantics and Hermeneutics," p. 93.

24. *Truth and Method*, p. 308–309.

25. *Truth and Method*, p. 308.

26. *Philosophical Hermeneutics*, "The Phenomenological Movement," p. 172.

27. *Philosophical Hermeneutics*, "The Phenomenological Movement," p. 172.

28. *Truth and Method*, p. 225.

29. *Truth and Method*, p. 307. Also: "The varied critique of this philosophy of absolute reason by Hegel's critics cannot withstand the logical consequences of total dialectical self-mediation that Hegel has set out . . ." (*Truth and Method*, p. 307). And "It cannot be denied that the objections of Feuerbach and Kierkegaard are already taken care of . . . by Hegel." p. 308.

30. This is the method of criticism which, according to Hegel, is the only suitable form of *philosophical* criticism: "With respect to the refutation of a philosophic system, I have elsewhere also made the general observation that one must get rid of the erroneous idea of regarding the system as out and out *false*, as if the *true* system by contrast were only *opposed* to the

false." Certainly, Gadamer cannot be accused of doing that. But: "Further, the refutation must not come from outside, that is, it must not proceed from assumptions lying outside the system in question and inconsistent with it. . . . The genuine refutation must penetrate the opponent's stronghold and meet him on his own ground; no advantage is gained by attacking him somewhere else and defeating him where he is not" (*Logic*, pp. 580–581). Thus, insofar as finitude as explicated by Gadamer is an 'assumption which lies beyond the system,' his critique fails as one which reflective philosophy is compelled to recognize as telling, and reflective philosophy and hermeneutics remain at loggerheads. That "reflection"—in the form of Hegel's systematic philosophy—itself has limits and acknowledges finitude is discussed in Chapter 6.

31. See especially the article "Hegel and Heidegger," in *Hegel's Dialectic*.

32. *Truth and Method*, p. 307. See also *Philosophical Hermeneutics*, pp. 50, 61–62.

33. *Truth and Method*, p. 310.

34. *Truth and Method*, p. 319.

35. "The claim which Hegel's philosophy makes contains in it an equivocation which in turn is responsible for the fact that this man assumes the historical role that he does" (*Hegel's Dialectic*, p. 101). Gadamer is referring here to Hegel's claim to have completed western metaphysics and to having achieved the consummation of philosophical thought. See Chapter 9 for a discussion of how Hegel may claim to have completed philosophy.

36. *Philosophical Hermeneutics*, "The Philosophical Foundations of the Twentieth Century," p. 128.

37. On Gadamer's appropriation and transformation of the Hegelian notion of dialectics, cf. especially *Truth and Method*, 414ff., in particular 421–423.

38. Hence: "Thus the question arises of the degree to which the dialectical superiority of reflective philosophy corresponds to a factual truth and how far it merely creates a formal appearance. For the arguments of reflective philosophy cannot ultimately conceal the fact that there is some truth in the critique of speculative thought based on the standpoint of finite human consciousness." *Truth and Method*, p. 308.

39. "Tradition is no proof and validation of something, in any case not where validation is demanded by reflection. But the point is this: where does reflection demand it? Everywhere? I would object to such an answer on the grounds of the finitude of human existence and the essential particularity of reflection." *Philosophical Hermeneutics*, "On the Scope and Function of Hermeneutical Reflection," p. 34.

Chapter 8, "The Critique of Marx and Marxist Thought"

1. Klaus Hartmann's *Die Marxsche Theorie* offers a thoroughgoing and important examination of Marx as a systematic philosopher. Robert Paul Wolff's *Understanding Marx* (Princeton: Princeton University Press, 1984), John Elster's *Making Sense of Marx* (Cambridge: Cambridge University Press, 1985), and Carol Gould's *Marx's Social Ontology* (Cambridge: MIT Press, 1978) are all recent works which testify to the increased interest in Marx on the part of philosophers.

2. The most recent attempt at a wholesale condemnation of Hegel's system and its dialectic is *Hegel's Dialectic and Its Criticism* by Michael Rosen.

3. Karl Marx, *Capital*, vol. 1, trans. B. Fowkes (Harmondsworth: Penguin Books, 1976), pp. 102, 103. For Marx's approving comments on Hegel see also the "Economic and Philosophical Manuscripts," p. 101 and "The Holy Family," p. 141, in *Karl Marx: Selected Writings*, ed. D. McLellan (Oxford: Oxford University Press, 1977).

4. Marx's conception of his project as an *Aufhebung* of Hegel's goes as far back as the "Notes to the Dissertation," pp. 13–15 in McLellan, *Selected Writings*, and is reinterated in *Capital*, vol. 1, p. 103. See also "Economic and Philosophical Manuscripts," pp. 104, 106 in *Selected Writings*.

5. Arguably, Marx himself might be said to belong to this tradition, owing to his stated objective of overcoming philosophy through its actualization, an issue I shall discuss subsequently. However, Marx still has at least one foot in the tradition, for he believes that reason is capable of attaining an adequate theoretical and critical understanding of the human condition. Thus he cannot be accurately classified with the numerous recent and contemporary philosophers who deny this and who attack the traditional goals of philosophy. (See the Introduction and Chapters 2 and 9.)

6. Marx acknowledges his debt to Feuerbach for originating this criticism of Hegel in the "Economic and Philosophical Manuscripts," *Selected Writings*, pp. 97 and 99; in a letter to Feuerbach, *Selected Writings*, p. 113; and in a letter to Schweitzer, reprinted in the *Poverty of Philosophy* (New York: International Publishers, 1963).

7. "My dialectical method is, in its foundations, not only different from the Hegelian, but exactly opposite to it. For Hegel, the process of thinking, which he even transforms into an independent subject, under the name of 'the Idea,' is the creator of the real world, and the real world is only the external appearance of the idea. With me the reverse is true: the idea is nothing but the material world reflected in the mind of man, and translated into forms of thought" (*Capital*, vol. 1, p. 102). See also the *Critique of Hegel's Philosophy of Right*, trans. and ed. J. O'Malley (Cambridge: Cambridge University Press, 1970), pp. 7f., 14, 15, 17, 100, 116, 122;

Poverty of Philosophy, pp. 108–109; *Selected Writings*, "Economic and Philosophical Manuscripts," pp. 100, 109.

8. That Marx does not see the problem as lying in dialectics itself, but rather in Hegel's version of dialectics, see the quotation from *Capital* in the previous note, and also the *Critique of Hegel's Philosophy of Right*, pp. 23, 24, 39, 40, 92. In a letter to Engels of the 14th of January, 1858, Marx writes: "In *the method of working* it was of great service to me that by mere accident . . . I leafed through Hegel's *Logic* again. If once again time for such work is at hand, I would have great desire to make available for common understanding on two or three sheets what is reasonable [*Rationelle*] in the method Hegel discovered and at the same time mystified."

9. *Capital*, vol. 1, p. 103. See also *Critique of Hegel's Philosophy of Right*, pp. 39, 40.

10. See the "Preface To A Contribution To The Critique of Political Economy," in Karl Marx, *Selected Works* (Moscow: Progress Publishers, 1968), p. 183; also *Poverty of Philosophy*, pp. 180–181; *Critique of Hegel's Philosophy of Right*, pp. 23, 24; Marx's *Grundrisse: Foundations of the Critique of Political Economy*, trans. M. Nicolaus (Harmondsworth: Penguin Books, 1973), p. 89, 102, 105, 107–108; "Towards a Critique of Hegel's *Philosophy of Right*," *Selected Writings*, p. 70; "The Holy Family," *Selected Writings*, p. 134.

11. See the *Critique of Hegel's Philosophy of Right*, pp. 39, 137; *Poverty of Philosophy*, pp. 180–181, 189; "The German Ideology," *Selected Writings*, pp. 164, 171.

12. See "Preface to A Contribution To The Critique of Political Economy," *Selected Works*, p. 183; also the letter to Weydermeyer, *Selected Works*, p. 679; *Poverty of Philosophy*, pp. 174, 181, 186; "The German Ideology," *Selected Writings*, p. 178; "The Holy Family," *Selected Writings*, p. 135.

13. *Capital*, vol. 1, p. 102.

14. Preface, the *Philosophy of Right*, especially pp. 10, 13.

15. "Theses on Feuerbach," *Selected Writings*, p. 158.

16. See the *Critique of Hegel's Philosophy of Right*, pp. 137, 141, 142; "A Correspondence of 1843," *Selected Writings*, p. 36.

17. See the *Critique of Hegel's Philosophy of Right*, pp. 137, 141, 142; "A Correspondence of 1843," *Selected Writings*, p. 36.

18. See the *Critique of Hegel's Philosophy of Right*, pp. 136, 137, 138; "The German Ideology," *Selected Writings*, p. 165; "A Correspondence of 1843," *Selected Writings*, pp. 36–38.

19. See the *Critique of Hegel's Philosophy of Right*, pp. 132, 136, 138, 139; "Economic and Philosophical Manuscripts," *Selected Writings*, pp. 77, 97.

20. See the *Critique of Hegel's Philosophy of Right*, pp. 137, 141, 132, 139; "The German Ideology," *Selected Writings*, pp. 175, 176, 178; "A Correspondence of 1843," *Selected Writings*, p. 36.

21. See the "Notes to the Dissertation," *Selected Writings*, pp. 13–15; "Economic and Philosophical Manuscripts," *Selected Writings*, p. 76.

22. See *Capital*, vol. 1, p. 103; *Critique of Hegel's Philosophy of Right*, pp. 33, 39, 64, 84, 109–09, 135, 136, 147; "Economic and Philosophical Manuscripts," *Selected Writings*, p. 106.

23. "The genuine refutation must penetrate the opponent's stronghold and meet him on his own ground. . . . The only possible refutation . . . must therefore consist, in the first place, in recognizing its standpoint as essential and necessary and then going on to raise that standpoint to the higher one through its own immanent dialectic." *Logic*, p. 581.

24. See the *Encyclopedia Logic*, Paragraph 213, p. 274ff.

25. See the *Encyclopedia Logic*, Paragraph 9, p. 13ff.; Paragraph 12, p. 16ff.; Paragraph 14, p. 19ff.; and the Addition to Paragraph 41, p. 66ff.

26. "The essential point of view is that what is involved is an altogether new concept of scientific procedure. Philosophy, if it would be science, cannot, as I have remarked elsewhere, borrow is method from a subordinate science like mathematics, any more than it can remain satisfied with categorical assurances of inner intuition, or employ arguments based on grounds adduced by external reflection. On the contrary, it can only be the nature of the content itself which spontaneously develops itself in a scientific method of knowing, since it is at the same time the reflection of the content itself which first posits and *generates* its determinate character." *Logic*, p. 27.

"For reason is unconditional only insofar as its character and quality are not due to an extraneous and foreign content, only insofar as it is self-characterizing [*sich selbst bestimmt*], and thus, in point of its content, its own master." *Encyclopedia Logic*, Paragraph 52, Addition, p. 86. See also *Encyclopedia Logic*, Paragraph 238, Addition, p. 294; Paragraph 9, p. 13; Paragraph 232, p. 289; Paragraph 4, p. 7; Paragraph 16, p. 20ff.; Paragraph 17, p. 22ff.; Paragraph 77, p. 110ff.; and the *Phenomenology*, p. 44.

27. "It is by the free act of thought that it [philosophy] occupies a point of view, in which it is for its own self, and thus gives itself an object of its own production" (*Encyclopedia Logic*, Paragraph 17, pp. 22–23). "The most perfect method of knowledge proceeds in the pure form of thought: and here the attitude of man is one of pure freedom." *Encyclopedia Logic*, Paragraph 24, Addition, pp. 41–42.

"Henceforth the principle of the independence of Reason, or of its absolute self-subsistence, is made a general principle of philosophy . . ." (*Encyclopedia Logic*, Paragraph 60, Remark, p. 93). " . . . the character of the rational . . . is to be unconditional, self-contained, and thus to be self-determining." *Encyclopedia Logic*, Paragraph 82, Addition, p. 120. See also *Encyclopedia Logic*, Paragraph 3, p. 5ff.; Paragraph 4, p. 7; Paragraph 6, p. 8ff.; Paragraph 28, p. 48ff.; Paragraph 60, p. 90ff.; Paragraph 238, Addition, p. 294; and the *Phenomenology*, pp. 32, 34, 40.

28. *Phenomenology*, p. 46.

29. *Phenomenology*, p. 49.

30. "Empiricism and the Philosophy of Mind," *Science, Perception and Reality*, p. 140.

31. See the *Encyclopedia Logic*, Paragraph 232, p. 289; Paragraph 1, p. 3; Paragraph 4, p. 7; Paragraph 74, p. 108; the *Logic*, pp. 824, 826, 830.

32. See Chapters 4, 5, and 9.

33. "Truth is first taken to mean that I *know* how something *is*. This is truth, however, only in reference to consciousness; it is formal truth, bare correctness. Truth in the deeper sense consists in the identity between objectivity and the notion. It is in this deeper sense of truth that we speak of a true state, or of a true work of art. These objects are true, if they are as they ought to be, i.e., if their reality corresponds to the notion" (*Encyclopedia Logic*, Paragraph 213, Addition, p. 276). But Hegel is also clear that the determination of whether reality corresponds to the notion is not a matter for philosophical science: "When understanding turns this 'ought' against trivial external and transitory objects, against social regulations or conditions, which very likely possess a great relative importance for a certain time and special circles, it may often be right. In such a case the intelligent observer may meet much that fails to satisfy the general requirements of right; for who is not acute enough to see a great deal in his own surroundings which is really far from being as it ought to be? But such acuteness is mistaken in the conceit that, when it examines these objects and pronounces what they ought to be, it is dealing with questions of philosophic science." *Encyclopedia Logic*, Paragraph 6, Remark, p. 10.

"Nothing can be more obvious than that anything we only think, or conceive is not on that account actual [*Wirklich*]; that mental representations *and even conceptual comprehension*, always falls short of being." *Encyclopedia Logic*, Paragraph 51, Remark, p. 84., translation revised, emphasis added; *Werke*, Vol. 8, pp. 135–136.

34. See the *Grundrisse*, pp. 102, 104, 105, 106; "The German Ideology," *Selected Writings*, pp. 164, 166, 171; *Critique of Hegel's Philosophy of Right*, pp. 39–40, 48; "Preface To A Contribution To The Critique of Political Economy," *Selected Works*, p. 182; *Poverty of Philosophy*, pp. 109, 173–174, 180, 183; "Economic and Philosophical Manuscripts," *Selected Writings*, p. 89; "The Holy Family," *Selected Writings*, p. 135.

35. See the "letter to Lachatre," *Capital*, vol. 1, p. 17; *Capital* vol. 1, p. 102; *Grundrisse*, p. 106; *Poverty of Philosophy*, p. 202; "Preface To A Con-

tribution To The Critique of Political Economy," *Selected Works*, pp. 182, 183.

36. See Hegel's letter to Schelling, November 2, 1800, in *Hegel: The Letters*, trans. Butler and Seiler (Bloomington: Indiana University Press, 1984), p. 63; and Ritter, *Hegel and the French Revolution*.

Chapter 9, "The Dead End of Postmodernism"

1. The joke is related by Alasdair MacIntyre in "The Relationship Of Philosophy To Its Past," in *Philosophy In History*, ed. Richard Rorty et al. (Cambridge: Cambridge University Press, 1984), pp. 39–40. According to MacIntyre, "the counter joke is: the people interested in philosophy now are doomed to become those whom only those interested in the history of philosophy are going to be interested in a hundred years' time."

2. See Finley's *Ancient History: Evidence and Models* (New York: Viking Press, 1986). Finley conceives of the proper nature of the historian's relation to the past in much the same way that the third group of philosophers, discussed below, see their relation to the dead, in terms of a dialogue. "The historians evidence (whether documents, literary texts or objects) propounds no questions. Or, insofar as a literary text does ask questions, they are those of an individual author, not identical with those of anyone writing an historical account, that is to say, an analysis suitable to a later age. Therefore, the historian himself must ask the right questions . . . and provide the right conceptual context. He must do that consciously and systematically, abandoning the stultifying fiction that it is the duty of the historian to be self-effacing, to permit 'things' to 'speak for themselves' (in Ranke's words)." *Ancient History*, p. 104.

3. *Encyclopedia Americana* (Danbury CT: Grolier Inc., 1988), p. 792.

4. In speaking of "objective truth" I mean, minimally, truth that is demonstrable, certain, and unconditional. I discuss a possible reconceptualization below.

5. *Contingency*, p. 97.

6. As I shall discuss below, this may set up a false dichotomy between an unobtainable objective truth as description and an obtainable non-objective truth. (Redescription is non-objective since, according to Rorty, we have no bases, save private, personal ones, for preferring one redescription to another.) The dichotomy may be a false one, for, as Hegel suggested in regard to Kant, we ought to be very suspicious of the adequacy of a notion of truth according to which truth turns out to be unobtainable by us. Rather than rejecting truth, we may need to reject the notion of truth in question.

7. *Contingency*, p. 97.

8. *Contingency*, p. 105.

9. *Contingency*, p. 106.

10. The notion of an abstract negation as contrasted with a determinate negation comes from Hegel. "All that is necessary to achieve scientific progress—and it is essential to gain this quite simple insight—is the recognition of the logical principle that the negative is just as much positive, or that what is self-contradictory does not resolve itself into a nullity, into abstract nothingness, but essentially only into the negation of its *particular* content, in other words, that such a negation is not all and every negation but the negation of a specific subject matter which resolves itself, and consequently is a specific negation, and therefore the result essentially contains that from which it results . . . " *Logic*, p. 54.

11. Is the manner in which postmodernism mounts its attacks— deconstruction—something radically new? I would suggest that it is basically a variation on the traditional philosophical procedure of an immanent critique. If deconstruction essentially consists in showing that the manner in which one's claims are asserted contradicts the claims made, then, for example, Hegel's critiques of Kant and the transcendental approach are deconstructive efforts.

12. No matter how the subject or object are more specifically construed— and this holds even if the object is construed as the knowing subject itself, as in absolute idealism—the sheer givenness of the object insures that certain knowledge of it cannot be demonstrated. Every attempt to compare a description of the object with the object 'itself' necessitates that we compare a description with another description. See Hegel, Introduction to the *Phenomenology*, and Davidson, "Empirical Content," in *Truth and Interpretation*.

13. The answer to this question is again based on the notion of a determinate negation of the traditional conception of cognition, and can be sketched out as follows: If failure to attain certain truth arose from the twofold presuppositions about truth mentioned above, then, in our consideration of the indeterminate as our subject matter, the refusal to proceed in the traditional fashion—refusing to regard the indeterminate as somehow already fixed in its determinacy as indeterminate just because it is an 'object' for our consideration—may lead to the discovery that the indeterminate cannot be conceived in its indeterminacy except through a contrast with what is determinate. This contrasting—the very procedure by means of which the indeterminate is being thought—would then be the first determination of the indeterminate. So, as noted in the text, cognition and its object here both come to be determinate at one and the same time. More extensive discussion of this procedure is to be found in Chapters 4 and 5. The idea is that by deliberately refraining from assuming that a

subject matter is already determinate as an object—by refusing to assume that the indeterminate is fixed in its indeterminacy because we are focusing on it as such—we may endeavor to engage in a consideration of this subject manner in such a way that no predetermination—antecedently given either in the subject matter itself or in the act of cognition—enters. We aim to insure this simply by focusing on what we have seen does lead to predetermination, and here refusing to cognize in this way. And it's just by moving in this fashion that the activity of the self-constitution of determinacies in this discourse is not arbitrary and radically idiosyncratic, even though not predetermined. In other words, focusing on the determinate negation, on what we know about how determinacy is *not* to be conceived if certain truth is to be attained, provides a negative framework for the constitution of this discourse by specifying just what must be avoided if determinacy is to be determined without predetermination. In this way the process has a specifiable procedure, a 'metarule for the avoidance of introducing antecedently determined rules' such that, armed with this rule, we can also examine efforts at self-constitutive discourse and make a determination as to whether they fulfill the demand for self-determination or not. It's because we thus have a way of assessing claims to what constitutes self-constituted discourse that the whole endeavor does not lapse into a radically arbitrary exercise of subjective positing in the style of Rorty's Nietzschean 'redescribing.'

14. For a brief consideration of how external determination could be kept out of the process, see note 13.

Chapter 10, "The Renewed Appeal to Transcendental Arguments"

1. In speaking of epistemic and metaphysical objectivity I am referring to the idea that neither reality nor knowledge are matters of opinion: that rigorous, nonrelative knowledge is possible, that the world exists and is determined independent of changing styles of discourse.

2. Davidson's antifoundational position is expressed most clearly in "On the Very Idea of a Conceptual Scheme," in *Inquiries*, pp. 183–198, and in "A Coherence Theory of Truth and Knowledge" and "Empirical Content," both in *Truth and Interpretation*. The extent to which Davidson agrees with this thumbnail sketch will be considered subsequently.

3. In both "Coherence Theory" and "Empirical Content" (pp. 312, 320), Davidson contrasts his coherence theory with the foundational view of knowledge. On his view of correspondence see especially "True to the Facts," in *Inquiries*. There (pp. 37–38) he writes, "In this paper I defend a version of the correspondence theory. I think truth can be explained by appeal to a relation between language and the world, and that analysis of

that relation yields insight into how, by uttering sentences, we sometimes manage to say what is true." Yet this is to be a correspondence theory without any comparisons, there isn't really to be any analysis of that relation: "A theory of truth can be called a correspondence theory in the unassuming sense of Essay 3 ["True to the Facts"], but that sense does not encourage the thought that we understand what it would be like to compare sentences with what they are about, since the theory provides no entities with which to compare sentences." Introduction to *Inquiries*, p. xviii.

4. See especially "Coherence Theory," pp. 307, 310. "Given a correct epistemology, we can be realists in all departments. We can accept objective truth conditions as the key to meaning, a realist view of truth, and we can insist that knowledge is of an objective world independent of our thought or language." p. 307.

5. For discussions of Davidson's transcendental approach see Michael Root, "Davidson and Social Science" and Carol Rovane, "The Metaphysics of Interpretation," both in *Truth and Interpretation*, and Richard Rorty, "Transcendental Arguments, Self-Reference, and Pragmatism," in *Transcendental Arguments and Science*, eds. Bieri, Horstmann and Kruger (Boston: D. Reidel, 1979).

6. To get clear on just what Davidson's understanding of foundationalism is, and just what he rejects in it, see "Coherence Theory," especially p. 312.

7. "What we have shown is that it is absurd to look for a justifying ground for the totality of beliefs, something outside this totality which we can use to test or compare our beliefs. The answer to our problem must then be to find a *reason* for supposing most of our beliefs are true that is not a form of *evidence*." "Coherence Theory," p. 314.

8. See the *Critique of Pure Reason*, pp. 345–347, A 369–A 372 for Kant's specific discussion of the reasons for adopting this approach.

9. See "True to the Facts."

10. "The approach to the problem of justification we have been tracing must be wrong. We have been trying to see it this way: a person has all his beliefs about the world—that is, all his beliefs. How can he tell if they are true, or apt to be true? Only, we have been assuming, by connecting his beliefs to the world, confronting certain of his beliefs with the deliverances of the senses one by one, or perhaps confronting the totality of his beliefs with the tribunal of experience. No such confrontation makes sense, for of course we can't get outside our skins to find what is causing the internal happenings of which we are aware. Introducing intermediate steps or entities into the causal chain, like sensations or observations, serves only to make the epistemological problem more obvious. For if the intermediaries are merely causes, they don't justify the beliefs they cause, while if they deliver information, they may be lying." "Coherence Theory," p. 312.

11. "As interpreters we have to treat self-ascriptions of belief, doubt, desire and the like as privileged; this is an essential step in interpreting the rest of what the person says and thinks." Davidson, "Empirical Content," *Truth and Interpretation*, p. 332.

12. It might be suggested that there is a radical difference between Kant and Davidson in that what I have been calling Davidson's domain of subjectivity—language—is construed by him as *inter*subjectively constituted, so that we're dealing with a plurality of subjects. In the essay "Rational Animals" (*Dialectic* 36:4 [1982]: pp. 317–327), Davidson indicates how this pertains to the issue of our—collective—knowledge of objectivity. But whether we are speaking of one subject or many, whether the subject is singular or collective, the question still remains—insofar as one holds on to correspondence—concerning how what is found within subjectivity can guarantee anything about objectivity.

13. " . . . a theory of truth helps us understand the underlying question how communication by language is possible . . . " "Reality Without Reference," *Inquiries*, p. 222.

That the relation of correspondence in question is internal to subjectivity, i.e., language: "What characterizes a theory of truth in Tarski's style is that it entails, for every sentence s of the object language, a sentence of the form: s is true (in the object language) if and only if p. Instances of the form (which we shall call T-sentences) are obtained by replacing 's' by a canonical description of s, and 'p' by a translation of s. The important undefined semantical notion in the theory is that of *satisfaction* which relates sentences, open or closed, to infinite sequences of objects, which may be taken to belong to the range of variables of the object language." "Radical Interpretation," *Inquiries*, p. 130–31.

"An important feature of Tarski's approach is that a characterization of a truth predicate 'x is true in L' is accepted only if it entails, for each sentence of the language L, a theorem of the form 'x is true in L if and only if . . . ' with 'x' replaced by a description of the sentence and the dots replaced by a translation of the sentence into the language of the theory. It is evident that these theorems, which we may call T-sentences, require a predicate that holds of just the true sentences of L. It is also plain, from the fact that the truth conditions of a sentence translate that sentence . . . that the theory shows how to characterize truth for any given sentence without appeal to conceptual resources not available in that sentence." "The Method of Truth in Metaphysics," *Inquiries*, p. 204.

14. On the inseparability of truth and translation, see "Conceptual Scheme," *Inquiries*, pp. 194–195, and "The Method of Truth in Metaphysics," pp. 204–205.

15. If "the conditions of the *possibility of experience* in general are likewise conditions of the *possibility of the objects of experience*" (*Critique of Pure Reason*, p. 194, A 158 B 197) then there would seem to be no need to worry about getting beyond experience to see if what is found within it corresponds to objectivity.

16. "Coherence Theory," *Truth and Interpretation*, p. 312. Also see the essays "Empirical Content," *Truth and Interpretation*, and "Reality Without Reference," *Inquiries*.

17. "Empirical Content," p. 332. Also see p. 331 and "Coherence Theory," p. 312.

18. "Coherence Theory," p. 312.

19. "Coherence Theory," p. 312; see "Empirical Content," p. 332.

20. "I have not said what is to count as evidence for the truth of a T-sentence. . . . What is clear is that the evidence, whatever it is, cannot be described in terms that relate it in advance to any particular language, and this suggests that the concept of truth to which we appeal has a generality that the theory cannot hope to explain. Not that the concept of truth that is used in T-sentences can be explicitly defined in non-semantic terms, or reduced to more behavioristic concepts. . . . [a] general and preanalytic notion of truth is presupposed by the theory. It is because we have this notion that we can tell what counts as evidence for the truth of a T-sentence." "Reality Without Reference," p. 223.

21. "Each individual knows this [that "the sentences that express the beliefs, and the beliefs themselves are correctly understood to be about the public things and events that cause them, and so must be mainly veridical"] since he knows the nature of speech and belief." "Empirical Content," p. 332.

22. See "Reality Without Reference," p. 224.

23. *Inquiries*, Introduction, p. xix. On the same page Davidson writes: "The question what objects a particular sentence is about, like the questions about what an object refers to, or what objects a predicate is true of, has no answer."

24. "Coherence Theory," p. 312.

25. *Inquiries*, p. xix.

26. "The Method of Truth in Metaphysics," p. 201.

27. "Coherence Theory," p. 307.

28. See "True to the Facts" and "The Inscrutability of Reference."

29. "Even those thinkers who are certain there is only one conceptual scheme are in the sway of the scheme concept; even monotheists have religion. And when someone sets out to describe 'our conceptual scheme,' his homey tasks assume, if we take him literally, that there might be rival systems." "On the Very Idea of a Conceptual Scheme," p. 183.

30. He presents much the same argument, briefly, in "The Method of Truth in Metaphysics."

31. "Empirical Content," p. 332.

32. "The Method of Truth in Metaphysics," p. 200.

33. To a certain extent he seems to realize this—that his own arguments against relativism also go against correspondence by undermining their common conceptual framework or model. See "Very Idea," p. 198.

34. "The Method of Truth in Metaphysics," p. 199.

35. "A Nice Derangement of Epitaphs," *Truth and Interpretation*, pp. 445–46. Speaking of Davidson's view ("True to the Facts") that "the whole web of sentences has to be true to the one fact, the fact of everything," Ian Hacking writes, "There is only total correspondence of all true sentences to the fact of everything; but this fact, the world, has no autonomy beyond what we say. That is one way in which 'coherence yields correspondence.' " *New York Review of Books* (December 20, 1984): p. 57. The tendency to eliminate a significant difference between language and the world—that is, a difference which we can make out at the epistemological level—is also suggested by remarks like the following: " . . . if reference is relative to my frame of reference as already embedded in my own language, all that can be provided to give my words a reference is provided simply by my speaking my own language." "The Inscrutability of Reference," p. 233.

36. "The Method of Truth in Metaphysics."

Chapter 11, "The Problematic Role of God In Modern Epistemology"

1. As will become clear subsequently, in speaking of the "role of God" I am only concerned with the use which some philosophers have made of the idea of a divine mind. Whether such a mind does or does not exist as a transcendent being is irrelevant for the purposes of this chapter.

2. By "foundational epistemology" I mean any project which purports to establish the nature, method, limits, and validity of a mode of cognition by means of an investigation into the conditions of its possibility. I distinguish such projects from descriptive epistemologies on the basis of whether or not the critical question of the legitimacy of cognition is at stake. Epistemic inquiries which do not raise that question I call descriptive, and I shall have nothing further to say about them here. What foundational epistemology entails more specifically I shall detail in Part I. Traditionally understood, epistemology has a positive goal of establishing that and how knowledge is possible, by laying out the foundations of knowledge. But, as I shall suggest in regard to Nietzsche, even those who purport to attack epistemology share certain basic assumptions with the foundational tradition they oppose.

3. See the *Introduction*.

4. The notion that an understanding of God, and more specifically, a Christian conception of the divine, lies behind and is intimately, albeit implicitly, interwoven with the emergence and development of modern philosophy is not new. It can be found in the work of Koyre, Burtt, and it was explored with considerable depth and acuity by Michael Foster in "The Christian Doctrine of Creation and the Rise of Modern Natural Science," *Mind* 63 (1934) (Reprinted in *Creation: The Impact of An Idea*) and "Christian Theology and the Modern Science of Nature," *Mind* (1935 and 1936). Foster was concerned with the nature and importance of the Christian conception of the divine in the attempts by modern philosophers to decipher, unpack, and justify the ontological and methodological presuppositions of modern natural science. Foster intimates that the demand for epistemology itself, as a distinctively modern project, arouse out of the need to account for the newly emerging and unGreek conceptions of nature and scientific method, conceptions which he sees as having their roots and finally their only possible justification in the Christian notions of creation *ex nihilo* and of revelation, respectively. According to Foster, modern science and philosophy alike failed to appreciate these sources for the modern world view, and the modern philosophical failure to provide adequate justification for the new notions of nature and scientific method stems from the inability to grasp the religious character of their origins and to rationalize or secularize them successfully. According to Foster then, the ultimate source for the long-perceived failure of modern philosophy to justify adequately these foundational assumptions stems from the origin of these assumptions in irreducibly religious conceptions which resist rational appropriation.

What I have to say does not presuppose that Foster is correct. Nonetheless, what I am doing can be seen as complementing his work, although my approach differs from his in that my concerns will be solely with the nature and the assumptions of modern epistemology seen as an entity in itself. Going beyond Foster and in a different direction, I shall argue that in the more narrowly conceived domain of modern epistemology as such, the presence of the Christian conception of the divine is not as hidden or as nearly implicit as he finds it in modern philosophy taken as a larger whole broadly concerned with grounding the assumptions of modern natural science. My contention will be that irrespective of the specific ontological and epistemological principles the modern philosophers wrestled with, the format of epistemology itself ordains the involvement of a notion or model of mind possessing the attributes associated with the Judeo-Christian God. My view is that what Foster scopes out as the hidden religious wellspring of the broader efforts of modern philosophers can be found to manifest itself more obviously, although in finally just as problematic a fashion, in the specific details of their epistemological efforts.

5. This seems to exclude coherence theories from the purview of epistemology. However, as Donald Davidson notes, coherence theories do not eliminate the comparison of a knowledge claim with a standard, it's simply that both knowledge claims and standard are construed as beliefs, rather than the standard being construed as an object which the belief must represent. I shall argue below that this feature—the comparison of the knowledge claim with an independently determined standard—is crucial to epistemological endeavors. If this is correct, even coherence theories are subject to the fundamental problem addressed in this chapter.

6. On the face of it, this description would appear to exclude Kant from being classified as an epistemologist, since he allows for a "subjective" dimension. I shall discuss this in the section on Kant.

7. "In this field [pure reason] nothing can escape us. What reason produces entirely out of itself cannot be concealed, but is brought to light by reason itself. . . . *Critique of Pure Reason*, p. 14, A xx.

8. I have spoken here of a cognitive agent as a mind, understanding, consciousness etc., since, during the historical period I shall consider, discussions of such agents, described in those terms, were part of the epistemological endeavor. As later epistemological developments have shown, one need not explicitly discuss epistemological matters in psychological terms nor even bring the nature of an agent explicitly into consideration. We can consider the purported truth-affording relation in term of language (rather than ideas or other mental entities) and objects; or, taking another step back, in formal terms of the relation of a metalanguage to an object language. Additionally, we can omit all discussion of the particular subjective conditions which make the language/object or language/world relation possible e.g., as Wittgenstein did in the *Tractatus*. There are very good epistemological reasons for making these moves (see Chapter 9). The question, which I shall not pursue here, is whether making such linguistic and formal turns really amounts to an escape from epistemological subjectivity and the problems associated with discussing knowledge in its terms, or whether it is merely a bracketing of subjectivity which preserves the other features—and problems—of the epistemological structure of cognition.

9. Two observations need to be made here. During the historical period under consideration purported knowledge was construed in mentalistic terms, as something 'of' and 'for' the mind which the mind (or understanding) had induitable access to. That against which this knowledge was to be measured was usually, albeit not always, taken as something which in most cases was nonmental, 'other' than the mind. But epistemology can, of course, be undertaken without any psychological considerations; indeed, without explicit reference to a mind or awareness at all. As I understand foundational epistemology, however, the difficulties associated with it can

be seen to arise whether there is any mind talk or not. We can construe the purported knowledge to be tested as an idea, or as a sentence, or proposition; the standard against which it is to be measured can be seen as an object in the straightforward, realistic sense, or as another idea, or as another language. Or we may choose not to draw any sort of an ontological distinction between purported knowledge and object, in an attempt to avoid the problems associated with connecting a mental and a physical domain. What is essential is that the distinction between purported knowledge, as the directly and unproblematically accessible, and its standard be maintained. Something must be taken to be unproblematically accessible; our epistemologist must hold something certain in order to have something to test at all. Correlatively, the standard must be construed as determined as what it is independently of the cognitive act; otherwise any possibility of its being a genuine, objective measure is lost.

10. If the agent/mode of cognition being tested is not the same as that effecting the test, the question immediately arises as to the certainty of any results: if the agency/mode is other than that being tested, what certifies the reliability of its results, save for another investigation into it, and so on ad infinitum? If it can be assumed that the testing agency is reliable, why not make the same assumption in regard to the cognition being tested and avoid the effort entirely? (See the Introduction to the *Phenomenology*.) What must not be forgotten is that the issue in epistemology is the possible legitimacy of any and all modes of cognition: Epistemology must hold that all modes of cognition are in need of legitimation, including the epistemological cognition itself; otherwise the whole enterprise is bootless. Yet how can the results be reliable if the testing agency/ mode of cognition is the same as that undergoing a test? Epistemology seems to require either an infinite regress or vicious circularity.

11. For the period in question, "subjective" indicates subjectivity: a mind, consciousness, or understanding. Independently of that meaning it can also signify more fundamentally, as it does in the immediate context, that domain whose access to the "objective"—in the sense of the standard or measure—is at stake.

12. Here is where epistemology and common sense part company decisively. I can check my belief about your phone number with the phone book. But epistemologically speaking, I am comparing one belief with another belief, and I am presupposing what epistemology aims to demonstrate: the veridical character of beliefs as such. But how can I compare a belief with something which is not a belief?

13. *Meditations on First Philosophy*, in *The Philosophical Works of Descartes*, vol. 1, p. 159.

14. *Discourse on the Method of Rightly Conducting the Mind*, in *Works*, vol. 1, p. 105.

15. *Meditation V* in *Works*, vol. 1, p. 185., cf. 183. See also *The Principles of Philosophy, Works*, p. 224, #XIII.

16. *A Treatise Concerning the Principles of Human Knowledge* in *The Works of George Berkeley*, ed. A. C. Fraser (Oxford: The Clarendon Press, 1901), vol. 1, p. 235.

17. *A Treatise, Works*, vol. 1, p. 260.

18. *A Treatise, Works*, vol. 1, p. 261.

19. Leibniz, quoted in Leroy E. Loemker, *Struggle for Synthesis* (Cambridge: Harvard University Press, 1972), p. 117. Leibniz, *Die Philosophische Schriften*, vol. 7, ed. C. I. Gerhardt (Berlin: 1875–1890), p. 264.

20. *Critique of Pure Reason*, pp. 495–531, A 583 B 617–A 642 B 670.

21. "Yet even he [Hume] did not suspect such a formal science, [as the critical philosophy] but ran his ship ashore, for safety's sake, landing on scepticism, there to let it lie and rot; whereas my object is rather to give it a pilot, who, by means of safe principles of navigation drawn from a knowledge of the globe, and provided with a complete chart and compass, may steer the ship safely wither he listeth." *Prolegomena to Any Future Metaphysics*, p. 10.

22. According to Kant "knowledge has to do only with appearances, and must leave the thing in itself as indeed real *per se* but as not known by us." *Critique of Pure Reason*, p. 24, B xx. Cf. p. 82, A 42, B 59; p. 83, A 43, B 60.

23. "Hitherto it has been assumed that all our knowledge must conform to objects. But all attempts to extend our knowledge of objects by establishing something in regard to them *a priori*, by means of concepts, have, on this assumption, ended in failure. We must therefore make trial whether we may not have more success in the tasks of metaphysics, if we suppose that objects must conform to our knowledge.... We should then be proceeding precisely on the basis of Copernicus' primary hypothesis."
        "... either I must assume that the *concepts* ... conform to the object, or else I assume that the objects, or what is the same thing, that the *experience* in which alone, as given objects, they can be known, conform to the concepts.... In the latter case the outlook is more hopeful. For experience itself is a species of knowledge which involves understanding; and understanding has rules which I must presuppose as being in me prior to objects being given to me, and therefore as being *a priori*. They find expression in *a priori* concepts to which all objects of experience necessarily conform, and with which they must agree." *Critique of Pure Reason*, pp. 22–23, B xvi–xviii.

24. *Critique of Pure Reason*, p. 148, A 126–127. Cf. p. 140, A 114.

25. *Critique of Pure Reason*, p. 140, A 114.

26. "Now we find that our thought of the relation of all knowledge to its object carries with it an element of necessity; the object is viewed as that which prevents our modes of knowledge from being haphazard or arbitrary, and which determines them *a priori* in some fashion. . . . All necessity, without exception, is grounded in a transcendental condition. There must, therefore, be a transcendental ground of the unity of consciousness in the synthesis of the manifold of our intuitions and consequently also of the concept of objects in general, and so of all objects of experience, a ground without which it would be impossible to think any object for our intuitions; for this object is no more than that something, the concept of which expresses such a necessity of synthesis." *Critique of Pure Reason*, pp. 134–136, A 104–106.

27. *Critique of Pure Reason*, p. 136, A 108; p. 135, A 105. Kant continues at A 108, "For the mind could never think its identity in the manifoldness of its representations, and indeed think this identity *a priori*, if it did not have before its eyes the identity of its act, whereby it subordinates all synthesis of apprehension (which is empirical) to a transcendental unity, thereby rendering possible their interconnection according to *a priori* rules." And we must "suppose that our representation of things, as they are given to us, does not conform to these things as they are in themselves, but that these objects, as appearances, conform to our mode of representation. . . . " (*Critique of Pure Reason*, p. 24, B xx). "The pure concept of this transcendental object . . . is what can alone confer upon all our empirical concepts in general relation to an object, that is, objective reality. This concept . . . refers only to that unity which must be met with in any manifold of knowledge which stands in relation to an object. This relation is nothing but the necessary unity of consciousness, and therefore also of the manifold, through a common function of the mind. . . . " *Critique*, p. 137, A 109.

28. "At this point we must make clear to ourselves what we mean by the expression 'an object of representations.' We have stated above that appearances are themselves nothing but sensible representations, which, as such and in themselves, must not be taken as objects capable of existing outside our power of representation. What, then, is to be understood when we speak of an object corresponding to, and consequently also distinct from our knowledge? It is easily seen that this object must be thought only as something in general = *x*, since outside our knowledge we have nothing which we could set over against this knowledge as corresponding to it. . . . But is clear that, since we have to deal only with the manifold of our representations, and since that *x* (the object) which corresponds to them is nothing to us—being, as it is, something that has to be distinct from all our representations—the unity which the object makes necessary can be nothing else than the formal unity of consciousness in the synthesis of the

manifold of representations" (*Critique of Pure Reason*, pp. 134–135, A 104–105). "The *a priori* conditions of a possible experience in general are at the same time conditions of the possibility of objects of experience." *Critique*, p. 138, A 111.

29. See note a at p. 169, B 158, for Kant's explicit denial that I can "determine my existence as that of a self-active being." He also asserts, "There are only two possible ways in which synthetic representations and their objects can establish connection, obtain necessary relation to one another, and, as it were, meet one another. Either the object alone must make the representation possible, or the representation alone must make the object possible. In the former case, this relation is only empirical, and the representation is never possible *a priori*. . . . In the latter case, representation in itself does not produce its object in so far as *existence* is concerned, for we are not here speaking of its causality by means of the will" (*Critique of Pure Reason*, p. 125, A 92, B 124–125). "Appearances are the sole objects which can be given to us immediately, and that in them which relates immediately to the object is called intuition. But these appearances are not things in themselves; they are only representations, which in turn have their object an object which cannot itself be intuited by us. . . . " *Critique*, p. 137, A 108–109.

30. *Critique of Pure Reason*, p. 244, B 274.

31. See *Critique of Teleological Judgement*, Part II of *Critique of Judgement*, trans. J. C. Meredith (Oxford: Clarendon Press, 1952), Paragraph 15, pp. 55–58.

32. *Critique of Pure Reason*, p. 27, B xxvi–xxvii.

33. Of course Kant denies such knowledge even to the transcendental philosopher. " . . . there are two stems of human knowledge, namely, *sensibility* and *understanding*, which perhaps spring from a common, but to us unknown root." *Critique of Pure Reason*, p. 61, A 15, B 29.

34. *Critique of Pure Reason*, p. 244, B 247ff. Also see Chapter 10.

35. According to Fichte, the question of the *Science of Knowledge* is that of the objectivity of knowledge. And " . . . it would be perfectly absurd to assimilate it to the question as to an existence unrelated to consciousness." *Fichte: Science of Knowledge (Wissenschaftslehre)*, eds. and trans. Heath and Lachs (New York: Appleton-Century-Crofts, 1970), p. 31.

36. " . . . whatever we may think, we are that which thinks therein, and hence . . . nothing could ever come to exist independently of us, for everything is necessarily related to our thinking." *Science of Knowledge*, p. 71.

37. *Science of Knowledge*, p. 48.

38. *Science of Knowledge*, p. 41. "The basic contention of the philosopher, as such, is as follows: Though the self may exist only for itself, there necessarily arises for it at once an existence external to it; the ground of

the latter lies in the former. . . . "*Science of Knowledge*, p. 33.

39. Schelling, F. W. J., *System of Transcendental Idealism (1800)*, trans. Peter Heath (Virginia: University Press of Virginia, 1978), pp. 26–27.

40. *Science of Knowledge*, p. 36.

41. *Science of Knowledge*, p. 110.

42. *Science of Knowledge*, p. 41, see also pp. 35–36.

43. "But the question now arises as to how the philosopher assures himself of this original act, [the absolute act of self consciousness through which everything is posited for the self] or knows about it. He obviously does not do so immediately, but only by inference." Schelling, *System of Transcendental Idealism*, p. 47. cf. Fichte, *Science of Knowledge*, pp. 83–84.

44. "The diminished activity of the self must find an explanation in the self as such; the ultimate ground of it must be posited in the self. This comes about in that the self, which in this respect is practical, is posited as a self that *ought* to contain in itself the ground of existence of the not-self, which diminishes the activity of the intellective self; an infinite idea, which cannot itself be thought, and by which, therefore, we do not so much explain the explicandum as show, rather, *that* and *why* it is inexplicable; the knot is not so much loosed as projected into infinity." *Science of Knowledge*, pp. 147–148. See also p. 164.

45. *Science of Knowledge*, pp. 231, 238.

46. *Of Human Freedom*, trans. J. Gutman (Chicago: 1936), p. 24.

47. *Phenomenology*, p. 9.

48. See *The Gay Science*, trans. Walter Kaufmann (New York: Vintage Books, 1974), Paragraph 344; *The Genealogy of Morals*, trans. Kaufmann (New York: Vintage Books, 1989), Third Essay, Paragraph 24; *The Will to Power*, trans. Kaufmann (New York: Vintage Books, 1968), Paragraph 15.

INDEX

Ackermann, Robert, 247 n10
action, philosophy of, 162, 164
Americks, Carl, vii
antifoundationalism, 1–13, 24, 47–
    49, 125, 156–157, 199–200, 207,
    217. *See also* deconstruction
consistency of, 6, 10, 11–12, 50,
    53–58, 185–186, 196
and foundationalism, 15, 31–36,
    51–59
antimodernism, 22–25. *See also*
    postmodernism
Apel, Karl-Otto, 243 n24, 253 n49
Aristotle, 25, 43
authority, legitimacy of, 11. *See also*
    philosophy, authority of
autonomy, 27, 168, 196

Baird, Davis, 251 n37
Bates, Norman, 179
Becker, Werner, 255 n6
Being and Time, 154
Berkeley, Bishop George, 60, 204,
    227–229, 230, 232, 236
Bernstein, Richard J., 239 n3
blasphemy, philosophical, 125–128,
    133–136, 140–141, 195
Blair, George, 179
Bloch, Ernst, 255 n6
Blumenberg, Hans, 245 n4
Bubner, Rudiger, 250 n25, 255 n6,
    256 n8
Burtt, E. A., 248 n14, 286 n4
Butler, Clark, 279 n36

Capital, 173
capitalism, 245 n2
Cartesianism, 3, 10, 147, 156, 157, 235
Clark, Malcom, 255 n5
Cohen, I. B., 249 n17
coherence theory, 8, 209–214
conduct, principles of, 26–29
contextualism, 4–5, 7
contextuality, 8
commodities, fetishism of, 172–173
consciousness, 203, 204, 220
    absolute, 148, 150, 155. *See also*
        knowledge, absolute
    finititude of, 131–134
    form of, 168. *See also* structure of
    structure of, 71, 72, 73, 74, 76,
        78, 81, 88, 89–93, 95, 102–106,
        109, 110, 114, 129, 191
    sublation of, 76
    suspension of, 91–92, 95
    truth of, 73, 76, 78–79, 109
Contingency, Irony, and Solidarity,
    183–185
correspondence, of knowledge and
    object, 90, 103–106, 130, 134,
    170, 171, 189, 190, 200, 202,
    205–206, 208, 209, 211, 212,
    213, 214, 215, 216, 220–223,
    224, 225, 226, 230, 231, 236, 237
    model of truth, 36
    theory, 7, 60, 61, 62, 63
critical theory, 147, 160, 162, 174–
    175, 177, 204 n6. *See also*
    Frankfurt School

293